THE FORBIDDEN SECRET

HOW TO SURVIVE WHAT THE ELITE HAVE PLANNED FOR YOU

Jonathan Gray

About the author

Jonathan Gray is a globally recognised researcher, author and speaker on international affairs. His world-wide radio audiences number tens of millions. The author has hosted newspaper columns and contributed to numerous magazines.

AuthorHouse™
1663 Liberty Drive
Bloomington, IN 47403
www.authorhouse.com
Phone: 1-800-839-8640

First published by AuthorHouse 4/18/2011

ISBN: 978-1-4567-4691-9 (e)
ISBN: 978-1-4567-4690-2 (sc)

Library of Congress Control Number: 2011903604

Printed in the United States of America

http://www.beforeus.com

If I have failed to credit any illustrations reproduced in this book, I offer my apologies. Any sources omitted will be appropriately acknowledged in all future editions of this book.

THIS COULD BE THE MOST IMPORTANT BOOK YOU WILL EVER READ

Are you ready for Operation Rescue?

Power-mad murder mongers have seized our planet. They don't want you to know the survival strategy that will defeat their plans for you.

WARNING: The contents of this book may be hazardous to your pre-conceived ideas

OTHER BOOKS BY JONATHAN GRAY

http://www.beforeus.com/shopcart_hc.html

Dead Men's Secrets
More Dead Men's Secrets
Sting of the Scorpion
The Ark Conspiracy
Curse of the Hatana Gods
64 Secrets Ahead of Us
Bizarre Origin of Egypt's Ancient Gods
The Lost World of Giants
Discoveries: Questions Answered
Sinai's Exciting Secrets
Ark of the Covenant
The Killing of Paradise Planet
Surprise Witness
The Corpse Came Back
The Discovery That's Toppling Evolution
UFO Aliens: The Deadly Secret
Stolen Identity: Jesus Christ – History or Hoax?
Who's Playing Jesus Games?
The Da Vinci Code Hoax
The Sorcerers' Secret
What Happened to the Tower of Babel?
The 2012 Prophecy
Welcome, Then Betrayal
How Long Was Jesus in the Tomb?
The Big Dating Blunder
The Weapon the Globalists Fear
Modern Religious Myths About Genesis
Will You Survive?

CONTENTS

PART FOUR – PLANET HIJACKED

PART FIVE – RESCUE PLAN

PART SIX – THE RESCUER'S NAME

PART SEVEN – THE RESCUER REJECTED

PART EIGHT – BACK FROM DEATH?

PART NINE – THE COVER-UP

PROLOGUE A: KIDNAPPED

Eleven year old Jaycee Lee Dugard was snatched at a bus stop. For the next 18 years, she was held in captivity, but apparently did not try to escape and, over time, developed a close relationship with her kidnapper. Her stepfather said that she "has strong feelings with this guy" and "feels it's almost like a marriage." (Laura Fitzpatrick, "A Brief History of Stockholm Syndrome," *Time,* Aug. 31, 2009)

After 10 months in the hands of a kidnapper, Shawn Hornbeck called police to report his stolen bike. The captive gave his first name, *Shawn,* and as his last name the surname of his abductor, *Devlin.* (*Ibid.*) He stayed with his captor three more years, never escaping even while the man was away working at his two jobs.

There are many reported cases of victims becoming bonded to and even feeling compassion for and loyalty to their captors.

In Stockholm, Sweden, two thieves held four bank employees hostage at gunpoint in the bank's vault for six days. "When the victims were released, their reaction shocked the world: They hugged and kissed their captors, declaring their loyalty even as the kidnappers were carted off to jail." (*Ibid.*)

Psychologists think the victim comes to perceive the captor as the one controlling survival and life itself. Thus the victim aligns with the captor out of pure self-interest.

We acquiesce to our controllers

Uncommon? No. In a broader sense, most of us without protest agree with those who have come to dominate our culture.

From infancy upward, external influences help shape our values. Most people do not question the worldview which is imposed upon them, assuming that what they think and practise is simply the way it is.

When challenged, they often defend themselves. They are held captive to their thinking – which they don't realize is often seriously off track.

Villains have seized control

Most are not aware that our world has been taken captive. Forces hostile to us have taken over our planet – our courts, our governments, science, education, the media, the entertainment industry, the medical industry, the legal and illegal drug trade, and they have infiltrated mainstream religion as well.

And we have fallen victim to the same syndrome as a kidnap victim, passively identifying with our malevolent captor!

Strange, but true! Our whole world has been held captive for thousands of years – and ***we have come to identify with our captors***.

Firstly, as New Zealand government figure Murray McLean admitted to me, “We are not the ones in control. We are following the directions of internationalists outside the country.” And they, in turn, are controlled by others …unseen, whom we shall identify later.

It is they who are plunging our world into its current financial crisis. They need to collapse every nation’s economy, so they can replace it with their

One World Government. A Conspiracy Theorist statement? No, it is a statement of fact.

They control the shadowy Bilderberg Group, a financial, political and corporate elite who, at a meeting in Greece in mid-May, 2009, agreed that in order to continue their drive towards a New World Order, the US Dollar has to be "totally" destroyed.

The extermination plot

Not only that. A frightening agenda is currently being put into operation – to eliminate most of this world's population. New World Order planners say this needs to be done, so they can have their Utopia world. In 1974, in an address to the National Security Council, former US Secretary of State Henry Kissinger presented 2 billion people as the desired level of reduction, but in fact the depopulation policy may seek a 2-4 billion reduction, or up to two thirds of the world's population. This depopulation policy is intended by the world's ruling elite to result in control of mineral and strategic resources and water and total control of the world's wealth. ("Implications of world wide population growth for US security & overseas interests", *National Security Memo 200*, April 24, 1974)

By 1979 depopulation was the top priority of US national security policy, as outlined in the national security paper *Global 2000* written by Rockefeller contractors Henry Kissinger, Z. Brzezinski, Gen. Alexander Haig, and Ed Muskie for President Carter.

We now see a progressive enacting of this plot in the stealthy release of biological/genetic/ recombinant DNA weapons, such as AIDS, swine flu, forced vaccinations in third world countries, and now systematic use of depleted uranium.

But an unseen bombshell is set to explode – and seal the fate of these plotters.

Plot uncovered

I placed my finger in the bullet hole.

Peter, a university lecturer and businessman from Perth, Western Australia, now in hiding, had called me to examine it.

"A helicopter flew low over our home," said Peter, "and lodged these bullet holes in our kitchen window. Then a sniper team from that tree on the hill fired into this same window. Police later said they knew in advance – but were ordered not to interfere."

You ask, why was Peter Golden targeted? In the process of dealing internationally in computer software, he had uncovered information – 11 months before the event – suggesting that men in the Australian government were involved in plans for the bombing of Australians in Bali, and also that individuals in the US government were plotting the 9/11 incident.

The motive: to provoke anger against the Muslim world which could lead to support for a war in the Middle East, the elimination of Muslims, and the seizing of their resources.

Within days of presenting a 5,000 page report to a highly placed government official whom he trusted, Peter was told he had to get out of Australia if he valued his life.

He fled to New Zealand – and from there he proceeded to alert officials in the New Zealand, United States and Australian governments. After each attempt, he became the target of death threats, break-ins and physical attacks on himself and his 6 year old daughter Katie.

Peter explained: "The physical fact was this: I had stumbled into New World Order plans for a major war in the Middle East – and the elimination of untold millions of innocent people. This was to be triggered by, firstly, an international baiting campaign to stir the Muslim world into a fury, then, secondly, a series of carefully engineered 'false flag' terrorist attacks, such as the Bali bombing, for which Muslims were to be blamed. When I unwittingly stumbled into this plot, the Globalist 'shadow government' needed to shut me up."

Are lying to us

On May 14, 2004, Dr Eugene Mallove was killed. The local police ruled his death a homicide. This occurred just as a discovery he had made was about to be vindicated.

Dr Mallove was a scientist and an engineer with two engineering degrees from MIT (1969, 1970) and a doctorate from the Harvard University School of Public Health (1975). He was also a regular science and technology broadcaster for The Voice of America.

Dr Mallove commented that if by chance you are one of those who believe "all is well in the house of science" and "official science" can be counted on to behave itself and always seek the truth – even in matters of central, overarching importance to the well-being of humankind – you are sorely mistaken.

Dr Mallove said it was time to "reconsider your opinion about who is telling the truth and who is defending falsehood."

The hijackers are manipulating science to mislead us. When you see a scientific claim in the newspaper, or in a textbook, on television or the Internet, you had better watch out! It is possible you are being conned – and you won't even know it! A major deception is being foisted on us all.

Thankfully, confessions like the following are leaking out concerning science text books:

> If [it] supports our theories, we put it in the main text. If it does not entirely contradict them, we put it in a footnote. And if it is completely 'out of date', we just drop it. (T. Save-Soderbergh and I.U. Olsson -Institute of Egyptology and Institute of Physics respectively, University of Uppsala, Sweden, "C14 Dating and Egyptian Chronology," in *Radiocarbon Variations and Absolute Chronology, Proceedings of the Twelfth Nobel Symposium*, Ingrid U. Olsson – ed,, Almqvist and Wiksell, Stockholm, and John Wiley and Sons, Inc., New York, p.35)

Just catch this shocking revelation from news reporter Hannah Devlin:

> **One in seven scientists say colleagues fake data...**
>
> Faking scientific data and failing to report commercial conflicts of interest are far more prevalent than previously thought, a study suggests. (*Times Online,* June 4, 2009)

Kenneth Kitchen, Professor of Egyptology in the School of Archaeology and Oriental studies, University of Liverpool, laments that

> scientific and archaeological research is not getting through to young people in schools and colleges. In some circles there even seems to be ***a deliberate withholding*** of such information, yet it is the fruit of leading scholars known for their restrained, moderate, factual presentation of their researches. (Forward to Victor Pearce's book *Evidence For Truth: Archaeology,* 2nd edition)

Money talks. Scientists who speak up are being shut out of funding for projects… misrepresented… ridiculed…fired. And much of their research has even been destroyed! Positions. Reputations. Opportunity for publication. Small and powerful groups control careers. If you want a university post, you need recommendations. To get your articles published in scientific journals, you must pass what is called "anonymous peer review". It is easy for a dominant group to control publication, research money and position. To "succeed", you have to go along with them. Or else, displaying the liberal tolerance we have all come to love, they will shut you out – despite your qualifications. The crowd in charge here is beyond the pale.

Destroying evidence

On August 12, 1989, at a conference in Dayton, Tennessee, Dr Don Patton showed compelling evidence that both human and dinosaur tracks were present at the Palaxy River, Texas, at what was known as the Taylor Trail. (Would it shock you to learn that ***dinosaurs and man have coexisted during the last few thousand years***?) (*The Discovery That's Toppling Evolution*, chapters 2 to 4)

Two well known "scientists" were present. At least one of them was conspicuously disturbed by this presentation. Both flew to Dallas the next morning and went immediately to the Paluxy River. They were seen in the river that afternoon with an 'iron bar'. And later extensive damage was noted to the prints.

But don't scientists accept evidence? It should be noted that a living scientist today is not the solid object he appears to be, but is really almost entirely empty space, a series of holes joined together by French knitting (spaced atoms). That is to say, the scientist is as human as the rest of us. Faking of science is the result of a plan that has been developing for several centuries.

An intellectual bomb let loose

We might be aghast at the dangers of the nuclear bomb in the hands of terrorists or renegade governments. Yet even more deadly than all of the above is an intellectual bomb that has been let loose on the race.

Hitler's atrocities were based on it. So were those of Stalin, Mao tse Tung and Pol Pot. Now it is the turn of the New World Order crazies.

What is this intellectual ticking bomb? Nothing less than the ***nihilistic mindset*** which has dominated scientific thought for the past century. Based on the popularised theory of evolution, nihilism is now in danger of committing mankind to a course of automatic self-destruction.

You may be surprised to learn that many leading scientists are now questioning the validity of evolution. But the damage has been done. It has had a free hand and little or no opposition in the universities and colleges, and through the press and television, all these years. It has resulted in reasoning which has brought the most disastrous consequences.

The "Big E" mindset of Hitler

The appeal of totalitarian systems such as Nazism, Communism and Secular Humanism, owe a great deal to the acceptance of the "Big E"... as do fascism, anarchism, atheism and militarism. Take away Evolution theory from these belief systems, and they effectively lose a central premise necessary for their coherence.

Yes, the "Big E" (Evolution) theory was a powerful influence on the mindset which dominated Nazi and Communist leaders. As the holocaust swept into action, Himmler regarded the victims as vermin, as though he was handling a biological disease. "Does a rat catcher think it is wrong to catch rats?" asked a Nazi defendant at the Nuremburg war criminal trials. So came the death camps, in which millions of men, women and children were exterminated. Gold watches, gold wedding rings, gold teeth and gold eye glasses that the victims left behind were deposited into the federal bank. One witness admitted it took an extra five minutes to kill the women, because they had to cut their hair off to be used in making mattresses.

Of course, we cannot blame Charles Darwin and his colleagues personally for such gruesome practices. But we need to recognise that unquestioning belief in evolution was a ***CENTRAL*** feature of the Nazi belief system, and ***not just incidental*** to it.

The "Big E" inspired Communism

Again, evolution theory was ESSENTIAL to the communist purges of 60 million in the USSR alone, and tens of millions more in China. The victims were regarded as nothing more than creatures expendable in the quest for a classless society. The central proposition of Class Struggle depended upon evolution theory for plausibility.

To be fair, one might not blame evolution theory for the inhuman and degrading acts carried out by Nazism and Communism. However, the impact of evolution needs to be placed in its proper context. We need to give it due recognition.

The "Big E" thinking inspires the Globalists

A major part of the Globalist hijackers' plans is to prepare us mentally to accept elimination of life as necessary. So to systematically dull down the minds of the masses, they have been carefully preparing and using a compliant servant team of "nice guy" educators whose doctorates, salaries and grants depend on toeing the line – who will parrot the ideology that "we're ***here by accident*** – not children of a Creator, but ***'useless eaters'*** that are ***expendable*** to evolutionary progress."

You realise, of course, that teachers, lecturers and textbook writers are just the front faces. Most are probably honest men and women who are unsuspecting that they are being used. And many of them would be aghast at the "expendable" idea. They haven't joined the dots. So they remain unwitting puppets.

Just like so many people in the media. It has been observed that "most journalists are so brain-dead themselves, so lacking in understanding of what they are part of, that they, like most of the population, play a part in advancing an agenda they do not even know exists." (*Uncensored* magazine, September-December 2009)

Most people are unaware

The propaganda has already moulded society's thinking. The people continue to remain, for the most part, blissfully unaware of what has happened and continue to believe the litany of Globalist lies being poured upon them by their propaganda media organs, never once raising any objection to billions of dollars being poured into perpetuating their ignorance.

No, the issue is NOT just a whole lot of different organizations. ONE CHIEF PLAYER and his gang ***controls them all.*** This chief player – the Lucifer Legion – has taken our planet hostage. Its human globalist puppets are now strategically placed throughout the highest levels of power. And, for the most part, we are acquiescing as they influence our lives. Unaware of the issues, most of us live in sympathy with our kidnappers.

There is a rescue plan

Why am I writing this? Because I hate to think that you and I are being cheated out of what a former editor of the *Los Angeles Times* called "***a world scoop***". Glimpsing its importance, he asked in astonishment, "***Why are you sitting on this? The world needs to know it!***"

There is a rescue program.

Ask yourself. If a credible, trustworthy and all-powerful world figure were to show you a foolproof strategy guaranteed to end the current violence, corruption and misery, would you be interested? And if he had also cracked the secret to life extension beyond your wildest dreams – with pain-free, productive, enjoyable living – what would that be worth to you?

Well, not only is such a rescue program currently under way, but the hijackers of our planet know it. They and their Globalist puppets are determined, if possible, to

(a) sabotage the operation, and

(b) stop us from learning about it.

That's why I have called this the *Forbidden Secret*. If you didn't know, it is so explosive that, when common people discover it, they become ignited, invincible and unafraid.

That's what the Globalist villains don't want - an informed, empowered and fearless population. They are obsessed with you becoming subdued, slumbering, and submissive to them, so that they can more easily execute their dark plans.

SUMMARY

1. **VICTIMS OFTEN ACQUIESCE TO THEIR CAPTORS**

2. **GLOBALISTS HAVE CAPTURED OUR SOCIETY. They have taken over the nations. Their agenda is to kill off most of us. They are lying to us.**

3. **THEIR PROPAGANDA HAS SHAPED OUR THINKING We have acquiesced to their control.**

4. **DIRECTING THEM ARE THE REAL HIJACKERS, THE LUCIFER LEGION**

5. **THERE IS A RESCUE PLAN**

6. **THEY ARE DETERMINED TO:**
   (a) sabotage that plan
   (b) even stop us from knowing about it.

PROLOGUE B: YOUR LIFE AND DEATH

"We buried Norman alive! We buried him alive!" The shocking news swept from house to house.

In 16th century England, some local folks were running out of burial space. So, they would dig up coffins, take the bones to a bone-house, then reuse the graves. On opening coffins, they found that 1 out of 25 coffins had scratch marks on the inside. To their horror, they had been burying people alive! So they began to tie a string on the wrist of the corpse, thread it through the coffin and up through the ground, then tie it to a bell.

Someone was appointed to sit out in the graveyard all night (the graveyard shift), to listen for the bell; thus, someone could be "saved by the bell" or was considered a "dead ringer".

I don't need to tell you. Of all things you possess, ***life*** is the most precious, right?

"My daughter is only 15," cried Moira. "She has a rare brain tumor that cannot be operated on. I don't want to lose her. What can I do?"

Fred slaved at his job. He planned to retire at 60. Missing time with his dear wife and children, he drove himself with the one thought… retire, then enjoy the remaining years. Fred was in a coffin before his 58th birthday.

If someone told you, "I'll guarantee to ***add 20 years to your life*** – 20 years of pain-free, productive, enjoyable living" – what would that be worth to you? Yet even better, what if you learned that there are some people now alive who will live to be 200, 300,

600 years old… no, more than that… some who will live on… and on… in glorious quality of life… without dying at all. Yes, you are right, it's hard to imagine. But there is a good chance that you could qualify to become one of them.

The colossal cover-up

However, there is a problem. There are powers that, for reasons which you might term philosophical, spiritual, or religious, want to keep the knowledge of this from you. That's why I've called this the *Forbidden Secret.*

And, as unlikely as the connection might seem on the surface, these people are right into the ***origins*** debate. As already noted, they ***control*** the scientific community, the education system, the media, the entertainment industry, the medical and pharmaceutical industries, and they have infiltrated mainstream religion as well.

They are aware that your knowledge or ignorance about your origins could definitely affect your chance of life extension. Why is this? You will see why, as we proceed. Sufficient to say, it's vital that first you get your origins facts right. No matter what the popular theories, it is the ***facts*** that decide the day.

Turned off by fake religious people? I understand. So am I. But this is not about religion or non-religion. It is not just about a religious viewpoint (atheistic, agnostic, New Age, Buddhist, Jewish, Muslim, Christian or whatever). It is not about that. It is about a ***spiritual war being waged against us***. It is happening in your own home town or district. This is a ***conflict of epic proportions***. And of such importance that not a single person alive on this planet should ignore it.

My investigations as a hard-nosed archaeologist over 44 years have been largely ***front-line***, dealing ***first-hand*** with ***on-site*** discoveries. And some of the ***evidence*** you are about to see may knock your socks off. It is still unknown to most people. Yet it is beyond successful contradiction.

Is this important? Yes – because it could affect your future… personally.

I promise you that a long, thorough investigation has been undertaken to guarantee the integrity of this information. Facts which ***can be tested*** underlie each point. So certain am I that ***the over-all thesis*** is correct that I hereby offer $100,000 to anyone who can ***disprove it*** – either to be retained by the claimant or donated to his/her nominated charity.

What's this all about?

Glad you asked. This is about ***evidence***. Here are the facts. (References relate to this current book, unless otherwise stated):

Facts at a glance

I submit that we shall materially and physically ***prove beyond reasonable doubt*** (sufficient to serve as actionable proof):

> * That we are here neither by evolution, nor by seeding from outer space, but by a direct creation of an intelligent Superior Being existing outside both space and time.
>
> *Demonstrated with evidence, not speculation.*

* That we are alienated from our Life-Giver. We suffer death and cannot save ourselves.

Demonstrated with evidence, not speculation.

* That, in His compassion, our Creator has provided a single means of rescue and restoration through His appointed Deliverer.

Demonstrated with evidence, not speculation.

That is the over-all thesis. Here it is in more detail:

1. **NO EVOLUTION**:
   Did life appear spontaneously then evolution take over?
   Documented and observable scientific ***evidence*** from DNA, biology and fossils, ***says no***. (Chapters 1-5)
2. **NO EXTRATERRESTRIAL START:**
   Did mankind originate by seeding from outer space? Physical and experimental ***evidence says no***. (Chapters 6-7)
3. **DELIBERATELY DESIGNED**:
   Observable scientific ***evidence*** indicates that an effect is not greater than its cause. It always takes a greater source of information to produce information. The intricate design of human life, intelligence and personality requires ***a cause*** which possesses life, intelligence and personality outside the creation itself. (See Chapters 8-9)
4. **HAS SPOKEN TO US:**
   This Superior Intelligence has demonstrated

ability to communicate messages to mankind and has sealed the authorship of certain messages in at least two ways that no human being can replicate:

(a) a 3500 year track record in prophecy - cold, hard, incontrovertible PROOF of accurate ***foreknowledge*** of consecutive world history (Chapters 11-12)

(b) a unique, DNA-style ***mathematical code*** within the structure of the written messages. (Chapters.13,43-46) Since the content of these messages is ***exactly consistent with observed fact***, then the most reasonable deduction from the ***evidence*** is that the messages are trustworthy.

5. **PLANET HIJACKED:**
There is demonstrable ***evidence*** that our world is held captive by forces ***hostile*** to the human race. (Chapters 14-18)

6. **SPIRITUAL WARFARE:**
Messages claiming to be from the Superior Intelligence reveal that a ***spiritual battle*** between the powers of good and evil is being waged for the future of each person on earth. One side uses force; the other does not. (Chapters 14-18)

7. **DEATH IS UNNATURAL:**
According to the ***evidence***:

(a) We are alienated from our Source of life.

(b) Cut off from this Source, our existence is fragile. We die.

(c) Death is not an inevitable, natural, essential part of our existence, but an intrusion, that need not be. (Chapter 16)

8. **RESCUE PROGRAM:**
FACT: ***The ancient nations universally claimed*** that the first great father was informed of a coming rescue program, which will result in abolishing death, and in the restoring of this world to its original perfect state. (Chapter 19)

9. **RESCUER'S NAME KNOWN:**
There is ***evidence*** that the name of the Rescuer was known from the earliest times and his name was recorded:
   (a) on the ancient sky charts (Chapter 27)
   (b) in the written text of the Tanakh (Chapters 24 and 25)
   (c) by various nations – for example, the Egyptians, the Celtic Druids and the Persians. (Chapters 26 and 27)

10. **RESCUER'S LOCATION KNOWN:**
Non-biblical sources show that ***the world's nations*** believed the Messiah was to make his appearance through the Hebrew branch of the human race. If this be true, then we might expect the ***more complete*** revelation of the Deliverer to be imparted to the Hebrews. Let's wait and see.

11. **MESSIANIC PROPHECIES SPECIFIC:**
Additionally, more than 300 prophecies concerning the Deliverer were recorded in the Tanakh, including
   (a) precisely ***when and where*** he would appear.
   (b) that he ***would be rejected*** by the nation of his birth.(Chapters 20-23,29)

12. **PROPHECIES WERE FULFILLED:**
There is solid ***evidence*** that at the precise ***place and time predicted,*** one bearing the ***prophesied name*** did appear, living out the prophecies one

by one - including those beyond human control, such as place of birth, manner of death, manner of burial, and so on, which no imposter could have acted out. (Chapters.22-23,28-32)

13. **THE RESCUER'S ROLE:**
The prophecies said ***his role*** would be to offer individuals:
(a) freedom from guilt
(b) power to live victoriously
(c) a restored personal relationship with the Creator
(d) the ultimate end to death
(e) a guaranteed place in the coming new world in which harmony, peace and joy will prevail.

14. **EVENT SEQUENCE:**
According to the prophecies, ***after*** Messiah's stand-in death for all, ***then*** the Second Jewish Temple sacrifices (which foreshadowed that event) would be terminated. (Ch..20) This timing is important in helping us to pinpoint the Messiah's identity.

15. **ANTI-RESCUE CAMPAIGN :**
Globally, on multiple fronts, a high-powered ***disinformation campaign*** has since swung into action against the rescue operation, along with a direct sabotage agenda to ***physically destroy or oppress*** *as many prospects as possible.*

Coincidences?

That brief overview now brings us to a bizarre set of historical "coincidences" that demand an explanation. Since no event is isolated and every effect has its cause, then what do these odd "coincidences" mean?:

COINCIDENCE 1: THE PASSOVER TIMING

FACT:

(a) The annual Hebrew ***Passover*** event (14th to 15th day of the month Nisan) centered around a lamb ***sacrifice.*** This symbolized a substitute death in the place of man, to free him from the penalty of his wrongs. (Exodus chapter 12; *Jewish Encyclopedia*)

(b) Jewish scholars expected the coming ***Messiah*** to bring redemption at that same time of the year – ***Passover.*** (*Cabalistae apud Fagium;* Abrabanal, *The Wells of Salvation*; Ex.12:1-6,11; Lev. 23:4,5; *The Jewish Encyclopedia*, art., "Atonement, Day of")

FACT:

(a) ***The one with the predicted name*** said he had come to fulfill the Passover symbolism, to ***sacrifice*** his life and free men from the penalty of sin. (Matthew 26:1-2,17-28; 1 Corinthians 5:7)

(b) Jewish leaders, charging that the "named one" "led astray Israel", condemned him to be ***executed*** on precisely the same day as the ***Passover lamb was sacrificed.*** (*Babylonian Sanhedrin* 43a, 95-110 AD)

Was it just coincidence that both…

* the Tanakh's prophetic date for Messiah to die violently, and

* the Passover "prophecy" date for the sacrificial lamb to die

…converged at the precise time that the "named one" died violently?

Or was something much bigger at work here?

COINCIDENCE 2: DEATH AND LIFE

FACT: After rejecting the "named one's" "how to escape" prophecy, 1,100,000 people died in the siege

of Jerusalem, AD 70. Their ***rejection of his message killed them.*** (Chapter 33)
FACT: Those who acted on the "named one's" prophecy did not die. They escaped. (*Encyclopedia Judaica*) Their ***acceptance of the "named one" saved them***.

Bold statements? Yes. An exaggeration? No. Both are documented history. Is there a connection?

COINCIDENCE 3:
REASON FOR THE DESTRUCTION:

According to the Hebrew Tanakh, the ***specific reason*** why the First Jewish Temple was destroyed in 586 BC and the nation ***scattered for 70 years*** was ***because*** they had ***rejected the prophets*** sent by God. (1 Chronicles 36:15-20)

Recognising the same spiritual laws to be operative, may we ask, what could be the enormity of the national sin which triggered the Second Temple's destruction in 70 AD and the people being ***scattered for 2,000 years***? Had they ***rejected a greater Prophet*** – even the Messiah himself? (Chapter 29)

COINCIDENCE 4:
DESTRUCTION DATE:

In 586 BC, the First Temple was burned by Babylonian armies on the ***10th day of the month Ab***.

In 70 AD, the Second Temple was burned by Roman armies on the ***10th day of the month Ab.*** (Josephus, *Wars of the Jews*, 6:4.5)

These two events: are they connected? Was there a supernatural element in the timing, to convey a message of extreme importance?

COINCIDENCE 5:
THE "FORGIVENESS" FACTOR:

Forty years before Jerusalem's destruction, the "named one's" public offer of the Creator's divine ***forgiveness*** to all who would accept, was officially ***rejected*** by the nation's leaders when they executed him as an imposter. (Chapters 23 and 29)

Forty years before Jerusalem's destruction, on the first annual Day of Atonement after their rejection of the "named one", the traditional red wool which always turned white (signifying divine forgiveness) now ceased to do so. According to the rabbis this was a supernatural omen that the nation's sins were ***no longer forgiven***. (*Babylonian Talmud,* Yoma chapter 39b.)

Coincidence? Or was there a supernatural connection in the timing?

Forbidden information destroyed

When news of the "named one's" death and resurrection, allegedly confirming him as the Deliverer, spread across the earth to challenge the legitimacy of Lucifer worship, sabotage campaigns were launched against it from two chief centers – ***Rome*** (the center of sun worship – Satan worship) and ***Alexandria, Egypt*** (the center of Luciferian pagan philosophy). (*The Da Vinci Code Hoax*, Chapters 4-7)

Acts of sabotage and cover-up included the following:

1. FIDDLING WITH MESSIAH TEXTS:

In ***Alexandria***, opponents infiltrated the "named one's" group of followers and surreptitiously ***mutilated selected Messiah texts*** in order to ***downgrade the "named one"***. Rome adopted and enforced these corruptions of text. (*The Da Vinci Code Hoax*, Chapters 4-7)

However, since most manuscript copies were beyond their reach, only 1 percent of surviving manuscripts are affected. (*The Da Vinci Code Hoax*, Chapters 17-18,20-21; *Who's Playing Jesus Games?* Chapters 12-15; *The Sorcerers' Secret*, Chapters 4-6)

2. PTOLEMY'S MUTILATED STAR CHART:

Between 127 and 151 AD, in that ***same center*** of undercover corruption – ***Alexandria*** – Ptolemy's historic map of the stars ***chopped out the prophecy of the "named one"*** which had been in the star maps for 4,000 years. (Chapter 27)

3. KEY WORDS CHOPPED OUT OF TANAKH

Around ***the same time*** (130 AD), Rabbi Akiva, "the father of the Mishnah", promoted a translation of the Tanakh which ***ripped out key words in certain messianic texts*** that were being linked with the "named one". (Chapter 27)

4. RABBIS FALSIFY CHRONOLOGY:

Rabbis Akiva and Ben Halafta also ***slashed out 160 years from the Persian/ Jewish calendar*** to nullify the "named one's" fulfillment of Daniel's 490-year prophecy. (Chapter 41) That's right, 160 years of real time was ripped out and thrown away!

5. CURSE ON MESSIAH PROPHECY:

Rabbi Samuel B. Nahmani placed a ***curse*** (recorded in the Talmud) on whoever would read the ***same prophecy*** of Daniel which pointed to ***the "named one"*** as the Messiah. (Chapters 21,23)

6. ***MESSIAH PROPHECY CUT OUT OF TANAKH***

The Isaiah 53 prophecy so clearly described the "named one" that some Ashkenazi Jews ***blasted this chapter right out*** of their Scriptures. However, the Sephardic Jews retained it. (Chapter 23)

Thought questions

Why such a desperate ***cover-up of that one single feature*** in all these different documents? Did ***evidence*** so clearly point to the "named one" as the Messiah, that rejectors had no option but to:

(a) ***chop out*** textual evidence
(b) ***falsify*** historical evidence, and
(c) ***curse*** whoever studied the evidence?

Shouldn't one feel sorry for them?

As the climax approaches

1. **OPPORTUNITY FOR ALL:**
   According to the prophecies, as the final showdown looms, every person will have opportunity to accept or reject the pending rescue.
2. **WE CHOOSE:**
   Inbuilt into each of us is the capacity for free choice concerning our destiny. (Chapter 15)
3. **FORBIDDEN NEWS:**
   The hijackers of our planet have admitted they will do whatever it takes to ***eliminate, suppress, or discredit*** the news of the rescue plan and the documents which alert us to it – so that you and I, deprived of its benefits, can be brought under their Luciferian New Age ***control***.

4. **THE RESCUER'S POWER:**
There is ***well-documented evidence*** that today in real life the name of the Promised One – and no other – is able to halt an alien abduction, free a victim from demon possession, and empower one to enjoy a new quality of life. (Chapters 48 and 49)

Sources identifying the Coming One

As already noted, the message of the Promised One was known to the ***nations of the world***, who testified that they had inherited this knowledge from the first great father. They knew that:

- Originally this was a perfect world with no suffering.
- There had been a rebellion in the heavens.
- Man had followed the rebels and had himself fallen.
- The Curer of all ills was coming to restore mankind.
- He was to appear in Judea – and have a Hebrew name.

We shall consult both ***non-biblical*** and ***biblical*** sources. Why biblical? some will ask. Firstly, because both the Globalists and the so-called UFO "alien" entities have adopted a particular ***stance toward the Bible*** as essential to their plans. Secondly, as the most widely trusted (and hated) book on the planet, what it says is directly relevant to our investigation.

How you can benefit

The best part of our topic will be this: You will be presented with ***actionable benefits*** in real life. (Chapters 47-49)

In contrast to the Globalist plan to annihilate millions, I shall show you how you can claim for yourself an extension of life.

Of course, there are laws of health that can enhance your quality of life now – and even extend your life-span to a certain degree. However, there is only one "bridge to eternal life" – and it does not involve preserving or repairing our present bodies. Death is ***not*** an engineering or ***biological problem***, it is a ***moral penalty***. Therefore the only solution to death has been provided by the Creator Himself.

I'm not always right. But with ***evidence*** like you're now about to see, I've never been more certain of anything in my life.

In assembling this report for you, I have been excavating deep for rock-solid ***evidence***. We need to be passionate about ***evidence.*** Speculation is out. ***Evidence*** is king.

If you just want to surface-scan this report and say 'I know all that', then stop right here. But if you're willing to ***drill into the facts*** and accept their challenge, then you are in for some mind-blowing ***evidence*** that can change everything for you – for the better!

No matter what you've thought, you want to know the truth, right? So please empty yourself of previous ideas and just look at the ***evidence.*** It might change your life.

Okay, are you feeling adventurous? Because we are about to embark on a grand discovery. For starters, let's explore a city…

PART ONE

EVOLUTION?

1

DNA: artefact of intelligence? -

BEYOND THE INCREDIBLE

The explorers could hardly believe their eyes.

Here was an unknown city. Martin just stood gaping. "Look!" he shouted. "Just see how all these pieces of machinery fit together!"

"So intricately designed," responded his companion. "Who could have made them?"

They surveyed the scene in wonder.

"Are you thinking what I'm thinking?" asked Martin.

His companion looked at him. "Our most brilliant modern engineers couldn't construct these."

Fantastic factory assembly lines... control centres... and transport centres... all unimaginably complex.

And packed into an area so tiny. All inside a *simple* cell. What simpleton made up that phrase... "***simple*** cell"?

* * * * * * *

What's inside your simplest cell?

Look magazine, in its January 16, 1962, issue declared, "The cell is ***as complicated as New York City."***

It is less than one thousandth of an inch long. And the more we study it, the more complex it is found to be.

Think of all the shops in your town. Shelves stacked with goods, display windows, check out counters, carpets, light fittings, telephones, and so on.

Now add in all the houses. Bedrooms, with beds, sheets, blankets, pillows, reading lamps, wardrobes, dressers, windows, doors. Lounge rooms, with chairs, wall pictures, TVs. Kitchens, sinks, tables, taps for hot and cold water, cupboards, frig., dishwasher, you name it.

Now all the factories with their complicated machinery. The automobiles, delivery trucks, with their pistons, radiators and… Oh, let's not get into this. It's endless. Every living human cell, like a city, contains multiplied millions of specially organized parts – just like that.

Your adult body contains as many as 100 trillion of these walled cities. Inside each one is activity which includes energy generators, transport systems, waste disposal systems, structural designers, invasion guards, food factories, protective barriers and communication links within and outside the cell city.

Michael Denton describes it so beautifully:

> To grasp the reality… we must magnify a cell a thousand million times until it is twenty kilometres in diameter and resembles a giant airship large enough to cover a great city like London or New York. What we would then see would be an object of unparalleled complexity and adapted design. On the surface of the cell we would see millions of openings, like the portholes of a vast space ship, opening and closing to allow a continual stream of materials to flow in and out. If we were to enter one of these openings we would find ourselves in a world of supreme technology and bewildering complexity. We would see endless highly

> organized corridors and conduits branching in every direction away from the perimeter of the cell, some leading to the central memory bank in the nucleus and others to assembly plants and processing units. The nucleus itself would be a vast spherical chamber more than a kilometre in diameter, resembling a geodesic dome inside of which we would see, all neatly stacked together in ordered arrays, the miles of coiled chains of the DNA molecules. A huge range of products and raw materials would shuttle along all the manifold conduits in a highly ordered fashion to and from all the various assembly plants in the outer regions of the cell.
>
> We would wonder at the level of control implicit in the movement of so many objects down so many seemingly endless conduits, all in perfect unison. We would see all around us, in every direction we looked, all sorts of robot-like machines....
>
> What we would be witnessing would be an object resembling an immense automated factory, a factory larger than a city and carrying out almost as many unique functions as all the manufacturing activities of man on earth. (Michael Denton, *Evolution: A Theory in Crisis.* Bethesda, Maryland: Adler and Adler, Publishers, Inc., 1986, pp. 328-329)

Amazing fact: Did you know that ***each cell*** in your body has the electrical potential of ***1.7 volts***. (And with up to 100 trillion cells, what is the electrical potential of your body?... you work it out!)

Your amazing genes

Within the nucleus of that little dot called a cell, 23 pairs of chromosomes are intertwined like a wad of spaghetti. These contain the ***master computer called***

DNA. And the DNA molecules contain ***thousands of genes***.

These genes

(a) programme all inherited characteristics, such as height and personality type.

(b) guide all growth processes, such as when and how baby teeth are pushed out by adult teeth.

(c) direct all structural and system details for every body organ.

You and I each came from a single fertilised cell. In the nucleus of that little dot, the master computer (DNA) contained the programming for every aspect of the yet-undeveloped person. Every organ, every nerve, every hair, skin colour, hair colour, behavioural patterns… are programmed in those amazing tiny chromosomes.

There is automated assembly, perfectly regulated and controlled… miniaturization… and ***incredible ingenuity***.

Each cell always "knows"

Were you aware that each and every cell in your body contains ALL the genetic coding for each of the other cells of your body?

There are ***instructions*** in your cells ***on how to*** manufacture and reproduce every different part of your body. The words are set out in sentences, and paragraphs and chapters.

- The genes are like sentences.
- Several genes together make a paragraph.
- Many paragraphs of gene clusters make a chapter.
- Many chapters make a book, which we call a chromosome.

- There are 23 chromosome books to make the whole encyclopedia of instructions.
- An encyclopedia comprises a complete person.

This is duplicated to make an identical copy, so that your body has two encyclopedias – that is, 46 books (chromosomes) in each human cell.

These books contain so many words that the human encyclopedia is more than ten times as long as *Encyclopaedia Brittanica.* To put this another way, ***over a million pages*** are needed for all human instructions.

And this DNA message is played back every time a new life is created, because its instructions are obeyed to the last letter.

This one million page DNA message book gives complicated technical instructions to make a plant or an animal or a man. They are ***more technical than*** any man-made computerised code for ***making a passenger airliner***, for example. They are more technical than any of the computers on our planet.

Think about this. Could a series of faults in instructions (mutations) make, by accident, such a technical code?

This code, like a Morse code of dots and dashes, ***needs to be translated*** before it can be used.

The truth is, this DNA code ***needed someone who knew the translation*** and then made a machine to translate it. That translation machine is included into every cell of your body, as well.

Think about this. Someone was needed to

(a) **know the code secret** and

(b) **make the code breaker**.

The theory of evolution ***cannot*** explain how this ***information*** arose.

As we have just noted, one process which the cell undertakes is the formation of new cells. This incredible process requires the cell to ***read itself*** and then ***reproduce itself***. And can you guess how fast it does this? The complete duplication is accomplished in just a few hours.

Would you like to attempt a job like that? And do it without mistakes.

To repeat: a living cell can do something that no man-made machine can do. It can make a perfect copy of itself in just a few hours!

Now think about this. Somehow, although each cell has such a vast encyclopedia of "blueprints", yet each cell "knows" its own special job and keeps it. For example, a cell on your skin at the end of your ear has the genetic information to produce a toenail cell… but it doesn't! Aren't you glad?

How small are your genes?

Now, have you stopped to consider that human DNA is infinitely more complex than our computers? As impressive as man-made microchips are, this bio-micro-circuitry is ***beyond the incredible***.

The programmed genetic coding for all of earth's 6.8 billion people would take up space less than the size of an aspirin tablet!

A single gene – can you grasp this – is estimated to be between 4 and 50 millionths of an inch across. And 500,000 genes would easily slide around in a hole made by an ordinary pinpoint!

The density of sub-microscopic information

In an interview with Benjamin Wiker, Dr Dean Kenyon, Professor of Biology at San Francisco State University, said:

> The number of bits of information stored in a cubic millimetre of tightly packed DNA exceeds, by many orders of magnitude, the information storage capacity of the same volume in any computer's memory.
>
> DNA's information density is 1.9 x 10^{18} bits per cubic millimetre – by far the highest density of information storage known to humans. (Paper: *A New Scientific Revolution)*

Kenyon observed that this had led many scientists to conclude that living cells were designed by a ***superintelligent Agent outside of nature***.

The incredible RNA

The messenger in a cell city is called RNA. Although it looks like DNA, is ***has a passport*** to leave the nucleus. And just listen to this:

Firstly, in a split second, the master DNA and the messenger RNA intertwine.

Then the DNA instantly imprints a section of its code on the RNA.

Then the DNA separates from the RNA.

Then the RNA rushes to the edge of the city. And there it transfers its code in rapid-fire succession to one enzyme after another.

This code tells each enzyme to do a particular job somewhere in the larger organism.

The whole mass of cells within a body ***somehow cooperate*** to act like a fish, a cat, a human, or whatever the total organism is supposed to be.

Protein forming so that DNA could be possible

Here's a puzzle for you. ***DNA cannot form without*** pre-existing protein. But ***proteins cannot form without*** pre-existing DNA!

So, can you answer me this: From where and how did the first protein originate, to facilitate the DNA code structure in each species?

Mathematical probability alone has shown that even if our earth and our universe were billions times trillions of years old, it would not even begin to scratch the odds of the simplest protein molecule forming by chance, much less an entire cell.

All DNA's interlocking, working parts must be 100% intact

And wonder at this! Inside the cell, one piece of machinery is manufactured, then transported to fit precisely into another waiting piece, then another, and another – each one designed specifically to fit and interact with that particular piece and no other.

We're talking about many parts of a complex machine, so small you can't see it with the naked eye!

Then what about this: DNA has to be ***totally 100 percent intact*** with all its ***interlocking, working parts***, *before* one living cell can even exist. Not only do you need the information in the individual genes. You also need the ***information*** that enables them to work together. Such masses of information do not emerge from chance random processes.

Our sophisticated machines can do nothing at all unless someone ***supplies a programme*** of code instructions. And the programmes must be developed by intelligent human beings.

Suppose I told you that my XP Windows computer, with all its interacting information software, just "happened" – that no one ever designed it?

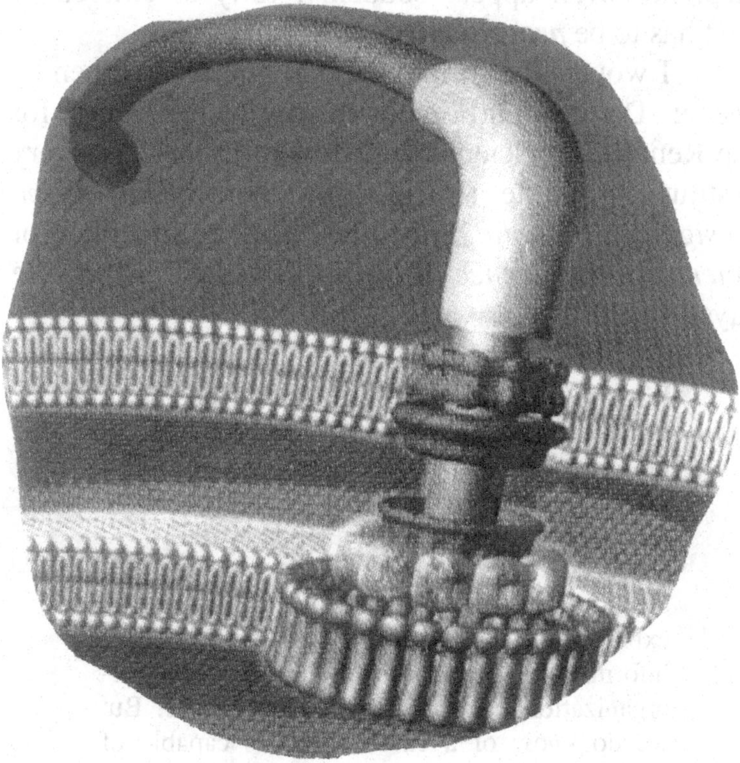

Each working piece of the machinery is designed to fit and interact precisely with another working piece. (Illustra Media)

You might be too polite to say, but I can guess what you'd be thinking.

How did this information evolve?

Now here's the big question. Do you have the answer?: DNA code, more complexly assembled than a computer… ***how did this information evolve?*** By a fluke?

I found myself unable to shrug this off. Information is not something that can evolve, step by step, nor even appear suddenly, fully assembled. It first has to be ***programmed***.

I would like to introduce to you Dr Stephen C. Meyer, Director and Senior Fellow of the Center for the Renewal of Science and Culture at the Discovery Institute in Seattle. (He is also author of *Darwinism, Design, and Public Education*, and is co-author of *Science and Evidence of Design in the Universe.)* He says:

> It's part of our knowledge base that intelligent agents can produce information-rich systems. So the argument is not based on what we ***don't*** know, but it is based on what we ***do*** know about the cause and effect structure of the world.
>
> We know at present there is no naturalistic explanation, no natural cause, that produces information. Not natural selection, not self-organizational processes, not pure chance. But we do know of a cause which is capable of producing information, and that is ***intelligence.***
>
> So when people infer design from the presence of information in DNA, they're effectively making what's called in the historical sciences an ***inference to the best explanation***. So when we find an information-rich system, in the cell, in the DNA molecule specifically, we can infer that an ***intelligence*** played a role in the origin of that system, even if we weren't there to observe

the system coming into existence. (DVD, *Unlocking the Mystery of Life*, Illustra Media, 2002)

In 2004, the scientific journal *Proceedings of the Biological Society of Washington* published an article by Dr Meyer, advocating that the complexity of living organisms could only have been deliberately designed – and that biological information could not have arisen from Darwinian evolution.

Like it or not, information has to be an ***artefact of intelligence.***

Scientist forced into a U-turn

Dr Dean Kenyon, Professor of Biology (Emeritus) at San Francisco State University, was one of the leading chemical evolution theorists in the world.

He co-authored *Biochemical Predestination*, which claimed that the evolution of life was inevitable… that proteins to produce living cells were formed directly by forces of attraction between their parts… that proteins are just formed together (self-assemble) in chains, directly from amino acids, without any DNA assembly instructions.

His theory was accepted with enthusiasm by the evolutionary scientific community. But within just five years after publishing, Kenyon suddenly had serious doubts.

It began when one of his students asked, "How could the first proteins have been assembled without the help of genetic instructions?" (Proteins were the necessary information to build the first cell.)

And then DNA was discovered. This would prove fatal to Kenyon's molecular evolution theory. Kenyon confesses:

> The more I conducted my own studies, including a period of time at NASA-AIMS Research Center, the more it became apparent there were multiple difficulties with the chemical evolution account. And further experimental work showed that amino acids ***do not have the ability to order themselves*** into any biologically meaningful sequences.
>
> The more I thought about the alternative that was being presented in the criticism, and the enormous problem that all of us who had worked on this field had neglected to address, the problem of ***the origin of genetic information itself***, then I really had to re-assess my whole position regarding origins. (*Ibid.*)

What he now had to address was this: What was the ***source*** of the biological information in DNA?

> If one could get at the origin of the messages, the encoded messages within the living machinery, then you would really be onto something far more intellectually satisfying than this chemical evolution theory. *(Ibid.)*

From Unlocking the Mystery of Life (Illustra Media)

The astonishing fact is that inside every microscopic-sized cell, ***machines*** work together to accomplish specific jobs and are shepherded by other specially shaped ***machines*** to precise locations where they are needed.

Learning this, Kenyon exclaimed, "This is absolutely mind-boggling, to perceive at this scale of size, such a finely tuned apparatus, a device, that ***bears the marks of intelligent design and manufacture!"***

Observable evidence of a Master Designer

What else can you call this but ***observable evidence*** of thoughtful, programmed designing by a Superior Mind? Evidence of intelligently organized patterns.

Obviously, such a Designer can only be greater than us. Greater than the creation itself.

Music in genes

Oh, and something else. Did you know this? It was recently discovered that DNA is linked to music!

If you like music, but think that you can't carry a tune, you may be wrong. Respected geneticist, Susumo Ono, believes he's discovered music in genes – particularly human genes, fish genes and rabbit genes. Susumo is a researcher in DNA.

He asked himself, If we were to assign a musical note to each chemical on the DNA strand and string those notes together and play them, what would DNA sound like?

So he did this – and the result was amazing. He discovered musical ***patterns*** of notes, that again reveal ***intelligence***. Susumo Ono was so astonished that he took his findings to musicians. And musicians, in turn, were astonished to hear echoes of Bach, of Schubert, of Mozart in DNA music.

Using the same formula for converting DNA into music, Dr Ono worked backwards and translated Chopin's funeral march into chemical symbols. It came out ***cancer!***

Skeptics naturally point out that these strands of DNA produce only a string of single notes; it is the musicians who fill in the rhythm and the harmony.

That's so. But the bottom line is this: Whichever way you look at it, the PATTERNS of single notes testify to ***intelligence*** as the source of DNA. Certainly it is not from a blind, accidental force in nature.

Identical to written language

But there's more, much more. Scientists at Bell Laboratories conducted studies on the ***mathematical language*** in the DNA molecule.

And what did they find? Its mathematical pattern is identical to that of conversational language.

Concerning DNA, Charles Thaxton states:

> A structural identity has been discovered between the genetic message on DNA and the written messages of a human language. (Charles Thaxton, "A New Design Argument," *Cosmic Pursuit* 1, no. 2, Spring 1998)

Hupert Yockey explains:

> There is an identity of structure between DNA (and protein) and written linguistic messages. Since we know by experience that ***intelligence*** produces written messages, and ***no other cause***

> is known, the implication, according to the abductive method, is that intelligent cause produced DNA and protein. The significance of this result lies in the security of it, for it is much stronger than if the structures were merely similar. We are not dealing with anything like a superficial resemblance between DNA and a written text. We are not saying DNA is like a message. Rather, DNA ***is*** a message. True design thus returns to biology. (Hubert P. Yockey, "Journal of Theoretic Biology". Quoted in Charles Thaxton, "A New Design Argument," *Cosmic Pursuit* 1, no. 2, Spring 1998. Emphasis mine.)

Since ***it takes intelligence to write a language***, is it not evident that it took intelligence to write the DNA code?

Intelligently designed 'sentences' impressed from the 'outside'

Dean Kenyon was asked if DNA comes in ***intelligently designed 'sentences'***. "Is it true that when scientists peer into the microscopic world of DNA, they find not mere random arrangements, but ***well-written 'instruction books'?"***

"Yes," responded Kenyon. ***"Masterpieces of immense intricacy and subtlety."***

"And you argue that these biological 'sentences' in DNA could ***not*** have arisen merely by material means, as evolutionists suggest?" asked the interviewer.

"No," said Kenyon. "Just as the chemistry and physics of ink and paper do not determine the order of symbols in a printed text, but that order must be impressed on the ink ***from the 'outside'***, so also the ***order of the*** bases, or ***sub-units***, in DNA [adenine, thymine, guanine, and cytosine, or A, T, G, and C as commonly represented] is not determined by the known chemical tendencies of these individual sub-units, but instead appears to have been ***impressed from the 'outside'*** on the sub-units ***to create just those sequences that make biological sense***."

It takes three billion (3,000,000,000) of those letters to represent a copy of you.

There is one of those 3-billion-letter messages inside each cell in your body.

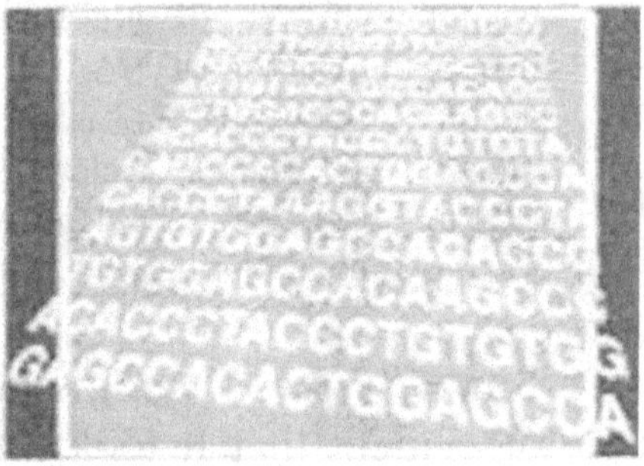

The fantastic complexity and orderliness of the DNA code – condensed into an incredibly tiny size – suggests the work of a ***brilliant intellect*** rather than chance processes. It suggests that ***much thought has gone into their design*** – just as human beings use intelligence to design and construct computers, Jumbo jets, space craft and other intricate equipment.

If radio signals were to be received from outer space, they would be understood as evidence of an intelligent source. Why then should we not regard the message sequence on the DNA molecule as prima facie evidence of an intelligent source?

Designed to NOT evolve

But that is not all! Gene code letters have ***built in error protection***!

Genes store information in long strings of DNA, in the form of chemical letters, called A, T, C and G. So that genes can be ***accurately copied,*** each gene consists of two parallel strands of DNA held together by links between the code letters of one strand and those of the other strand. The two strands are not identical. That is, A's do not link to A's, and so on. Instead, they are complimentary. A's link to T's; C's always link to G's.

Donail MacDonaill of Trinity College, Dublin, studied that pattern of linkages between letters. And he found that they form a ***parity code*** similar to computer codes, to minimise mistakes during the electronic transfer of information. (*Nature* science update, www.nature.com/nsu September 18, 2002)

Now is the moment of truth. No one would be so naïve as to believe modern electronic ***parity codes*** could have evolved by chance. They were carefully planned by software designers. Could the parity code found in DNA be further evidence that the genetic code was ***deliberately created?***

DNA is designed to maintain accurate copies and ***avoid changes*** in the information it carries. ***This means it was designed to NOT evolve.*** But rather to reproduce its own kind forever. Doesn't this make evolution scientifically impossible? The genes of fruit flies were manipulated to produce flies with no eyes. When these were interbred their offspring also had no eyes. But after several generations eyes started to reappear due to this fail-safe mechanism, ***reverting back*** to a normal fly. In other words, no evolution!

A miracle – nothing less

Microbiologist Dr Michael Denton challenges the scientific community to address the impossibility of a single cell being thrown together, unless by an occurrence "indistinguishable from a miracle." (Michael Denton, *Evolution: A Theory in Crisis*. Bethesda, Md.: Adler and Adler, 1986, p. 264)

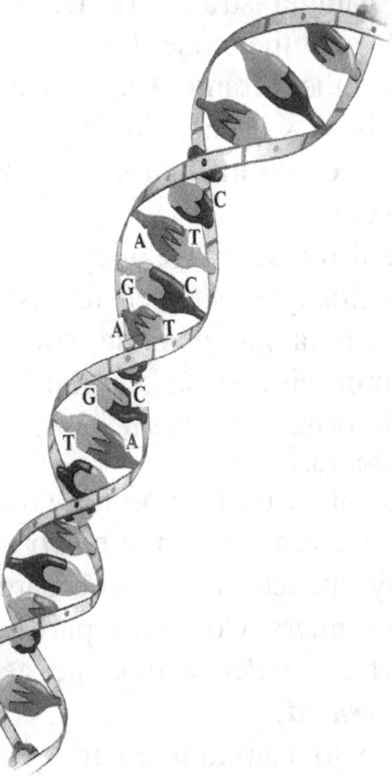

Each nucleotide base (or letter) on one DNA strand interlocks with a specific partner on the other strand.

Together they then form a base pair of letters.

*Three pairs of letters form a code for one **amino acid**.*

The order in which the pairs are arranged on a DNA strand determines the information contained in that strand.

Genetic information is contained in the myriad combinations of pairs throughout the length of the DNA molecule.

*A **gene** is a particular sequence of letters which codes for a specific protein.*

Is it any wonder that mathematicians can have serious doubts about evolution? Mathematician I.L. Cohen, a member of New York Academy of Sciences, writes:

> …any physical change of any size, shape or form is strictly the result of purposeful alignment of billions of nucleotides [in the DNA]. Nature or species do not have the capacity to rearrange them nor to add to them… The only way we know for a DNA to be altered is through a meaningful intervention from an outside source of intelligence – one who knows what it is doing, such as our genetic engineers are now performing in the laboratories. (I.L.

Cohen, *Darwin Was Wrong; A Study in Probabilities.* New York Research Publications, Inc., 1984, p. 209)

He adds:

> …every single concept advanced by the theory of evolution (and amended thereafter) is imaginary as it is not supported by the scientifically established facts of microbiology, fossils, and mathematical probability concepts. Darwin was wrong. *(Ibid.)*
>
> …The theory of evolution may be the worst mistake made in science. (*Ibid.*, p. 210)

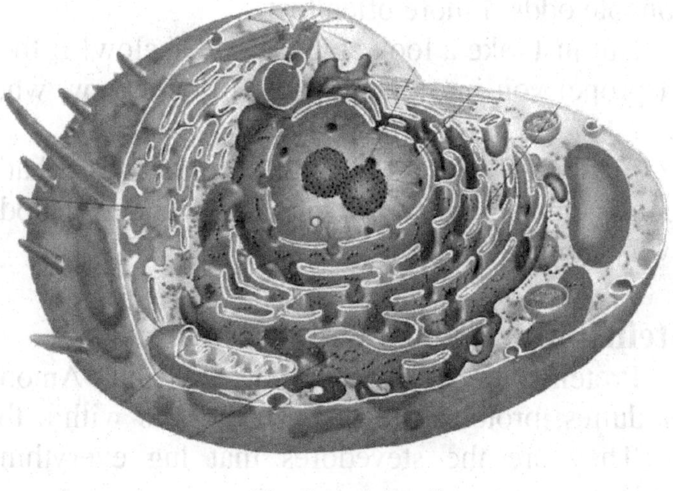

The "simple" cell

2

Impossible odds -

COULD YOU WIN A $MILLION LOTTERY A MILLION TIMES?

I used to love betting on horses. What excitement to buy a newspaper, work out a winning system... and listen to the race! To increase the excitement, I might sometimes go to the track. Those last few moments were so tense! Even with reasonable odds, I more often lost.

But just take a look at these odds below! If they don't propel you into outer space, I don't know what will.

First, let me tell you something that's happening inside every cell of your wonderful body this very moment.

Proteins: intelligence with no brains

Proteins are workers inside the cell. Among other duties, proteins are the *transporters* within the cells. They are the stevedores that lug everything around.

Who tells them what, where, when, and how much to carry?

I will tell you the answer to that one, yet it only presents a bigger question: Another protein (often a constructor) moves over to the transporter, touches him momentarily, and the transporter then knows exactly what to get and how much is needed.

Each protein is carefully assembled by another protein – which was itself assembled only a short time before. It does the assembling job from materials lying around. And it never makes a mistake.

Who taught the protein how to assemble another protein?

Each protein has a very complex structure. It is made up of hundreds of organic amino acids, arranged in a totally complicated order.

There could be only one correct arrangement of each protein – yet there are millions of wrong ways it could be arranged.

The utter randomness of evolution could never come up with the right combination for each protein.

If the *constructor* protein finds he does not have the right amount and combination of amino acids lying around, he tells another protein to bring him some more!

The messenger goes to the edge of the cell and tells the *gatekeeper* (another protein) to bring them in, which he does.

This is going on millions of times a minute in every cell of your body.

Each little protein molecule does the most fabulous things. It carries out complicated tasks which require great intelligence. The problem is there is not a nerve cell anywhere in its body. No brains.

Armies of proteins carry out complicated series of actions. Every step is complex, yet the finished result is always perfect.

I ask you, how can this be done, when different proteins which never meet each other take part in the different steps? As you know, none of the proteins lives very long. And none of them teaches the new proteins they construct how to do the work they are going to do! There are no classroom teachers in the cell, for all the students have ***no brains***, yet they know exactly what to do!

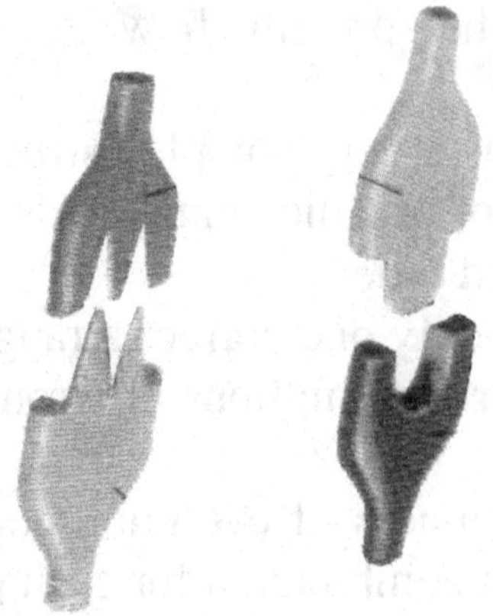

And now consider this: Even if, just one time, evolution could produce one correct protein – how on earth could it keep repeating the fluke again and again, which ***it would have to do*** in order to replicate that correct protein in making millions more of it?

Something else. The simplest form of DNA complex is a virus. But for a virus to reproduce it needs to enter a living cell to utilise energy from mitochrondria and the ***protein-producing*** ability of the host cell. It is ***unable to reproduce on its own.***

Enzymes: mathematical odds

Enzymes are proteins of high molecular weight. Sir Fred Hoyle and Professor Wickramasinghe write:

> Biochemical systems are exceedingly complex, so much so, that the chance of their being formed through random shufflings of simple organic molecules is exceedingly minute, to a

> point where it is insensibly different from zero. (F. Hoyle and C. Wickramasinghe, *Evolution From Space*. Dent, 1981, p. 3)

They explain that there are perhaps 10^{80} (10, followed by 80 zeroes) atoms in the universe and 10^{17} seconds have elapsed since the alleged 'big bang'. The number of independent enzymes necessary for life is about 2,000. The probability of building just one of these enzymes cannot be better than one in 10^{40000} This outrageously small probability could not be faced, even if the whole universe consisted of organic soup.

> If one is not prejudiced either by social beliefs or by a scientific training that life originated on Earth, this simple calculation wipes the idea entirely out of court. *(Ibid*, p. 24)

Fred Hoyle, writing in *New Scientist*, repeated that 2,000 different and very complex enzymes are required for a living organism to exist. Then he added that not a single one of these could be formed by random, shuffling processes in even 20 billion years!

Our existence on earth is as if we had won a million-dollar lottery a million times in a row.

Amino acids: impossible odds

There are 20 amino acids. There are 300 amino acids in a specialised sequence in each medium protein. There are billions upon billions of possible combinations!

The right combination from among the 20 amino acids would have to be brought together in the right sequence – ***in order to make one usable protein.***

The possible arrangements of the 20 amino acids is 2,500,000,000,000,000,000.

If evolutionary theory is true, every protein arrangement in a life form has to be worked out by chance until it works right – first one combination and then another until one is found that works right.

By then the organism will have long died, if it even had been alive! It's becoming embarrassing… The sheer amount of speculation… the ***myriad "blind chances"*** needed to support the evolution thesis… I need a glass of water!

All need to exist together, instantly!

DNA only works because it has enzymes to help it; enzymes only work because there are protein chains; protein only works because of DNA; DNA only works because it is formed of protein chains. They all have to be there together, immediately, at the same time.

But the enzymes only work because the protein chains are coded in a special sequence by DNA. DNA can only replicate with the help of protein enzymes. We are really in a chicken and egg situation. (E. Ambrose, *The Nature and Origin of the Biological World*, p. 135)

Outmoded theory

Yes, it appears we are now in the soup with this evolution theory. We are stuck with an outmoded mid-19th century idea that was devised when almost nothing was known about proteins, genetics, or microbiology.

Do experiments suggest we could create life?

Dean Kenyon is a fellow of the Discovery Institute's Center for the Renewal of Science and Culture, an Intelligent Design think-tank based in Seattle, Washington. He is a Professor of Biology at San Francisco State University. He holds a PhD in biophysics from Stanford University. He has been a National Science Foundation Postdoctoral Fellow at the University of California at Berkeley, a visiting scholar at Trinity College, Oxford University, and a visiting Research Associate at NASA-Ames Research Center.

The following extracts are from an interview he did with Benjamin Wiker.

Wiker: According to the standard materialist account of evolution, billions and billions of years ago there was on earth a kind of chemical "soup" and from this lifeless soup somehow living things arose. What discoveries in particular led you to reject this account?

Kenyon: The standard account has many flaws – not the least of which is the fact that there is no geochemical evidence for the existence of a prebiotic soup!

Wiker: But how do you account for those experiments which supposedly showed that we can create the building blocks of life, amino acids, out of just such a chemical soup?

Kenyon: Stanley Miller's famous experiment, first performed in the early 1950s, presumably simulated the earth's primitive atmosphere. Using a mixture of methane, ammonia, molecular hydrogen, and water vapour, and supplying energy with an electric discharge, he produced small amounts of a few amino acids and other substances which occur in living cells.

But less well known is the fact that the dominant trend of the chemistry occurring in these experiments is toward non-biological material – that is, amber gunk which coats the inside of the apparatus.

Moreover, such experiments routinely leave molecular oxygen out of the apparatus even though geological evidence suggests that oxygen may well have been present in the earth's early atmosphere.

Wiker: Why do they leave oxygen out of such experiments?

Kenyon: If molecular oxygen is present, then it destroys, by oxidation, any biochemicals that form. Of course, we should add that if both hydrogen and oxygen are together in a mixture of gasses supplied with electric sparks, the apparatus might explode!

Wiker: So the Miller-type experiment does not, in this regard, match the actual chemical environment of the early earth?

Kenyon: Correct. In this instance, the oxygen is left out of the experiments because of a requirement of chemical evolution theory, not because we have evidence that it was absent from the primitive atmosphere.

And there are many more difficulties. For example, the energy used to initiate the chemical reactions in these simulation experiments – electric sparks, ultraviolet and other types of radiation, heat – would actually have destroyed the more complex products they presume were created.

The energy sources, rather than being creative, would have interacted with the presumed prebiotic carbon compounds in such a way that the destruction of chemicals would have predominated over their synthesis.

Finally, we have no plausible naturalistic account of the prebiotic origin of genetic information – that is, of the origin of specific biologically meaningful linear sequences of nucleotides in DNA and RNA.

These are just some of the reasons why I think the empirical case against a chemical evolutionary origin of life is overwhelming.

Life created in the laboratory?

But couldn't life be created in the lab? After all, scientists have created some building blocks of life – amino acids.

Not so fast! Firstly, it has been done by men with intelligence, under artificial laboratory conditions far different from those on the early earth. And secondly, amino acids are only a tiny part of the necessary components for life. It would be like claiming that accidental laboratory production of a speck of black ink proves that the *Encyclopaedia Brittanica* randomly evolved.

Why Kenyon had to repudiate evolution

Wiker: I'm taking it that it has not always been this way – that you were not always so skeptical about the claims of evolutionary theory. You were co-author of the best-selling, advanced textbook on chemical evolution in the 1970s.

Kenyon: Yes, that's right.

I did postdoctoral research in Melvin Calvin's lab at the University of California at Berkeley, and collaborated there with Gary Steinman in writing *Biochemical Predestination.*

It wasn't until after I taught the evolution course at San Francisco State University for ten years that I began seriously to doubt the evolutionary account.

I had growing doubts about the transition series of fossils and about the chemical evolution experiments – such as Miller's – and became increasingly uncomfortable making the standard evolutionary claims to students because these claims could not be supported in the scientific literature. (Interview by Benjamin Wiker. Paper: *A New Scientific Revolution*)

Some other honest scientists speak up

Evolution theory is scientific? Where is the science? I can assure the reader the American Kennel Club would not certify an ***ancestor of your dog*** based on evidence such as paleontologists present. (Isaac V.Manly, M.D., Harvard Medical School. *God Made: A Medical Doctor Looks at the Reality.* Joplin, MO.: College Press, 1994, pp. 15,117,228)

I believe that one day the Darwinian myth will be ranked ***the greatest deceit*** in the history of science. When this happens, many people will pose the question: how did this ever happen? (Saltationist Soren Lovtrup, Professor of Embryol-ogy, University of Umea, Sweden. *Darwinism: The Refutation of a Myth.* New York: Chapman Hall, 1987, p.422)

So we can sleep well tonight. Our children's education is in the good hands and sticky fingers of honest "experts".

Now comes my next question to test the imaginations of these mighty thinkers…

3

How did information evolve? -

ORIGIN OF THE UNIVERSE

"Keep it up, boy!" Little Jamie bent down again and tugged on his shoe laces. He pulled and pulled until he was out of breath.

"Why can't I pull myself off the ground?" he cried in frustration.

Well, you know the answer to that. If you pull up on your boot straps for ten trillion years you still won't lift yourself off the ground. The law of gravity stops you.

So here were two questions niggling at my mind:

1. Firstly, were the Laws of the Conservation of Energy and of Matter ***suspended*** long enough for Empty Space to give birth to a rock?
2. Secondly, would the rock get wet (for no reason), and then give birth to an amoeba?

Er, yeah… sure it would, if you sort of screwed up your eyes and crossed your fingers!?

No one disputes that the origin of the universe involved physical matter ***appearing from nothing***. Yet there is no scientific mechanism that could have caused it to occur.

But physical matter has appeared. Because we are here!

Pure lottery. What if a billion, billion, billion black balls were mixed together with one white ball, and I had to reach, blindfolded, and pick out the white one? What if my life depended on it? Pick out that white one or be killed.

If I reached, blindfolded into those zillions of black balls and discovered I had pulled out the one and only white ball… yes, I would rightly suspect that the whole thing was rigged.

I pulled it out by pure accident? What do you think? Wouldn't you call me nuts if I told you I picked it first time by chance!

Origin of life

But that's not all. What about the odds of ***life*** happening? Mathematically, it was simply impossible. When you consider the ***hundreds*** of factors required to produce life or even a planet capable of sustaining life as we know it – factors as diverse as the decay rates of elements and the distance of a planet's orbit to its sun – and multiply them by the scientific and mathematical odds of those factors being right, it just doesn't work. ***We shouldn't be here.***

That brings to mind something that Sir Fred Hoyle said. That honoured British astronomer calculated that the odds of only ***one*** factor necessary for life coming together by chance – the enzymes needed to perform the chemical functions needed to produce the most simple living creature – were one in $10^{40,000}$. That's mathematical shorthand for 10 followed by 40,000 zeros, enough to fill 20 pages of this book…000000000000 and so on.

(For perspective, mathematicians consider any probability of less than one in 10^{50} to be impossible.)

1. Did DNA just evolve?

Now just consider the ***origin*** of one living cell.

What were the odds of ***the first simple cell*** forming? Just ask a statistician.

Produce a simple cell by chance? You are living in a dream world, he'll reply. Do you know what you're asking?

Even the simplest cell you can conceive of would require no less than 100,000 DNA base pairs and a minimum of about 10,000 amino acids, to form the essential protein chain. Not to mention the other things that would also be necessary for the first cell.

Bear in mind that ***every*** single base pair in the DNA chain has to have the same molecular orientation ("left-hand" or "right hand")? As well as that, virtually ***all*** the amino acids must have the opposite orientation. And ***every one*** must be without error. Every single one of the ten thousand.

Now, to randomly obtain those correct orientations, do you know your chances? It would be 1 chance in $2^{110,000}$, or 1 chance in $10^{33,113}$!

To put it another way, if you attempted a trillion, trillion, trillion combinations every second for 15 billion years, the odds you would achieve all the correct orientations would still only be one chance in a trillion, trillion, trillion, trillion ... and the trillions would continue 2755 times!

It would be like winning more than 4700 state lotteries in a row with only a single ticket purchased for each. In other words...***impossible.*** Would you please read that over again carefully and think about it?

2. How is 'life' added?

But to orientate the molecules correctly is ***just one*** of the hurdles to be overcome for life to appear randomly.

Here's another: ***How do you add 'life'*** to non-living matter?

And that's only for the first, simplest cell. You still have the problem of the developing of more than 1.7 million highly complex species.... With even greater odds against it happening. As a statistician will assure you, random evolution is utterly impossible.

At school we were taught about the "simple cell"... Oh go on!... we have now discovered it to be more complex than New York's vast transportation network at rush hour. To appear accidentally was ***a mathematical absurdity***.

We've already noted this, but a brief review is in order here.

The DNA *machinery* inside each cell had to be totally ***100 percent intact*** with all its interlocking, working parts, ***before one living cell*** could even exist.

Fascinating, you might say. But just wait till its implications hit you...

Firstly, DNA comes in ***intelligently designed sentences***. It is not LIKE a language. It IS a language. Much thought has gone into the design of the DNA code.

Secondly, this molecular machine has the ***ability to make functional copies of itself***. And to do this it would ***have*** to be extremely complex.

Thirdly, the DNA molecule which tells every part of the cell "city" which different job to do, is the most complex storage system in the known universe.

Fourthly, in every cell, microscopic-sized factories endlessly retrieve, process and store food. And highly efficient power plants burn the food to produce and store energy – all without over-heating the delicate temperature-sensitive machinery.

3. How did the first information evolve?

Each of these things needs to receive information on how to do its job. That's a gigantic hurdle... ***information***.

How did genetic information evolve? And where did it come from, in the first place? From dead matter? That was the very question that would finally stump me.

I ask you, how on earth could this complex coded information evolve, ***instantly perfect***? Do you have the answer to that?

A world leader in the field of "information science" was Dr Werner Gitt, a director and professor at the German Federal Institute of Physics and Technology. According to Dr Gitt, science makes one fact absolutely certain: information cannot emerge from disorder by chance. It ***always takes a greater source*** of information to produce information. And ultimately, information is the result of intelligence. ("How Would You Answer?" <www.answersingenesis.org/docs/3270. asp#r16>, March 13, 2003)

> A code system is always the result of a mental process (it requires an intelligent origin or inventor).... It should be emphasized that matter as such is unable to generate any code. All experiences indicate that ***a thinking being*** voluntarily exercising his own free will, cognition, and creativity, is required. (Werner Gitt, *In the Beginning Was Information*. Bielenfeld, Germany: Christliche Literatur-Verbreitung, pp. 64-67. Emphasis mine)

> There is no known natural law through which matter can give rise to information, neither is any physical process or material phenomenon known that can do this. (*Ibid.*, p. 79)

Bad news for evolution?

As if that wasn't enough... Just factor this in. Simultaneously, you would need a totally functional system able and ready to ***write, read and use*** that information. In other words,

- the writing mechanism,
- the reading mechanism, and
- the mechanism to use it,

these ***must all be present at the same very first moment*** that the information appears. If one of these components is missing, the whole system will fail to work. Here was a case of "irreducible complexity".

Could this just happen? Could mere chemicals just on their own change into living systems? Not a snowflake's chance.

How much information?

Do you have any idea as to how much information is continuously programming, constructing and reproducing your body?

For starters, your body contains 75 trillion or more cells. Just suppose that you could stretch out and join up all the DNA in those cells end to end, do you know how far that would reach? Get this: 94 billion (not million, but billion) miles. Or 150 billion kilometres. That's a thousand times the distance from the earth to the sun. Or 3½ million times around our earth's equator! It would take a beam of light 5½ days to travel that far.

Does that make your head spin? If all the DNA in just your body was placed end to end, that's how far it would reach! No kidding. Read the last paragraph again.

Okay, then, what is the probability of ***just one – just one – just one – of those DNA molecules*** forming by chance? The late astrophysicist Sir Fred Hoyle put it this way:

> Now imagine 10^{50} blind persons [that's 100,000 billion billion billion billion billion people – standing shoulder to shoulder, they would more than fill our entire solar system] each with a scrambled Rubik cube and try to conceive of the chance of them all simultaneously arriving at the solved form. You then have the chance of arriving by random shuffling [random variation] at just one of the many biopolymers on which life depends. The notion that not only the biopolymers but the operating program of a living cell could be arrived at by chance in a primordial soup here on Earth is evidently nonsense of a high order. (Fred Hoyle, "The Big Bang in Astronomy," *New Scientist*, vol. 92, no. 1280, November 19, 1981, p. 527)

It has been estimated that the 3 billion letters of information in just one human cell of DNA are equivalent to 1,000 encyclopedia-sized books of information. ("Human/Chimp DNA Similarity," <www.answersingene sis.org/docs/2453.asp#f6>, March 13, 2003)

Optimum design perfection

Oh, something else. The DNA code for information storage and translation, contains the ideal number of genetic letters.

This threw me. You see, the copying mechanism of DNA, to meet maximum effectiveness, requires the number of letters in each word to be an ***even number***. Of all possible mathematical combinations, the ideal number for storage and transcription has been calculated to be ***four*** letters.

And this is exactly what has been found in the genes of every living thing on earth – a four-letter digital code. "The coding system used for living human beings is ***optimal from an engineering standpoint.*** This suggests it is a case of purposeful design rather than a [lucky] chance." (Dr Werner Gitt, *In the Beginning Was Information*, p. 95. Emphasis mine)

Here, then, is what I have found myself needing to face:

1. Scientists have ***never*** observed chemicals forming themselves into complex DNA molecules.
2. Life ***cannot*** arise spontaneously from non-life.
3. The simplest living organisms show ***irreducible complexity.***
4. DNA molecules ***do not*** produce new genetic information. They only reproduce it.

The bottom line is this: There are ***no natural processes*** that could account for it... ***no scientific mechanism*** that could have caused it to occur.

Sorry, skeptics. That leaves you and me with only one rational alternative... that ***the first life*** must have been designed, then created.

1. Such organisms were ***fully formed from the first moment*** they appeared.
2. The first life must have been ***programmed***, like a computer chip, with the original code (or life-information) loaded into it by the designer.

So life was ***deliberately created***?

Well, then, after life was created, did evolution follow? Did an original living organism evolve upward into the many varieties we have today?

Let's investigate...

4

Mutations, natural selection, and variations -

MAKING EVOLUTION POSSIBLE?

Jack's business was selling raincoats. He bought them for $69, then sold them for $62.50

"If I sell enough of them, I'll be able to upgrade to a new car," he said.

What was wrong with Jack's plan? Of course you know! A business can't make money by losing a little at a time.

And what has this to do with our subject? You'll see…

The thought arises, perhaps DNA ***was*** created, but then after that evolution took over?

How? By mutations, dummy! Isn't that what we were taught in school?

Mutations do not add information needed for evolution

Okay, stop right there. Mutations? What are they, anyway? If you didn't know, mutations are genetic ***copying mistakes!***

Mistakes? That's right. Copying mistakes. Now, please help me here, if I'm missing something. Do you honestly think that ***mistakes*** would ***produce*** the intelligent ***organized information*** required for evolution?

You want it straight? There's no need to guess. There is ***observational evidence.*** And it says ***no***.

OBSERVED FACT ABOUT MUTATIONS: In every case known to science, there has been a ***loss of genetic information.***

Wake up, Suzie! We now know that DNA molecules ***do not produce*** new genetic information. They only ***reproduce*** it.

Confirmed? Yes. As Dr Lee Spetner, biophysicist and information theory specialist, and a former professor at John Hopkins University, reveals:

> All point mutations that have been studied on the molecular level turn out to reduce the genetic information and not to increase it. (Lee Spetner, *Not by Chance*. Brooklyn, NY.: The Judaica Press Inc., 1997, p. 138)

> Information cannot be built up by mutations that lose it. A business ***can't make money by losing a little at a time***. (*Ibid.,* p. 143. Emphasis added)

Well, who could argue with that?

Inherited back-up template can correct mutations

As I was mulling over this, there came the shocking news of a discovery made by plant scientists at Purdue University.

Well, what had the scientists discovered? It was a plant containing a template – that is, a master genetic blueprint – that ***can correct defective genes inherited from its parents.***

What!

Yes, it's true. They examined the offspring of two mutant plants which had a malfunctioning gene. And they found that 10 percent of their offspring don't have this malformation, but rather are like the normal (non-mutant) grandparents. As *New York Times* science reporter Nicholas Wade announced:

> The discovery also raises interesting biological questions – including whether it gets in the way of evolution, which depends on mutations changing an organism rather than being put right by a backup system…. The finding poses a puzzle for evolutionary theory because it corrects mutations which evolution depends on as generators of novelty [new features]. ("Startling Scientists, Plant Fixes Its Flawed Genes," *New York Times*, March 23, 2005)

Even Robert Pruitt, the discoverer of the phenomenon, was puzzled. As he admitted:

> This challenges everything we believe…
>
> It seems that these [mutant gene]-containing plants keep a cryptic copy of everything that was in the previous generation, even though it doesn't show up in the DNA, it's not in the chromosome. Some other type of gene sequence information that we don't really understand yet is modifying the inherited traits. (Quoted by Susan Steeves, "Plants Defy Mendel's Inheritance Laws, May Prompt Textbook Changes", *Purdue News Services*)

Scientists do not yet know how many living organisms contain this master back-up copy. But the search has begun.

I can tell you this. One will be hard pressed to explain how such a mechanism could have been created in a Darwinian step-by-step fashion – and inherited not from parents, but from grandparents or distant ancestors!

We noted earlier that there is a complex mechanism within the DNA of every cell that corrects mutations. Remember the flies that lost eyes and got them back again after several generations?

Mutation only within the species

And, in any case, when a mutation occurs, the change is still within the DNA of the species. The change is ***within*** the basic type of organism, ***not transferred from one basic type into another.***

If half developed: no survival value

You know as well as I. Of the many thousands of living things, ***every one*** is today ***perfectly designed*** for its environment. There is a happy state of dependability and workability throughout nature. And it is persistently so.

Does anyone want to quibble over that? So do you mind me asking, if evolution is occurring now, where is it? I've looked high and low. There should be thousands of partly evolved features. There are none! Not one life form has a half developed organ, or an organ superfluous to its needs. Nothing is unfitted, or out of place.

Instead, what do we see? Thousands of amazing creatures doing highly specialised jobs that ***demonstrate intelligence*** – which they ***don't have***. Not only that, they also possess highly specialised organs which are vital to their survival – organs which could ***not*** possibly be the outcome of long and gradual 'chance mutations'.

Common sense tells us that these millions of 'specialised organs' are so highly complex that to be useful and functional, every one of their interlocking parts had to ***all*** come into existence at once.

You don't need to be smart to realise that numerous precision components ***had to work perfectly***

from the very start of any organism's existence. No process of gradual change from generation to generation could ever create any apparatus with all its ***inter-dependent working parts***.

Not until the ***entire*** mechanism was complete would the arrangement have any practical value to an animal or plant. Meanwhile, mutations which led to the useless intermediate stages, having ***no survival value,*** would be ***removed*** by the so-called "natural selection" process. And the final, complete mechanism would never have been able to appear.

We've already referred to the term ***"irreducible complexity"*** – which means that systems needed to appear in an organism already ***complete*** if they were to function at all.

When you think about it, there's nothing really simple. Even the simple mousetrap is a combination of several different things – a block of wood, the spring latch and the hammer. If one is missing, the mousetrap is useless.

Evolution theory would require that each element of the mousetrap developed on its own, separately. But how could that make sense? Because the trap wouldn't work ***without all*** three parts there at the ***start***.

Have you ever studied the human ***eye***? It's not simple like that mousetrap. The eye is made up of ***millions of parts*** – the pupil, lens, muscles, optic nerve, and millions of rods and cones. All parts were needed at once. So how did that come about? Could evolution answer this? Yeah. And pigs will fly.

To design something like an eye you'd need a clever-minded engineer.

Again, Michael Behe, a biochemist and professor at Pennsylvania's Lehigh University, explained that genetic information is primarily an ***instruction manual:***

> Consider a step-by-step list of [genetic] instructions. A mutation is a change in ***one*** of the lines of instructions. So instead of saying, 'Take a ¼ inch nut,' a mutation might say, 'Take a 3/8 inch nut.' Or instead of 'Place the round peg in the round hole,' we might get 'Place the round peg in the square hole'... What a mutation ***cannot*** do is change all the instructions in one step – say, [providing instructions] to build a fax machine instead of a radio. (Michael Behe, *Darwin's Black Box*, 1996, p. 41)

What about "punctuated equilibrium"?

The theory goes like this. Perhaps the major evolutionary changes occurred quite rapidly, while the population levels were low. So the gaps might be due to such periods of 'explosive evolution', which occurred so rapidly they left no trace in the fossils.

In other words, extremely fast evolution occurred in small isolated communities. So it was NOT recorded in the fossil strata.

In that case, evidence should not even be expected. Um, okay.

Great theory. But evidence? Can't find a shred of physical evidence for it. Frankly, it's an argument from silence. You just have to trust it by faith.

You are probably going to tell me that a theory which predicts it will have no evidence hardly qualifies as a scientific theory. And I must agree with you.

Punctuated equilibrium doesn't even have a mechanism. Even the promoters themselves admit that.

You mean experiments have not been able to show any means by which evolutionary jumps can occur? Not one.

So it's ***not scientific observation***. We're asked to believe that evolution occurs so slowly today that we cannot detect it, and so rapidly in the past that we cannot detect it!

Then I came upon a copy of *Science News.* The report mentioned how the AIDS virus was shown to mutate up to a million times faster than the DNA for other organisms. So in one year the virus went through the equivalent of one million years of mutation at the usual rate. (*Science News*, June 28, 1986, p. 410)

Great! Here's a good way to test the "punctuated equilibrium" theory. Here's an example of what would actually happen if very fast development ***did*** occur in a small isolated community, as some have suggested.

Hopefully this helps the theory? Oh, bother! Even with the mutation process speeded up a million times, the AIDS virus only 'evolved' into another form of AIDS virus and nothing else. *(Ibid.)*

Now you know. This observed evidence actually ***refutes*** the idea of ***punctuated equilibrium.***

Darn it! Fossil evidence shows the same for other creatures that experience numerous mutations in a short period. The first spiders mutated and selected into the forms they have today. They remain spiders. And the same with everything else.

Here is no joy for "punctuated equilibrium" as a means of evolution. Punctuated equilibrium? That's the kind of evolution you have when you don't actually have any evolution!

Does that leave you with a kind of empty feeling inside?

My final question on punctuated equilibrium is this: Just how could these big jumps occur genetically? How could the ***genetic code for fully functioning organs*** suddenly appear out of nowhere?

What about natural selection?

We all know that variation exists among living forms. Variations are the result of what we call ***natural selection.*** What is natural selection? It is the process by which heritable traits are ***selected from*** the parent gene pool, that make it more likely for an organism to survive in a particular circumstance.

There's an oft-recited myth that natural selection is "the mechanism by which evolution occurs."

Why a myth? Because of…INFORMATION. Since information ***cannot be added***, then at the very ***start,*** the parents must have possessed ***enough variety of information*** so their descendants could ***select*** what was needed to help them adapt to a wide variety of environments. For example, antibiotic resistance, or long beaks may become dominant features in generations that follow. But, bad luck… ***the gene pool has been reduced.***

Why? Because it is a selecting of only ***some*** of the parents' gene pool. Thus the original information is thereby reduced, and ***that is the opposite of evolution.***

But let facts get in the way? Never. This evolution theory has become an institution. (And some say that's where it belongs.)

Variations = evolution? No!

In every case, the descendants, despite all their variations, continue to be of the same basic type. The DNA ensures that. All today's dog breeds came from an original dog. And that original dog possessed all of the genetic information required to produce the varieties of dogs we now see. But all its descendants, no matter what their appearance, are still – every one of them – dogs. No amount of variation will mutate a dog into a horse, or anything else.

So, really, is ***variation*** evolution? Another disappointment. It's not evolution, but adaptation.

What about when some varieties become extinct and others survive? Sorry, ***extinction is not evolution***. The bottom line is that the information has been ***reduced***. The gene pool has been ***reduced.*** And that is the ***opposite of evolution.***

Total re-design needed

For one creature to change into the other (for example, a reptile into a winged bird) is not a modification, it is a ***cancelling*** of one perfect design and ***starting*** with another. And if only ***part*** of the new design system is complete, then the total organism will fail to function. In that single lifetime it would become extinct. ***Inter-dependence*** of every part – we cannot shrug this away.

Do similarities prove evolution?

But what about similar design of body parts shared by different creatures? Isn't this a hint of a common evolutionary ancestor?

As an intelligent person, just think it through. Again, the answer is: OF COURSE NOT! Common sense tells us that similar parts more likely had ***a common designer***. And an efficient design will be used constantly. If a wheel is useful for a motor car, a wheel will also be useful for a skateboard, or a bicycle. The skateboard did not beget the car.

Quick summary

DON'T VARIATIONS PROVE EVOLUTION? No. Whether mutations or natural selection, they only reduce the information to each new variety. They do not add information for upward evolution to occur.

DON'T SIMILARITIES PROVE EVOLUTION? No. Parts similarity only indicates an efficient design – and very likely a common designer.

In any case, for evolution to happen, you need two essentials:

1. a CODE to direct evolution, and
2. an ENABLING MECHANISM.

But neither of these has been discovered.

Theories… but not evidence

As you can see, there is no shortage of theories… nothing more than a bundle of changing guesses! Isn't there something wrong with a theory – any theory - if one needs to ***invent unknown*** and ***never-seen*** mechanisms to support it?

Okay then. But what about fossils? Don't we hear so often that they prove evolution?

Ah, that's a good question…

5

Fossils and evolution -

DEAD IN THE WRONG PLACE

Do you remember sitting in school and being taught about "the geological column"? The chart went something like this:

THE GEOLOGICAL TIME-SCALE		Estimated years ago
Age of Man 	Recent (Neolithic, Bronze, Iron) Pleistocene or Glacial (Paleolithic)	25,000 to 5,000,000
CENOZOIC Age of Mammals	Pliocene Miocene Oligocene Eocene	12,000,000 to 65,000,000
MESOZOIC Age of Reptiles	Cretaceous Jurassic Triassic 	65,000,000 to 248,000,000
PALEOZOIC Age of Invertebrates, Fishes, Amphibians 	Permian Carboniferous Devonian Silurian Ordovician Cambrian	248,000,000 to 590,000,000
AZOIC Primitive life	Pre-Cambrian	590,000,000 to 1,800,000,000

The story goes that after the first simple cell, more complex life forms evolved… amoeba… trilobites… coal 280 million years ago… dinosaurs 135- to 65 million years ago… and man more recently, say 5- to 1 million years ago.

There you are. Evolution did occur. And that's the sequence. Just believe the chart!

The world's best known living atheist, Richard Dawkins recently said, "I challenge anyone to submit 'out-of-sequence' fossil finds that disprove evolution."

And his buddy Warwick Don added, "Evolution would be falsified if even one out of sequence fossil were ever found in the fossil record, e.g. a fossil 'human' in the Carboniferous [coal]… No such anachronistic fossils have ever been found." (*Investigate* magazine, January 2010)

So evolution theory is secure. Fold your arms, lie back and all is well.

Oh bother! Who's this spoilsport rocking the boat? Oh, some unimportant guy by the name of Ed Conrad.

What has he done?

Near Mahanoy City, between coal veins in the anthracite region of Pennsylvania, he has discovered a fossil human skull and other human parts, as well. That's right, in coal-bearing strata.

Have they been scientifically examined? Indeed, they have. Bones, teeth and/or soft organs found in this Carboniferous strata have been subjected to independent scans and tests at

* American Medical Laboratories in Chantilly, Virginia, considered the world's foremost medical lab.

* Yerkes Regional Primate Research Center at Emory University in Atlanta, Georgia, considered the world's foremost facility for primate research.

* National Taiwan University geology department.

* Alberta Research Council in Canada.

From more than 20 fossils thin sectioned and examined and more than 1,000 microscopic pictures taken, the verdict, proven beyond doubt, is that humans were entombed in Carboniferous strata! They were buried the same time as the trees that formed the coal.

So, ***as our evolutionist friends Dawkins and Don themselves tell us,*** such a discovery ***falsifies evolution***. (Please read my 58 page scientific report - <http://www.beforeus.com/man-in-carboniferous.pdf>)

Controversial? You bet! So we must rubbish these finds every way possible. (Never mind the certified test results.)

Portion of the human skull from Carboniferous strata

Okay, I'm feeling in a generous mood. So let's scrap Conrad's discoveries. Will that help us? Um… er… it sort of gets worse…

HUMAN REMAINS

Pleistocene	Skull	Olmo, Italy
	Skeleton	Clichy, France
	Skeleton	Gally Hill, England
	Pelvis	Natchez, North America
	Jaw	Abbeville, Africa
	Upper arm bone	Kanapoi, Africa
Pliocene	Skull	Calaveras, California
	Skull	Castenedolo, Italy
	Skull	Table Mt., California
	Jaw	Foxhall, England
	Footprints	Laetolil, Africa
	Footprints	Tulsa, Oklahoma
	Sandal prints	Carson City, Nevada
Miocene	Skull	Stanford, California
	Jaw	Tuscany, Italy
	Shoe print	Gobi Desert, Asia
Eocene	Skull	Germany
	Tooth	Bear Creek, Montana
Paleocene	Cast iron cube	Wolfsegg, Austria
Cretaceous	Skeletons (2)	La Sal, Utah
	Skull	Gilman, Colorado
	Tooth;footprints	Glen Rose, Texas
	Foot,shoe prints	Carrizo Valley, Oklahoma
	Castmetal nodules	Saint-Jean de Liver, France
Jurassic	Leg & foot bones	Spring Valley, Nevada
	Footprint	Parkersburg, W. Virginia
Triassic	Sandal footprint	Pershing County, Nevada
	Footprint	Mt. Victoria, Australia
Permian	Footprints	St. Louis, Missouri
Carboniferous	Footprints	Bera, Kentucky
	Iron pot	Oklahoma
	Tools	Aixen-Provence, France
	Gold chain	Illinois
	Footprints	Missouri
	Hieroglyphics	Hammondsville, Ohio
	Inscription	Philadelphia, Pennsylvania
	Imprinted slab	Webster City, Iowa
	Concrete wall	Heavener, Oklahoma
Devonian	Precision pattern	Pittsburgh, Pa.
Silurian	Skeleton	Franklin County, Mo.
Ordovician	Sandal print	Lake Windermere, England
	Metal Hammer	London, Texas
Cambrian	Sandal,footprints	Antelope Springs, Utah
	Iron bands	Lochmaree, Scotland

In all geological strata types

The chart above illustrates the problem. Not only have numerous other human remains been discovered in Carboniferous strata – including complete skeletons (Macoupin County, Illinois – *The Geologist*). But they're also in EVERY other so-called geological "age", as well. Those listed are a mere sampling of finds – commonly reburied, "lost" in museum basements, or suppressed. That's why you seldom hear of them.

In 1912, at the Municipal Electric Plant, at Thomas, Oklahoma, fireman Frank J. Kenword split a large piece of coal and discovered an ***iron pot*** embedded inside. The source of the coal was the Wilburton, Oklahoma, Mines. The pot is on display at the Miles Musical Museum in Eureka Springs.

At Meeting House Hill, Dorchester, Massachussetts in 1851, a ***metallic vase*** was blown out of an immense mass of solid rock. The rock was said to be ***Precambrian***, "over 600 million years old." (That's worse than being found in Carboniferous!) Made of an unknown metal, the artefact was beautifully inlaid with pure silver. It portrayed six figures of a flower, a bouquet, and a vine or wreath. The chasing, carving and inlaying are cleverly and exquisitely done. (*Scientific American*, Vol.7, p.298, June 5, 1852) Vol.7, p.298, June 5, 1852)

Summarising the fossils

It is not just physical finds such as these that scream out against evolution. Here are summarised for you eight major fossil facts that, quite frankly, are alarming.

1. Complex fossils appear suddenly in the *"earliest"* strata, ***already fully formed,*** with ***no evidence of ancestors.***
2. Each plant and animal type appears abruptly in the ***subsequent*** fossil record, with ***no evidence of any previous transitional form leading up to it.*** At its first appearance it is an ***already complete***, functional unit – and optimal from an engineering standpoint. Thus there are persistent, ***unbridgeable gaps*** or chasms ***between*** different major types of organisms. – between, for example, reptiles and birds. The same gaps between organisms that we witness today, are likewise in the fossil record of the past. No links.
3. Fossils in the "wrong" order. All over the world, what the evolution theory classifies as "older" and "younger" are found mixed ***in any sequence –*** no evolutionary progression.
4. Although, theoretically, millions of years of deposits make up the different strata, in the real physical world of remains there is ***no visible time lapse*** between them.
5. Polystrate fossils: All over the world, ***individual fossils penetrate several strata***. For example, in the picture below you see Jeff Smith, long time industrial chemist, standing beside a fossil pine tree in the Pilot coal seams south of Newcastle, Australia. Its trunk penetrates vertically through ***fourteen*** different coal seams, each of which

was, according to evolution theory, formed slowly over thousands or millions of years. But, horror of horrors, here is one tree going through all of them. The coal seams are

interspersed with layers of sand. How on earth could any tree trunk survive the ups and downs while waiting to get buried? But the ***evidence*** is that that tree had no time to decay before it was buried. Such polystrate fossils are common, all over the world. Strata was ***formed rapidly***.

6. There is ***not one geological site*** on earth that has the full evolution fossil sequence palmed off to us in text books. Not anywhere! It's in their heads, not in the rocks.
7. "Index fossils" (fossils assumed to have lived exclusively in a particular era and which were thus used to date rock layers in which they appeared) are now found still alive. These ***living fossils*** falsify the "indexed" age of the rocks.

8. Today's living organisms are basically ***unchanged from their first fossil ancestors***. Just look at the flatworm. With its short lifespan we can watch it go ***through thousands of generations,*** which, according to evolution theory, should be enough to show evidence of evolution. But not so!

It is necessary to keep the information concerning these eight fossil facts brief here, but for in-depth ***evidence***, may I recommend *Surprise Witness*, chapters 14 - 17 (<http//.www.beforeus.com/second.php>) and *The Discovery That's Toppling Evolution*, chs. 3 - 9 (<http://www. beforeus.com/evol.php>)

No transitional remains found

To comment briefly on Point 2, have you ever gone through a museum and noticed how with no real links between life-forms, someone had tried to "fill in the gaps" with artists' sketches?

The evolutionist's sketches normally portray an ape-like creature that turns into a man – a theory arrived at presumably after extensive self-examination. Of course, like the frog-into-a-prince tale, you can draw a picture of anything.

This lack you can correctly view as an enormous problem. A true transitional link would be something with a non-functional "partial" something – like a partially formed feather. However, among the millions of fossils found, one finds evidence of ***only totally functional components*** – all from the very start, fully perfect.

The "prehistoric man" myth

Evolutionists segment history into ages – such as the "Stone Age" for "prehistoric" times. Yet this is useless for determining a chronological history because, as they admit, these ages may not be sequential, but actually contemporary! Today, while we live in our age of space exploration, the Internet, and nuclear power, we have other people living in a primitive "stone age" culture in tropical rainforests. It was almost always so. Man started off intelligent. After natural or man-made disasters, survivors had to get by with more primitive tools of survival – yet preserving the memory of their ancestors' past achievements. Indeed, you might well ask, Was there ever a Stone Age? The answer is NO! Have there been ***stone cultures***? Yes. (Please study the evidence in my book *Dead Men's Secrets,* Chapters 5 to 7.)

More complex first

Regarding Point 3, evolution theory says that simpler organisms evolved first, followed by more complex. Logic tells us that plants would need to come first, so that animals could feed on them.

But did you know that plant cells are more complicated than animals' cells? Each plant cell has 20 to 100 sub-units, called chloroplasts. And each chloroplast contains about 45 sun traps. These sun traps are like solar panels on the roof of a house, to:

(a) receive and convert the sun's rays to energy
(b) absorb carbon dioxide, and then
(c) give out oxygen into the air for animal life to breath.

Every solar panel in a plant contains a green pigment called chlorophyll. This greenness soaks in the sun's energy.

Now, here is the crunch. Evolution theory says the simpler systems came first and the more complex systems came later.

But this chloroplast discovery means that, contrary to evolution theory, ***the more complex systems came first.***

Animal cells do not have these complicated sun-converting panels. Yet, without these, animal life could not have started or survived.

Darwin: "Fossils will prove or disprove my theory"

Darwin predicted that the evidence for evolution would eventually be found in the fossils buried in the earth's strata. (Darwin, Charles. "On the imperfection of the geological record," Chapter X, *The Origin of Species* London: J.M. Dent & Sons Ltd., 1971, pp.292-293)

And Darwin's champion, T.A. Huxley, had said, "If evolution has taken place, there will its marks be found; if it has not taken place, there will be its refutation."

So what has since been found? The sad fact was admitted by Niles Eldridge, curator of New York's Natural History Museum: "The fossil record we were told to find in the past 120 years [since Darwin] ***does not exist.***" (*New York Times*, November 4, 1980).

And some 30 years after that, nothing has changed.

When anyone tells us the fossils prove evolution, we are being lied to, because the hoped for evidence for evolution in the fossil record does not exist. (For a great deal of scientific documentation, see my two books *Surprise Witness*, chs. 14 - 17 <http//.www.beforeus.com/second.php> ; *The Discovery That's Toppling Evolution*, chs. 3 - 9 <http://www.beforeus.com/evol.html>)

Yet, even as the theory crumbles, its promoters cling on with religious tenacity. Why do they keep flogging a dead horse? Honest evolutionists like Dr. Michael Walker, Senior Lecturer in Anthropology, Sydney University, have put their finger on it:

> One is forced to conclude that many scientists and technologists pay lip-service to Darwinian theory only because it supposedly excludes a Creator. (Michael Walker, Sydney University *Quadrant*, October, 1981, p.44)

Yes, many accept evolution theory not from a careful evaluation of the data, but because of a bias against the supernatural. The real reason why these people want to believe in evolution is ***to get God out of their lives***. If you admit evolution is false, then you have to deal with God. The theory of evolution is there to eliminate God out of peoples' lives. Darwinism has become something close to a religion or a worldview.

The cover up

Then how are scientists in general reacting to such recent discoveries? Combing through the literature, one finds that these facts have came as a surprise to most scientists – because evolution was all they were taught.

Others know about the latest discoveries but are playing dumb – fearful of bucking the establishment! Scoundrels – all of them! Sure, many mean well. But they still hide the facts. Reputations, careers, and financial research grants are at risk. And so this shabby pseudoscience has acquired a blind popularity.

Thousands of scientists abandoning evolution

But truth can't be suppressed forever. Meanwhile, many highly qualified scientists are openly rejecting evolution. In the United States alone, tens of thousands of them.

One of the most renowned atheists of the 20th century was Dr Antony Flew of the University of Reading, in England. Flew is arguably the best-known atheist in the academic world of the last 50 years. He helped set the agenda for atheism with his paper *"Theology and Falsification"*. That was the most widely reprinted philosophical publication of the last half century.

Well, in 2004 Dr Flew startled the scholarly world by announcing he had now accepted the existence of God, largely due to his study of DNA. Here are his own words: "I think that the most impressive arguments for God's existence are those that are supported by recent scientific discoveries ... I think the argument to Intelligent Design is enormously stronger than it was when I first met it." (Richard Ostling, " Leading Atheist Now Believes in God," *Associated Press* report, Dec. 9, 2004).

He then stated: "As people have certainly been influenced by me, I want to try and correct the enormous damage I may have done." (Stuart Wavell and Will Iredale, "Sorry, Says Atheist-in-Chief, I Do Believe in God After All," Dec. 12, 2004). There's an honest man.

Majority of medical doctors

In a survey of 1,482 physicians (the type of people most familiar with the wonders of the human body), the majority rejected strict Darwinism. The poll was conducted by HCD Research and the Louis Finkelstein Institute for Religious and Social Studies.

"Of course, most doctors are skeptical of Darwinism," said Dr Robert Cihak, M.D., former president of the Association of American Physicians and Surgeons and a medical columnist for JewishWorldReview.com. "An eye surgeon knows the astonishing intricacies of human vision intimately, so the vague, just-so stories about eye evolution don't fool him. And the eye is just one of the countless organs and interdependent systems in the body that defy Darwinian explanation." (Discovery Institute, "Nearly Two-Thirds of Doctors Skeptical of Darwin's Theory of Evolution," May 31, 2005)

Unscientific

The evolution theory contradicts these known scientific laws:

1. FIRST LAW OF THERMODYNAMICS: Energy or mass are neither created nor destroyed. Energy and mass cannot originate from nothing, by natural processes. The universe could not have begun itself. EVOLUTION SAYS matter and energy created itself from nothing.
2. BIOGENESIS: Life comes ONLY from life. This tells us that life cannot and never did originate by natural processes. EVOLUTION SAYS life originated from non-life.
3. SECOND LAW OF THERMODYNAMICS: With time, a closed system (like our universe) will become more random and disordered. Things wear out and break down. Ask any engineer or home owner. EVOLUTION SAYS

the universe began as disorder (the big bang) and became orderly over time.

4. CAUSE AND EFFECT: An observed event can be traced to an event that preceded it. EVOLUTION believes in NO 'First Cause' for the universe.

12 Questions that demand an answer:

1. What scientific laws support the theory of evolution?
2. How did life originate?
3. How did energy originate?
4. How did mass originate?
5. How did DNA information code originate?
6. How did the code to translate it originate?
7. MAN SINCE THE START OF LIFE?: If man evolved from earlier forms, then why are ***human remains*** found ***in all "ages"*** of strata, even with the "first and earliest" fossil life forms?
8. COMPLEX LIFE AT START?: Why do ***complex fossils*** appear in the "earliest" strata, with ***no evidence of ancestors?***
9. REQUIRED LINKS NOT FOUND: Why are there ***persistent gaps between*** major types of organisms – with no evidence of transition from one type to another?
10. STRATA RAPIDLY FORMED?: Why does a single fossil commonly ***penetrate through multiple "ages"*** of strata?
11. UNCHANGED OVER THE AGES: Why are today's basic types ***unchanged*** from their first fossil ancestors?

12. EVOLVING OF INFORMATION: How does new ***information*** evolve?

It seems to me that fossils and DNA kill evolution stone dead.

(a) DNA tells me evolution ***couldn't even get started.***

(b) Fossils tell me that whatever we started with ***has not evolved since then***.

* * * * * * *

For more detailed information, see
The Discovery That's Toppling Evolution, 218 pages.
Surprise Witness, 216 pages
<http://www.beforeus.com/shopcart_ebooks.html>

PART TWO

ALIENS?

6

From outer space? -

THE SUMERIAN TABLETS SHOCK

Erich von Danicken caused a sensation in the seventies when he claimed that sophisticated ancient relics were the result of a space visit to earth.

Now is the time for the truth.

Von Danicken, like others, assumed that early man struggled for endless millions of years as a primitive dumb and stupid creature, unable to accomplish anything on his own.

Then we find man quite suddenly (in the last few thousand years) nurturing a technology so intricate, so sophisticated, that it suggests intellectual maturity from the start.

You don't have to be smart to sense there is something wrong here.

So, faced with the new evidence of high technology in ancient times, and realizing that man could not have obtained such advanced thinking capabilities and complex technology simply by evolving from nothing, Von Danicken's camp suggested that maybe galactic visitors were responsible. These alien giants crossbred with primates to produce modern man, then left behind artefacts from their visit.

Did they? You have to admit, it's an interesting theory.

The Planet X – Anunnaki shock

And then there's the Planet X story.

It's the kind of story you might want to believe. A certain popular writer, describing himself as an expert on ancient texts, tells us that beyond the planet Pluto there is an outer planet called Nibiru.

Nibiru was populated by a reptilian super race, the Annunaki.

The Anunnakis' own planet was dying. So the Anunnaki came to Planet Earth to attempt a rescue of their planet. The gold on Planet Earth was needed to create a shield for preserving Nibiru's dwindling atmosphere.

One can actually feel sorry for the Anunnaki.

Anyway, this Planet Nibiru, in its orbit, came close to Planet Earth.

A group of 50 astronauts from Nibiru, with their leader called Enki, splashed down in the waters of the Persian Gulf. Some Anunnaki were sent to mine gold in Africa.

When the toil became unbearable, Enki 'created' 'primitive workers' by mixing the genes of male Anunnaki with the eggs of early female hominoids, to bring about Homo sapiens - you and me.

This sudden speed-up given to our evolution explains how the Sumerian civilization began suddenly, fully developed, with no evidence of a primitive beginning.

You can credit these extraterrestrials for jump-starting it, this popular writer says.

Oh, and something else. The orbit of Nibiru (which some label Planet X) brings it into our solar system every 3,600 years. It will return to Planet Earth very soon.

Well, that awakens my interest. How about you?

Mr S: "It's on the Sumerian tablets"

In any case, this gentleman, whom we shall call Mr S, assures us that this is what the Sumerian clay tablets say. In fact, he has been heavily promoting this topic.

In contrast to the airy speculation of von Danicken, Mr S claims to be a scholar. He graduated in economics. But he claims to be an expert in ancient Sumerian texts and Hebrew.

You have to admit, an argument appealing to ancient clay tablets does sound somewhat scholarly.

Oh well, you must have guessed by now who Mr S is, so I might as well name him. But I shall make it absolutely clear that what follows is not about the man. It's about the subject. I have no problem with Zecharia Sitchin as a person. He's probably quite a nice guy. (Later note: Sitchin died soon after I wrote this report.)

As it was, for a number of years I accepted this gentleman's claim that the above story was in those ancient Sumerian records. After all, you just don't make up such things, do you?

When Mr S first spun his exciting story to us, how many of us had access to all the Sumerian texts?

What he had right

From my years of independent research, I knew that Mr S had at least one thing correct – that, from earliest times, the Sumerians enjoyed a very high standard of civilization.

As you know, in today's world, where we are taught that early man was primitive, it is rare to hear about high technology in the ancient world. So I felt a measure of rapport with Mr S.

For this reason, my customary cautious approach softened toward this man. And I did enjoy reading his books. So I let down my guard just a little to give the "facts" in his books due respect – in particular, the claim that certain ancient texts existed that backed up his story.

Accepting his claim also to be a responsible scholar, I went as far as to quote him a couple of times in my book *Dead Men's Secrets.*

BUT THEN SOMETHING HAPPENED…

People begin asking

Over a period of time, I received an increasing number of emails asking me about

* Planet Nibiru (Planet X)
* The Anunnaki
* The Nephilim
* The 3,600 year orbit of this planet, which is said to bring destruction each time its passes close the earth.

So I felt an increasing obligation to dig deeper.

Investigation results bother me

Well, I was checking carefully through the story. And an irritating anomaly cropped up. Assuming Mr S's story were true, such mis-fitting data made no sense. It should not exist!

Naturally, this bothered me. Shrug it off as an isolated problem? Perhaps. But it did cry out to be resolved.

Nevertheless, pursuing this matter was not so easy. You see, very soon another inconsistency surfaced then another and another.

Bother! The problem was not just one, but a growing procession of non-fitting pieces.

That's when it struck me that the problem might be not with the inconsistencies, but with Mr S' story.

Three problems arise

Here are some of the serious questions that arose:

1. Mr S said that the ***Anunnaki*** come from the planet Nibiru (a 12th planet). How do we know this is so? According to our friend, it's in the Sumerian texts.
   PROBLEM: Search, search and search! But, no matter where one might turn, it was absolutely ***impossible to find even one such Sumerian text!***
2. ***Nibiru*** is a planet beyond Pluto. How do we know? According to our friend, the Sumerian texts say so.
   PROBLEM: Again, I could find ***not one single Sumerian text that says anything like this.***
3. This planet Nibiru cycles through our solar system ***every 3600 years***. According to Mr S, the Sumerian texts say this.
   PROBLEM: But try as one might, ***no such Sumerian texts*** could be found! Not anywhere!

The Sumerian texts displayed a distressing habit of being ***not there***.

So could the problem be with me?

More awkward questions

As I scratched my head over this, a few more awkward questions began to nag at me:

* Why did Mr S claim that the biblical pre-Flood "sons of God" who married the daughters of men" were called "***nephilim***" –

when the Genesis text itself said ***something very different?***

* Why did Mr S say that "***nephilim***" means "***people of the fiery rockets***" and also "***those who came down from heaven***"? – when, in the Hebrew language, the word "*nephilim*" meant nothing like this.

* Why did many of Mr S' vital ***translations*** of Sumerian and Mesopotamian words, ***differ so much*** from Mesopotamian cuneiform bilingual dictionaries?

Why... why... why? Here was a whole mass of questions now crying out for an answer.

Facts above theories

You should understand something here. Experience in front line archaeology has taught me that ***evidence*** must always override theories. If a theory says yes, but the confirmed facts say no, then the theory is wrong. That is plain common sense.

In an investigation, there may be hundreds of information bits to consider. One starts out imagining a scenario, but when all the facts are in, the final picture may turn out to be quite different.

Let's say you have hundreds of torn-up bits of newspaper scattered over the table, and you want to fit them together to form a page. But after working for hours, you discover the pieces just do not fit. Well, that's where I was with the many pieces to Mr Sitchin's theory. They just did not fit.

I write to the Nibiru man

So what would you do? What better than to ask the man who gave us the pieces? So I sat down and wrote to Zecharia Sitchin, asking him to help me clarify these matters.

Surely he would substantiate his story better than anyone. Perhaps he had sources not available to the rest of the world? With Mr Sitchin's help, this bothersome matter could be resolved.

Below is the letter I wrote to Zecharia Sitchin:

Jonathan Gray
PO Box 785
Thames 3540
New Zealand
Email: info@archaeologyanswers.com
Phone +64 7 869 0405

Mr Zecharia Sitchen
PO Box 577
New York, NY 10185
USA
March 2, 2010

Dear Mr. Sitchin,

I have enjoyed reading your work and have quoted from you in a couple of my own books.

With respect, I would appreciate you helping me with some information. When I quote you, some people raise questions.

This is not intended to be critical, but rather stems from a desire to understand better the propositions which you raise.

Here are my questions.

1. I notice you translate "nephilim" as "people of the fiery rockets" and also "those who came down from heaven" (as closely as I remember the wording) Could you please explain how this is arrived at, using the rules of Hebrew morphology? Where do you get your understanding that "naphal" has to do with fire or rockets? In what ancient text does naphal have to do with fire or rockets?

2. Which Sumerian text says that the Anunnaki come from the planet Nibiru - or have a connection to Nibiru, a 12th planet, or some other planet? Also that Nibiru is a planet beyond Pluto?

3. Why do many of your important word meanings or translations of Sumerian and Mesopotamian words, differ so much from Mesopotamian cuneiform bilingual dictionaries?

Thank you for your patience. I am sure there are good answers, but I need to be able, as one who quotes from you, to answer others. I appreciate you taking the time to respond.

Sincerely,

Jonathan Gray

I "bit on my fingernails"... and waited...

Seven weeks passed...

I recall vividly that Tuesday morning at the Thames post office. My heart was thumping heavily as I tore open the envelope. And there, inside, was a photocopy of my letter, with Mr Sitchin's few brief notes scribbled over it.

They consisted of only a few words. It was evident that the dear man was stumped to produce any of the claimed Sumerian texts. Sure, as he said, it was in his "books", but not in the Sumerian texts! Well, I had already been through his books. (You will find the details of his brief reply to each of my questions in my special 224 page report, *Just Sitchin Fiction?)*

What you should know about the Sumerian texts

Further investigation, without Mr Sitchin's help, turned up the fact that all of the Sumerian texts discovered by archaeologists have now been translated and catalogued. No longer a secret, they are finally accessible to us – and even on the Internet.

So are you ready for this? Examination shows that there is ***not one Sumerian text*** that says those things. Not one anywhere. In my book *Just Sitchin Fiction?* I show you how to check for yourself all the Sumerian texts online. The truth is that in the entire cuneiform record there is ***not one single text*** that says any of these things Mr Sitchin was claiming they did. These texts do not exist. ***They are all made up***!

Except one. And that is a cylinder seal known as "VA243" (so named because it is number 243 in the collection of the Vorderasiatische Museum in Berlin). But, contrary to Mr Sitchin's claim, this seal does not show a 12th planet at all, but is the record of a grain harvest offering to a god.

What about the good Mr Sitchin's Sumerian word translations? Same problem. They are just made up.

How can we be sure? Surprise! Not only do we now have access to the Sumerian texts, but also to 4,000 year old Sumerian word dictionaries. That's right. The Sumerians kept their own dictionaries. And we have these now! And what is their verdict on the "alien-favoring" meanings that Mr Sitchin has been giving us? The words do not mean those things at all! The actual meanings are very, very different.

What about Mr Sitchin's Hebrew word translations? Sorry to be a spoilsport, but these are likewise fictitious. (So that you can check it all for yourself, I now offer you a free 224 page e-book in which you can go through each of these in detail. See below.)

Honesty is a treasure. But I am sorry to state that Mr Sitchin has

(a) served up to us fictitious word meanings so that we would accept his theory, and

(b) he has also "made up" Sumerian documents which do not exist.

He asks us to accept such scholarship as his evidence. If the "evidence" for a theory is bogus, then, may I ask you, what of the theory?

Millie, bring me an aspirin!

* * * * * * *

FOR MORE INFORMATION

For detailed evidence on the Sumerian texts and Zecharia Sitchin's claims, see my free special 224 page report, *Sitchin Fiction?* <http://www.beforeus.com/sitchin.pdf>

7

From outer space? -

DID ALIENS CREATE US?

"Oh, what a journey that was!" sighed the weary spore as it landed on earth with a bounce. "70 zillion light years – and I've made it at last! Now let's raise the Pleiades flag and claim this planet!"

So, could that have happened? Could life have already existed in outer space, and then somehow got here?

Life spores drifted from outer space?

Some keen minds have been asking whether life might have first appeared on some other planet, then drifted from planet to planet as naked bacterial spores, eventually ending up on this earth?

An interesting idea! But it seems Isaac Asimov has already covered that one. Experiments have shown that ***ultraviolet light (UV) would quickly kill such spores.*** In space, UV is much more intense.

Also there are other forms of radiation that would kill off any microscopic spores. The big problem would be the accumulated dosages over an extended time period.

But we still get back to this: ***matter itself contains no information that can produce life*** in the first place. So it boils down to these two facts:

1. No DNA information comes from non-living matter, to even create the spores to start with.
2. Outer space radiation would kill spores travelling toward earth. End of story.

DNA brought by aliens?

Then what about this idea? Might already-intelligent aliens have introduced the DNA on earth – and then let evolution take over?

Despite the *Sitchin Fiction* fiasco, is it still possible that aliens may have interbred with primates to produce modern man?

The quick answer is: I ***do*** accept that there are other intelligent beings "out there". But unfortunately, ET (extraterrestrial) "seeding" would not answer the ***origin of ET intelligence*** in the first place - whether on this earth, or on some other planet.

You can work this out for yourself. ETs from another planet also needed a beginning. They needed to be programmed with *their* DNA from somewhere - before they could even exist! And then, if you expect similar results time and again on numerous planets… the odds against that ever happening by chance become so exponentially remote as to be impossible.

Scientists have never ever observed chemicals forming themselves into complex DNA molecules. Life cannot arise spontaneously from non-life.

Just as for us on this earth, the odds for ETs to exist on some other planet would be as if they had won a million-dollar lottery a million times in a row.

Could genetic engineering occur? Yes. But again, even if by some long-shot miracle earth primates were given an extraterrestrial DNA boost artificially, any subsequent upward evolution ***would require continual adding of genetic information***. However, as we saw in an earlier chapter, there is ***no*** natural mechanism that can add this information.

So with upward evolution impossible, aliens would have needed to create 100 percent fully fledged, intelligent modern humans ***in one hit***. And the same applies to all other life forms, as well. The whole multitude of them ***complete and functioning***.

Could not just evolve - whether here or in outer space

The more you think it through, the clearer it comes.

Evolution? Not here – or anywhere! If ***evolution*** cannot account for the ***programming of intelligence*** (or life itself) on this planet, it is equally impossible to explain a more highly intelligent man ***evolving*** on some other planet.

If ***evolution*** of original cells is ***impossible,*** then aliens with physical bodies could not be the product of evolution either. Aliens could not themselves have created the matter from which they ultimately came.

The more we discover about the complexity of life, the more one is forced to concede that ***no form of evolution*** is an adequate explanation.

There is no escaping it. This planet's complexity of life - as evidenced by ***DNA*** and the remains of ***fossils*** – shows all signs of having "burst" into existence fully formed. It shows ***no evidence of evolutionary ancestry.***

And if matter ***could not arrange itself*** into complex life by natural processes, then even the ***ETs would need a Creator.***

Evolution of intelligent life is so improbable that it is unlikely to have occurred on any other planet in the entire visible universe.

So, it all gets back to the question, ***who, then, was responsible for life?***

A Superior Designer

Like it or not, this requires an ultimate Master Creator, a Superior Designer working to a pre-organized plan. Someone who was ***not one of us, but much greater than us*** – someone greater than any extraterrestrials, ***greater than the creation itself.*** Someone OUTSIDE OUR TIME AND SPACE arena.

No help needed from ETs

A Supreme Creator ***outside time and space*** would be totally adequate to account for

(a) the origin of life on earth;
(b) man's original intelligence; and
(c) early man's advanced civilization.

No need for ET help. Civilization did not suddenly drop into the Middle East from some star.

DNA changes the whole game. It means ***man was already intelligent from the first cell.*** Man had the ***information*** ability from Day 1 to invent his own technology and high civilization. All it would require were enough people to support a culture.

6 other things worth remembering

Here are a few other things to bear in mind:

1. None of the out-of-place artefacts is composed of material unknown to earth.
2 Their technological makeup conforms with the development of our own modern civilization.
3. For sexual interbreeding to produce ***fertile offspring,*** aliens would (a) need a carbon-based physiology; (b) need to be physically adapted for entering the human female; and (c) their

chromosomes would have to be interchangeable, even for artificial insemination. Chromosomes and genes must *both* match up, which is extremely unlikely and does not happen even between animals and humans of the same planet!

Simply put, each separate type has a distinct set of chromosomes which holds its genetic makeup. For example, cats have 19 pairs, rabbits 22 pairs. Each parent donates a chromosome to make each pair. With most species, after fertilization, when the cell starts to divide, there would be an uneven number of chromosomes that needed to 'pair up.' The cell would die. There are rare exceptions. Domesticated horses have 32 pairs, and donkeys 31 pairs. Their offspring (mules) have 31.5. Mules are infertile – no offspring. Like zedonks and tigons, their chromosomes match up just enough to allow for interbreeding between similar species. ***And then*** (with rare one generation exceptions) ***full stop***. However, the location of a gene is not in the same place on the same chromosome between species. Chromosome A on a rabbit might hold the genetic codes for ear size, hair color and bone configuration, but chromosome A on a cat might hold the genetic codes for vision, tail length and brain size. They could never match up.

4. And of course you realize that if these were to match, they would already be of the same or closely related species—and man would be ***already*** intelligent.

5. Still unresolved, the problem of the origin of intelligence is only removed to another planet. You have to account for civilizations on two worlds now, instead of one, and you still have to find out how the first began. Now naturally, if evolution cannot account for it on this planet, it is equally impossible to explain a more highly intelligent man evolving on some other planet.
6. Memories of "gods" from the skies are explainable as the recollection by primitive people of visits from contemporary civilizations who had aircraft. Similar reactions have occurred in our day.

With whatever good intentions, the "space gods" theory was born in careless research; since then it has been perpetuated through the use of faulty reasoning and sensationalism.

Then what are UFOs, and from where?

Quite apart from any secret advanced military technology, are UFOs real? Yes, there are real UFOs.

Are other worlds inhabited? ***Yes***, there are other inhabited worlds.

Are aliens visiting this earth? ***No***, aliens are not visiting our little planet.

Who, then, are the "aliens" that people keep reporting?

The subject is much more complex than any of us imagined. It has ***paranormal aspects*** but certainly it has very real ***physical aspects***, too.

Few have studied this question better than J. Allen Hynek who founded the Center for UFO

Studies (CUFOS) along with the now noted UFO researcher Jacques Vallee.

When interviewed by *Newsweek*, Hynek expressed this theory:

> UFOs, he says, may be ***psychic phenomena*** and the 'aliens' ***may not come from outer space*** but from a 'parallel reality.' (Hynek, *Newsweek*, November 21, 1977. Emphasis mine)

We shall address this more comprehensively in a later chapter. Meanwhile, here are a few quick facts to think about. The evidence from millions of observations suggests that:

1. They are here – emanating, apparently, from our own planet Earth.
2. Although visible, they may not be physical entities. They appear to be ***not*** bound by the same material, physical laws.

UFOs can

- ***make 90 degree turns*** at impossible speeds
- make other ***maneuvers impossible in the physical realm***.
- ***change shape*** before our eyes
- ***melt away*** into nothing in front of us
- apparently '***materialize***' (take physical form)
- ***Two distinctly different UFOs*** hovering in a clear sky will converge and eventually ***merge into one object.***

These all hint at another dimension. The ***weight of evidence*** suggests these are paramountly ***not physical, but spiritual*** manifestations. (In a later chapter, we shall examine this closely.) Extraterrestrials? No. ***There is a better explanation.***

Then what about the seeming traces of physical landings?

An engineer with an understanding of physics will find no problem with this. They could be explained as ***manipulation of mass and energy***.

Bearing in mind that all solid objects have a vibration frequency within the range perceptible to the human eye. What if the vibration frequency could be altered into vibrations outside the visible range? Some scientists consider it possible.

Many open-minded scientists are, in fact, concluding as much - that the cosmos consists of frequencies or dimensions of life that share the same space, just as radio and television frequencies do.

Reason for the "aliens created us" theory

So how came the theory that we are the result of alien intervention? This theory stems from the ***same mindset as the evolution theory*** – which is basically a resistance to the idea of an Eternal Being who, by creating us, has a claim on us. We want to do our own thing, and banish the idea that one day we might have to account for our behaviour. That's the bottom line.

Its promoters are correct, however, on one point: ***Human intelligence*** cannot be the product of chance evolution. Man did appear suddenly—at the top, not at the bottom. Man is a created artefact, far more wonderful than any computer. He was carefully planned and endowed with the gift of language and the most amazing intellect, as well as a feeling for handcrafts and technology.

And something else was implanted within man: both the capacity and the need to communicate with his Maker, the prime Intelligence. Consequently, there is a part of every person which is restless, seeking unattainable goals, yet experiencing futility and emptiness until it finds identity and peace with the Creator. And that makes all the difference.

Belief in someone you cannot see?

QUESTION: Is it reasonable to believe in a Being I cannot see?

You ask Australian atheist Philip Adams, and he may tell you that any who believe in a Creator "*have bats in their belfry*". They are "*gullible*", "a growing multitude of *dimwits*" in need of "psychiatric help," and that it's a "*looney proposition.*" (Adelaide *Weekend Review*)

ANSWER: Very early every morning someone delivers my newspaper. I've never seen him. But the paper is always there. Should I believe that no one has been delivering the paper?

In this world we have full confidence that many people we have never seen, do exist.

Why? Because there is evidence of their presence. So if our world reveals evidence of an architect behind it, is it any less reasonable to believe in a God I have never seen?

"I'm an atheist"

My neighbour Bernie came straight out and said it: "I'm an atheist."

"Well, an atheist is one who ***knows*** there is no God. Do you know all there is to know?"

"Of course not."

"Would it be generous to say you know half of all there is to know?"

"That would be very generous."

"Then, if you know only half of all there is to know, wouldn't you have to admit the possibility that God may exist in the body of knowledge you do not have?"

"I never thought of that," mused Bernie. "Well, I'm not an atheist, then I'm an agnostic."

"Now we're getting somewhere. Agnosticism means you don't know." (I didn't tell him, but the Latin equivalent means "ignoramus." However, that wouldn't be nice.) "An agnostic is a doubter," I said.

"Well, that's what I am."

"There are two types of doubters – honest and dishonest. The honest doubter doesn't know, but he wants to know. The dishonest doubter doesn't know because he doesn't want to know. He can't find God for the same reason that a thief can't find a policeman. So which kind of doubter are you?"

Bernie's face softened. "I never really thought about it. I guess I never really wanted to know."

"Bernie, if a man honestly wants to know what is true, then if there is a God He will reveal His reality to that man." I looked Bernie straight in the eye. Yes, I thought, he's basically an honest man.

"Okay, Bernie," I said, "Would you do this: Would you be willing to write this down and sign it?" This is what I suggested:

> God, I don't know whether you exist or not, but I want to know. And because I want to know, I will make an honest investigation. And because it is an honest investigation, I will follow the results of that investigation wherever they lead me, regardless of the cost.

Bernie studied his shoes. Then, after a pause, he again looked up. "Yeah, I'll do it!" And what happened in the end? Bernie was not disappointed. He says his whole life now has purpose.

It is laughable, when you think about it. We have sneered at miracles... but all that time we have believed in the self-creation of life (a miracle, if ever there was one!).

We have mocked at the creation of the world by a God... yet we have spoken learnedly of unconscious matter producing consciousness, of a primal cell that created itself!

We have maintained the self-beginning of life, and denied the possibility of Creation!

When God is defined as the Creator of the universe, we are immediately faced with the mutually exclusive alternatives as to whether the universe came about through a random process or by special creation (by God). We have already proved mathematically that random evolution is impossible. This leaves the existence of God as the only option.

Where did this "God" come from?

But where did "God" come from? Have you ever asked that? I did.

Then it struck me. Everything that we experience – whether time or distance – has a beginning and an end. So that's all we understand.

But would an Entity ***outside time and space***, Creator of ***all things***, be limited by beginning and an end? Not at all! He would exist through all time – past, present and future. Yet, let's face it. Our brains have no way to put that into meaningful perspective.

By definition God is the uncreated creator of the universe, so the question *Who created God?* is illogical, just like *To whom is the bachelor married?*

So a more sophisticated questioner might ask: If

the universe needs a cause, then why doesn't God need a cause? And if God doesn't need a cause, why should the universe need a cause? The answer, is, of course, that:

1. Everything ***which has a beginning*** has a cause.
2. The universe has a beginning.
3. Therefore the universe has a cause.

The universe requires a cause because it had ***a beginning***, as will be shown below. God, unlike the universe, had ***no beginning***, so doesn't need a cause. In addition, Einstein's general relativity, which has much experimental support, shows that time is linked to matter and space. So ***time itself*** would have ***begun*** along with matter and space.

Since God, by definition, is the creator of the whole universe, he is the creator of time. Therefore he is not limited by the time dimension He created, so has ***no beginning*** in time. God inhabits eternity. Therefore he doesn't have a cause.

In contrast, there is good evidence that the universe had a beginning. This can be shown from the ***Laws of Thermodynamics***, the most fundamental laws of the physical sciences.

* 1st Law: The ***total*** amount of mass-energy in the universe is ***constant.***

* 2nd Law: The amount of energy ***available for work*** is running out. That is to say, ***entropy*** is increasing to a maximum.

If the total amount of mass-energy is limited, and the amount of usable energy is decreasing, then the universe cannot have existed forever, otherwise it would ***already*** have exhausted all usable energy in the the universe. For example, all radioactive atoms would have decayed, every part of the universe would be the same temperature, and no further work would be possible.

So the obvious corollary is that the universe began a finite time ago with a lot of usable energy, and is now running down.

It is self-evident that things that begin have a cause. We call this ***the law of cause and effect***. Without this, all law enforcement would break down – such as if the police didn't think they needed to find a cause for a stabbed body or a burgled house.

Thus, the universe cannot be self-caused. Nothing can create itself, because that would mean that it existed before it came into existence, which is a logical absurdity.

It boils down to this: *I cannot use my limitations of time and space to measure God's existence.*

One sunny afternoon, I plopped myself down on the grass to watch a baseball game. For a brief moment my attention was attracted to a tiny ant battling heroically through the grass. That little ant moved around beneath the turf, the blades of grass overhead, the soil beneath, and the tinier life forms all around. That's the world the ant understands.

As a baseball game unfolds, this little ant may see an occasional shadow moving above him, or hear the thud of giant feet and feel the ground shake. But he has not the foggiest idea what is going on in that world above him. He crawls around the grass shoots, virtually unaware of anything but his own world.

Could you explain that baseball game to that ant? We might smile. That little ant would be incapable of comprehending.

Come to think of it, are we not like that little ant, when it comes to understanding the Supreme One? Indeed, if I could fully understand God, I should either be a god myself, or God Himself would cease to be God. Just because I live in ***my*** reality is no reason to dismiss another reality of existence.

So because I'm ever so inquisitive (that's why I am a field archaeologist), I now invite you to come with me as we follow Ken Gaub along a road near Dayton, Ohio…

PART THREE

A SUPREME BEING?

8

A personal, caring Creator? -

DESPERATE PHONE CALL

"I don't know what to do!" exclaimed Ken. "Perhaps I need a change."

For quite a while now, Ken Gaub's time had been spent giving a boost to others... helping those who were hurting... trying to influence their lives in a positive way.

With this in mind, he and his family had travelled, both across the United States and overseas. He had also established a counselling service on radio and television.

But that day in the 1970s as Ken, his wife Barbara and their children drove their two buses down 1-75 just south of Dayton, Ohio, Ken was feeling drained and discouraged.

"Oh," he cried, "Am I doing any good, travelling around like this? God, is this what you want me to do?"

His thoughts were suddenly interrupted. "Hey, Dad, let's get some pizza!"

Ken turned off at Route 741. There was sign after sign, offering fast food.

"A sign," mused Ken. "That's what I need... a sign."

As Ken's family poured out, and across to the pizza parlor, Ken announced, "I'm not really hungry. I'll just stretch my legs."

He grabbed himself a soft drink and ambled back to the bus. Was it burnout? He was just plain exhausted.

A persistent ringing broke into Ken's concentration. He looked across at the outside phone booth. The attendant seemed oblivious to the sound.

Ken grew impatient. "Why doesn't someone answer it?" he wondered. "What if it's an emergency?"

Nine rings. Ten…Fifteen…

His curiosity perked up. He shuffled over to the booth and picked up the receiver. "Hello?"

The operator's voice came through. "Long distance call for Ken Gaub."

Ken was dazed. "No," he heard himself saying. "You are crazy!" And then, realising how rude that must have sounded, he apologised and tried to explain. "I was just walking down the road here. And the phone was ringing…"

The operator simply asked again, "Is Ken Gaub there? I have a long distance call for Ken Gaub."

Oh, this must be *Candid Camera*, he thought, instinctively. Ken ran his hands through his hair. But no camera crew appeared.

He looked toward the pizza house. The family was still inside. They were at this restaurant only on a whim. It was randomly selected. And no one knew they were here. No one.

"I have a long distance call for Ken Gaub, sir." The operator sounded quite insistent now. "Is Mr Gaub there or isn't he?"

"Operator, I'm Ken Gaub." Ken could make no sense of this whole thing.

"Are you sure?" asked the operator. Then suddenly there was another woman's voice on the phone.

"Yes, that's him, Operator!" she exclaimed. "Mr Gaub, I'm Millie from Harrisburg, Pennsylvania.

You don't know me. But I'm desperate. Please help me."

"How can I help you?" And Ken heard the operator hang up.

The woman at the other end was weeping now. Ken patiently waited. Finally, she gained control. "I'm at the end of my rope. I was about to kill myself. I started to write a suicide note. Then I began to tell God I really didn't want to do this."

In her despair, Millie recalled that she had seen Ken on television. Oh, if she could only talk to that kind, understanding person....

But that was impossible. There was no place she knew, to reach him. Millie spoke a little more calmly now. "So I began to finish the note. And then some numbers came into my mind, and I wrote them down." Millie was weeping again.

Silently Ken prayed. "Show me how to help this woman."

Through her tears, Millie went on. "I looked at those numbers. And the thought came... wouldn't it be wonderful if God has given me Ken Gaub's phone number? Oh, Mr Gaub, I just can't believe I'm actually talking to you. Are you in your office in California?"

"No," responded Ken, "I do not have an office in California. It's in Yakima, Washington."

"Then where are you?" called the woman, bewildered.

Even more puzzled was Ken. "Millie, it was you who made the call. Don't you know?"

"No, I have no idea what area this is," said Millie. "I just dialled the long-distance operator. I gave the numbers to her, and made it a person-to-person call."

Daub advised Millie what to do. And it was to take her into a successful new life.

Still stunned, Ken hung up.

"Barb," enthused Ken as his family climbed back into the bus, "you won't believe this! God knows where I am!"

This incident was reported by Nancy Leahy to Joan Wester Anderson and appeared in the #1 *New York Times* bestselling *Chicken Soup for the Soul*, by Jack Canfield and Mark Victor Hansen.

Some questions

- Who was it that arranged those events in such a manner that Ken and Millie should meet on the phone exactly at that hour?
- Who prompted Ken's son to ask for pizza exactly when he did?
- Who led Ken to pull into that precise restaurant?
- Who persuaded Ken to stay outdoors near the payphone booth?
- Who gave Millie the exact sequence of numbers that would ring that precise telephone beside the road?
- Who imparted these "impressions"?
- ***Who answered both their prayers with one "miracle" connection?*** To each separately an electrifying response.

And that again raises the BIG question…

- Who programs those many DNA machines, all so different from one another, to ***inter-connect*** inside a cell? Could it be ***the same Superior Intelligence*** that ***connected*** Ken and Millie to the pay phone?

Is this evidence of a Designer who cares about his creation?

Speaking of this God that thousands of scientists now believe they can pray to, if this God can not only plan, design and create, might he also be able to hear?

You may ask, If God exists, how on earth could he be concerned about every human being in the world?

Why does a mother love her baby? She can give no reason, except that it belongs to her. The chemicals comprising its body are worth only a few dollars. It weighs perhaps eight pounds of flesh. That tiny baby causes trouble, disrupts the family routine and deprives her of sleep. But he belongs to her and she loves him.

Suppose you have five children. Did you love your first baby? Naturally you did. Did you love the second child only half as much? Of course not. So what about the third? You loved it just as much as the other two. What if you had twenty children? You would love each child just as much as the others.

Think now. If you and I, limited as we are, could have hearts big enough to love all our children, why would a limitless God find it difficult to love all of his children on this planet?

In our computer age, what's the potential for programming information? By pressing a few keys, one can already gain information about the financial situation of people with credit cards from all over the world. Conceivably, in a few years from now, everyone on earth will have a number – by which all their information will be stored on one machine. Now if such a vast storage of information can be memorised on one inorganic electronic brain, surely it is conceivable that there is a supernatural being that understands us in greater detail?

"Not testable"

A guy called DL heard another guy Mark Harwood mention God – and was he upset! "The god proposition does not appear reasonable," said DL. "It's both untestable and founded upon lack of knowledge. How can one rationally be expected to believe (have faith) in untestable propositions."

"Well," said Mark, "we all have faith in nontestable propositions every day of our lives. Rather than being based on lack of knowledge, our faith is usually based on very real experience.

"For instance, the room you are sitting in is part of a larger building. Can you see the architect and the builder? Have you met them? How do you know they exist? You know the building had a designer and a builder because in your experience you observe that buildings do not make themselves. They all have a designer and builder.

"So, you have faith that the designer and builder have existed, because the building exists and your faith is based on knowledge. But the existence of the designer and builder is ***not scientifically testable***! It would be irrational to assume there was no designer or builder just because you can't see them now.

"In exactly the same way, we look around at the amazing diversity and complexity of living things and we know there must have been a designer and builder.

"One of the sure evidences of design is the presence of information in the genetic code of living things. The coded information is not inherent in the physics or chemistry of the DNA molecule, just like the information in a book does not reside in the ink and the paper. Instead, the information resides in the way the base pairs of the DNA are arranged, and in the way the ink makes shapes on the paper, so that the code is intelligible and meaning is transferred.

"Therefore, the inference that the universe has a Creator who is outside of what has been made, in other words, a supernatural Being, is entirely reasonable and soundly based on knowledge and experience."

DL: "I'll only believe what is testable. Is there any scientifically testable evidence for the existence of any spiritual being?"

MARK: "The answer is clearly 'No'. But the problem is you are asking the wrong question. Perhaps you could ask:

1. Do you only consider something to be real if it is scientifically testable?
2. Is love real?
3. Are historical events real?

"Clearly, there are very real things that are not accessible via scientific experiments. Most importantly, past events can only be determined by historical records as they are not available for observation and are therefore not accessible by science."

And I believe we do have such historical records…

9

Communication -

WOULD HE WANT TO SPEAK TO US?

We have a beautiful Labrador dog. After feeding him, do we take no interest in talking to him? We hear his cry, we experience the joy in his eyes, we feel him licking our hand. Do we never want him to experience the love that is in our hearts for him? Don't you ever want to let your pet know that you love him?

Of course you do! And who implanted that ability and desire into your heart?

We have already considered a Supreme Being's ability and willingness to hear us. But, since we are designed to receive information, then might our Maker desire to communicate with us – to send us messages? Would that make sense?

Ability to speak to us?

But would He ***be able*** to communicate to us? Think now! Here is this Master Designer who has ***inter-dimensionally transmitted coded data*** into our DNA molecules. He has programmed our DNA to send millions of messages a second throughout our bodies. And we think He cannot pass on additional information in other ways to us? Even to guiding human minds to write down messages?

The personality question

That naturally raises the question as to whether God is just some impersonal force or a personal Being.

Ask yourself: Did your personality come from impersonality? Is the Intelligent Programmer who planned and produced your DNA – who designed you to be a personal, intelligent, thinking, speaking, communicating being – does that Designer have LESS ability than you?

Would not our Maker possess the same ability to think, speak and communicate, that he has given us? The Intelligence that made the ear, can he not hear? Whoever designed the eye, can he not see?

Observable ***scientific evidence*** indicates that an effect is not greater than its cause. It always takes ***a greater source*** of information to produce information. On this basis, the design of living, intelligent, and personal human beings requires ***a greater cause*** outside the creation itself which possesses life, intelligence and ***personality*** – a Superior Intelligent Being.

It makes sense that such a Supreme Creator would be able to – and desire to – communicate with creatures He has made. And would ***not need*** a space ship to do it, either.

Again, wouldn't it make sense that humans were created, not for what they can do for their Maker (or even He for them), but for an enduring relationship of love, fellowship and interaction with Him? And that this relationship defines the ***purpose*** of human existence and gives it ***meaning***?

In fact, might He even document ***evidence*** of our origins, and stamp the document with His signature in ways that no human being could replicate? So that none of us would have any rational reason for doubting?

Actually, there does exist a document that 3,800 times makes the outrageous claim to be not man-made, but the Creator Himself speaking to us – and it even ***challenges us to disprove it***. So why don't we accept this challenge?

If the document's claims can be disproved, fine. But if we can establish its credibility, then might it contain information relevant to our subject?

Remember, we're talking about ***evidence***, not preconceived ideas.

So what is this document? And how accurate is it? In the next four chapters we shall see…

10

Archaeology's verdict: –

PHYSICAL EVIDENCE

The desert pushed right down to the water's edge. And as Sayid, our Egyptian friend, packed the sleeping gear on to the roof rack of our expedition vehicle, Paul watched the sun climb over the sea.

If we were not mistaken, there was something quite startling down there on the floor of the Red Sea. And we were about to investigate.

But this whole saga began much, much earlier… in that land of romance and mystery, ancient Egypt.

Some 3,500 years ago, in the most glorious era of her history, Egypt was the granary of the world. She was eminent in science, the arts, luxury and magnificence. Egypt was, in a sense, the super power of that day.

Slaves' baby becomes a prince

And this is where we stumble upon a fascinating old story. Was it just a myth, or did it really happen? Here's the story, anyway…

In 1526 BC was born a baby who, according to the Old Testament account, was to dramatically alter Egypt's super power status. Moses was born to Israelite parents in humble surroundings. But by a bizarre twist of circumstances, he grew up to be trained as "the son of Pharaoh's daughter".

Because of his relation to the throne, Moses had all the might and wealth of Egypt at his fingertips. He became a great statesman and general. Yet he had learned that the thousands of slaves working in the brick-pits were his people, and that his destiny was linked with theirs.

The time came for Moses to make his decision. He could choose to become king of what was the world's greatest empire, or to be numbered among the sweating and grumbling slaves.

Red Sea crossing

The biblical book of Exodus tells us that the Hebrew slaves, led by Moses, escaped from Egypt, but they were pursued by the pharaoh's army. When they found themselves trapped at the Red Sea, a strong wind blew from the east, opening up a passage for them to escape across a dry sea bed, with a frozen wall of water on either side. But, as the Egyptian army pursued, the sea collapsed upon the army and every man in it was drowned.

Now, my work requires that I deal with ***evidence.*** So was there any truth to this old story? Or is it just a colorful myth?

Well, at the alleged site, the Gulf of Aqaba arm of the Red Sea, we have had at least 30 international divers scouring the sea floor. Most of our dives have been on the Egyptian side.

And – hold your breath - we have actually found the remains of chariot cabs and wheels intermingled with skeletal parts of horses and men, scattered across the sea bed.

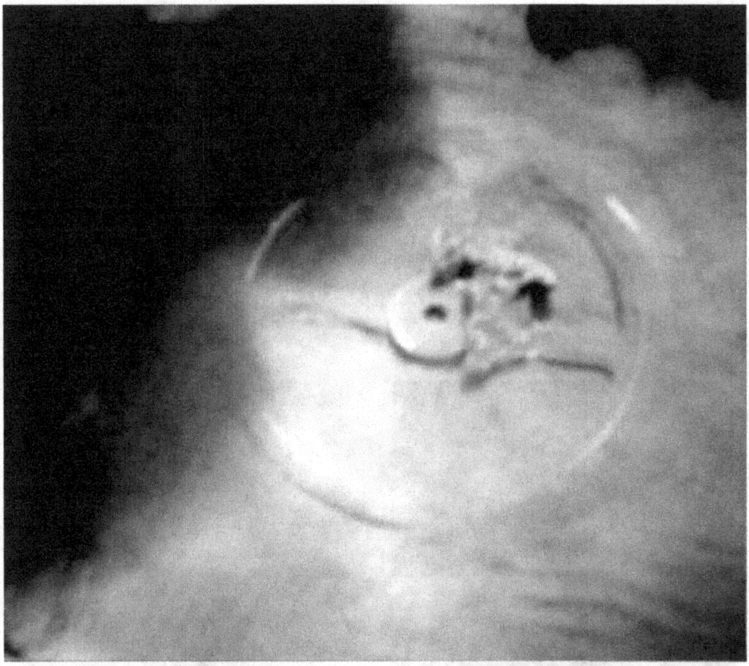

These chariot remains were not in perfect condition and required careful examination to see exactly what they were. They were covered in coral, which at first made it difficult to see them clearly. The coral was the agency that had preserved them!

There were numerous wheels. Some were still on their axles, and some were off. There were chariot cabs without the wheels.

Meanwhile, Viveka Ponten, a Swedish lady with a work permit in Saudi Arabia, dived on the Saudi Arabian side and found and photographed more remains. These were similar to those we found on the Egyptian side… wheels and skeletons. All mixed together across the seabed.

A portion of one wheel was taken up from the sea floor and presented to Nassif Mohammed Hussan, of the Egyptian Antiquities Department in Cairo. He pronounced it to be from the same period given in the Bible for Moses and the Exodus.

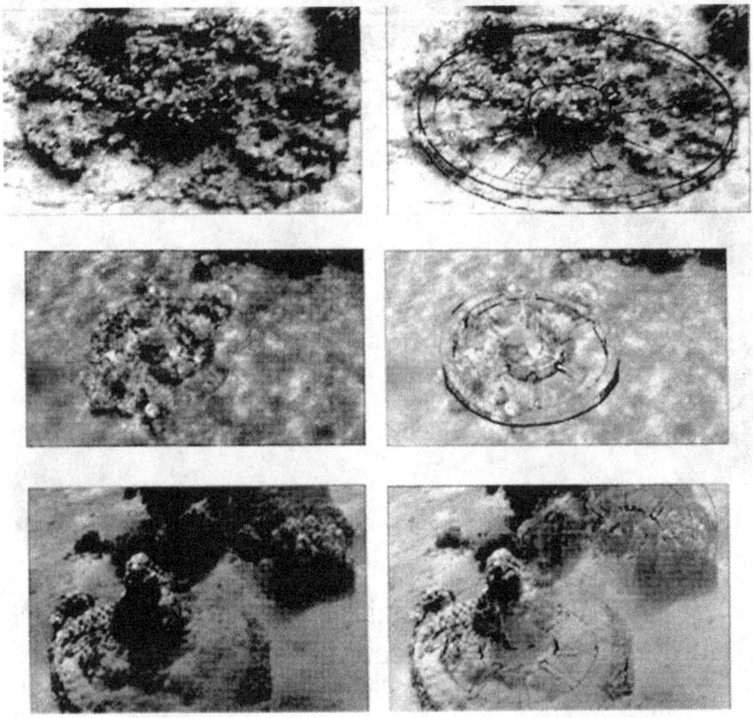

Pre-judging

For many today, the study of history is incorporated with ideas that there is no God, miracles are not possible, we live in a closed system and there is no supernatural.

With these presuppositions they begin their 'critical, open and honest' investigation of history.

When they study, for example, the story of Moses and the crossing of the Red Sea, they conclude it was not a miracle or even a real event, because we know (not historically, but philosophically) that there is no spiritual dimension. Therefore, these things cannot be.

They rule out the Exodus of the Israelites even before they start an historical investigation of the Exodus.

These suppositions are not so much scientific biases, but rather, philosophical prejudice. Instead of beginning with the scientific and historical data, they preclude it by prior speculation.

But now we have seen ***physical evidence*** to convince any unbiased, thinking person that the Bible is ***real history***.

Why introduce the Bible?

When I mentioned to an email correspondent my plan to reveal the "forbidden secret" and expose those who were suppressing it, he asked, "Why introduce the Bible into the discussion?"

This was my answer: As an experienced hands-on archaeologist, I have learned that:

(a) to ignore the biblical writings is to deprive oneself of a ***valuable source of information***, and

b) an amazing 3,800 times the Bible claims to offer vital intelligence data ***beyond what man can discover on his own***.

So would common sense prompt us to at least investigate?

Yes, we might as well admit it. The ***real truth*** concerning our topic will ***never*** be found in the ***opinions*** of the present world system. The best it can offer is the convenience of thousands of people blundering in and out of theories, as through a revolving door. It is also a fact that if you do not start with the right premise, there is no way you can come up with the right answer.

Now, let me share with you a trade secret. When we decided to take the Bible "myths" literally, our archaeological teams began discovering ancient remains that others had been missing. Its clues gave us an outcome more solid than expected. We also found long-forgotten scientific secrets within the Bible.

I now believe it will throw some light on our topic, the "***forbidden secret***." But first, let's do some more tests on its accuracy.

Crossing the River Jordan

I love skeptics. (I was one.) And I loved the man who smirked as he said, "So you've confirmed one story. But what about this: The Bible says that, after the Exodus, the Hebrews came to cross the Jordan River. It was flood time… but that river – in flood, mind you – suddenly dried up so they could cross over! A tall tale, if ever there was one! Impossible!"

You would have to agree, that's quite a story.

"Well, let's see how you'll wriggle out of that!" he chuckled.

As it turns out, there's something interesting about the geography in that area. Sixteen miles upstream from Jericho there's a place called Damieh (the site known as Adam in the biblical incident). At that spot, the limestone cliffs rise hundreds of feet high, forming a deep, narrow gorge through which the stream flows rapidly, especially at the season of floods.

Due to erosion or earth tremors the cliffs at this point sometimes collapse, completely blocking the river with a natural dam. It may interest you to know that the River Jordan has ceased to flow on at least three different known occasions in history. These were AD 1267, 1907 and 1927. The 1927 event was actually witnessed by archaeologist Professor John Garstang. Newspapers reported that the waters from the upper stream were blocked for 21 hours, so that many people crossed and re-crossed the Jordan on foot.

Stopping the river flow for the Israelites to cross over was really a miracle of timing. Could not the Creator control of the laws of nature He created? We now have ***evidence*** that such an event could happen.

Critics "had a ball"

More and more we've been discovering that the biblical record stands up remarkably well to the missiles shot at it by critics.

For many years, attacks on the Bible by the higher critical scholars of Europe stood unchallenged. That was because so many biblical names and stories were found nowhere else except in the Bible. And it certainly did appear that its stories were 'made up'.

For example, the Bible mentioned a nation called 'Hittites'. But they were unknown to history. So critics could boldly claim that the Hittites simply had not existed.

Then, in 1879, A. H. Sayce and W. Knight identified strange hieroglyphic inscriptions found in northern Syria and Anatolia as monuments of the long-lost Hittites. In 1860, the *Encyclopaedia Brittanica* had devoted to the Hittites a mere eight lines on one column. But its 1947 edition would give over ten full pages of two columns each to an article dealing with Hittite history, culture and religion. More widespread digging began to take place in the Middle East. And the deciphering of cuneiform inscriptions started to furnish ***evidence*** which would leave the critics dumbfounded.

Jericho's walls tumble down

Another apparently wild Bible story concerned the city of Jericho, on the Jordan's West Bank.

After the river crossing, Jericho was the first outpost standing in the way of the Hebrew tribes occupying the Promised Land of Canaan (Palestine). The Bible says that the Hebrews, led by Joshua, camped nearby. Then they marched around the city every day for a week. Then, on the seventh day they marched around it seven times. Yes, seven times in a single day. They then blew a chorus of trumpets. And the walls surrounding Jericho came crashing down.

Seven times around a city in one day? Oh, come on!

Well, today, you can see what remains of ancient Jericho. Archaeological ***evidence*** confirms that an earthquake did actually bring down the walls of Jericho. According to Dame Kathleen Kenyon, who excavated the site in the 1950s, scorching and ashes throughout the city prove that "the destruction of the walls was the work of enemies."

This is precisely how Joshua's capture of Jericho is portrayed in the Bible – an earthquake that broke down the city walls and the whole city burned to the ground. (Joshua 6:24)

During his excavations of Jericho (1930-1936), John Garstang found something so startling that he and two other members of the team prepared and signed a statement describing what was found. In reference to these findings Garstang says:

> As to the main fact, then, there remains no doubt: the walls fell outwards so completely that the attackers would be able to clamber up and over their ruins into the city. Why so unusual? Because the walls of cities do not fall outwards, they fall inwards. And yet in Joshua 6:20 we read, "The wall fell down flat. Then the people went up into the city, every man straight before him, and they took the city." The walls were made to fall outward.' (John Garstang, *The Foundations of Bible History; Joshua, Judges*. New York: R.R.Smith, Inc., 1931, p.146)

The fallen walls of Jericho seen today are precisely those that came tumbling down in the face of Joshua's army.

Kenyon's expedition uncovered a portion of a house wall and floor, with an oven and a small jug, which appeared to be "part of the kitchen of a Canaanite woman, who may have dropped the juglet beside the oven and fled at the sound of the trumpets of Joshua's men". (Kathleen M. Kenyon, *Digging Up Jericho,* p. 263) The single dipper juglet was beside the oven, lying on the floor. It was found *in situ.*

It turned out that archaeological digs substantiated the Bible story in a number of ways.

1. There was a king for each of the small Canaanite city-states, just as the Bible suggests.
2. There were double walls.
3. Only one gateway was found. This harmonizes with the biblical comment about 'shutting of THE gate.'

Unlike the ruins of other ancient Middle Eastern cities, all of the city of Joshua's time (and parts of even earlier levels) was eroded away. This is not surprising, since the crumbling mud-brick structures were not preserved by being built upon by later inhabitants, because the city was unoccupied for centuries after Joshua's time. (Joshua 6:21) Pottery finds in the tombs outside the city, indicate that Jericho was inhabited in the 14th century, just as the Bible states.

Seven times around in one day

But what about the "impossibility" of marching around this city seven times in one day?

Some time ago, I explored those ruins. And it is evident that Jericho was actually a collection of tiny dwellings compactly crowded together on such a scale that you can easily walk around the foundations in 30 minutes or less! Yes, the city's total size was less than 8 acres. Seven times around would be less than 3 miles. Well, it seems the biblical history has stood the investigation better than the opinions of the scholars!

14th century date for conquest of Canaan

While some critical scholars have been fond of saying there was no Hebrew (Israelite) Exodus, there have been others who did accept such an event, but rejected the biblical dating of 1400 BC. They preferred to place the Hebrew Exodus and the subsequent conquest of Canaan, as late as 1200 BC.

So who was right? The answer came with the discovery in Egypt of a complete royal archive. This comprises hundreds of official letters received by the Egyptian kings Amenhotep III and IV from their Palestinian and Syrian vassals.

Known as the Amarna Letters, these documents ***prove*** Egypt was politically weak in the 14th century BC, the very time which the Bible claims the Hebrews were invading Palestine (Canaan).

Some of these letters come from the king of Jerusalem, Abdu-khepa – a Hittite. He pleads for weapons and soldiers from Egypt to defend his city from the invading ***Habiru***. He writes that the "*Habiru*" have already taken over great parts of the country, and that they threaten to overrun the whole land. So what do we have here but a description of the ***Hebrew*** conquest of Canaan as the Canaanites saw it.

And knock me down, we've stumbled upon further ***evidence*** that the Hebrews were ***already*** in Canaan in the 13th century BC – long before the time claimed by critical scholars.

The Egyptian pharaohs frequently erected monuments in the form of high stone pillars to commemorate their victories and political successes. One such stele set up by Pharaoh Merneptah mentions Israel as a people he had defeated in a battle in one of his Palestine campaigns. This bears witness to the existence of the Israelites in Palestine in the 13th century, just as the Old Testament says.

Archaeology furnishes evidence of biblical persons, places and events

As noted earlier, because so many names – and events – were ***known only from*** the Bible, these were blasted by critics as pure myth. But now archaeology has turned the whole situation around. Here is a sampling from the almost countless examples:

- Pharaoh Shishak's Palestinian campaign in the fifth year of King Rehoboam: a fragment of his victory monument found at Megiddo, confirms the biblical account. (1 Kings 14:25,26)
- Many fragments of beautifully carved ivory plaques from Ahab's palace, described in the Bible as an ivory palace. (1 Kings 29:39)

- Assyrian inscriptions of Sennacherib's siege of Jerusalem in 701 BC, against Hezekiah again confirm the Bible record. (2 Kings 18:13 to 19:36)
- Assyrian inscriptions mentioning the biblical kings Joash, Azariah and Manasseh, Ahab, Jehu, Jehoash, Menahem, Pekah and Hoshea.
- Babylonian receipts confirming the exile and food rations of Judah's king Jehoiachin. (2 Kings 24:8-15; Jeremiah 52:30-34)
- Excavations at Susa in Iran, show the layout of the Persian palace in such perfect agreement with the biblical description of it in the Book of Esther that scholars have been led to admit that only someone well acquainted with the palace, its environs, its divisions, and its court ceremonial could have written it.
- Almost every Assyrian, Babylonian, or Persian ruler mentioned in the Bible has been rediscovered in contemporary documents – Shalmaneser, Tilgath-pileser, Nebuchadnezzar, Belshazzar, Cyrus, Darius the Great, Xerxes, Sargon, and many others.
- Even officials whose names are in the Bible, such as Nebuzar-adan (2 Kings 25:8) or Nergal-sharezer (Jeremiah 39:3) are met with in the official documents of their time.

Babylon's fiery furnace

The Bible speaks of three young Hebrew men being thrown into a fiery furnace by Nebuchadnezzar, king of Babylon (Daniel ch. 3) …and others "*whom the king of Babylon roasted in the fire*" (Jeremiah 29:22) Excavators in the ruins of Babylon City uncovered a peculiar cone-shaped structure that appeared to be a firing-kiln for the production of brick or pottery. But when the cuneiform figures were deciphered, linguists were astonished to find this inscription:

> *This is the place of burning where men who blasphemed the gods of Chaldea died by fire.*

That the incidents recorded in the Bible concerning punishment in a fiery furnace were in keeping with the times is also shown by an inscription of the Assyrian king Ashurbanipal:

> *Saulmagina my rebellious brother, who made war with me, they threw into a burning fiery furnace, and destroyed his life.*

Nebuchadnezzar's son-in-law, in one of his royal inscriptions, claims to have *"burned to death adversaries and disobedient ones."* ***Evidence*** that the Bible record is real history.

Daniel in the lion's den

The biblical book of Daniel also records that the Hebrew captive Daniel was tossed into a den of lions. (Daniel chapter 6)

That such 'lion's den' punishment was in keeping with the times is now ***proven*** by the discovery of that same inscription of Ashurbanipal that we just mentioned. It continues thus:

> *The rest of the people who had rebelled they threw alive among bulls and lions, as Sennacherib my grandfather used to do. Lo, again following his footsteps, those men I threw into the midst of them.*

On one occasion, as the famed excavator Marcel Dieulafoy was digging amid the ruins of Babylon, he fell into a pit that appeared like an ancient well. After being rescued by his companions, he proceeded with the work of identification. How astonished was he to find that the pit had been used as a cage for wild animals! And upon the curb was this inscription:

> *The Place of Execution, where men who angered the king died torn by wild animals.*

Nebuchadnezzar was Babylon's great builder

The book of Daniel identifies Nebuchadnezzar as the builder of mighty Babylon. (Daniel 4:30)

An inscription by Nebuchadnezzar found among Babylon's ruins and now in the Berlin Museum states:

> *I have made Babylon, the holy city, the glory of the great gods, more prominent than ever before, and have promoted its rebuilding.*

In fact, numerous bricks have been found in the ruins of Babylon, stamped with Nebuchadnezzar's name. ***Evidence*** of biblical accuracy.

Belshazzar, Babylon's last king

According to the Bible, the last king of the Chaldeans was Belshazzar. (Daniel 5:2,30,31) This name was unknown outside the Bible (or works based on it). So, for centuries, scholars hotly denied Belshazzar ever existed. All secular histories dealing with that period listed the last king as Nabonidus. Therefore the book of Daniel was said to be a forgery, written not when claimed, but by some later ignorant writer. It was not until the 20th century that contemporary records bearing the name Belshazzar surfaced for the first time in archaeological digs.

In 1924, Sidney Smith discovered a tablet in the British Museum which showed that Belshazzar was the eldest son of Nabonidus and that in 'the third year' Nabonidus 'entrusted the kingship' to his eldest son (as coregent) and also placed the army of Babylon under his command.

This was a severe blow to critics who claimed the biblical book of Daniel to be a product of the 2nd century BC, and not a 6th century eyewitness report. (*Babylonian Historical Texts.* London, 1924, p. 88; Latest trans. By Oppenheim in *Ancient Near Eastern Texts*, ed. By Pritchard. Princeton, 1950, p. 313)

According to Cuneiform sources, Nabonidus was absent from Babylon at the time of its capture.

A prayer tablet of Nabonidus says: "*As for Belshazzar, the first-born son, proceeding from my loins, place in his heart fear of thy divinity; let him not turn to sinning; let him be satisfied with the fullness of life.*" Evidently the old king was quite worried over his wayward son.

That Belshazzar was merely a co-ruler in Babylon is also indicated by the fact that in the Bible (Daniel 5:29) Daniel is referred to as ***third ruler in the kingdom.*** So two other rulers are implied. Who were the other two? Nabonidus and Belshazzar!

Intricate detail puzzles skeptics

Professor R.H. Pfeiffer was typical of those who did not accept the book of Daniel as genuinely written in the 6th century BC, but claimed it to be a 2nd century BC forgery.

However, his skepticism raised a problem for which he could find no answer. The mystery facing him was how on earth could accurate information about Belshazzar have been put into the book of Daniel at a time when this king had been so completely forgotten in the ancient world that not one of the Greek authors mentions him?

Therefore he wrote:

> We shall presumably never know how our author learned... that Belshazzar, mentioned only in Babylonian records, in Daniel, and in Baruch 1:11, which is based on Daniel, was functioning as king when Cyrus took Babylon in 538. (R.H. Pfeiffer, *Introduction to the Old Testament.* New York: 1941, pp. 758,759)

If one accepts the book of Daniel as genuine – that it was written when it says it was – the problem disappears.

On the other hand, if a scholar does not want to give up his critical attitude, he finds himself in a serious dilemma. He cannot understand how a man of the Maccabean age (2nd century BC) could be so accurately informed about the historical events that took place 300 years earlier, ***when no reliable source material of that period existed any more.***

Kings of Israel

My friend Hugh dropped by the other day, carrying a book written by a well known modern author. Hugh wanted to know whether some claims made in that book were backed up by archaeological discoveries or not?

Well, I took a good look. And here is one statement that jumped off a page:

> Did MOSES, SOLOMON and King DAVID exist? I would say categorically no. (David Icke, *The Biggest Secret*. Bridge of Love Publications USA, Wildwood, MO, USA, 2001, p. 82)

King David

It is true that until fairly recently, there was no evidence outside the Bible for the existence of King David.

But in 1993, a team of archaeologists in Israel led by Professor Avraham Biram, were excavating Tel Dan. This was a beautiful mound at the foot of Mount Hermon in northern Galilee, beside one of the headwaters of the Jordan River.

Anyway, on July 21 that year, they came upon a triangular piece of basalt rock, measuring 23 x 36 centimeters. Inscribed in Aramaic, it was eventually identified as part of a victory pillar erected by the king of Syria and later smashed by an Israelite ruler. The inscription on the stone dates to the 9th century BC. This was about a century after David was believed to have ruled Israel. The inscription includes the words *'Beit David'* (which means 'House' or 'Dynasty of David') and also refers to 'King of Israel'.

So you see, the inscription refers not simply to a David, but to the House of David, the dynasty of the king. This reference to David does strongly indicate that a king called David established a dynasty in Israel during the period that the Bible states.

But that's not all. In the inscriptions on a stele known as the Moabite stone, another scholar found the name 'House of David'. This is similarly from around 900 BC, a hundred years after the alleged time of King David. So I ask you, how did King David's name appear in historical records if he were no more than a later literary invention?

As time passes, more such ***evidence*** involving Bible names and places is being discovered. And, like it or not, the skeptics are constantly having to retreat.

Very well, so King David is real history. But where's the evidence for Solomon? Because I notice that our friend Icke, in his book, says, 'Solomon – it's all invention.' " (*Ibid.*, p. 87)

King Solomon

Pardon me if I now ask, ***who is really inventing*** tales? Because archaeologists have been stumbling upon ***evidence after evidence*** of King Solomon.

Temple Hill tablet: Israeli geologists announced on January 12, 2003 they had examined a stone tablet dating to 800 BC which detailed repair plans for King Solomon's Temple. Tests confirmed this Temple Hill Tablet to be authentic. (Laurie Copans, The Associated Press, January 14, 2003) Some stone tablet 'finds' are later presumed to be forgeries. But not this one. We must be careful not to confuse the two.

Phoenician treaty record: The Bible speaks of a treaty that Solomon made with Hiram, king of the Phoenician city of Tyre. (1 Kings 5: 1,12) The historian Josephus informs us that a thousand years later, independently kept copies of this Phoenician treaty with King Solomon could be read in the public archives of Tyre in Phoenicia. (Flavius Josephus, *Antiquities of the Jews*, Book VIII, Chapter II, Section 7)

Ethiopian record: Furthermore, an independent Ethiopian epic, the *Kebra Nagast*, written about 850 BC, tells the story of an Ethiopian queen's visit to King Solomon of Israel and of the enormous riches and gifts that he showered upon her.

Indian record: Then there is a mountain in Srinagar, India, called Tahkti Suleiman ('Solomon's Mountain'). Very strange, don't you think, that a mountain in India's highlands should be named after a Hebrew king – except that an ancient tradition declares that King Solomon came there and arranged for the construction of the temple on the summit.

Red Sea inscription: In 1984 a commemorative pillar was found on the eastern shore of the Gulf of Aqaba… close to chariot remains on the seabed. It bore an inscription in archaic Hebrew: "*MIZRAIM (Egypt); SOLOMON; EDOM; DEATH; PHARAOH; MOSES; and YAHWEH*". Was this erected by Solomon to mark the Israelite crossing of the sea? Of course, I will still respect the critic's right to say that Solomon never existed. You can't take the Bible literally? Here is some more ***evidence:***

THE BIBLE SAYS	SCIENCE CONFIRMS
After the Deluge (Global Flood) the human race divided into 3 families. (Genesis 9:19)	All mankind has stemmed from one origin, in 3 main branches (*Royal Anthropological Institute Journal*)
This physical division of mankind took place during a forced scattering 5 generations after the Flood. (Genesis 10:22-25)	National genealogies show a unity until the 5th post-Flood generation, then they diverge. (meticulously kept pagan Irish, Anglo-Saxon, Norwegian, Danish and Iceland royal genealogies)

Customs are described concerning the duty of a childless wife; the precedence of an oral will; giving up an inheritance by barter; titles inscribed on dolls, and so on. (Gen.16:1-4; 27:1-33; 25:29-34; ch.31)	These customs fit no other period of ancient history (1911-1750 BC) and were later forgotten - indicating they were written by persons familiar with those events. (Code of Hammurabi and Nuzi texts prove these customs were unique to that period.)
Jerusalem's original name was Salem. (Gen.14:18)	Confirmed by one of the Ebla tablets (c. 2000 BC).
Five Jordan plain cities were Sodom, Gomorrah, Admah, Zeboiim, Bela (Zoar). And the king of Gomorrah was Birsha. (c. 2000 BC) (Genesis 14:2)	Five Jordan plain cities were (in the same order) Sodom, Gomorrah, Admah, Zeboiim, Bela (Zoar). And the king of Gomorrah was Birsha. (Ebla Tablet no. 1860)
Burning sulfur balls from the sky turned 5 Jordan plain cities to ashes (1893 BC). (Genesis chapter 19)	Five sites turned totally to ash have been discovered on the Jordan plain, peppered with sulfur balls. (*The Weapon the Globalists Fear,* ch.14)
The price of slaves in 1728 BC: Joseph was sold for 20 shekels of silver. (Genesis 37:28)	Matches the price of slaves during 18th + 19th century BC (Mari texts) By the 8th century BC the price was 50-60 shekels, and by 5th c. BC it was 90-120 shekels.
In Egypt seven years of plenty were followed by 7 years of famine (1715 BC). (Gen.41:29,30)	Egyptian inscription tells of a 7 year famine and 7 years of plenty. (Rock inscription at Sihiel, below First Cataract)

The Hebrew people in Egypt were placed under bondage of physical labor (1470 BC) (Exodus chapter 1)	Egyptian monuments depict people called "Apiru" or "Habiru" doing manual labor during the reign of Thutmoses III (1400s BC)

Well, you get the picture. The parade of archaeological discoveries revealing the Bible to be accurate history just goes on and on. So does anyone still dare tell us it's just "myth or allegory"?

Yeah. And I'm the tooth fairy!

Critics jump the gun

A serious anti-Bible campaign got off the ground in the 1800s. When Darwin postulated random evolution, many of his contemporaries, turned off by a hypocritical church, jumped onto the bandwagon, believing they had been given an 'out' from belief in a Creator.

Predictably, it wasn't long before the Bible was placed under the microscope – and found to be 'inaccurate', 'mythical' or 'allegorical'. Some critics deemed the Bible writers totally uninformed, foolishly imagining things that did not exist.

And so many, acting with woefully incomplete information, rushed into judgment.

At that time, there was virtually no modern archaeology to "test" their assertions. What the critics did not expect was that hundreds of later historical and archaeological discoveries would support the Bible's astounding accuracy. And often in minute detail.

Now we have ***evidence*** that the people, places and events they wrote about were indeed real.

From my firsthand experience as a field archaeologist, leading or participating over the years in at least 25 hands-on expeditions, here is the bottom line: Beyond reasonable doubt, the Bible is better informed than its critics. The historical setting is true to fact and the events described ***did really happen***.

Nelson Glueck, one of the world's most eminent Middle Eastern archaeologists, would tell you much the same:

> It may be stated categorically that no archaeological discovery has ever controverted a Biblical reference. (Nelson Glueck, *Rivers in the Desert: History of Negev*. Philadelphia: Jewish Publications Society of America, p.31)

Confronted with the ***evidence***, the "myth" charge has failed. It seems we need to update our opinions. I submit to you that the authority of the Bible as literal history is substantiated not by academics in their ivory towers, but by hands-on archaeologists who follow the book's directions and find physical remains from mentioned events. ***Actionable proof in real life.***

****

A small boy was sitting on a park bench, exclaiming excitedly, "WOW! That's fantastic!"

A 'learned' gentleman, a skeptic, approached. "Well, son what are you getting so excited about?"

"Oh, Sir, I am reading how God made the waters of the Red Sea stand up and let all the Israelites cross on dry land, and then when the 600 Egyptian soldiers in their horses and chariots tried to follow them, God let the waters go back to normal and drowned them all."

"Oh come now, son," said the man pontifically, "the Bible is mistaken, it wasn't the Red Sea, but the Reed Sea and it's only 6 inches deep. When it says they walked on dry land, that means the water was only ankle deep." And having set the boy straight, he continued on his way, only to hear "WOW! That's awesome!"

So he turned back and asked the boy, "What are you carrying on about now?"

"Isn't God great," answered the boy, "He managed to drown all 600 soldiers and their horses and chariots in only 6 inches of water!"

Now we come to the acid test. If you want to discredit the Bible, I'll now show you now precisely how to do it.

FOR FURTHER INFORMATION

What OTHER ARCHAEOLOGICAL ***evidence*** sheds light on the Bible record? See these books:

- *Ark of the Covenant*
- *The Corpse Came Back*
- *The Weapon the Globalists Fear*
- *Discoveries: Questions Answered*
- *The Ark Conspiracy*
- *Sinai's Exciting Secrets*
- *What Happened to the Tower of Babel?*
- *Solomon's Riches*

Has the Bible been TAMPERED WITH, ALTERED, CORRUPTED? – see what the ***evidence*** reveals in:

- *Who's Playing Jesus Games?*
- *The Sorcerers' Secret*
- *The Weapon the Globalists Fear*

11

Prophecy's verdict: –

AMAZING PROPHECIES

On April 23, 1989, Harold Costar was murdered on his way to consult an astrologer about his future! No matter, his horoscope predicted a good day.

Astrology is big business – but I'll show you something with a better track record.

QUESTION: What is the best ***evidence*** that the Bible is a reliable source of information?

ANSWER: Its fulfilled prophecies. An absolutely stunning performance! Prophecy can be tested. ***It is as rigidly demonstrable as geometry***. Other evidence can be falsified, changed, or lost. Memory may fail, conflicting statements may cloud the issue. Passion, self-interest, or dishonesty may impair proofs. But prophecy relates to history, and history is recorded fact. Did you know that the Bible stakes everything on its ability to foretell the future? It claims God gave the information – and that only He can foretell world history.

> *Who, as I... shall declare... the things that are coming, and that shall come to pass, let them declare.* (Isaiah 44:7)

Has any skeptic a case to present? Hear the challenge:

> *Produce your cause, saith the Lord; bring forth your strong reasons... Declare to us what shall*

> *happen: declare you... things to come.* (Isaiah 41:21-23)

Let's be honest about this. Usually we can't even foretell the outcome of a horse race a minute before it ends. We can guess and hope. But we cannot know.

But if world history has been declared accurately and clearly for thousands of years in advance… what then? Notice this claim:

> *I am God, and there is none like me,* ***declaring the END from the BEGINNING,*** *and from ancient times things that are NOT YET DONE.* (Isaiah 46:9-10)

The challenge: proof of a Supreme Being?

Does not this make the Bible unique? No other book on Planet Earth has the audacity to place its veracity on its record of fulfilled prophecies. Not the *Koran* of Islam, the *Veda* or the *Bhagadgita* of the Hindus, nor the *Book of Mormon*, claim such.

The Bible claims that the Eternal One selected men of integrity and revealed messages to them – and that, as they wrote, they were under His direction. Did you know that expressions such as "*God said*", "*the Lord commanded*", and "*the word of the Lord*" occur in the Bible more than 3,800 times?

Are its predictions vague? Not on your life! They are specific. And in some cases they pinpoint precise dates far into the future – even to naming names.

We're not talking about an odd prophecy or two, but ONE THOUSAND or more of them! One analyst has catalogued 8,362 predictive verses, which include 1,817 specific predictions on 737 separate matters. (J. Barton Payne, *Encyclopedia of Biblical Prophecy*) The accuracy of their fulfillment is enough to give you goose pimples. Let's look at a few examples:

TYRE

For 2,000 years the Phoenician city of Tyre grew in importance until she was mistress of the sea, the commercial center of the world, the New York of Asia. Carthage, the rival of Rome, was only a colony of Tyre. Ships from all nations anchored in her harbor and their passengers bartered in her streets.

Ancient Tyre on the eastern coast of the Mediterranean Sea

An unlikely prophecy

About 590 BC, while Tyre was at the height of her glory and power, when it seemed she ***must*** stand for ever, along came the prophet Ezekiel, and said:

> *They shall destroy the walls of Tyrus, and break down her towers: I will also scrape her dust*

from her, and make her ***like the top of a rock.*** *It shall be a place for* ***the spreading of nets in the midst of the sea:*** *...thou shalt be* ***built no more.*** (Ezekiel 26:4-14)

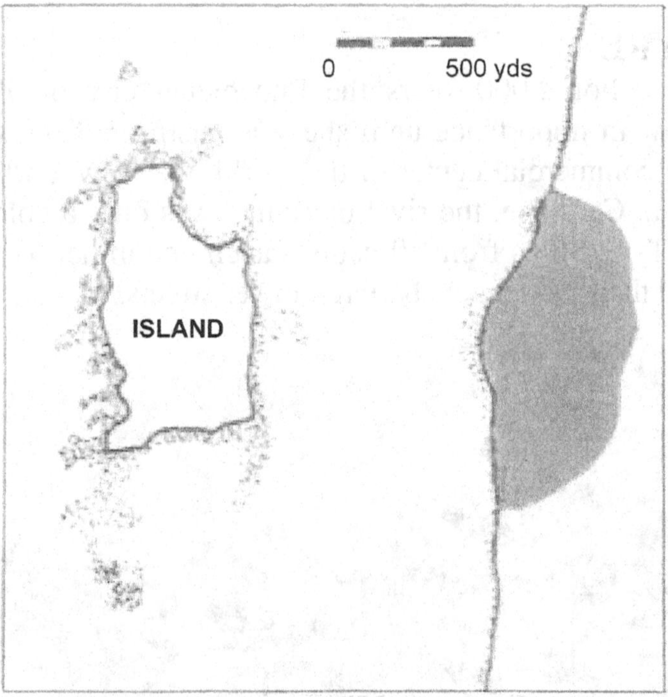

Tyre's location on the mainland Phoenician coast

Soon after that prophecy was made, Nebuchadnezzar of Babylon attacked Tyre. After a 13 year siege, he left it in ruins.

Stones, timber and dust to be laid in the water, leaving the bare rock

Yes, Nebuchadnezzar left the old city in ruins. But the prophecy declared that the timbers and rocks and even the very dust were to be cast into the sea, leaving a ***bare rock***.

The only known portrait of Nebuchadnezzar

It seemed improbable that this would ever happen, because if Nebuchadnezzar, in his anger, had taken full vengeance, and had not thought of this, who was likely to care enough about the ruins of a deserted city to be so violently destructive? It would be needless and crazy.

Two and a half centuries passed, and still the ruins stood, a challenge to the accuracy of prophecy. Then in 332 BC Alexander the Great marched down the coast toward old Tyre.

He saw its ruins. But the people had moved onto an island. Half a mile of water surged between him and the island.

Having no ships, Alexander planned a different strategy. He took the walls, towers, timbers, and ruined houses and palaces of the ancient Tyre, and dumped them in the sea to form a solid causeway to the island. So great was the demand for material that the very dust was scraped from the site, and laid in the sea.

And so the site of Tyre became ***like the top of a rock*** – just as the prophecy foretold.

I have been there. With my own eyes I have seen the fulfillment of this prophecy. From out of the sea, beside Alexander's causeway, I have picked up pieces of beautiful colored glassware, porcelain, and tile that once adorned mainland Tyre.

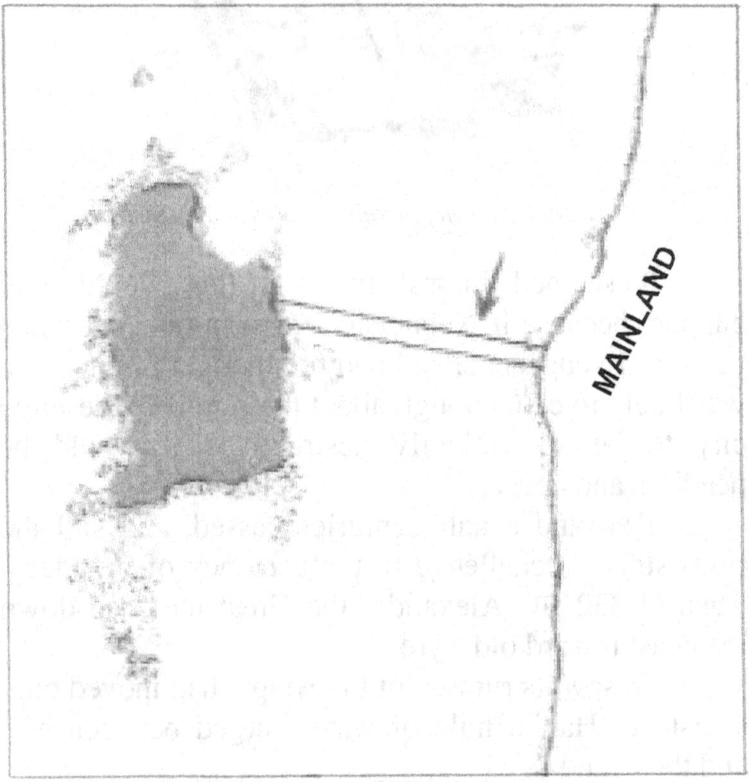

Alexander scraped the timber, stones and dust of old Tyre into the sea to build a causeway out to the island (see arrow).

Original Tyre will never be re-built

This old mainland city of Tyre continues a daily defiance to every unbeliever. *"Thou shalt be built no more: for I the Lord have spoken it,"* says the prophecy. (Ezekiel 26:14)

Yet it's a habitable site: ten million gallons of water daily gush from the springs, and fertile fields stretch clear to the distant mountains. Since there are millions of determined doubters who write numberless books to ***disprove the Bible***, how did any prophet have the breath-taking daring to utter such a defiant prophecy? For 2,000 years no skeptic has dared say the prediction is untrue.

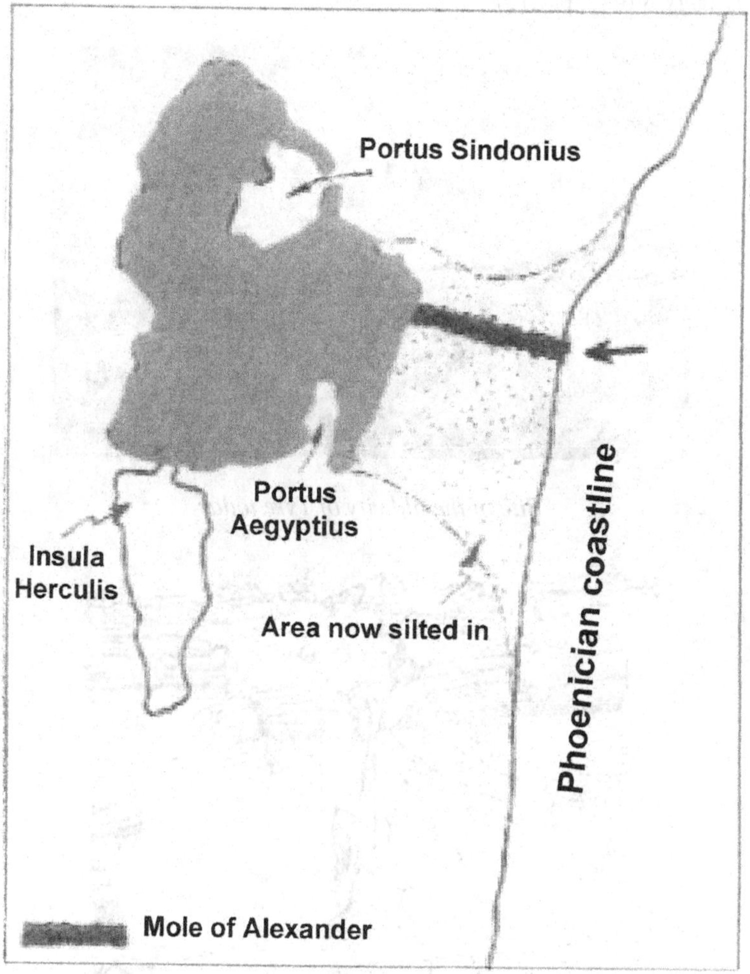

Today the area around the causeway has silted in and the island is now a peninsula.

A place to spread nets in the midst of the sea

The prophecy says "*it shall be a place for the spreading of nets in the midst of the sea.*"

Volney, the French skeptic, tells of visiting this spot and observing fishermen drying their nets on the rocks, just as the prophet said they would. (Volney, *Travels*, Vol. 2, p. 212)

Site of the old city of Tyre today

Fisherman's nets drying on the causeway in the midst of the sea (sketch from a photo)

Every year, every day, every minute that mainland Tyre has continued in utter ruin it has ***disproved*** the assertion of skeptics that Bible predictions are vague.

You can check on this, if you like. No person outside of the Bible ever made a solitary correct forecast covering hundreds of years concerning any city on earth. Now tell me, how is it that ***only*** Bible writers are able to 'guess' with perfect accuracy 2,000 years into the future?

OBJECTION: Well, it would be natural for a writer, looking upon a ruined city, to assume, hence to predict, that it would never again be inhabited.

IN REALITY: Such an assumption, however natural, would have plunged the Bible prophet immediately into serious difficulty.

Sidon: Blood in her streets, the sword on every side

And here's why. Ezekiel turned his attention to Tyre's still more ancient sister city only 30 miles distant. While Tyre was still glorying in the splendour of its heyday, Sidon had for centuries been declining in power.

Now, according to skeptical critics, Ezekiel was written as late as 330 BC, at least after Alexander's time. But accepting their dating for Ezekiel's writing adds strength to my contention, for while Sidon was still in a state of decay it was taken by Artaxerxes Ochus, king of Persia, in 351 BC, and destroyed!

So if the prophet were ***judging by appearances*** in 330 BC, as our skeptic claims he did judge, he would have pronounced complete oblivion as the inevitable fate of Sidon, for nothing seemed more certain than its utter eradication. But Sidon still remains, even now possessing thousands of people.

Would you notice the prophet Ezekiel's words:

> *The word of Yahweh came unto me, saying, Son of man, set thy face toward Sidon, and prophesy against it, and say, Thus saith the Lord Yahweh: Behold, 1 am against thee, 0 Sidon.... For I will send pestilence into her, and* ***blood into her streets;*** *and the wounded shall fall in the midst of her,* ***with the sword upon her on every side****.* (Ezekiel 28:20-23)

Observe that the ***predicted future*** of Sidon was not utter extinction like that of mainland Tyre, but only ***blood*** in her streets, ***wounded*** in her midst, the ***sword on every side***.

And do you know that no other city on earth, with the possible exception of Jerusalem, has had so much suffering and been so often destroyed and rebuilt. Yet Sidon has survived continuously right to this day.

Now, suppose Ezekiel had said that both Tyre and Sidon were to be destroyed and would be built no more, then every one of the thousands of inhabitants of Sidon would be a living proof of the falsity of the prophecy.

Or suppose that the prophet had said mainland Tyre was to survive, but undergo great suffering, while Sidon would be utterly destroyed and never be rebuilt? What then? Wouldn't the skeptic have a ball? And with good reason!

How did it happen that the prophet was exactly right in both cases? How is it that the city that never has been rebuilt is the city of which this fact was foretold, and that the city which has continued to exist with age-long suffering is the one which the prophet foresaw would continue to exist even to our day?

When the skeptic has explained this satisfactorily, he has a still harder question to answer.

Sidon, like many other ancient cities, might have sunk into insignificance, so that in its utter defencelessness it could have offered no resistance to even a feeble enemy, and would have tempted no invaders.

How did Ezekiel know that, in spite of many terrible experiences, it would continue as a place of strength which, age after age, would be fought for, and passed on, ***wet with blood***, from one conqueror to another?

It has been bitterly fought over by:

Syrians… Egyptians…Persians… Romans…
Crusaders… Muslims… Mongols… Turks…
English… French… New Zealanders and
Australians… Israelis.

In 1982, Sidon was the southern Lebanese headquarters for the PLO – a prime Israel target. *Time* magazine reported that it was ***the most completely destroyed town of the war.*** Not one unscathed building remained. And it remains in the firing line.

The future of Sidon, according to Bible prophecy is: ***"blood into her streets;*** *and the wounded shall fall in the midst of her,* ***with the sword upon her on every side".*** (Ezekiel 28:20-23)

EGYPT

When the biblical writers Isaiah, Jeremiah, and Ezekiel lived, Egypt was then so ancient that she boasted ***a longer unbroken line of kings than did any other nation.***

In their day, 600 BC, Egypt was eminent in science, in the arts, in luxury and magnificence. Egypt was a leader of civilization. For many centuries those artificial mountains, the famed pyramids, had stood as proud sentinels of a mighty super power.

Like its monuments, Egypt seemed to defy the tooth of time. She had the unity, repose, and calm majesty of conscious power, the grandeur of great age. There was not the faintest cloud on the horizon to threaten the peace and power of Egypt.

It would have been natural to predict for her, unending prosperity.

Then came the Bible prophets, foretelling many amazing things concerning Egypt, which would reach more than 2,000 years beyond their death! I shall share with you a handful of the more outstanding predictions:

> *It **shall be the basest of the kingdoms**; neither shall it exalt itself any more above the nations: for **I will diminish them,** that they shall no more rule over the nations.' 'I will . . . sell the land **into the hand... of strangers**: 1 the Lord have spoken it. . . . And there shall be **no more a prince of the land of Egypt.*** (Ezekiel 29:4,15; 30:6,7; 32:15; 30:12,13)

Egypt: "Not to be destroyed"

While prophecy, in speaking of other kingdoms of the Middle East, predicted their destruction and obliteration, of Egypt is predicted that she ***will remain, but decline***.

The prophecy said it will become a (base) lowly nation.

Egypt was to continue a nation, but it was no longer to rule others. On the contrary, it was to be ruled by cruel foreigners. This prophecy could not have been the result of mere human foresight. Even 600 years later, in the time of Jesus, Egypt was still very powerful.

Egypt to be ruled by strangers

I will make the land waste...by ***the hand of strangers***. (Ezekiel 30:12)

Long after that prophecy was given – for the past 2,500 years - Egypt has been ruled by strangers - Persians, Greeks, Romans, Byzantine Greeks, Saracens, Turks, French, British and Arabs - strangers, just as the prophecy predicted.

Will "diminish the Egyptians"

I will diminish them. (Ezekiel 29:1)

Biblical prophecy is turning out to be full of surprises. The fulfillments are stunning! Did you know that today Egypt, although the most heavily-populated nation in the Middle East, is populated ***mainly*** by Arabs, ***not Egyptians***?

According to *Encyclopaedia Brittanica*, the Copts in Egypt, not the Arabs, are the racial representatives of the ancient Egyptians.

> The Copts have undoubtedly preserved the race of the Egyptians as it existed at the time of the Arab conquest in remarkable purity. *(art.: "Copts")* The Copts are direct descendants from the ancient Egyptians. *(E.A. Wallis Budge, The Nile, p.331)*

In their own country the descendants of the ancient Egyptians are outnumbered an estimated 12 to 1 by Arab foreigners who have come in and taken over the country. The prophecy said God would '***diminish***' the Egyptians. How true!

"No more a native prince"

The prophecies become even more amazing:

There shall no more be a prince of the land of Egypt. (Ezekiel.30:13)

When recorded, this prophecy would seem absurd. Mighty Egypt had a line of kings such as no other nation under heaven had possessed, and it seemed as though this would last forever.

Even today, Egypt has had a ***longer line of kings*** than any other country. Yet, since 400 BC - that's for 2,400 years! - none of Egypt's kings have been Egyptians!

The land of the Pharaohs has been ruled by foreign overlords, Persians, then Greeks, Romans, Saracens, Turks, French, British and Arabs. King Farouk, Egypt's last king, who ruled until just after World War II, was not an Egyptian, but an Albanian! And Naguib, the man who led the revolt to depose Farouk, was not Egyptian, but Sudanese! Likewise, Presidents Nasser, Sadat, Mubarak, and so on, none of them has been Egyptian, but of Arab descent.

How astonishingly accurate is this prophecy! In all world history, ***never has any nation*** been subject to foreign governments and foreign rule so long as Egypt has been.

THE JEWS

Will be scattered across the world

> *I will scatter you among the heathen; thou shalt be removed into all the kingdoms of the earth.* (Leviticus 26:33; Deuteronomy 28:25)

Today, wherever mankind is found, whether it be barbaric or highly civilized, there you will find the Jew. He is in every land and every race.

Will be oppressed and slaughtered

> *Thy life shall hang in doubt before thee and thou shalt fear day and night; and ye shall have no power to stand before your enemies. And they that are left of you shall pine away in your enemies' lands. (*Leviticus 26:33,36,37,39; Deuteronomy 32:24; 28:66,67)

Wherever the Jews have set foot, they have felt the cruel stroke of persecution. On several occasions, atrocious massacres have almost secured their complete extermination. Their history has been one long, bloody commentary on the uncanny accuracy of this prophecy. The Nazi holocaust still makes one's flesh creep.

Will be wanderers

> *They shall be wanderers among the nations.* (Hosea 9:17)

This prophecy hardly needs comment. We know the expression "wandering Jew". There is even a vine with that name!

Will be a proverb and a byword

> *And thou shalt become an astonishment, a proverb, and a byword, among all nations whither the Lord shall lead thee; a reproach and.. a taunt.* (Deuteronomy 28:37; Jeremiah 24:9)

Wherever he has wandered, the Jew has been taunted and reproached. Through history, when one wished to express contempt for a person, he would call him a Jew. Who has not heard such derogatory expressions like "as mean as a Jew", and so on. All too frequently, I'm afraid – and often undeserved.

But the inspired biblical prophets foresaw it. And their enemies fulfill the prophecy even as you read this.

Not be totally destroyed

> *I will make a full end of all the nations whither I have driven thee, but I will not make a full end of thee.* (Leviticus 26:44; Jeremiah 46:28)

The Jewish nation has survived more dispersions, persecutions, and martyrdoms, than any other people on the face of the earth. The amazing preservation and longevity of the Hebrew race is a standing enigma, a curious paradox, to the world. It is significant to notice that every nation that has persecuted the Jews has, in time, crumbled and vanished. Two nations around Judea that remain today, Persia and Greece, were those who befriended the Jews.

Jerusalem, though repeatedly taken by foreigners, will remain

> *Jerusalem shall be trodden down of the nations until the times of the nations be fulfilled.* (Luke 21:24)

Present-day Jerusalem is the 17th edition of the original city! There is no spot on earth so blood-soaked as Palestine, Jerusalem City has suffered 40 major sieges, been partly destroyed 35 times and totally destroyed 4 times. But while great cities such as Babylon, mainland Tyre, and other named cities, were prophesied to disappear, Jerusalem would remain.

Is it ***evidence*** you want? Then now you have it. ***Evidence, evidence, and evidence.*** Evidence of prophecy which is so accurate, it is uncanny. Thorough research will confirm there is nothing like this on earth. Not anywhere. The often touted prophecies of Nostradamus and others pale by comparison.

So, why don't we now investigate a prophecy which outlines the history of a whole succession of nations, beginning 2,500 years ago and ***reaching to the present moment***?

12
Prophecies –

PROPHECIES REACH TO OUR DAY

Were you aware that the story of the decline and fall of the Roman Empire was first written, not by Edward Gibbon in the 18th century of our era, but by the Bible prophet Daniel in the 6th century BC?

And Gibbon the skeptic used six large volumes in telling us in detail how accurate were the predictions of Daniel the prophet.

Date of the prophecy

IT IS CLAIMED: The book of Daniel speaks of the Roman Empire, which did not arise until 168 BC. Such future knowledge is impossible, so the book must have been written after Rome arose – not by Daniel at all, but by some unknown author after 168 BC.

IN REALITY: Yes, the book of Daniel does describe the Roman Empire. But the ***evidence*** is conclusive that Daniel was indeed written as early as the 6th century BC. It is not within the scope of this present work to lay out the evidence for this. But you will find this ***evidence*** in my book *Stolen Identity*, chapter 21. Sufficient to state here that the skeptic's charge that Daniel was written after 168 BC is falsified by the fact that the book of Daniel was included in the *Septuagint* (LXX), a translation of the Hebrew Bible into Greek, the date of which, 283 to 180 BC, is not disputed.

The heavy artillery of the critics has been directed against the book of Daniel simply because the accuracy of Daniel's descriptions cannot be denied.

It is a fact that Daniel chapters 2 and 7 contain such clear predictions of world history, beginning with Babylon and reaching to the present moment, that the most skeptical have been hard placed to account for them… unless they admit supernatural knowledge on the part of the prophet.

And understandably, critics have tried hard not to face such an admission. They seem to think that if they can only show that Daniel never wrote a word of the book, but that it was composed much later, its prophecies will be invalidated.

However, for our purpose we shall accept the skeptic's date, and will care not who wrote it.

To go into the amazing details of all Daniel's prophecies could take a complete book on its own. But we shall examine just a few.

All who have read Daniel – skeptics or not – admit that the book teaches this: that ***beginning with Babylon there shall be just four great world powers in succession - four and no more – and then the sequence will be broken.*** (Daniel 7:23-27; 2:39-45)

World power 1 - Babylon

The writer of Daniel claims he was informed by his divine messenger that the empire of Babylon (ruling in his day) would be overthrown. Other details of this coming event were pre-recorded by the Bible prophets Isaiah and Jeremiah. Something like 60 prophecies were made concerning Babylon. We shall look briefly at five of them.

Ancient Babylon in its glory

1. Babylon's river will be dried up

I will dry up thy rivers....I will dry up her sea.
(Isaiah 44:27; Jeremiah 51: 11,36)

The city of Babylon was extremely well fortified. From their lofty walls, the inhabitants mocked the invading Medes and Persians. Not only was the city impregnable, but it contained enough provisions to last for 20 years.

There was no entrance into Babylon except where the River Euphrates entered and emerged, as it passed under the walls.

Aware that he could not take the city by force, the Persian king Cyrus decided on a clever plan. He would turn away the water from its channel through the city. So at a given time, he diverted the river upstream into a lake.

The river below soon became shallow enough to ford and his soldiers followed the river bed under the gate, into the heart of the city of Babylon.

(Herodotus, i.190,191; Xenophon, *Cyropaedia*, vii.5.1-36). The prophecy was amazingly fulfilled.

Medo-Persian armies enter Babylon on dry river bed under the gates

2. The gates will be left open.

> *Thus saith the Lord to Cyrus. I will open before him the two leaved gates; and the gates shall not be shut.* (Isaiah 45:1,2)

On each side of the river through the city were interior walls of great height. In these walls were enormous gates of brass, which, when closed and guarded, debarred all entrance from the river bed to any of the streets that crossed the river.

Had the gates been closed at this time, the invaders might have marched in vain along the riverbed between the walls and out again. But, feeling secure, the Babylonians had that very night put on a great feast. In their abandoned carelessness, these internal river gates were left open so that the citizens could cross the river at will. Another fulfillment of prophecy.

3. The city will be captured during a festival.

> *I will make drunk her princes, and her wise men, and her captains, and her rulers, and her mighty men, and they shall sleep a perpetual sleep, and not wake, saith the King, whose name is the Lord of hosts.* (Jeremiah 51:39,57)

Even the attempt to capture Babylon by means of the river bed would have been in vain, had not the whole city given itself over on that fateful night to drunken revelry. Prophecy fulfilled!

4. It will be taken without a fight.

> *The mighty men of Babylon have forborne to fight, they have remained in their holds: their might hath failed; they became as women.... One post shall run to meet another, and one messenger to meet another, to show the king of Babylon that his city is taken at one end.* (Jeremiah 51:30)

No one noticed the sudden subsidence of the river. No one saw the entrance of the Persian soldiers. No one took care to close and guard the river gates. No one cared for anything that night except to plunge into the wild celebrations. That night cost the Babylonians their kingdom and their freedom. They went into it subjects of mighty Babylon. They awoke from it slaves to the king of Persia.

Every detail of those four prophecies was fulfilled precisely.

5. Arabs will not pitch their tents in Babylon

> *Neither shall the Arabian pitch tent there. (Isaiah 13:19)*

Some years ago, a Dr Cyrus Hamlin was in Istanbul (then known as Constantinople) visiting with a colonel of the Turkish army.

Dr Hamlin asked the colonel if he had ever been to Babylon.

"Yes," replied the colonel, "The ruins of Babylon abound in game, I engaged a sheik and his group, and went to those ruins for a week's shooting."

He described to his guest some of the thrills of his recent lion-hunting expedition to the ruins. "And I will tell you a curious incident," he said. "Each morning and evening, I had to do a long walk over the desert, all because of my Arab guide's refusal to camp overnight in the ruins.

"At sundown the Arabs, to my amazement, began to strike their tents, getting ready to leave. I went to the sheik and protested. But nothing I could say had any effect. 'It is not safe,' said the sheik. 'Nor mortal flesh dare stay here after sunset. Ghosts and ghouls come out of the holes and caverns after dark, and whomsoever they capture becomes one of themselves. ***No Arab ever has seen the sun go down on Babylon.***'"

Dr Hamlin showed interest and excitement. Taking out his copy of the Bible, he read from it:

> *And Babylon, the glory of kingdoms, the beauty of the Chaldees' excellency, shall be as when God overthrew Sodom and Gomorrah* ***neither shall the Arabian pitch tent there.*** (Isaiah 13:19)

"That is history you are reading," said the colonel.

"No," answered Dr Hamlin, "it is prophecy. Those words were written when Babylon was in all her glory."

The colonel was silent, and they never met again.

Now, I ask you, how did the Bible prophet know the Arabian would continue to exist after Babylon had become dust?

Although a few humble Arabs lived in tents about Babylon 2,500 years ago, the Babylonians were the haughty rulers of many nations. Yet the utter extinction of that ruling race was foretold. Have you ever met a solitary living Babylonian? In effect, the prophet said this: "While the most powerful race on earth will become extinct, together with their world-ruling city, this small, insignificant, nomadic race of Arabs will continue on and on for thousands of years, long after this proud city has crumbled to ruins and its very site is almost forgotten."

For that matter, how did Isaiah know that the Arabs would continue to live near Babylon? Yet the prophecy clearly implies this. Since they were a wandering race, it would be logical to suppose that in time they would either leave the vicinity of such a desolate place as it is now, or would themselves become extinct. But how did Isaiah know they would remain about Babylon's ruins? That they would be there today? Imagine the jeering sarcasm of skeptics if there were not an Arab within a thousand miles of Babylon! And what a field day skeptics would have if all Arabs had become as extinct as the dodo, before Babylon sank into oblivion!

Oh, and something else. How did Isaiah know that Arabs would continue to live in tents? And how did he know that the Arabs would not make use of the ruins of Babylon for shelter?

Many other explorers and excavators have reported the same fact – that it is impossible to get Arabs to remain on the site of this ancient city overnight. One explorer, Captain Mignan, says that he was accompanied by six Arabs completely armed, but he "could not induce them to remain toward night, from apprehension of evil spirits. It is impossible to eradicate this idea from the minds of these people." (Mignan, *Travels,* page 235) And all this, despite the fact that Arabs are fearless fighters, dangerous warriors.

Again, when Saddam Hussein was attempting to rebuild Babylon, using bricks with his name inscribed on them, his workmen would not stay the night in that place.

It is a fact that this prophecy about the Arabs is amazingly unique in every particular - and each passing day serves only to strengthen its force.

World power 2 – Medo-Persia

The prophecy of Daniel stated that Babylon would be overthrown by a kingdom inferior to it. (Daniel 2:38-39) The Medo-Persians, who took Great Babylon in 538 BC, were indeed a less powerful force.

The Bible prophet Isaiah actually stated ***the name of the coming conqueror of Babylon***. He would be a man named Cyrus. (Isaiah 45:1)

More amazing still, this prophecy concerning Cyrus was made in the late 700s BC, long before Cyrus was even born! (The dating of Isaiah in history is well established.) Cyrus did not conquer Babylon until 539 BC, which was more than 150 years after the prophet Isaiah mentioned him ***by name***!

World power 3 – Grecia

Daniel's prophecies stated that the next great empire – the one that would overthrow the Medo-Persian Empire – would be Greece (then relatively weak). (Daniel 8:3-7,20-21) This was accurately fulfilled by Alexander the Great in BC 331.

Both Medo-Persia and Grecia were ***identified by name*** – and, in the struggle, the winner and the loser were respectively named.

The prophecy also stated that Greece's ***conquests would be rapid.***

Here is what eventually happened. In BC 332, Alexander the Great swept through the Tyre and Gaza region in his march toward Egypt.

During his campaign he turned toward Jerusalem. Alexander had already demanded men and supplies from the Jews, who were under the rule of Alexander's enemy, the Persian king Darius. The high priest hesitated, saying that while Darius lived they would remain loyal to him. Alexander was angry and began to move upon Jerusalem.

Well aware of the danger, the high priest Jaddua and the other priests went out of the city to a carefully chosen place to meet the king. Alexander approached the high priest and members of the procession and greeted them.

The priest invited Alexander into Jerusalem and the temple, where, as the noted first-century historian Josephus records, he was shown Daniel's prophecy, written several centuries earlier, which foretold the rise and conquests of Alexander.

> And ***when the book of Daniel was shewed him,*** wherein Daniel declared that one of the Greeks should destroy the empire of the Persians, he supposed that himself was the person intended; and as he was then glad, he dismissed the multitude for the present. (Flavius Josephus, *Antiquities of the Jews,* Book 11, chap. 8, sec. 5, William Whiston translation, 1981)

Many scholars regard Josephus as a reputable historian on the same footing as other ancient authorities such as Tacitus.

I ask you, how did Daniel know, 200 years earlier, that one of the Greeks should destroy the empire of the Persians? (Daniel 8:4-7,20-21) Who imparted these "impressions"?

Daniel was also told to write that this "first king" of the Grecian empire (Alexander) would have a sudden end, dying while in his prime. (Daniel 8:8,21) And Alexander did die suddenly at age 33.

Daniel also wrote that after Alexander's death, the Grecian Empire ***would break up into four divisions***. (Daniel 8:22) It did. I ask you, how did Daniel know all these details?

World power 4 – Rome

The prophecy continued, stating that a fourth empire would replace the Grecian. Its numerous characteristics were described. The Roman Empire ***fulfilled the role exactly as predicted***. (Daniel chapter 7)

If Daniel lived in 600 BC, then he foretold the rise and fall of the three empires beyond his day who were to follow Babylon. That's a marvellous series of predictions.

In order to deny that these are prophecies written before the events, skeptic writers have contended that the Book of Daniel must have been written in 168 BC - after Rome had acquired rulership.

Prophecy: "previous pattern of history will be broken"

Let's grant the skeptic his date for Daniel as168 BC.

IF WRITTEN 168 BC: But does this help his case? Sorry, if Daniel was written in Roman times (168 BC), so that it comes after the events predicted, then the skeptic faces Problem No. 1.

It means that the writer of Daniel had knowledge of the fact that in just four centuries (538 BC to 168 BC) four empires (Babylon, Medo-Persia, Greece, and Rome) had ruled in succession.

But now we see him predicting that, ***contrary to the analogy of all previous history***, there will not be a fifth world power to succeed the fourth!

Here are the details of Daniel's prophecy:

(a) the fourth empire (Rome) ***will not be conquered by a fifth power***, ***but will***

(b) ***fall apart*** into a motley group of nations, some strong and some weak. (Daniel 7:24; 2:41-42)

(c) ***There will be attempts to weld it together again.***

(d) But the territory of the old Roman Empire will ***remain divided until the end of time***.

What daring to suggest that right at this point after the fourth empire, the past pattern of history would end! This is what no philosopher, using past history to judge the future, would ever dream of doing.

It would be natural to guess that the coming centuries would repeat the pattern of the past centuries; because then, as now, ***it was believed that history repeats itself***. Since the Babylonian Empire was conquered by the Persian, the Persian by the Grecian, and the Grecian by the Roman, would it not be natural to expect the Roman Empire to be conquered also by some other world power?

No, said Daniel. Precisely after the fourth empire, the pattern will change. The fourth world empire will ***not*** be conquered by a fifth.

> *The kingdom **shall be divided.*** (Daniel 2:41)

I ask you, did the writer of ***Daniel have some other source of information*** not accessible to anyone else?

IF WRITTEN c. 600 BC This is the other option for the date the prophecy was written. If Daniel was written about 600 BC, one must concede that the descriptions of events are too amazing to be explained away easily. A skeptic is faced with Problem 2: ***accurate foreknowledge***.

The critic loses, either way.

So whether the Book of Daniel was written about 600 BC or 168 BC, the problem of prediction remains unsolved.

The prophecy continues

But this is not all. We have already noted that there would be only four world powers in direct succession, one conquering the other. FOUR AND NO MORE.

And then that fourth power (the Roman Empire) would be ***split up into ten*** nations or groups of nations, and these would ***remain divided until the end of time.*** (Daniel 7:23,24; 2:42-44)

And as every schoolboy knows, in a consecutive series of four, Rome was the fourth great empire.

You can read any history written by anyone. But, in particular, read from one of the greatest unbelievers - Gibbon's *Decline and Fall of the Roman Empire* - and you will see that this 'immortal' work is an unwitting commentary on Daniel's accuracy.

Indeed, the fourth empire, the Roman, was not succeeded by another empire, but, under the onslaught of fierce northern tribes, Rome simply broke up into a mass of smaller kingdoms.

The historian Machiavelli names these ten kingdoms as the Ostrogoths, Visigoths, Franks, Vandals, Suevi, Huns, Anglo-Saxons, Heruli, Lombards, and Burgundians. Seven of these are represented by present-day nations. The prophet said these smaller nations would ***continue to exist*** (with three exceptions noted by the prophet himself – Daniel 7:8,24), to the end of time.

Prophecies in Daniel 7 and Revelation 13 and 17 complement this prophecy of Daniel 2, and plainly reveal that the Roman Empire, although officially dead, would enjoy ***seven temporary resurrections***. These have been fulfilled in the several successive attempts to reunite Europe.

Prophecy of intermarriage

The prophecy went further. It suggested that, in order to weld the divided nations of the old Roman Empire together, alliances would be attempted – even ***by intermarriage.***

> *They shall mingle themselves with the seed of men.* (Daniel 2:43)

Well known is Napoleon's arrangement of marriages between the various royal families of Europe, with the result that their ***seed*** is now virtually all ***intermingled***. A remarkable fulfillment of prophecy.

But would bonds of unity among the nations by intermarriage prove successful? The prophecy says no:

> *... but **they shall not cleave one to another,** even as **iron** is not mixed with miry **clay** (Ibid.)*

When the call to war was sounded, cousin fought cousin. The bonds of international marriage, forged in the attempt to consolidate Europe, snapped apart in the face of war.

7 powerful words that stopped dictators

A recurring theme of the past 1,500 years has been the repeated attempts to unify Europe.

Successive attempts to break the prophecy of Daniel were made by the mighty Charlemagne, the swift Charles XII of Sweden, the ambitious Charles V, the proud Louis XIV, and the resistless, eagle-eyed Napoleon.

However, these seven fateful words in Daniel's prophecy stopped each of them:

> *... but they shall not cleave one to another. (Ibid.)*

Now, what if some conqueror had re-cemented all the nations of the old Roman territory into one successful mighty empire subject to his sovereign will - what could one say? But can anyone produce any such failure of Daniel's prophecy?

Napoleon's attempt

As Napoleon's conquering forces invaded Russia, they were suddenly devastated by the ***coldest winter in all Russian history***. This was a turning point in Napoleon's campaign. Then, at Waterloo in 1815, a ***mighty downpour of rain*** bogged down Napoleon's big guns and gave time for reinforcements to bolster Wellington's troops and save Britain from defeat.

If he had read Daniel first

Believe it! The prophecy of Daniel was stronger than all the might of Napoleon.

When an exile on the drab and drear island of St. Helena, Napoleon read the book of Daniel, and for the first time understood why he had so miserably failed to weld the broken bits of the old Roman Empire into his cherished empire. The priceless lives of thousands, the wasted mints of money, the misery and tragedy that resulted, might have been spared if Napoleon had consulted Daniel first.

World War I attempt

Just before World War I, in 1914, Kaiser Wilhelm of Germany was shown this same prophecy in the Bible. He responded, ***"It does not fit into my plans."***

Subsequently, the German army swept all before it into the heart of Belgium and France, and on toward the English Channel, prompting Kaiser William to declare, "I will have Christmas dinner in Buckingham Palace."

The British people realised that only divine help could save them, and the nation humbly knelt in prayer.

In the sky appeared what are today known as the "***Angels of Mons***". More than once they appeared, causing the Germans to halt and retreat in disorder, and their horses to panic. The "Angels of Mons" incident was observed by many British troops. Admittedly, the phenomenon has been debunked by some.

However, as I write this, my colleague John Paige, a man of proven integrity, has reported to me, "My father Phillip was there and confirmed the angels' appearance." Confirmation also came from Captain Haywood of the British Intelligence Service.

On April 22, 1915, Germany launched her first gas attack. The ***wind direction*** was supposed to be settled for the next 36 hours, but it ***suddenly reversed*** and the gas was blown back to the German lines with disastrous results. (The Bible speaks of God's dealing with the wind, 116 times.)

The Kaiser missed his dinner in Buckingham Palace. In fact, he died in exile, chopping wood. Those ***seven prophetic words*** beat him.

World War II attempt

Next came Hitler's hordes sweeping across Europe. The Nazi dictator boasted, "***Where Napoleon failed, I will succeed.***"

Hitler brought up a host of secretly built weapons to destroy Britain. These included the mighty Luftwaffe (the biggest air force in the world); the world's largest battleships; powerful rockets; and the pilotless "doodlebug".

The Nazi forces over-ran nation after nation. France, Holland and Belgium fell and Britain was next for defeat!

As the planet trembled at the march of the Nazis, scholars who knew Daniel's prophecy were opening it up and reassuring audiences around the world that "***Hitler will not win.***"

In May, 1940, Nazi Panzer tank divisions in France were closing in on the British troops. All 350,000 of them, hemmed in on the beach at Dunkirk, were trapped.

Suddenly Hitler ordered the Panzer divisions to halt and draw back. His generals were speechless. Now the Luftwaffe (the Nazi air force) was to take over. It looked as though the trapped Allied forces would be destroyed by the Luftwaffe.

A day of National Prayer was proclaimed for May 26, 1940, led by King George VI, prime minister Winston Churchill and members of the British Cabinet, in Westminster Abbey. Also, throughout the Commonwealth, millions committed the cause in this dark hour to the Almighty One.

Within 48 hours, a ***great storm*** broke over Flanders, giving cover to the British forces and hampering the enemy. General Halder, Chief of the German General Staff, complained in his diary for

May 30, 1940: "Bad weather has ***grounded the Luftwaffe*** and now we must stand by and watch countless thousands of the enemy getting away to England right under our noses."

At the same time, the English Channel, which is notoriously rough, became ***miraculously calm***, enabling hundreds of small craft from Britain to come over to France and assist in evacuating the troops from Dunkirk.

Why such a simultaneous miracle of opposites – a ***storm*** to ground the Luftwaffe, and a ***calm channel*** for the rescue of doomed men? Because *"The scripture cannot be broken."* (John 10:35) It stated emphatically, ***"They shall not cleave one to another."***

Hitler now attacked England from the air. After two months of this, both the Luftwaffe and the RAF (England's Royal Air Force) were at the point of exhaustion. However, unbeknown to Hitler, the Luftwaffe – with their superior numbers – was close to overcoming the RAF. Then suddenly, Hitler ordered them to stop attacking the RAF!

After bombing England for a while, he turned and started to attack the Soviet Union. The fleeing Russians burned their crops so as to leave no food for the advancing Nazi forces. Then it suddenly ***started to rain***. The whole invading army got bogged down in the mud. Then it turned cold and the tanks could move again. Then it got unbelievably cold - 67 degrees below zero. Now the most ***devastating winter freeze*** since the year of Napoleon's invasion fell upon the German troops. And they were still in their summer uniforms. Just 20 miles from Moscow, the German general sent out the word, "We can go no further. This is the end."

Hitler was beaten by "little things" – drops of water. Why? Because *"the scripture cannot be broken."*

Back in England, the troops who had escaped from Dunkirk re-grouped, were re-armed and helped to overthrow Hitler and bring deliverance to Europe.

Communism's attempt

Before the collapse of the Soviet Union and the fall of the Berlin Wall, I personally addressed audiences on "Why Russia Cannot Win". Again, Daniel's seven words ***"they shall not cleave one to another",*** stopped Communism's nefarious ambitions cold. Here was prophecy in action – ***actionable proof in real life.***

European Union attempt

In the past, uniting Europe was temporary and always accomplished by force. Today the nations of Europe are coming together voluntarily, forming an ever-closer union as they integrate economically, politically and militarily.

But Daniel's prophecy says it will be like a mixture of "*iron*" and "*clay*", making it "*partly strong*" and "*partly broken*".

Mull over that for a moment. Is there a more apt description of Europe today?

Politically and economically, Europe is a continent of iron and clay – some nations strong and robust, others weak and fragile. The European Union is a mixture of iron and clay, making it "partly strong" and "partly broken".

The prophecy says they ***will be integrated*** – but only ***for a brief moment***. Based on this, you can count on the emergence of a short-lived and crumbly union

– yet powerful, possessing the strength of iron. While Europe will unite, its bonds will be weak and short-lived, like clay and iron, which cannot mix.

If you think on it for a while, this truly is mind-staggering. This prophecy was written more than 2,500 years ago, yet it describes today's Europe perfectly.

And of this you can be sure. Upon those same seven fateful words that defeated previous attempts, ***the European Union will collapse*** also. During its brief life – involving a resurrection of the "holy Roman Empire" led by a major religious power – an enormous crisis will develop, involving the suffering of a large number of people. Then it will be terminated suddenly. And the emerging New World Order will be short lived. Just wait and see. Bible prophecy has spoken.

The prophecy then moves on to its final stage – forecasting a sudden end to human history. "*In the days of these kings shall the God of heaven set up a kingdom that shall never be destroyed... it shall break in pieces and consume all these kingdoms, and it shall stand forever.*"

The One directing the Bible writers actually claimed to be the Creator of heaven and earth. And He instructed them to write down this challenge to the unbeliever, either to

(d) make similar prophecies of world history or to
(e) break one of His.

No man or woman on the planet has been able to do either.

I submit to you that each fulfillment of prophecy on its own is a strong point in favor of divine wisdom, but each additional fulfilment increases the strength of the ***evidence***, not by addition, but by multiplication.

It seems ***evident*** that someone with Intelligence is behind all this. History is ***His*** story.

And, as in the case of Ken Laub and Millie (see Chapter 8), He knows each of us personally, and works through his influence in our daily activities. Here is a providence that we often don't recognise. But it is operating all the time.

If you only knew, "impossible" events which suggest Intelligent Intervention are occurring every day, all over the planet. Believe me, it's so. I have experienced them myself.

And honestly, I would rather live my life as if there is such a God, and die to find out there isn't, than live my life as if there isn't, and die to find out there is.

Prophecies fulfilling now

Of numerous other Bible prophecies, just look at these few:

- The "time of the end" will see fast travel and an increase in knowledge. (Daniel 12:4)
- Wheeled vehicles "shall rage in the streets; they shall jostle one against another in the broad ways; they shall seem like torches, they shall run like the lightnings." (Nahum 2:4)
- A young, peaceful power will arise in the New World, attain global dominance, then undergo a change of character to enact oppressive laws. (Revelation chapter 13. See the detailed fulfillment of this prophecy documented in *Welcome, Then Betrayal*.)
- A Middle Eastern group of nations "will be against every man, and every man's hand against" them. (Genesis 16:12. See the fulfillment of this prophecy documented in *The Weapon the Globalists Fear*, chapter 22.)

- A religious power in the city of the seven hills, will direct the emerging World Order. (Daniel 7:23-25; Revelation 17:3,9,18; chapter 13. See the fulfillment of this prophecy documented in *Welcome, Then Betrayal*)
- This European power will establish a base in Jerusalem. (Daniel 11:45. See steps that are being taking to fulfill this prophecy in *Ark of the Covenant,* chapter 47.)
- Finance - buying and selling - will become globally controlled. (Revelation 13:14-17. See steps in the fulfillment of this prophecy in *Welcome, Then Betrayal.*)
- This end times will be characterised by a proliferation of wars, famines, plagues, earthquakes, raging seas and fearful sights in the sky. (Luke 21:10,11,25)
- Mankind will actually acquire the capability to destroy the earth (Revelation 11:18), opening up the danger that none might survive. (Matt.24:21-22)
- Fear will grip the nations, with no apparent way out. (Luke 21:25-26)
- The world will be plunged into a time of trouble such as never was. (Daniel 12:1; Matthew 24:21,22)
- Man will not be permitted to wipe out all life. For the sake of those who live in harmony with him, the Creator will intervene. The earth's cities will fall. Man's dominion will end. (Daniel 12:1; Matthew 24:21,22)
- Out of the ashes of the old, the Creator will bring forth a new earth which shall last forever... a world in which eternal youth, loving concern and security are the norm; where transformed individuals are able to live in harmony and love. (Daniel 2:44; Isaiah 24:1-6,19-22; 26:20-21; Jeremiah 4:23-28; Isaiah 11:4-9; 35:1,5-7,10; 65:17-25; 66:22-23; Malachi 4:1-2)

Bible prophecy has a 3,500 year track record of never being wrong – with cold, hard, incontrovertible

PROOF! There is ***no easier way*** to know what's coming.

A climax is approaching. Every remaining major Bible prophecy is presently taking shape before our eyes.

An integrated message system

A careful investigation will confirm beyond reasonable doubt that the biblical prophecies are ***inter-connected***. There is an amazing unity between them – evidence that what we have here is ***one*** book, an ***integrated message system.***

More than that, its coverage of world history, given in advance, compels us to consider that the Bible has been supervised by One who ***knows the end from the beginning*** - outside our time domain.

At the very least, you can safely accept the Bible as ***an authoritative source***, an *Intelligence Report* par excellence.

Are you ready for this? Here comes a little-known discovery that will set your head into a spin. I believe it seals the ***authorship of the Bible*** beyond question…

13

The author's signature -

YOU CAN'T WRITE THIS BOOK!

"Yeah, that's right," said Dean. "The Bible is just a compilation of men's allegories or myths."

Um, okay.

I love people like Dean – not just for their probable sincerity, but because I love watching the wonder in their eyes when they suddenly catch onto what you're about to see.

Believe me, this is going to be an adventure. You're about to discover that ***no one person nor group of persons in the world could have created the Bible***, even had they wanted to.

May I impress the need for very careful concentration. We shall be exploring a unique phenomenon. And it lies deep ***below the surface*** of the *Intelligence Report.*

No, we are ***not*** talking about Michael Drosnin's Bible code. But it is a discovery that has staggered the cleverest brains in the world. Are you ready?

Number design in nature

For starters, you may be aware of a numeric scheme that runs through nature, right?

"Of course," you reply, "everything operates according to mathematical laws."

Good. Then were you also aware that the human body seems to be stamped with the number SEVEN?

Just think about it. Your body consists of 7 main parts – head, neck, trunk and four limbs – 7 in all. Did you know that the development of the human embryo is in exact periods of 7s, such as 28 days (4 x 7)? Ask your doctor to explain. You'll be amazed at the accuracy of this law. Is this arrangement of 7s merely accidental?

Are you familiar with the fact that this same number or its multiples marks the period of gestation and incubation of many birds and animals?

The common hen sits on its eggs 21 days (3 x 7); the pigeon, having laid its eggs, sits on them for 14 days (2 x 7). The duck takes 28 days to hatch its eggs (4 x 7); the goose 35 days (5 x 7); the swan 42 days (6 x 7); hundreds of varieties of small birds have been checked at 14 days (2 x 7); larger birds, such as the emperor penguin, ostrich or emu 49, 56 or 63 days (7 x 7…8 x 7 …or 9 x 7). If the hen leaves her eggs on the 20th day, there'll be no chicks.

The seal calves on the rocks and suckles its young for 14 days (2 x 7). The ova of salmon are hatched in 140 days (20 x 7). The gestation period of the mouse is 21 days (3 x 7); the rabbit 28 days (4 x 7); the cat 56 days (8 x 7); the dog 63 days (9 x 7); the lion 14 x 7; the sheep 21 x 7; the cow 40 x 7; the elephant 90 x 7. And so on. The ova of the glow worm occupy 42 days (6 x 7), and of the mole cricket 28 days in hatching (4 x 7). The period of the bee in the larva is 7 days. In moths it is 42 days (6 x 7).

Come to think of it, in chemistry, music and art, we find the same number 7 playing a key role. Both sound and light are subject to the law of 7. How has it come about, for example, that the human ear responds to 7 distinct intervals in a scale of one octave? In the rainbow are 7 colors –red, orange, yellow, green, blue, indigo, violet.

Might some call such persistence of sevens ***intentional design***?

The "watermark"

But, more to the point, did you know that this very same 7s design has been found embedded both ***on and beneath*** the surface of the Bible?

I wouldn't blame you for being a little skeptical. After all, we're breaking new ground here. But you're about to discover this for yourself. It seems that both the Bible and nature bear ***similar identification marks*** – just as surely as various papers from the same mill bear beneath their surface the watermark of ***that mill alone.***

The truth is that quite independently of the biblical text is a "watermark" design woven through the surface message –a ***pattern of 'seven'***, if you please!

If you didn't know, the Tanakh (also known as the Old Testament of the Bible) was composed in ***Hebrew***, a language in which every letter of the alphabet also doubles as a number. Thus every letter, word and sentence has a numeric value, the sum total of each letter value.

"Like Latin?" someone asks, "where V equals 5; X is also 10; C is 100, and so on?" That's right. Except that in Latin only some letters are numbers. In Hebrew (and also in Greek) it is every letter. So when you read a word or sentence, you are simultaneously looking at a string of numbers. And that brings us to a discovery made by a Russian scientist, Ivan Panin.

Dr Ivan Panin was one of the ten top mathematicians of his day in the United States. He taught in universities and knew up to 14 languages. He loved playing with numbers.

The "sevens" sub-surface pattern

Anyway, one day in 1882, that mathematical genius found himself experimenting. Knowing Hebrew, Aramaic and Greek, he began reading the Bible in ***its original languages***. He experimented by replacing the letters in the Bible with their corresponding numbers. Suddenly his excitement began to well up. His trained mind was seeing a mathematical pattern! He kept experimenting. And after a few hours he was totally amazed. The passages he had studied revealed unmistakable evidence of an elaborate numerical pattern. This was far beyond random chance, nor human ability to construct.

On the surface runs the message in everyday words, as in any other book. But the substructure of individual letters spells out a complex mathematical code – an interlocking pattern of ***sevens***.

A juggling game that defies the world's cleverest men

Take, as an example, the very first sentence in the Bible: *"In the beginning God created the heavens and the earth."*

	God	created	In the beginning
את	אלהים	ברא	בראשית
400 1	40 10 5 30 1	1 200 2	400 10 300 1 200 2

the earth	and	the heavens
הארץ	ואת	השמים
90 200 1 5	400 1 6	40 10 40 300 5

Actually, there are ***dimensions*** to this creation account which go well beyond the surface story. A whole mass of vital scientific statements is sealed by the numeric design ***exactly fitted within the statement itself.*** But to cover this aspect is not within the scope of the present work. (See my book, *The Weapon the Globalists Fear,* chapter 21, section: "21st century science in Genesis.")

What I would like you to notice is this amazing sevens design:

- This sentence contains exactly ***seven*** Hebrew words.
- These comprise 28 letters (4 x 7).
- The three nouns (God, heaven, earth) have a total numeric value of exactly 777.
- The first three Hebrew words (containing the subject) have exactly 14 (2 x 7) letters.
- The fourth and fifth words have exactly 7 letters.
- The fifth and sixth words have 7 letters.
- The Hebrew words for the two objects "the heavens and the earth" ***each*** have exactly 7 letters.
- The numeric value of the first, middle, and last letters is 133 (19 x 7).
- The numeric value of the first and last letters of all 7 words is 1,393 (199 x 7).

- The value of the first and last letters of the sentence is 497 (71 x 7).
- So the value of the first and last letters between is 896 (128 x 7).
- The last letters of the first and last words have a numeric value of 490 (70 x 7).

In fact, there are over 30 different numeric features of ***seven*** in the first simple sentence of the Bible. These ***seven*** Hebrew words were so chosen and arranged that the number ***seven*** is literally woven into them ***in every conceivable way***.

These 7s are so deeply concealed that special searching, investigating and counting is necessary to find them. They are not seen by ordinary reading.

Another type of 'sevens' feature

So much for the first sentence in the Bible. What about the first book as a whole? Yes, the entire book of Genesis is signatured in every conceivable way with the number 7.

So it should not surprise us to discover that it also comprises exactly 78,064 Hebrew letters. Just look what makes up this number:

* 77700	=	**100 x 777**
* + 343	=	**7 x 7 x 7**
* + 21	=	**7 + 7 + 7**
Total:		78064

Would you just look at that once more… carefully. Can you imagine a sevens design more perfect?

But just get this, will you? ***Every paragraph, passage and book*** in the Bible is constructed in the same astonishing way. Amazingly, there is not a single paragraph out of the thousands in the Bible that is not constructed on exactly the same plan. The Old Testament, in Hebrew, is ***like a single skilfully designed artefact***… nothing less than the product of a supremely intelligent and purposeful mind. So: ***Whose Mind***?

As we shall discover in later chapters, this is a deliberate structuring that is ***far beyond human possibility to invent***. You see the problem now, don't you? We're no longer talking about an ordinary piece of literature.

Impossible to replicate

Scholars who have set out to accomplish a similar thing admit that after struggling for days their efforts were in vain without reducing the passage to a meaningless jumble.

Here you have something that is scientifically testable. You can try it yourself. But I assure you that repeated scientific, mathematic demonstrations prove that humans cannot replicate it. If you want ***actionable proof in real life,*** here it is.

In no other books on earth

This interlocking numeric phenomena is found ***in no other literature.*** Mind you, there have been sincere efforts to find such numerics in the Greek classics (Homer's *Iliad* and others), the *Septuagint*, the *Apocrypha,* the *Koran* and other works, but they have proven unsuccessful. So what kind of book have we here? Is this from God Himself, as it claims?

The most reasonable conclusion from the evidence is that its claims are true. That is, you can accept Bible ***testimony*** to be as reliable as any ***evidence*** outside the Bible. No… more so!

Accurately transmitted

There is good historical evidence that the original text of the Tanakh (Old Testament) was carefully preserved until the time of Jesus. (See my book *The Weapon the Globalists Fear*, chapters 19 and 20.)

1. Ancient literary aids, obsolete names and cuneiform usages are still discernable in the books, which clearly reveal the purity of the text and the care with which it has been handed down to us, step by step, from the very first tablet.
2. Another check on the integrity of the Scripture is in the Israelites' extreme reverence for the sacred writings – an obsessive reverence for every letter and word. For this reason, scribes made copies of the Tanakh manuscripts in a way which is quite unique. They preserved them as no other manuscript in history has been preserved. Why? Because these documents played an important role in Israelite culture and government.

You see, religion was ***their ruling passion***. They believed that the Bible was not of human origin, but was directly inspired by God Himself. Therefore every letter and word had to be regarded with the highest reverence. And this could allow no changes. Modern critics are so blissfully ignorant of this ancient Hebrew mind-set – which is so different from their own.

Josephus testifies: "We have given practical proof of our reverence for our own Scriptures. For, although such long ages have now passed, no one has ventured either to add, or to remove, or to alter a syllable. (Flavius Josephus, "Flavius Josephus Against Apion" *Josephus, Complete Works*, pp.179,180)

From 100 to 500 AD, in transcribing the scrolls, the Talmudists allowed no word or letter, not even a yod, to be written from memory, without the scribe looking at the codex before him. Between every consonant, new section, and book, a precisely-stipulated space must intervene. (Samuel Davidson, *Hebrew Text of the Old Testament*. 2nd edition. London: Samuel Bagster and Sons, p. 89)

They were followed by the Masoretes (AD 500-900), who counted the number of times each letter of the alphabet occurs in each book. They numbered the verses, words and letters of every book. They calculated the middle word and middle letter of each book. of the entire Hebrew Bible. (F.F. Bruce, *The Books and the Parchments*. Rev. ed. Westwood: Fleming H. Revell Co., 1963, p. 117)

In 1947, the Dead Sea Scrolls, including a complete Hebrew manuscript copy of the biblical book of Isaiah, were discovered. Dated around 125 BC, it was found to be ***in precise agreement*** with the text of 1,000 years later. Yes, you CAN be certain that the Hebrew Bible text has been transmitted accurately. (For more detailed information on this topic, see *The Weapon the Globalists Fear*, Chapter 20.)

And that does raise this interesting question: Might it then just hold ***the key*** to events shaping up right now on our planet?

Exposing the forbidden secret

Just suppose you discovered that persons ***mistaken for outer space aliens*** were actually the brains behind the New World Order – and that they had sinister plans for you and your family?

In the next few chapters, after identifying these gangsters beyond reasonable doubt, we shall progressively reveal the ***forbidden*** information that they don't want you to know – and you will see clearly ***why*** they want to keep it ***secret*** from you.

WARNING: This may be hazardous to your preconceived ideas. Are you ready for this?

PART FOUR

PLANET HIJACKED

14

From another dimension? -

WHO ARE THE ALIENS?

For over 20 years, J. Allen Hynek was a scientific consultant for the U.S. Air Force on Project Blue Book. His instructions were to study UFO reports and determine whether an astronomical object, such as the moon or the planet Venus, might explain them.

Whilst Blue Book listed 12,618 reports (of which 701 could not be explained) it concluded that UFOs did not pose a threat to national security. Without saying what they were, the government by this means got itself "off the hook". The later Condon Report announced the same conclusion.

Although a UFO skeptic at the start, Hynek became convinced that a certain percentage of claimed sightings were worthy of serious study.

In 1973, he founded the Center for UFO Studies (CUFOS) along with the now noted UFO researcher Jacques Vallee.

There was, by this time, some collateral physical evidence that seemed hard to explain. This included depressions in the ground, scorch marks and burnt or damaged plants that might take longer than normal to recover.

Hynek and Vallee considered that where there was smoke there was fire.

In 1976, Hynek made this observation:

> The conclusion I've come to after all these years is that first of all, the subject is much more complex than any of us imagined. It has

> ***paranormal aspects*** but certainly it has very real ***physical aspects***, too. The attitude we're taking in the Center for UFO Studies is that since we're going to have scientists involved, we will push the physical approach as hard and far as we can – instrumentation, physical evidence, photographs, radar records. If we are finally forced by the evidence itself to go into the paranormal, then we will. (J.Allen Hynek, *Fate*, June 1976, cited in Ronald D. Story, editor, *The Mammoth Encyclopedia of Extraterrestrial Encounters*. London: Constable & Robinson, 2002, pp. 304-305. Emphasis mine)

Extraterrestrial, or parallel reality?

The following year, he was quoted as expressing these views during an interview:

"HYNEK: [The extraterrestrial] theory runs up against a very big difficulty, namely, that ***we are seeing too many UFOs***.

The Earth is only a spot of dust in the Universe. Why should it be honoured with so many visits?

"INTERVIEWER: Then what is your hypothesis?

"HYNEK: I am more inclined to think in terms of something metaterrestrial, a sort of ***parallel reality."*** (Hynek, Lumieres dans la Nuit, No. 168, October 1977, cited in Ronald D. Story, editor, *The Mammoth Encyclopedia of Extraterrestrial Encounters*. London: Constable & Robinson, 2002, pp. 304-305. Emphasis mine)

When interviewed by *Newsweek*, Hynek repeated this theory:

> UFOs, he says, may be ***psychic phenomena*** and the 'aliens' ***may not come from outer space*** but from a 'parallel reality.' (Hynek, *Newsweek*, November 21, 1977. Emphasis mine)

As already noted, Hynek was formerly a skeptic. He was also the author of numerous technical papers and textbooks on astrophysics. Surrounding himself with credible and reliable scientists, he investigated UFOs for nearly 40 years.

> Hynek submitted that perhaps UFOs were ***part of a parallel reality, slipping in and out of sequence with our own***. This was a hypothesis that obviously pained him as an empirical scientist. Yet after 30 years of interviewing witnesses and investigating sighting reports, radar contacts, and physical traces of saucer landings no other hypothesis seemed to make sense to him. (Douglas Curran, *In Advance of the Landing: Folk/Concepts of Outer Space*. New York: Abbeville Press, 1985, p.21. Emphasis mine)

The findings of numerous other researchers tend to support this conclusion. Prominent UFO researcher John Welldon has noted that:

1. In all the millions of sightings, there has never been even one radar detection of a UFO entering our atmosphere from outer space.
2. "ETs" appear quite able to breathe in Earth's atmosphere without respiratory equipment.
3. Although fired upon many times by Russian, Canadian and American pilots, never has a UFO been brought down.
4. Startlingly, no UFOs seen at different times ever look exactly alike. (John Ankerberg and John Weldon, *The Facts on UFOs and Other Supernatural Phenomena*. Eugene, OR.: Harvest House Publishers, 1992, p. 12)

These observations would suggest that:

1. They are here – emanating, apparently, from our own planet Earth.

2. Although visible, they may not be physical entities. They appear to be ***not*** bound by the same material, physical laws.

Materialise and dematerialise

Here are some other characteristics noted by Hynek and Vallee. We hinted at them briefly in an earlier chapter, but now is the time to address them in more depth:

> If UFOs are, indeed, somebody else's 'nuts and bolts hardware,' then we must still explain how such tangible hardware can ***change shape*** before our eyes, ***vanish*** in a Cheshire cat manner (not even leaving a grin), seemingly ***melt away*** in front of us, or apparently '***materialize***' mysteriously before us without apparent detection by persons nearby or in neighbouring towns. We must wonder too, where UFOs are 'hiding' when not manifesting themselves to human eyes. (J. Allen Hynek and Jacques Vallee, *The Edge of Reality.* Chicago, IL.: Henry Regnery Company, pp. xii-xiii, cited in "The Premise of Spiritual warfare," www.alienresistance.org/ce4premise.htm, March 7, 2003. Emphasis mine)

Did you get that? Here are scientists admitting that UFOs apparently ***materialize and dematerialize***. That indicates another dimension.

Merge into one object

But there's more, much more. Hynek reveals that "There are quite a few reported instances where ***two distinctly different UFOs hovering in a clear sky will converge and eventually merge into one object.*** These are the types of psychic phenomena that are confronting us in the UFO mystery." (J. Allen Hynek, interview in *UFO Report Magazine*, p. 61, August 1976)

And John Keel, famous UFO researcher (author of many UFO books, including *The Mothman Prophecies 1975,* later made into a Hollywood movie of that name) concurs:

> The UFOs do not seem to exist as tangible, manufactured objects. They do not conform to the natural laws of our environment. They seem to be nothing more than transmogrifications tailoring themselves to our abilities to understand. The thousands of contacts with the entities indicate that they are liars and put-on artists. (John Keel. *Operation Trojan Horse.* Lilburn, GA.: Illuminet Press, 1996, p. 266)

Researchers Ankerberg and Weldon also note:

> ...it seems evident that these phenomena are produced in the same manner that other occult manipulations are produced. They involve dramatic manipulations of matter and energy. Although they originate from the spiritual world, they can produce very powerful, temporarily physical manifestations at the material level.... However the UFO is produced, it is frequently of small dimensions – an area where an extremely large amount of energy is concentrated. (John Ankerberg and John Weldon, *The Facts on UFOs and Other Supernatural Phenomena.* Eugene, OR.: Harvest House Publishers, 1992, pp. 36-37)

The weight of evidence suggests these are paramountly ***not physical, but spiritual*** – inter-dimensional – manifestations.

Then what about seeming traces of physical landings? An engineer with an understanding of physics will find no problem with this. They could be explained as ***manipulation of mass and energy***.

Not only that, many UFOs demonstrate the ability to make 90 degree turns at impossible speeds, as well as other maneuvers considered impossible in the physical realm.

Could it be that one needs to wear "spiritual glasses" to understand what was going on here... to understand who these entities are... and what is motivating them?

The reality of another dimension

Is it reasonable to assume that the objects we see with our eyes are the only ones which exist?

Bearing in mind that all solid objects have a vibration frequency within the range perceptible to the human eye, what if the vibration frequency could be altered into vibrations outside the visible range? Some scientists consider it possible.

It is not always easy to adjust one's thinking. But the evidence now pressing itself upon us is that there has to be ***another dimension***, from which these non-human aliens are orchestrating their control and manipulation. The evidence is pointing more and more in one direction – to the possibility of a spirit "world" existing as another dimension all around us.... not in some far-off place. Many open-minded scientists are, in fact, concluding as much - that the cosmos consists of frequencies or dimensions of life that share the same space, just as radio and television frequencies do.

Not space travelers

You are familiar with that word *psychic.* It means spiritual (or spirit). Beyond doubt, so-called "alien" encounters do have a spiritual nature - and abductions have a spiritual effect! Increasingly, the evidence suggests that these entities are ***not*** real physical ETs from other worlds in space. Rather, they are emanating from another dimension!

And this is precisely what so many UFO researchers ***from different sides of the fence*** are coming to realise… well-known researchers like Vallee, Keel, Mack and others.

Psychiatrist John Mack of the prestigious Harvard University founded the Program for Extraordinary Experience Research (PEER). To explain abduction claims, Mack, initially a skeptic, looked hard for any and every psychological root cause he could, including childhood abuse.

From 1990, he began interviewing abductees. Over the next few years he would interview more than 100 of them, practising, as he described it, a thorough psychoanalysis of each one. His conclusion? That these folk were solid citizens, of a sound mind. And he became convinced that something real – and important – was going on.

"These abduction accounts," said he, "are so congruent among healthy people, from all over the United States – people who are not in touch with each other, who have ***nothing to gain and everything to lose by telling their stories."*** ("Are Aliens Already Here? Harvard's Controversial John Mack. Interview with John Mack, <www.skepticfiles.org/misctext/mack.htm>, July 29, 2003)

His years of research led Mack to a conclusion similar to that of other researchers - that the visitors are ***inter-dimensional…*** from another reality or spiritual realm.

Aliens change their story

And the aliens' story line? There was something suspicious about the aliens' claims.

It was common in the early days of UFO contacts for aliens to claim they were visiting from Venus. An example was Frank Strange's 1959 encounter with a "Venusian" calling himself Val Thor.

That was ***before*** the space program sent out probes to that region. But nowadays, most aliens are purporting to come from further away, somewhere else in the galaxy ***where we cannot test their claims***.

These intruders – these aliens – are changing the identity of their home planet so we cannot check up on them. Something fishy here? And what about this…

Their common obsession

UFO researchers Ankerberg and Weldon ask:

> … how credible is it to think that literally thousands of extraterrestrials would fly millions or billions of light-years simply to teach New Age philosophy, deny Christianity, and support the occult….? (John Ankerberg and John Weldon, *The Facts on UFOs and Other Supernatural Phenomena.* Eugene, OR.: Harvest House Publishers, 1992, p. 13)

So what is the truth? Is it that they did ***not*** have to fly here? They are already here… of course! The thought may be startling. But the increasingly the evidence suggests that they've been emanating ***from our own planet Earth***!

Many of them claim to be here to "save" us from looming disaster. And they speak "good" things to us. Others appear to be non-friendly. ***Don't be*** *fooled*. Things are not always what they appear to be. There is evidence that these are simply two "fronts" to a clever game orchestrated by the same group. They are intelligent and able to communicate with us. But they are liars and con artists. You could never trust them.

But there is good reason to believe that it goes much deeper. The entities can be identified as the Legion of Lucifer, who are filled with insane hatred for the human race. Their aim is our eventual destruction. In fact, the current wars, crime and corruption in our communities point straight at this sinister and deadly organization exerting their control in the highest echelons of government, business, science, religion and medicine, worldwide. If you didn't know, a master plan is in place to bring down America, China… the whole world, very soon. Don't let your preconceptions blind you to this reality.

Why is government silent?

So why do governments have nothing to say in this matter? Since the claims are occultic or spiritual in nature, could it be that governments do not want to admit that they are unable to explain what is really occurring? Just imagine the public disquiet should leaders openly admit that something is happening, but "we don't know what and we are powerless to do anything about it"! No wonder, then, that we receive the blanket response, "UFOs pose no threat to national security."

Despite government denials, there can be no doubt that, from behind the scenes, these mysterious entities are extending their tentacles into all spheres, influencing world events, and dragging us down to a planned climax. Stay tuned.

IMPORTANT WARNING: The drama now moves into a sphere with which some may feel uncomfortable, because it will appear to have a more religious tone.

However new this may be to you, the information now to be presented is as ***rock solid*** as that in the earlier chapters – based on testimony ancient and modern, as well as a source we have now ***established as credible*** – the Bible record itself.

Why is it necessary to present this? Firstly, because the ***New World Order*** (which will affect you and those you love), has a sinister hidden base which is ***religious***. And behind it is a major religion. Secondly, because you need to have an informed understanding of the Legion of Lucifer (who are ***really*** pulling the Globalist strings) and what they plan. ***You need to know your foe***. Then you are better equipped to withstand him. In later chapters we shall establish beyond reasonable doubt the ***startling connection*** between the so-called "alien" phenomenon and the Legion of Lucifer.

15

The original "star wars" -

LEGION OF LUCIFER

Go Back!

If you started reading this book only five minutes ago and you are already here, I want you to go straight back to Chapter 1. If you do not first read carefully the preceding chapters, you may neither understand nor accept the truth of what follows. And in that case you will not be qualified to make a rational judgment concerning this vital information.

* * * * * * *

Okay, are you ready for this? Here comes the BIG news.

Behind the scenes, a cosmic drama is being played out. It is much BIGGER than you and I ever suspected. The action is on this planet, but involves the whole universe.

Did you know that our earliest civilizations - your ancestors and mine – believed that a rebellion had occurred "out there"? And that the banished rebels had hijacked this infant planet?

A ***Babylonian*** tablet calls it "The Revolt in Heaven". ***Mexican*** tradition likewise recounts the war in heaven, the fall of Zontemonque and the other rebellious spirits, the Creation, and the subsequent entrapment of mankind by the rebel.

It was universally understood by the ***ancient civilizations*** that there was ***a conflict*** raging between two major personalities and their followers. Today it continues. America, Obama, the European community, Arabs, Israelis, the Pope, or China are really just minor players. But all of us are caught up in it.

We are involved in a drama that is being watched with breathless interest by all the universe.

Fantasy? No, it's fact!

And that brings us back to the *Intelligence Report*. It deftly draws aside the curtain to inform us that there is not only a ***physical realm***, but also a ***spiritual realm***, or kingdom, unseen by the human eye. Both were created by the Eternal One. That spiritual reality also has kings, rulers and authorities reigning over it. (Colossians 1:15-16)

Heart of the universe

We might as well be realistic about this. Most facts concerning the universe are still unknown to science. It would be presumptuous to imagine that we know as much as one octillionth of what the universe holds in store.

Our planet is just a speck near the edge of our Milky Way galaxy. But there is good reason to believe that all the galaxies revolve around a central axis. This grand central region – the crown jewel of the universe, and the governing center – is frequently given the name "heaven". Get out of your mind the notion that this is some "pie in the sky" fantasy. It is a real location in our universe. (See nuclear physicist Dr Robert Gentry's DVD, *Center of the Universe*)

According to the *Intelligence Report*, just as Planet Earth is inhabited by "humans"; heaven is home to billions of celestial beings called, in our language, "angels". The term actually means "messengers", since these beings travel on errands between the worlds. They also exercise abilities superior to ours.

Let's be rational about this. If we have no trouble believing that extraterrestrials exist, what is so difficult about accepting the biblical claim concerning angels?

It began out there!

In any case, according to ***the ancient ancestral memory*** of all nations – which harmonises with the Bible record, as well – there was a rebellion. It occurred at a real place, at the governing center of the universe.

Lucifer, brilliant, handsome and powerful, occupied a high position of trust. But he had a problem – pride. Though respected and loved, that seemed not enough. It was unlimited power he wanted. (Isaiah 14:12-17; Ezekiel 28:11-19)

Charismatic in personality, and respected, he managed to convince a third of the angels that his way of self centeredness was better than the Creator's way of unselfish service.

"The Supreme One does not care for His subjects," he asserted. "His laws are not in our interest." You see, Lucifer's desire to ***get*** came into conflict with the Creator's law of love, a law of ***give***.

Lucifer now desired to take over the heavenly domain. And a great spiritual battle took place.

Perhaps you've imagined a mythical devil with horns, hoofs and a pitchfork. Forget it.

Lucifer was a superbly beautiful and intelligent being. He was invested with power above all the other created beings. His name Lucifer means "son of the morning", "bright and shining one". He was a free moral agent with the power of choice. But he became filled with ambition to be higher than his Maker.

The result was spiritual mutiny. "*And there was war in heaven: Michael [the Prince of God] and his angels fought against [Lucifer]; and [Lucifer] fought and his angels.*" (Revelation 12:7)

This was ***not*** a war fought with ***physical weapons***, but a ***battle for the mind*** – for the loyalty – of each member of the heavenly host.

Lucifer would subsequently become known as Satan (meaning "opponent").

Did God create evil?

A university professor challenged his students with this question. "Did God create everything that exists?"

A student bravely replied, "Yes, he did!"

The professor answered, "If God created everything, then God created evil, since evil exists. And according to the principle that our works define who we are, then God is evil."

Another student raised his hand.

"Yes?"

"May I ask you a question, sir?"

"Of course," responded the professor.

The student rose to his feet. "Professor," he asked, "does cold exist?"

"What kind of question is this? Of course cold exists! Have you never been cold?"

The young man replied, "In fact, sir, cold does ***not*** exist. According to the laws of physics, what we consider cold is, in reality, just the absence of heat. We can only study something when it has energy or transmits energy. We cannot study cold. Absolute zero (-460 degrees Fahrenheit) is the total absence of heat.

All matter becomes inert and incapable of reaction at that temperature. Cold does not exist. We have created this word to describe how we feel if we have no heat."

The student continued. "Professor, does darkness exist?"

"Of course it does," replied the professor.

The student looked at him. "Once again you are wrong, sir. Darkness does not exist, either. Darkness is, in reality, the absence of light. We can study light, but not darkness. In fact, we can use Newton's prism to break white light into many colors and study the various wave lengths of each color. You cannot measure darkness. A simple ray of light can break into a world of darkness and illuminate it. How can you know how dark a certain space is? You measure the amount of light present. Isn't this correct? Darkness is a term used by man to describe what happens when there is no light present."

Finally, the young man asked the professor, "Sir, does evil exist?"

Now uncertain, the professor responded, "Of course, as I have already said. We see it every day. It is in the daily example of man's inhumanity to man. It is in the multitude of crime and violence everywhere in the world. These manifestations are nothing else but evil."

All eyes were on the student as he responded, "Evil does not exist, sir. Or at least, it does not exist in itself. Evil is simply the absence of God. It's just like darkness and cold – a word that man has created to describe the absence of God. God did not create evil. Evil is not like faith, or love, that exist just as do light and heat. Evil is the result of what happens when man does not have God's love present in his heart. It's like the cold that comes when there is no heat, or the darkness that comes when there is no light."

The professor sat down, stunned. The young student's name was – Albert Einstein.

Evil = absence of God

Have you ever wondered, did God create a devil? The answer is, NO. Lucifer, by choosing open rebellion – by choosing to sever his connection with God – turned himself into a devil.

Evil itself is a mystery, but it is ***not*** another face of God, the good Creator. Evil is the exclusion of good – separation from God. Just as darkness is simply the absence of light, or cold is the absence of heat, so evil is the absence of God.

Another name for "evil" is "sin". Just as "*crime*" is a violation of a nation's laws, so is "*sin*" a violation of divine laws.

The fate of the universe at stake

So Lucifer had rebelled. What would God do now? Not only had His government been challenged, but His very character had been called into question. His reputation for truthfulness and for concern about His subjects was at stake.

Here was a conflict involving not a single world, but the entire universe. The fate of all who were loyal to the Creator was at stake.

The stain

Those who were loyal must have had problems. After all, such an accusation as Lucifer had made would inevitably leave a ***stain*** that could only be erased by a long and careful demonstration of integrity, concern and wisdom.

Would the Creator respond with His superior power? Would He snuff out opposition with one great mushroom cloud?

An unknown deadly "virus"

Yes, why didn't God do just that – snuff out rebellion before it got worse? In the future, it might have saved us all a lot of pain, right?

The truth is, God was wiser than that. You see, when the rebellion began, it seemed incredible that "sin" could be as dangerous as the Eternal One said it was.

Just suppose He had destroyed Lucifer there and then. Consider now, those who were still loyal. They might well have concluded: "See what God has done! Could it be that Lucifer was right, after all? God ***must*** be a tyrant." And they would have remained loyal out of fear.

No. If we are to believe the *Intelligence Report*, the Creator decided to fight the rebellion with LOVE. Lucifer's character must be UNMASKED. This mysterious virus of "sin" must be allowed to show its results to all. The Creator would place Himself on trial before His subjects and let them see just who it is that cares. (Revelation 15:3)

He wanted His creation to regard Him with love, not fear. No wonder, then, that He had to give this "sin" virus a chance to develop – to show to the onlooking universe the true effect of this spirit of evil. Its character had to be understood, for the future security of all.

The Creator would demonstrate a "hands off" approach, to allow Lucifer opportunity to "prove" his claim that he could set up a better government than

God. Then, when He finally destroys the rebel and his gang, no one will have any doubts about justice.

Banished

So Lucifer was not blotted out of existence. He and his sympathisers were banished from the heavenly domain.

Now they were bitter and simmering for revenge.

The knowledge of this event is ***recorded in the traditions of many ancient races***, as having been revealed to them. (Also in the *Intelligence Report* - Revelation 12:7-9; Luke 10:18; 2 Peter 2:4; Jude 6)

But it gets more interesting…

****

In my 452 page book, *UFO Aliens: The Deadly Secret*, is documented a horror story of these malicious entities who pose as extraterrestrials – beings with questionable origins who abuse people and treat them with disdain. They are inextricably linked to present day world events, for which you will see evidence as you continue.

PLEASE NOTE: This information is well documented ***solid fact*** and very important.

16

Planet Earth hijacked -

PLANET IN REBELLION

The scene now shifts to Planet Earth.

The couple's wedding day was sheer bliss. Deeply in love… A bright future together… Setting up home… And then came the bombshell – CANCER!

Death brings an end to everything we've got.

And even if we don't get carried off suddenly, the time comes when the hair begins to grey, the wrinkles appear, the teeth start falling out, and the back becomes stooped

And before we know it we are carried off in a box.

Is that how it was meant to be?

* * * * * * *

There was a Golden Age, says the *Mahabharata*, an epic ***Indian*** poem containing the history of the world. In that First Age there was no disease, hatred or evil.

The same idea was echoed by the ***Greeks***, of an original Golden Age when human beings lived with no evil desires, without guilt or crime.

The ***Chinese*** likewise recall that First Age as one of perfect harmony.

And the ***native Americans*** speak of an Age of a First People who were happy and at peace with each other. All food was plentiful, with no need to plant or work to get food.

The ancient ***Sumerian*** writings speak vividly of a time when animals were neither wild nor harmful, when there was no rivalry or enmity among men, when there was plenty, security, harmony, everywhere. (S.N. Kramer, *Sumerian Mythology*. Philadelphia, Frontispiece. For corrections made after additional fragments of the same story were found, see Kramer, *Journal of the American Oriental Society*, vol. 88, 1968, p. 109)

Indeed, there is a common racial memory of a once perfect world… of an age that ***did not know suffering***.

As you are very much aware, this is a very different beginning from what we were told in school, that the sordid and wasteful mechanism of evolution (embodying tooth and claw, painful upward struggle) was used to produce mankind.

Of course, some will assume that God Himself used evolution to produce mankind. But if God did that, then He was a "cruel Creator". You cannot call Him a God of love.

But in any case, the racial memory of mankind and the *Intelligence Report* are in agreement about the fact that ***all was perfect in the beginning***. Don't ignore this. It's in our history.

A rival government set up

However, it changed when Lucifer's mob dropped in. Bitter and simmering for revenge, these rebels looked for a new homeland. They were attracted to Planet Earth, newly created, singing with life.

This would become Lucifer's battlefield. From here he would set up a kingdom according to his rules.

Although the main stage of the war now shifted to earth, the target of Lucifer's rage was still the One who threw him out, the Prince of God.

Plot to hijack a planet

In this beautiful world, our first parents had everything perfectly fashioned for their needs and enjoyment.

But Lucifer, his heart bitter for revenge against God, was determined to wreck this state of happiness. And he soon planted in their minds his own attitude of "***Get***". "Go it alone," he urged. "Be independent. You don't need God."

So foolishly they joined the rebellion.

Why not make evil to be impossible?

Wait a minute! Is our Creator all powerful, yet uncaring? Or, if He's benevolent, is He powerless to help? Why didn't He make it impossible for mankind to fall?

And for that matter, why did God Himself create the tree they were forbidden to touch? Didn't He thus create the temptation that was the cause of the ultimate curse?

The truth is, God surrounded them with evidences of His love. He warned them concerning Lucifer, and then drew what we might call a line in the sand. He gave them an instruction by which they could confirm their allegiance.

In the face of Lucifer's slander, it was reasonable to require from our first parents not just a promise of loyalty, but a demonstration of loyalty.

And for this to occur, they needed to be faced with a definite test. (And there's nothing wrong with tests. When we measure up, they can make us stronger.)

Okay, think now. Just suppose you had a fourteen year old daughter, would you let her ski?

Sure. You'd tell her to be careful. You'd give her some good advice. Then you would tell her to go off and ski.

Would you run behind her and molly coddle her? What if she fell and skinned her face?

She would learn to be more careful.

So although you have power to intervene – and even to prevent her pain – you would show your respect for her by allowing her to make her own mistakes and learn from them. Does that make sense?

And it makes sense that if God loves what He has created, then He'll also want us to experience the greatest happiness possible, right?

So – and we know this is a fact – He gave to each of His creatures free will. Freedom to acknowledge His existence or deny it. Freedom to love Him or to spit in His face. Freedom to run the world and even to make a mess. Unless you can CHOOSE, you can never know optimum happiness.

Who would want to be a robot? Would you like to be married to a robot chatty doll?... so that whenever you pulled a string you would hear the mechanical words, 'I love you?'

Man, what kind of love would that be? Love is voluntary. That's what makes it so beautiful.

Yes, He could have made us as robots, but that would have robbed us of freedom of choice… and ***a free heart***.

Honestly, I think that this must be one of the most winsome, beautiful and basic things about our Creator – His love of liberty. Ability to choose has been inbuilt into us. The greatest power you have is the power to choose.

Cause of evil and suffering – man, not God

But He has not left us without some guidance and protection. Along with physical laws by which this universe is run, He has given us spiritual laws for our well-being.

We know from experience that ***physical laws*** operate (so if you jump off a roof, gravity will pull you to the ground, or if you put your hand on a fire you will get burned).

Spiritual laws are likewise experienced (so that if you sow joy to others you will reap joy from them, or if you treat others violently, you will bring ultimate suffering upon yourself).

These spiritual laws are just as real as the physical. If I disregard them I will suffer the consequences. Live in harmony with them and well-being results.

So it makes sense that the basic ***reason for suffering*** in the world is ***our abuse of these laws***. We have exercised our free choice to cut ourselves off from our Maker. That's our responsibility, not God's.

Racial memory of it

Would it surprise you to learn that nearly all writings of ***ancient peoples worldwide*** tell the same story of ***a fall*** from the original paradise state of peace, love and happiness?... a departure from harmony with the Creator?

The "Fall" as it was termed, became fixed in our racial memory. It is described as the origin of our sense of separateness, our sense of being alienated and at odds with each other.

From ***Sumeria*** to the ***Americas***, art and literature recorded this Fall. In ***China***, ***Egypt*** and

Babylonia, indeed among ***all peoples***, this tragedy of Satan's invasion is ***the oldest racial memory***.

The loss of immortality caused by man's disobedience to divine law seems to have been keenly felt by more than one ancient writer. (For example, the Mesopotamian *Temptation Seal* – now in British Museum. Also *Adapa Myth* and the *Gilgamesh Epic*. A translation of the Adapa Myth made by E.A. Speiser is found in J.B. Pritchard, ed., *Ancient Near East Texts Relating to the Old Testament,* 3rd ed. Princeton, N.J., 1969, pp. 101-103. A translation of the *Gilgamesh Epic* made by Speiser is found in *Ancient Near East Texts Relating to the Old Testament*, pp. 72-79. See especially, pp. 88,90,96. Alfred Jeremias, *Das Alte Testament im Lichte des Alten Orients,* 4th ed. Leipzig 1930, p.99. W. H. Prescott, *Conquest of Mexico,* vol. 1. London: J.M. Dent and Sons Ltd., 1948, p.380)

Many prayers and hymns of the ancients impressively reveal how these people clearly understood the principles of the Ten Commandments and knew quite well what was right and wrong. (Jonathan Gray, *Ark of the Covenant*, page 56) They were fully conscious of their rebellious condition and were longing for forgiveness.

In ancient ***Babylon***, man was felt to live under a curse, a spell, from which only a divine act of cleansing could free him.

Egyptian writings reveal a similar understanding: that the people were aware of a condition of wrong doing, that they had a longing for eternal life and even felt a need for some kind of rescue.

Since the Fall, human nature had become so weakened through habitual wrong-doing that it was impossible in one's own strength to resist the power of ***the Lucifer Legion***.

Alienated and dying

The tragedy had begun with our first parents. Up to that time, they had lived in innocence. They were able to commune direct with their Maker. He had surrounded them with evidences of His love.

Yet they had listened to the enemy's slander – and doubted their Creator's integrity. They had failed Him. Their wrong-doing marred the harmony and biased them against the divine law.

From now on they and the entire human race would no longer enjoy that luxury of direct contact.

At first, they were clothed with a glory of visible light perhaps similar to that with which He communicated Himself to them.

The Creator's glory would then have no ill effect on the two. But now this cover of glory faded, revealing to their startled eyes their now naked bodies.

At first, they hid, possibly realising that they would no longer survive in His presence.

But there was also another dreadful result of this loss of their glorious covering. Their bodies would no longer be protected from the effects of external forces and the entrance of disease. They had lost the immunity provided by their 'glory' covering. In other words, they had now commenced to die.

Death is not natural

We are so used to death that we take it for granted that death is a natural, normal, essential part of our existence. But it was not always so. The fact is, death is an enemy, an intrusion, that need not be.

Dr Linus C. Pauling, world-renowned chemist and winner of two Nobel prizes, provides an insight into the reality:

> Death is unnatural.... Theoretically, man is quite immortal. His body tissues replace themselves. He is a self-repairing machine. And yet he gets old and dies, and the reasons for this are still a mystery.

Yes, life should have continued joyously, on and on. But now, separated from the Life-Giver, the natural consequence would be death. There you have the reason why we die. And so, from that day, the process of dying commenced within their bodies, cell by cell. This process would be passed on to all their children.

Because God could not use trickery, Lucifer had won the first round. Man was now in his grasp, alienated from his Creator.

The Creator's intervention

What would the Creator do now?

Two things.

Firstly, limit the human life span. They were now subject to ***the curse of death.***

How could a good God institute such a penalty, you ask? Answer: to limit pain. Yes, He knew what He was doing. Even today, so much evil is messing up the world from men and women with brief life spans – up to the day they die. If we were to live forever, this world might well have been destroyed ***by us*** long ago.

It was an act of mercy for the Creator to bar them from endless life. If He had not done so, and they had continued to live endlessly, they would gradually have become ***more and more ill*** as time passed. Then no matter how agonising their illness became, they would have still lived on with no possibility of any release from their suffering. Death, then, became an act of mercy on the part of our

Designer – to place a limitation on the pain that was about to come… pain resulting from mankind's choice to sever himself from God.

Now, just a minute!

None of us is blameless. Each of us has gone his own way. I remember protesting, "But I'm a good person…I don't steal… or commit adultery…I'm a good neighbour. I even solicit funds for the Blind Society."

"That may be true," said my friend. "but have you ever wished someone bad? Have you ever told a 'white lie'? Ever been impatient with your spouse? Have you ever wanted to have your neighbour's house or car? You have broken the spiritual laws."

I looked at him aghast, while he laid it straight on me, "If you commit only three sinful acts each day, you would be guilty of 1,095 sins each year. Multiply that by your age.… and you have some idea of how sinful you may be! SHOCKING, ISN'T IT?"

Well, as much as I hated to admit it, he was right. It is good to recognise we have a sin problem. Then we can seek help.

Suppose a person with ***cancer*** never recognises his or her condition, or seeks help?

Let's face it. If I say I have no sin I am deceiving myself.

Yes, by violating His law, we have severed ourselves from our only source of all life; cutting ourselves off means death. What a predicament we are in! We are doomed to die. And we cannot extricate ourselves from this. We are trapped. We sure need help.

Satan, Prince of Earth

Our first parents were appointed custodians over this planet. But they gave in to Lucifer – and he took over the world. That makes him the defacto prince of this world, even its pseudo-god. (John 12:31; 2 Corinthians 4:4; Ephesians 2:2; 6:12; Revelation 12:9)

As descendants of Adam, we inherit a weakened moral nature, the tendency of which is to do evil rather than good. Our surrender to Lucifer's mob has brought death to everything upon earth. ***What the Bible says about this is exactly consistent with observable fact.***

Since he hijacked our planet, subsequent history is a story of moves and counter-moves. Behind the interplay of nations, the two unseen major players – God and Lucifer – are guiding history to its PLANNED CLIMAX.

You'd better believe it. Though normally invisible to us, these other forces – ***inter-dimensional*** beings – are indeed here with us. And they're intensely active. The messengers of light and the messengers of Lucifer are engaged in a relentless conflict. And they are in a tug of war for every person on earth.

Notice this comment in the *Intelligence Report*:

> *We are not struggling against people made with flesh and blood, but against persons without bodies – the evil rulers of the unseen world, those mighty satanic beings of darkness who rule this world; against huge numbers of wicked spirits in the spirit realm.* (Ephesians 6:12)

Clearly, we're not up against mere human enemies, but opponents who are not human – spirit enemies, diabolical and powerful.

These malicious spirits are in rebellion against the Supreme One. And they've brought their rebellion to this planet.

Unseen powers behind the scenes

In mercy, their forms are beyond the light spectrum, so that we are not able to see them. Nevertheless, they are, by condensation, capable of visibility. And in spiritualistic séances, this occurs.

Lucifer and his gang can materialise (take physical form) and interact with our dimension. They are as real as you and I. They have consciousness and personality, just as we do.

And this earth has become the theater of a drawn out, incessant battle with those hijackers. ***These are your so-called aliens.***

Planet Earth placed into quarantine

It is of the utmost importance to recognize that when Lucifer overcame our first parents, the Creator immediately quarantined sin! It was isolated to Planet Earth!

This cut off all contact between our planet and other galaxies – until the earth would be restored.

This meant that rebellion could not be allowed to infect the rest of the universe. The *Intelligence Report* infers that outside of Planet Earth, the "sin" thing does not exist. ***No other planet*** in the universe is ***contaminated*** by the rebellion of Lucifer.

This is a crucial point in understanding about UFOs and so-called ETs.

To recognize this helps us to refute their claim to be from other worlds – and it identifies them without question. They are members of Lucifer's demonic legion.

Alien visitors *not* from other planets

The living beings on other planets are beautiful, pure, perfect, radiant beings. They are clothed in garments of light. And they are tall and majestic, compared with us. There is peace throughout the universe.

Only on earth is there found war, envy and conflict.

Compare this with what the so-called ETs look like, say and do, and it becomes clear that ETs ARE NOT, cannot be from other planets as claimed.

Earth became the stage

We raised this matter earlier, but it bears repeating. Because Lucifer claimed he could set up a better government than God's, such a demonstration needs time for its results to be evident to the watching universe. The Wise One, in giving Lucifer (Satan) the freedom to prove his character – and then, by contrast, demonstrating His own matchless love in stooping down to rescue people, the truth will become evident to all.

When the rebellion began, it had seemed incredible that the "sin" virus could be as dangerous as the Supreme One said it was. It would take time for the Legion of Lucifer to be discredited.

But as the universe proceeded to watch the centuries of hatred, heartache and death on planet Earth, they would begin to understand. They would watch Lucifer's kingdom in operation.

And they would see the Creator's eventual rescue bid. Nevertheless, it would take a whole long series of events to be enacted out before God's love for His creatures could be vindicated.

So Earth became the lesson book to the universe concerning this "sin" thing and where it would lead, the theater where the drama was to be acted out, scene by scene. As Shakespeare perceived, "All the world's a stage and men are only players." To let it play out its course, was the only way the lesson could be learned.

The Creator's "hands off" strategy to allow Lucifer the freedom to discredit himself, will ultimately be seen as the wisest. He will not intervene in our lives without our permission.

When things go wrong, we judge things by the short term. Isn't it a common knee-jerk reaction to blame God?

But listen, if your dog bit you, would you kick your wife? Of course not. Then, why don't you and I stop blaming God for the world's problems? Let's be fair. Place the blame where it belongs.

As we are about to discover, there may be someone else close to you trying to manipulate events in your life – someone you might never have suspected…

17

ETs and the occult -

DEAD LOVER RETURNED?

I received a newsletter the other day from my friend Evan Sadler, of Dunedin, New Zealand. He told me of a lady he knows well, whose boyfriend was killed in an accident. Some time passed. Then late one night he "appeared" to her and said he was in heaven, and that he still loved her. She was so overwhelmed with joy that they had sexual relations together. If that girl had only known the truth! She was ***had...*** by an impersonator.

There are many astonishing tales of supernatural encounters with "dead loved ones". Grieving wives or husbands have had their "deceased spouse" talk with them in the night and in some cases they have materialised and cuddled.

Impersonating the dead

In séances, these evil agents play the ultimate cruel trick, posing as departed loved ones to the bereaved who grope for comfort. This gives them a direct line to the soul. Then it is but a short step to CONTROL.

Spiritism is very attractive because it promises knowledge of the future and communication with dead loved ones.

Today countless messages from the spirit realm are accepted simply because they contain information ***that supposedly nobody else but a loved one would know.*** But wait! Are you sure that nobody else knows those family secrets? If evil spirits are out of sight but observing us all the time, then don't you suppose they know as much as we do?

When the medium at a séance enters a trance, a control spirit takes over and allegedly introduces the spirit of a dead person. In reality, the unseen visitor is a "familiar spirit" who intimately knows the dead person. Apparently these familiar spirits accompany a person throughout life, becoming so well acquainted that they can convincingly imitate the dead person's mannerisms and knowledge of personal details when called upon at a séance. In this way even close relatives are tricked into believing they are hearing their dead loved one.

If these spirits are ***willing to lie*** (as psychics themselves admit), they have all the cards – shrewdness, convincing information, a willingness to lie, and the advantage of being invisible. By revealing hidden things of the past, the spirit inspires confidence in his power to foretell things to come.

Thousands today – it may be unwittingly – are playing games with the perpetrators of a ***giant cosmic hoax.***

"Mother, is that you?"

A typical encounter was that of Edward B. He went to a séance and "saw" his deceased mother appear, clothed with light. She drifted across the room to him, stopped, and gave him a gentle smile. He impetuously leapt up, shouting "Mother!", only to have her disappear.

The *Intelligence Report* is emphatic that the dead know nothing and cannot return to visit the living.

There is good ***evidence*** that the spirits who appear at séances are rebel angels… the Legion of

Lucifer… the ones who "kept not their first estate", but were banished from Paradise. (Revelation 12:7-9; Jude 6)

"Killed in Vietnam"

An American soldier was reported killed in Vietnam. His grieving mother was told by a friend that if she came along to their meeting she would meet her dead son.

At the meeting, her friend was proved "right" when the "dead son" appeared before his emotional and happy mother.

They hugged and kissed, and told each how much they loved one another. Then the "son" said, "I must return to heaven."

The mother went home that night the happiest mother in the whole of North America. Some time later, she answered a knock on the door. When she opened the door, there was her son, dressed in his military uniform.

He had just returned unexpectedly from Vietnam.

What a shock!

Her son explained how his group had been cut off by the Viet Cong and captured. The United States Army had reported them dead. But now they had been found, rescued and given an immediate pass for home leave.

"But who was it?" she gasped. "Who was it that I hugged and kissed down at the local charismatic church?"

Who was that non-human being who resembled him in every minute detail… from the smile, the dimple and even the voice? Certainly not her son!

If only the mother had acquainted herself with the *Intelligence Report*, passages such as these could have alerted her to the clever séance deception:

> *For the living know that they shall die: but* ***the dead know not anything****.... Also their love, and their hatred, and their envy, is now perished; neither have they any more a portion for ever in any thing that is done under the sun.... Whatsoever thy hand findeth to do, do it with thy might; for there is no work, nor device, nor knowledge, nor wisdom, in the grave, whither thou goest.* (Ecclesiastes 9:5,6,10) *He that goeth down to the grave shall come up no more. He shall return* ***no more to his house****, neither shall his place know him any more.* (Job 7:9,10)

Some, under the effects of anaesthetic, have thought they had died and were looking down on their bodies on the operating table. Later, they were not quite sure about their experience. The truth is, they had not died.

A teacher's son was killed in Vietnam. Years later, the teacher was awakened to hear his dead son's voice and see his smiling face. He asked his father to give him a hug. The sleepy father desired to embrace him, but he quickly awoke and responded, "It is written, the dead know nothing."

The "son's" smile turned into a terrible sneer, and he vanished.

Believe it! The aim is to trick a bereaved person, open a direct line to the heart and then gain total CONTROL.

So who are those "spirits and ancestors" who manifest themselves among people belonging to traditional religions in Africa, "Folk-Islamic" Muslims in the Middle East, Hindus in southern Asia, and

Christians in the West? None other than these same fallen angels in disguise! Satan (former head of the angelic hosts), commands them.

Whether in the sophisticated West or in cultures where spiritual forces play an important role in daily life…whether by spiritism or by alien impersonation, the actors are the same… the Legion of Lucifer. And their aim is the same… CONTROL.

We are dealing here with something real and tangible, something that cannot be explained away.

Every person who honestly investigates spiritism and phases of the occult with a degree of thoroughness comes to the place where he has to admit that there is a supernatural power involved.

We have already noted the existence of another real dimension which contains entities, both good and malicious. They have consciousness and personality, just as you and I do. And they are intensely active, affecting the lives of millions on this planet.

And yes, it is from this other dimension that modern satanists summon their demonic entities in black magic rituals.

Unseen powers behind the scenes

Many people think that spirit phenomena are accomplished by trickery, sleight of hand, or black magic.

"Yes," concedes former spiritist Victor Ernest, "it is true that many mysterious happenings associated with prominent psychics and small-town fortune-tellers are hoaxes – perhaps 85 percent of them. But I believe the rest are actual deeds of evil spirits….

"At one trumpet séance, to prove there was no hocus pocus involved, the control spirit sent the trumpet sailing between the rungs of the chair on which I was sitting. Since I was in my own home, I knew no props had been arranged and that no strings were attached." (Victor H. Ernest, *I Talked With Spirits*. Wheaton, Illinois, Tyndale House Publishers, 1972, p.35)

Granted, spiritists have used sleight-of-hand methods to deceive. Also, mass hypnotism can make people see things that do not exist. Yet, there are some things which cannot be explained by trickery, but prove, rather, an intelligence behind them.

The spirits involved can speak. They can send messages through spirit mediums. They can slam doors, move furniture, and toss things through the air, hurl objects across a room, press hands around your neck to choke you and leave finger mark bruises as evidence. These are not imagination. They are definitely REAL!

The noted spiritist, Thomson Jay Hudson, in his book *The Law of Psychic Phenomena,* correctly states: "The man who denies the phenomena of spiritism today is not entitled to be called a skeptic, he is simply ignorant."

An important question

Now comes a crucial question: What ***evidence*** is there that spiritualism (spiritism) has anything to do with the "alien" phenomenon and with present world events?

Are you ready for this? The ***evidence*** may shock you.

18

ETs and the occult -

CLINCHING CLUES

Modus operandi. That is a term understood by police detectives who are tracking down a serial killer. To identify the guilty one they will assemble clues which indicate a pattern of behaviour. It is a procedure that often enables them to identify their man.

Edward Gein's modus operandi was to skin his victims, exhume corpses, and decorate his home with parts of his victims' bodies. Human skin was used to make dust bins, furniture, and even clothes.

Ted Bundy had a unique modus operandi in luring his victims. He would drink alcohol before approaching potential victims, even in a crowd or in broad daylight, and gain their trust by faking an injury with his arm in a fake cast or a sling. He would at times act as a policeman or fire department personnel. After luring victims to his car, he would hit them on their head with a crowbar. He then raped and assaulted them sexually before strangling and mutilating them.

John Wayne Gacy lured his victims into handcuffs in the pretext of showing them a pair of trick handcuffs he used in his clown act. He'd then dare the youth to free themselves. Once the boys were handcuffed, he would use either a rope or a board across their throats to kill them while he raped them.

Each man's unique pattern of behavior enabled each of these monsters to be identified and caught.

You and I shall now be detectives. We shall fit into place some patterns of behavior that will enable us to identify the UFO aliens beyond any reasonable doubt. Why is this important? Because our so-called "aliens" are not what they claim, but are members of the Lucifer Legion – the invisible rulers of this world and the emerging New World Order. We need to know this. It is very important. Our future is wrapped up in it.

The links:
ET encounters - and séances

Now this may surprise you. Are you sitting down? There is a ***confirmed connection*** between ***UFO*** occupants conversing with men, and the various experiences associated with modern ***Satanism*** and the ***occult.***

On Monday, September 7, 1992, a television program, *Inside Edition*, aired a story about six people – five men and a woman – who were in the United States Air Force, stationed in Germany. They were there to gather highly secret information for the Air Force. Then one day they suddenly disappeared. An all-points bulletin was issued to find them, capture them and return them to the Air Force authorities. Should they resist arrest, they were to be "exterminated".

They were finally found in Florida, in a small town near Fort Walton Beach, when one of them was stopped for a minor traffic violation.One of the men, a USAF officer, finally consented to an interview. He talked with the *Inside Edition* investigative reporter, but would tell only a bare minimum. However, the little he did say was most revealing. It supports my contention that ***saucers and aliens are linked with spiritism.***

The six of them had been playing with a Ouija board (a ***spiritualist*** method of "contact" disguised as a game). The message was spelled out to them that they were to go to a certain town in Florida to meet the "christ", who would be coming in a ***flying saucer***. (Devon Grey, *Comings.* Middleton, Idaho: CHJ Publishing, 1997, pp. 95-96)

In case you didn't know, Avitar, witchcraft's "christ" is also the "christ" of the New Age movement. ***Witchcraft*** believes that this Avitar will come in a ***saucer*** and precede the coming of the New Age Christ.

Roger Morneau, when in the Church of Satan, heard the high priest explain that Satan and his host were going to land on the earth in UFOs and tell world leaders that the world will be destroyed by a cosmic calamity, but if they cooperate with them, the world can be saved.

The connection with witchcraft is unmistakable. In Ohio ***witches*** routinely "conjure up" at their covens (meeting places) ***spacecraft*** and their aliens. Every time they do this, there is a rash of UFO sightings. The Ohio town where this occurs is known for frequent sightings of saucers. Many photos of saucers have been taken by observers here. The ***Ouija board connection*** is proof positive of the nature of the saucers. They emanate from the same source.

Same physical abilities: both ETs and séance spirits

Just notice these points of convergence.

1. Both UFO aliens and séance spirits appear temporarily as physical beings

Although this may be new to you, here is a reality we shall have to face. What we call "aliens" can be present with us in an invisible state. They can make themselves only partially visible. Or they can appear temporarily as totally physical.

This is true both of UFO occupants and the appearances at spiritistic séances. As UFO researchers Ankerberg and Weldon concur:

> ...it seems evident that these phenomena are produced in the same manner that other occult manipulations are produced. They involve dramatic manipulations of matter and energy. Although they originate from the spiritual world, they can produce very powerful, temporarily physical manifestations at the material level. (John Ankerberg and John Weldon, *The Facts on UFOs and Other Supernatural Phenomena.* Eugene, OR.: Harvest House Publishers, 1992, pp. 36-37)

Many characteristics attributed to aliens conform precisely to the biblical "spiritual yet physical" descriptions of angelic beings.

Angelic beings are mentioned on dozens of occasions in the Bible. The Bible states that angels are spirits. (Hebrews 1:14) However, as visible messengers of God they appear to mankind as men. (Genesis 19:1; Luke 24:4) And so physically real can they appear that we do not recognise them as angels. (Genesis 18:1-16; Hebrews 13:2)

As the clues emerge we shall discover that our so-called "aliens" are the rebellious ***fallen*** angelic beings, the Legion of Lucifer.

2. Both UFO aliens and séance spirits appear in any number of guises and shapes

(a) **They can create an illusion.** They can control what we think we see. You should be aware that these entities can impersonate or take any physical appearance they choose. They have enormous mind abilities. They have the ability to use their minds to project physical images for people to see. Everything in energy vibrates at different speeds. If you could use your mind to re-vibrate that energy to a different resonance – that is, to change the sound range of the body - you could appear in any form you wanted.

These entities have had thousands of years of practice at manipulating man's senses, causing him to see, hear, feel, smell and taste things that are not real.

(b) **They can manipulate vibrational frequency.** Physical matter is the result of sound resonating energy into form. This is simply the natural laws of creation at work. Hence the Legion of Lucifer can materialize or dematerialize. They can appear in any form - as humans, or as snarling, hideous creatures. But that is just a vibrational overcoat.

Of this you can be certain. These entities do ***not*** have the ability to create something from nothing. But they ***can*** materialize existing matter. They can manufacture UFOs and juggle genes.

Abductees claim that the aliens have sometimes ***disguised*** themselves as Jesus, as well known celebrities, the pope, and even the ***dead spouses*** of the abductees. Let a spiritualist tell us:

> Sometimes this was done in order to get the cooperation of the abductee, even to the extent of having sexual intercourse with him or her. (Dr Karla Turner, "Aliens – Friends or Foes?" UFO Universe, spring

1993, cited in "The Premise of Spiritual warfare,"<www.alienresistance.org/ce4prem ise. htm >, March 7, 2003)

This is true both with regard to UFO occupants and with the appearances at spiritistic séances. Not limited physically, as are we, they can impersonate or take any physical appearance they choose. And they can also materialize inanimate objects. Spirit beings have that ability. They can appear with Eurasian features, with Caucasian features, as long and spindly, or short, and pumpkin-headed.

Others are somewhat large-headed, with small, thin slit-like mouths, small nose slits, no ears to speak of and large slanted or round eyes. These are reported in about 90 percent of abduction cases. These are the so-called bad guys, who perform surgery on abducted humans.

The rest of the ETs appear as peace-loving, concerned and interested in our welfare. They claim that their master has sent them to warn the world to change its ways, or disaster will befall us. Again, this is a charade.

3. Both UFO aliens and séance spirits often appear as reptiles

Abductees often report aliens appearing as ***reptiles.*** Significantly, this is the trademark, or symbol, of Lucifer, "*the great **dragon**... that old **serpent**, called the Devil, and Satan, which deceiveth the whole world.*" (Revelation 12:9)

Francie Steiger, first wife of well-known writer Brad Steiger, claimed that an angelic being named Kihief had channelled messages through her. UFO researcher William Alnor reports that

> Kihief gave her an alternative history of the world and explained a way of salvation – a different gospel from the one outlined in the Bible and believed by Christians for twenty centuries…. According to Kihief, the ***serpent people***, who, he says, were represented by the ***serpent*** described in the biblical Garden of Eden, ***helped create humankind.*** Francie Steiger says we should believe him because 'he speaks only of God and of goodness.' (Brad Steiger, *Gods of Aquarius*. New York: Berkeley Press, 1983, p. 115, Emphasis mine)

Should we be surprised that Kihief presents himself as a good guy? You will observe that he redefines the evil ***serpent*** of the Garden of Eden (Lucifer) as being a good character. I perceive here a parallel to those people who rewrite history by saying that "Hitler was just a misunderstood genius." Similar corrections of history are reported by many channelers and contactees.

4. Both UFO aliens and séance spirits visibly change shape

Just as in spiritistic séances, where a spirit looking intinially like an elegant woman can then suddenly change into the appearance of a snarling animal, so in ET encounters.

The spirit being can use an apparent human form to hide his true nature. There are numerous encounters in which the spirit or alien has later changed his appearance. Some people who have been abducted by ETs have recalled how their abductors at first looked quite human, but then changed to look like humanoid ***reptiles***. Changing from one shape to another is true both with regard to UFO occupants and with the entities at spiritistic encounters. The term for this is "shape-shifting".

5. ***Both UFO aliens and séance spirits can appear as beings of light***

Not only do UFOs commonly manifest as objects of light, but contactees have described some aliens as changing into "beings of light". This gave the illusion of a divine encounter.

The name *Lucifer* literally means "lightbearer" or "shining one". Speaking of Lucifer, the Bible alerts us that "*Satan himself masquerades as an angel of light*" as do his agents. (2 Corinthians 11:14,15)

This is true both with regard to UFO occupants and with the appearances at spiritistic séances.

6. ***Both UFO aliens and séance spirits can pass through walls***

Aliens have been reported as passing through walls – just as spirits in a séance materialise through walls.

Same messages: both ETs and séance spirits

Now let's compare briefly what they are saying. The messages reported by numerous people from séance sessions and from UFOs are often of the same nature.

1. ***Both UFO aliens and séance spirits say they are here to help us***

"ETs" pretend to be the good guys. They say they are here to help us. That's precisely what Lucifer did when he hijacked this planet. He cast doubt on the Creator's integrity, then told Eve that he was there to help her achieve something better.

2. ***Both UFO aliens and séance spirits tell us we can be as gods***

Lucifer aimed to sabotage God's purposes for man by telling our first parents that they had the potential to reach godhead. "You shall be as gods," was his classic yarn. (Genesis 3:5) This is ***basically the same message*** the aliens bring today.

3. ***Both UFO aliens and séance spirits give identical predictions***

In May, 1967 UFO contactees were told to expect a large power failure. On June 5 in the northeastern U.S. a massive power failure did occur. Guess who planned and triggered it?

Other prophecies were given, with New York City to slide into the ocean on July 2… the pope to visit Turkey and be assassinated, and so on.

An interesting point here is that trance mediums and automatic writers were also receiving the same messages from "spirit guides". Sometimes the **PHRASING WAS IDENTICAL.**

4. ***Both UFO aliens and séance spirits reveal information known only to the hearer***

   The "space brothers" must be genuine, some think, because they sometimes impart life histories and incidents from an individual's past that only that individual could know are true. This is identical to disclosures in spirit séances.

   DON'T BE FOOLED. Things are not always what they appear to be! Your intimate details may be known to them.

Same medical and emotional effects: both ETs and séance spirits

1. ***Both UFO aliens and séance spirits can "possess" their victims*** Victims of spirit possession (demonomania) suffer the same medical and emotional symptoms as UFO contactees. Many victims of repeated abductions give themselves completely over to their abductors. They become continually ***possessed.***

   In New Age terminology, experiences of demonic possession are styled as "walk-ins". It is thought that a more evolved or "ascended" alien entity has literally taken over a person. This is the same as satanic spirits ***possessing*** humans. Frequently, they overshadow and control people. Basically spirit entities can live within a person's physical body. And sometimes speak out of it, using their own voice. As far as the human is concerned, we would call this outright possession.

Many of the possessed persons have no clue that this is so. However, their thoughts are the spirits' thoughts and they act in ways that advance the Lucifer agenda, without realizing it.

Some psychiatrists who do not especially care for spiritual realities at the personal level, yet often grudgingly acknowledge the very real possibility of demon possession in some patients.

2. ***Both UFO aliens and séance spirits sometimes speak through trance mediums***

UFO entities talking ***through*** people? Just as in spiritualistic séances? That's right. Such an incident from Project Bluebook is reported in my book *UFO Aliens: The Deadly Secret.* A major source of influence in the UFO/New Age movement is the practice of channelling, or communicating with "spirits", "vibration", "frequency", "a higher evolution", and so on. This is unmistakably a mark of spiritism.

The same 3 words "spook" them

Both UFO aliens and séance spirits are defeated by the same identical phrase. That is, the same three words that can stop spirit possession can also stop alien abduction – the very same three words.

This is a powerful clue to ***their common identity***. (We shall investigate this later in the book.)

Identical features

So there you have it – the identical ***modus operandi*** of the UFO phenomenon and that of spiritism. Stunning, isn't it?

Coldness of heart

Pro-UFO writer Thomas Bullard acknowledges this concerning the "space brothers":

> Though polite, the outward courtesy of the beings hides an innate coldness. They show little concern or understanding for human feelings and care only for accomplishing their mission. (Ronald D. Story, *The Mammoth Encyclopedia of Extraterrestrial Encounters*, in an article by Thomas Bullard, pp. 4-10)

Opponents of the Creator

Here is one factor that many researchers miss. The aliens expend ***great effort*** to promote the idea of an ***impersonal god or force*** behind the universe, rather than a Supreme Creator.

You may wonder why.

Clearly they do believe in God, otherwise they would not be expending such an ***immense effort*** to convince us otherwise. The simple truth is, they are trying to get ***revenge*** on God for their earlier defeat.

UFO researchers have noted that they also seem to be ***obsessed with the Bible***. Again, you may wonder why. The answer, again, is simple. This is the Book that reveals a divine rescue plan for the human race and ***exposes the nefarious agenda*** of these aliens, the

Legion of Lucifer, *"who deceives the whole world."* (Revelation 12:9)

The Bible speaks very plainly against them and warns us not to dabble in their affairs. (Deuteronomy 18:10; Ezekiel 13:6) Why? Because flirting with the occult opens the door to immense danger.

WE CAN KNOW that their master is the father of lies, Lucifer. They are operating UNDER A MASQUERADE. Sometimes they will ***confess*** their real identity. Other times they will ***deny*** who they are.

"Our leader is Lucifer"

Edwardo Dingaosen had just a month earlier moved into a New Guinea village.

One day, while he was some distance from the village, a messenger brought an urgent request that he return home. Arriving home, he found Sima, a 19-year-old domestic, lying on her mat, terrified. The reason for her fear was that voices were coming from her body.

"What's going on?" asked Edwardo.

A deep voice responded, "We are spirits and we have taken possession of this girl. We do not want her to study the Bible with you as she has been doing." They claimed to be five spirits.

Naturally, this caused excitement in the village and people came to see her.

One villager asked the spirits, "Do you have a leader?"

"Yes," came the answer.

"What is the name of your leader?"

A husky voice responded, "His name is Lucifer."

"We were cast out of Paradise"

Another villager asked where they came from.

"We were originally in Paradise," was the response. "But we chose to follow Lucifer and were cast out of heaven. For a time we went to other worlds, but now we spend all our time on earth. Wherever our leader tells us to go, we go."

Other ***confessions by these entities*** that they belong to the Legion of Lucifer (Satan) are documented in my book *UFO Aliens: The Deadly Secret.* (<http://www.beforeus.com/aliens.html>)

Many reports of alien encounters resemble ancient reports of what the Bible calls "demons", "liars", "seducing spirits", "spirits of devils". (Revelation 16:14; John 8:44; 1 Timothy 4:1)

It seems incredible that so many researchers have noted this similarity, yet they have ignored the world's most famous and best-selling book, which explains their identity and origin.

Divine response

But did our Creator just ABANDON rebellious man and leave us to suffer the consequences?

Indeed not! Firstly, we noted two chapters ago that a ***divine response*** to man's rebellion was to ***limit the lifespan***. But there was a ***second response*** from the Creator. This was ***a promise of hope and rescue.*** And this is where it gets interesting…

PART FIVE

RESCUE PLAN

19

Sacrifice of love –

OPERATION: RESCUE

A young couple excitedly bring their baby home from hospital.

But within a few days the infant begins to cry day and night with a severe case of colic.

They follow the doctor's advice. But nothing seems to help. They walk the floor with the baby until they are exhausted.

But not once do they consider giving the child away or leaving her to suffer alone.

WHY?

Because they LOVE her!

They love that helpless little child they've produced all the more because of the pain and suffering she has to endure.

Our Creator is the source of all love. His children on earth developed the colic of sin. And the pain and suffering they have endured because of it has only intensified God's love for them. Never has God considered abandoning us.

He wants us to turn from our self-destroying ways and live. Regardless of how good or bad you think yourself to be, His love for you is constant.

As the *Intelligence Report* keeps telling us: *"The Lord God [is] merciful and gracious, abounding in love and faithfulness, maintaining love to thousands, forgiving wickedness and rebellion and sin. Yet he does not leave the guilty unpunished."* (Exodus 34:6,7)

The BEST NEWS of all is that our loving,

forgiving, compassionate Maker found a perfect way to rescue us.

First, He would provide a stand-in to suffer the penalty for our wrongs, so we can live.

And ultimately He would restore endless life as a GIFT!

This gift is so priceless that you and I could never earn it. No good works of our own will get us out of our mess. We are totally dependent upon our Creator's LOVE, FAVOR and GENEROSITY - *which are FREE!*

If a friend gave you a birthday present…would you think you had to pay him for it?

The promise

Yes, God could have wiped out our first parents, there and then - and started over again. But He loved the man and woman He had created. And that was when God's rescue plan clicked into operation.

That spiritual law which had been violated could not be altered to save the rebels. Since it is the standard on which harmony throughout the universe rests, it must remain.

To abolish the law would have immortalised rebellion… and along with it the misery.

In any case, human nature was so weakened by wrong-doing, they had no strength to resist the power of the Lucifer Legion. Our first parents were now in a hopeless situation. No matter what good things they might do, they could not rehabilitate themselves.

But the Creator had a solution. He told them that someone called "the Seed" would come, stand in for man, endure the same struggles that each person faces, and in his own life defeat the Legion of Lucifer.

(Genesis 3:15) Then this Prince of God, his blamelessness still intact, would secure pardon for each person by taking upon himself the penalty of that violated law.

Thus the law would stand unshaken, even though it cost the life of the Deliverer.

All races knew of the Coming One

This, the world's oldest prophecy, given to our first parents, was to be handed down to all their descendants - the prophecy of a Deliverer. ***All nations separately*** knew it.

You'd better believe it, this is real. Archaeology has uncovered solid ***evidence*** that civilizations all over the world recorded this ancient promise concerning the Coming One. Among the ancient ***Babylonians***, ***Persians***, ***Chinese***, ***Hindus***, ***Germans***, ***British***, ***Romans***, ***Egyptians and others***, there was the expectation of this Great One who was coming to cure all ills.

The Roman historian Tacitus refers to this expectation among the nations. (Tacitus, *Histories*, v.13. See also Suetonius, *Vespasian*, iv)

Dupuis, in *L'Origine des Cultus*, has collected a vast number of traditions prevalent in ***all*** nations concerning a divine person, born of a virgin - that is, without an earthly father – who would come from heaven for the purpose of delivering mankind. (Dupuis, *L'Origine des Cultus, on Religion Universelle.* 12 vols. in 8vo,. Paris: 1794)

He would lay down his life once for all, but rise to life again and ultimately bring a new world.

Notice how an ancient poet contemplated these prophecies:

Hail, great Physician of the world! all hail!

> Hail, mighty Infant, who, in years to come, Shall heal the nations and defraud the tomb!... Thy daring art shall animate the dead, And draw the thunder on Thy guilty head; For Thou shalt die, but from the dark abode Rise up victorious, and be twice a God! (Joseph A. Seiss, *The Gospel in the Stars*. Grand Rapids, MI.: Kregel Publications, 1982, p. 48)

Likewise, in the earliest Egyptian texts are found prophecies proclaiming the coming of this Savior of the human race - prophecies that were already ancient. (Seiss, *The Great Pyramid: A Miracle in Stone*. New York: Harper and Row, 1973, p. 66. D. Davidson, *The Great Pyramid: Its Divine Message*. London: William and Norgate, Ltd., 1936, pp. 369,528)

Think now. Would such a "promise of rescue" be just suddenly "imagined" by all these different nations? They were in agreement that the Creator had made the promise to their common first ancestor. Can you think of any rational reason to doubt their harmonious testimony?

They held that this Prince of God was ***coming to confront Lucifer*** head on. In the process, he would sacrifice his life. But also he would conquer death and restore what was lost.

Every single person on earth would be offered the choice to accept this amazing rescue. And indeed, the whole world was waiting for these events.

The first animal sacrifice

On the day that the Eternal One reveals this rescue promise to our first parents, He then does something seemingly bizarre. He instructs the man to lay his hands on an animal (probably a lamb) and take its life.

The man does as instructed, and the first blood ever shed spurts out upon the ground.

Death is unknown until this moment. Can you imagine how terrible it must have been for our first father to shed the blood of that innocent creature? What horror and grief as he snuffed out the life of that animal he had named, nurtured and loved!

Now the promise is powerfully driven home. Just as this innocent animal now dies, so the innocent Deliverer will die to free guilty man from the curse of death.

It was spelled out clearly that the Eternal One is not a distant, aloof sovereign. He is not only aware of suffering. He feels it.

A teaching device

Someone will surely ask, Is not animal sacrifice a rather gory way to teach a lesson? Indeed, on the surface, it might appear so. But now ask yourself, What was the sacrificial system designed to achieve in the heart of the wrong doer?

We should not get the idea of a bloodthirsty God, demanding appeasement. Far from it, the Creator was to ***sacrifice His own*** Son for the benefit of humans who were under the death penalty. Why, then, was the sacrificial system instituted? It was an unforgettable teaching device.

First lesson

Firstly, man needed to feel a **HORROR** for wrong-doing, a desire to turn away from it.

Just visualise the situation. A man is sorry for a wrong he has committed. He brings an animal for sacrifice to the altar. He lays his hands on the animal and personally takes a knife and kills it. He himself kills it. By laying his hands upon the animal, the wrong-doer now symbolically transfers his own guilt to the innocent victim — and the animal becomes, as it were, a substitute for him.

Can you see the man shuddering as he gazes upon the lifeless form of that animal, realizing that his own act has just caused the death of an innocent creature? The sacrificial act was a constant and vivid reminder of the terrible cost of wrong-doing. The death of the sacrifice drove home the painful truth that the result of sin is death. Wrong-doing causes death so irrevocably and inevitably that the Creator cannot merely overlook it. It was going to cost Him dearly to save men and women.

Second lesson

A second reason for the sacrifices was that mankind needed **HOPE**. He must be reminded that his wrong-doing would one day cost the life of the innocent "Lamb of God". The slaughtered animal represented the DEATH of the Coming One.

The ritual was an act of ***faith,*** an ***acceptance*** of future deliverance. It had to do with the restoring of broken relationships.

The sacrificial system was a teaching device, ***to help*** the father of the human race and his descendants ***understand the rescue plan***.

Of course the sacrifice itself could not rescue a person any more than staring at a picture of a salad could fill an empty stomach. Rather, ***the sacrificed lamb*** was ***symbolic*** of the Coming One, who would, at the appointed time, be "led as a lamb to the slaughter". (Isaiah 53:7)

The *Jewish Encyclopedia* comments on this:

> The laying of hands upon the victim's head is an ordinary rite by which the substitution and the transfer of sins are effected. In every sacrifice there is the idea of ***substitution***: the victim takes the place of the human sinner. (*The Jewish Encyclopedia,* art., "Atonement, Day of")

It is about ***a substitute*** dying for us. The sacrifices anticipated the future supreme sacrifice of all time. We are beneficiaries of a love story, written in the blood of the coming Messiah.

The substitute payment

An American television personality was stopped for speeding. As the officer wrote out the ticket, the celebrity handed him his driving license.

The officer, suddenly recognising him, exclaimed, "My wife loves your show. She watches you all the time. Here's what I'll do. I can't tear up the ticket. The law must be enforced. But let me pay the fine for you. Here's the $50. Now please don't speed again."

That was the message of the sacrificial system. The Prince of God – the Law-Giver Himself - will pay the penalty and free the guilty from the curse of death.

Why not just say "you're forgiven"?

We might wonder, Why would the Divine Deliverer have to die? Couldn't God just say to people, "You're forgiven?"

Think about it this way. What if a judge said to a car-stealer, a drug dealer, or a psychotic murderer, "I'm going to forgive you. Just try not to do it again." What would happen to our society? There would be chaos, right?

That's the situation with which our universe was faced.

But the Deliverer would do more than just pay the ***penalty***. He would also ***provide power*** for individuals to achieve the standard of right living, so we would not mess up again, when all is restored.

The global practice of sacrificial rites is ***evidence*** of their common origin. Among the nations of the world it was always held that the institution of sacrifice was ***as old as the days of the first great father***. And they deemed it to be expiatory (atoning for man's wrongs). (George Stanley Faber, *Origin of Pagan Idolatry*. London: F. and C. Rivingtons, 1816, pp. 463-472))

In summary

- The global extent of the sacrificial rite is a proof of its ***common origin***.
- The institution of sacrifice is ***as old as*** the days of ***the original great father***.
- Various nations independently testify to this position. So do the Hebrew Scriptures.
- The ceremony was designed to impress a horror of the results of wrong-doing.
- The ceremony was a teaching device, that the Creator would forgive one who genuinely turns from his wrongs.
- Each sacrifice foreshadowed the future sacrifice of the Messiah.
- The ancient races looked forward to ultimate resurrection from death through him and the restoration of all that was lost.

Legion of Lucifer response

How would you expect the Lucifer Legion to respond to such an intervention plan? In their seething hatred for the human race and for the Prince of God, the Lucifer mob were filled with fury over the rescue plan. And, to get revenge for what happened in heaven, they determined to do all within their power to either thwart or discredit the plan.

They have already revealed themselves and what they hope to accomplish. We do know they hold some mean grudges.

Their strategy

1. ***Assassinate*** the Prince Messiah.
2. ***Exterminate*** by any means all who acknowledge the Divine One's sovereignty and who accept the rescue offer.
3. ***Eliminate*** most others – and that probably includes you and your family. As an earlier Prime Minister of Britain, the Marquis of Salisbury, acknowledged, "We are in the presence of forces far larger than we can wield." Have you wondered at the insanity that seems to be driving world events? Men in high places driven by a madness that seems non-human?

   As early as 1971, the renowned British astrophysicist Fred Hoyle told a London press conference that an unseen force was controlling the world. And "they" could manifest in many forms. To astonished journalists he announced, "They are everywhere, in the sky, in the sea and on the earth." He asserted that they control the human race through the mind.
4. ***Seize control of the information sources***, education, science and religion, to promote a long-term misinformation campaign which will

"discredit" the rescue offer. Then, ultimately, ban its public discussion.

This was set into motion very early in world history. It would be accomplished in several ways, two of which were:

1. Knowing that mankind has implanted within him a desire to communicate with his Maker, it was decided very early to set up ***decoy organisations*** to distract man's attention from the hated rescue plan. How to do this? By setting up ***subtle religious counterfeits*** which would incorporate elements of the original "Christ" prophecy – but reduce this coming "christ" to being only a teacher, not a rescuer. There's no rescue plan. You save yourself by your own good works. And this will effectively nullify the rescue message in the minds of multitudes.
2. For the many others who would not fall for the religious approach, the solution is simple: Just put out the idea that ***God has nothing to do with*** affairs on earth. Man simply got here by accident or by alien cross-breeding. And we've evolved upward since then. There is no need to consider God in our thinking. No divine laws to live by. We can do whatever we feel like doing without moral restriction. We have not fallen from an original perfect state. Death is an essential part of life. So there is nothing from which to be rescued. (This development was predicted in 2 Peter 3:3-7)

Either way, Lucifer would get his revenge, subvert the rescue plan, and protect his tyrannic rule over the planet.

His unwitting puppets do his will. This scam goes on every day… in the controlled universities, the media and in religious seminaries. A man might be listed in *Who's Who*, but he doesn't know what's what.

There's no rescue program. You're okay. Believe our lies. Just stay under our control. And most of us have been gullible enough to fall for it.

Taking full advantage of the weaknesses of human nature, Lucifer holds the kingdoms of this world captive under his control and is able to give them to whomever he wishes. (Matthew 4:8-9) The inhabitants of this world are his captives. And, like those who fall victim to ***the kidnapper syndrome***, they unknowingly identify with their kidnapper more than their Creator – preferring to believe his lies and even adopting his cunning, subtle and deceitful ways. Lucifer's attitudes permeate the world.

The fruits of his reign

Living under Satan's rule has brought mankind untold heartache and suffering.

Since Satan is a murderer, it's no surprise that we live in a world overflowing with violence and mayhem of every kind. It's no wonder that human history is written in blood, with the record of human existence being largely a chronicle of war after war after war. War is simply murder on a massive scale! Satan is behind genocide and the murder, manslaughter, beatings and assaults that plague many countries. We're appalled by the headlines. Even our popular entertainment is often *filled* with violence!

Where does this evil influence come from? It comes from the one who "was a murderer from the beginning"!

He is also "the father" of lies. Is it any wonder we see so much deception of every kind all around us? Should we be surprised that lying is so commonplace? We lie to each other. Our governments lie to us. We lie to our governments. Our various forms of media lie to us. Countries lie to other countries. Again, there is a reason for this—the father of lies who is behind it all.

Why do we see so much rebellion, resentment and suffering throughout the world? There is a powerful spirit influence behind it all. The world is imprisoned by an evil, malicious captor whose ***attitudes permeate society***. He has deceived the world, and those who are deceived, of course, *do not know* they are deceived — or they wouldn't be deceived.

The document they hate

A key part of this strategy is to discredit the hated Bible – since it focuses on the detested Prince of God and inspires its readers to resist the Lucifer strategy. Have you ever been a victim of this?

The good news

Nevertheless, as I shall soon prove to you, there is enough ***evidence*** that this divine rescue plan is on track… enough ***evidence*** to convince any honest, thinking person.

Which raises the obvious question: If the promise of a Deliverer is genuine, just ***when*** may we expect it to occur?...

* * * * * * *

FOR FURTHER INFORMATION
ON THE SACRIFICIAL SYSTEM

and how paganism corrupted it
into human sacrifice, see

Ark of the Covenant
Stolen Identity

http://www.beforeus.com/shopcart_ebooks.html

20

The prophecy -

WHEN WILL HE COME?

Suppose you opened a centuries-old book, and there was your whole life story published before you were born… your name… your birthplace… your achievements… and even the precise time you will die?

Most unlikely, you would say. And you would be right. But it has happened just once in history – a man's life story written before he was born. And this we shall now ***prove*** beyond reasonable doubt.

Progressive thread of prophecy

The prophecy of a coming Deliverer, or Messiah, spans some 4,000 years. Over the centuries, more information is received concerning this coming person. The simple outlines of the first prophecy become progressively more detailed as some Supreme Mind inspires different prophets in succession. Each new messenger is like a painter who uses the brush to put in details — until at last the word painting is finished and the full picture of the coming Messiah stands out perfect and complete.

His whole life story - including the ***precise time*** he would appear, was written down hundreds of years in advance.

The most common theme of the entire Bible is this Coming One called the Messiah. If you didn't know, he is the key that unlocks all mysteries found within the Bible.

The Messiah will be a human being

Although it may seem obvious to many that the Messiah would be a human being, it is necessary to reaffirm this fact – because we live in a day when religious thought is influenced by science fiction.

Indeed, many allusions to a Messiah figure can be found in science fiction films and books. But no, the Messiah could neither be an angel, nor some kind of extraterrestrial humanoid. He had to be human.

If the Messiah was to inherit our human weaknesses, defeat Lucifer from the same position as our first parents fell, then, as our stand-in substitute, suffer the penalty of our wrongs, he would need to be human like us. Thus the prophecies declare that

* he is the *"seed"* of the woman (Genesis 3:15), and

* *"to us a child is born, unto us a son is given."* (Isaiah 9:6)

The Messiah will be more than a man

However, the Scriptures say also that the Messiah will be called God. Several passages often used by Jewish rabbis in reference to the Messiah clearly teach this:

* *"This is the name by which he will be called: The Lord [Yahweh] our righteousness."* (Jeremiah 23:5-6)

* *"And he will be called Wonderful, Counsellor, Mighty God, Everlasting Father, Prince of Peace."* (Isaiah 9:6)

* *"Whose goings forth have been from the days of eternity."* (Micah 5:2)

The picture gradually forms

You will notice how a progressive thread of prophecy unfolds:

1. The Flood survivor Noah, in addressing his three sons (progenitors of the three racial branches of mankind) speaks specifically of "*the Lord, the God of* ***Shem***" (ancestor of the Semites). This suggests that the descendants of Shem will play a special role in relation to God's plan for the world. (Genesis 9:26)
2. The One who is coming to bless "the nations" will be a ***descendant of*** the Semite ***Abraham***. (Genesis 22:18)
3. Of Abraham's two sons, the Messiah will come from "the seed of ***Isaac***". (Genesis 26:4; 17:19)
4. Of Isaac's children, the Coming One will appear through "the seed of ***Jacob***". (Genesis 28:13,14)
5. The prophecies narrow it still further. Of Jacob's twelve sons, the Deliverer will be born of the tribe of ***Judah***. (Genesis 49:8-11)
6. Of all the families in Judah, he will appear through the family-line of ***Jesse***. (Isaiah 11:1,10)
7. Jesse had at least eight sons. Now a prophecy eliminates all of them except one — ***David***. The Messiah will be a descendant of King David. (Jeremiah 23:5,6; 2 Samuel chapter 7)
8. He will be ***born in Bethlehem*** — and a particular Bethlehem at that. You see, there were two towns called Bethlehem. There was Bethlehem of Zebulon, 70 miles to the north in Galilee; but this was not where the Messiah would be born. The prophesied place was "*Bethlehem Ephratah... in Judah*". (Micah 5:2) So now the Divine Forecaster eliminated all the cities in the world, except one, for the entrance of the Promised One.

The time: before the Jewish temple is destroyed

When was this to happen?

9. Here is a clue from the prophet Malachi (440-400 BC): "*the Lord, whom ye seek, will suddenly come to his temple.*" (Malachi 3:1) When Malachi wrote, the First Temple was already destroyed. This prophecy relates to the Second Temple. It says that Messiah will appear BEFORE the Second Jewish Temple is destroyed and the Jews finally exiled.

This, along with three similar prophecies (Genesis 49:10; Haggai 2:9; Daniel 9:25-27), required that the Messiah ***come while the Second Jewish Temple was still standing.*** The time factor was clearly spelt out. This is of great significance when we understand that the Second Jewish Temple was destroyed by the Romans in AD 70.

After the 586 BC destruction of Solomon's Temple, when a Second Temple was being constructed in Jerusalem by Zerubbabel, many sorrowed over the fact that it was inferior to Solomon's Temple. But the prophetic compensation to those who sorrowed over that inferiority, was that the glory of the latter house should exceed the glory of the former house (Haggai 2:9), since the Messiah would come to that Second Temple (Malachi 3:1). He had to come BEFORE the destruction of that temple — or the prophecy would fail.

Another of the prophecies states: "*And after the sixty-two weeks Messiah shall be* ***cut off*** ["***cut off*** *out of the land of the living*" – Isaiah 53:8], *but not for himself; and the people of the prince that shall come shall* ***destroy the city and the sanctuary***." (Daniel 9:26)

This is a remarkable statement! You will notice that a time sequence was specified:

First, Messiah is cut off (dies). ***After that***, the city (Jerusalem) and sanctuary (temple) is destroyed.

Jerusalem and the temple were destroyed by General Titus and his army in AD 70. Therefore, if Messiah did not come first, he never will come – and any who wait for him will do so in vain.

If you think that is sticking out one's neck, then what about this?:

The time: before tribe of Judah loses its judicial power

"The scepter [tribal staff] *shall not depart from Judah, Nor a lawgiver from between his feet, Until Shiloh* [the Messiah] *comes."* (Genesis 49:10)

There was no ambiguity about this. Jewish rabbis understood that "*Shiloh*" (*"His gift", "the one to whom it belongs," "wished for"),* was the coming Messiah.

* The Targums, or Chaldee Paraphrasis of Jerusalem, renders this prophecy "until the time when King Messiah shall come." (E. C Ettmann, *Messianic Evidences,* Melbourne, Australia: Presbyterian Women's Missionary Union, p.18)

* Onkelos (60 BC): "until Messiah comes, whose is the kingdom."

* The Talmud: "Shiloh is reckoned among the names of Messiah."

* The Targum Pseudo Jonathan on Gen-49:lla states: "How noble is the King, Messiah, who is going to rise from the house of Judah."

(For another example, see the quotation below.)

You will notice that two signs were to occur soon ***after the arrival of the Messiah:***

1. Removal of the scepter or identity of the Hebrew tribe of Judah.
2. Suppression of the judicial power ("lawgiver").

It is important to note that right through history (even during the captivity in Babylon in the 6th century BC), the tribe of Judah never lost its "tribal staff" or "national identity". They always possessed their own lawgivers or judges, even while in captivity. (Ezra 1:5,8)

It was not until AD 11 that the Roman procurators took away the power of the Jewish Sanhedrin (ruling council), to exercise the *jus gladii* (the sovereign right of life and death) themselves. This deprived the nation of Judah of its ability to pronounce capital sentences. (Flavius Josephus, *The Antiquities of the Jews.* New York: Ward, Lock, Bowden & Co., 1900, Book 17, Chap. 13, 1-5)

The Jewish *Talmud* itself admits that this occurred. (*Talmud*, Jerusalem, Sanhedrin, fol. 24, recto.) Rabbi Rachmon says:

> When the members of the Sanhedrin found themselves deprived of their right over life and death, a general consternation took possession of them; they covered their heads with ashes, and their bodies with sackcloth, exclaiming: ***'Woe unto us, for the scepter has departed from Judah, and the Messiah has not come!*** (M. M. LeMann, *Jesus Before the Sanhedrin.* Trans. By Julius Magath. Nashville: Southern Methodist Publishing House, 1886, pp. 28-30)

Did you notice? Once the judicial power was suppressed, the scepter was removed and Judah lost its royal or legal power. And the Jews ***knew it*** themselves!

The ancient prophecy said this would occur only ***after*** the Deliverer had arrived! Had the Messiah already come, and they didn't know it?

According to eyewitnesses of the time, he certainly had arrived:

"He came unto his own," says one contemporary writer, *"and his own received him not."* (John 1:11). If true – if the long awaited rescue plan was now being activated – this blindness of mind by his own people is about the saddest story in thousands of years of history!

Taken by surprise

So, if we are to credit the prophecies, the Deliverer must have come, covering his divinity in human flesh. But it took them all by surprise. Very, very few had the slightest idea that their long-awaited Messiah would come to them in such humble guise.

Of course, the fulfillment of a single prophecy or two might not count for much.

But a meticulous search, it is calculated, will turn up 332 distinct predictions, whose combined strands together form an ***unbreakable rope of evidence***. Can you imagine one person fulfilling all of these? It would be absolutely stunning.

Now may I ask three sensitive questions:

1. Why did a group of rabbis place a ***curse on a prophecy*** that foretold the specific arrival time of the Messiah Deliverer?
2. Why did this prophecy provoke others to ***cut 160 real years out*** of their national history?
3. Why has this same prophecy struck skeptics speechless?

Shall we explore this astonishing prophecy now? Are you ready for this? It's a prophecy, which, when you read it carefully, furnishes ***absolute mathematical proof*** of the Messiah's identity.

But first, my simple question to you

Pardon me issuing this caution, but if this is to benefit you – be you open-hearted, or the most hardened skeptic on earth – there is a question you need to address. Here it is: ***If you could convince yourself*** that the evidence now to follow is valid, and that the predicted Messiah is identified beyond reasonable doubt, would you follow him?

(You don't have to tell me. Just make a pact with yourself about this.)

* * * * * * *

FOR MORE INFORMATION

on the prophecies of the Messiah, see

Ark of the Covenant

<http://www.beforeus.com/sitchin.pdf >

Modern Religious Myths About Genesis

<http://www.beforeus.com/ebooks.html>

21

Mathematical proof 1 -

THE RABBIS' CURSE

In 1656, a dispute arose in Poland between some distinguished Jewish rabbis and some students of the book of Daniel. The dispute concerned Daniel's "70 weeks" prophecy.

"Look," said the students, "this prophecy proves Yeshua to be the Messiah. It tells exactly when the MESSIAH was to suffer."

The rabbis were so hard pressed by this argument, it was embarrassing. So they broke up the discussion.

The rabbis then held a meeting. As a result, they pronounced a curse upon any Jew who should attempt to work out the chronology found in this prophecy.

This was their curse:

MAY HIS BONES AND HIS MEMORY ROT
WHO SHALL ATTEMPT TO NUMBER
THE SEVENTY WEEKS.

Does this curse sort of arouse your curiosity? It did mine. So I undertook a long, careful investigation… and discovered that in Daniel 9:24 we are given the actual length of time from a confirmable specified event in world history, to the predicted year for Messiah to appear.

Background to the prophecy

In 586 BC, the Babylonian armies laid waste the land of Judah and dragged its people into captivity. Their capital city, Jerusalem, lay in ruins. About 70 years later, the Hebrew prophet Daniel, a captive in Babylon, was poring over a prophecy penned by an earlier prophet, Jeremiah, which stated that after 70 years of desolation, the captivity would come to an end. (Jeremiah 25:11,12; 29:10; Daniel 9:2) Confessing the wrongs of his people which had brought such disaster upon them, he prayed that the fulfillment of this prophecy for Jerusalem's restoration would not be delayed. (Daniel 9:3-19)

Daniel records that, in response to his prayer, a heavenly messenger named Gabriel appeared to assure him that his people would return and Jerusalem would be rebuilt.

Some details of the prophecy

Outlining a succession of events to occur in the future, Gabriel also pinpointed the time in Roman history when the Messiah would appear.

In a later visit to Daniel (Daniel chapter 11) he even described the emperor who would be reigning when the Messiah would die a violent death.

And to top it off, there were other Old Testament prophecies that identified not just the year, but the precise month, day and hour in history when that event would occur. (See documentation for this in my book, *Ark of the Covenant*, pp.182-188. <http://www.beforeus.com/aoc. html>)

Here follows Daniel's mathematical prophecy:

Seventy weeks are determined...[for the coming of the Messiah, the Promised One].

Know therefore and understand, that from the going forth of the decree to ***restore and build Jerusalem*** *UNTO MESSIAH THE PRINCE shall be seven weeks, and sixty-two weeks: the street shall be built again, and the wall, even in troublous times.*

And after the sixty-two week period ***shall Messiah be killed****, not for himself [but for others]:* ***after that*** *the people of a coming prince* ***shall destroy Jerusalem*** *and the temple; and at the end of the war, its desolation shall come like a flood.*

For one week, the Messiah shall confirm with many God's promise of rescue for man: and half way through the week he shall bring the sacrificial system to an end, and because of its abuse he shall destroy its temple, until the end of time, when the judgment which is decided shall be inflicted upon the desolating power. (Daniel 9:24-27)

"70 weeks" = 490 years

Here is an outline of a prophecy that was to be fulfilled during a period of "seventy weeks", along with other events which are not confined to the "seventy weeks" but are related to them.

This prophecy unveiled the future history of Israel and the precise time of Messiah's appearance.

How good are you at maths? Oh, that doesn't really matter. You'll probably find this quite easy – and fun, as well.

For starters, how many days are there in a week? Seven, you say. How many days in 70 weeks? 7 x 70 = 490, that's easy.

According to this prophecy, how many things are going to happen during "seventy weeks"? For one thing, ***a whole city built.***

Now just do a little figuring here. Think about that and you will see that we are dealing with a period of time that has to be longer than just 490 days.

Numerous Jewish scholars are clear on the fact that this prophecy is speaking of "***weeks of years***" in which every day of the prophetic week means a year. This is in harmony with the bible's own explanation of prophetic time.

The Hebrew for "seventy weeks" literally means "***70 sevens***". This is recognised by scholars to mean 70 sets of 7 years, a total of ***490 years*** - each day representing a year.

The ***year-for-a-day principle*** appears in the Bible as a divinely established identity in prophetic symbolism: "*I have appointed thee each day for a year.*" (Ezekiel 4:4-6; Numbers 14:34)

On "seventy weeks" (70 x 7 years), Jewish commentator J.J. Slotki states: "The cryptic phraseology may have been suggested by the seven-year cycle of Lev. xxv. The expression 'week of years' occurs in the Mishnah (*Sanh.* v.i)." (J.J. Slotki, *Daniel, Ezra, and Nehemiah,* p.77a)

One could compare the expression "*weeks of years*" with "*seven sabbaths of years..., seven times seven years;... forty and nine years*" in the book of Leviticus. (Leviticus 25:8)

Other Jewish scholars concur:

- On "*he shall confirm the covenant with many for one week*" (Daniel 9:27), *Midrash Rabbah* reads: "'Week' represents a period of seven years." (*Lamentations*, Soncino ed., p.65, note 3)
- On this same reference (v.27), the *Talmud* says: "'One week' in Dan. ix means a week of years." (*Yoma* 54at Soncino ed., p.254, note 6)

- On *"seventy weeks are determined"* (v.24), the *Talmud* states it to be "490, i.e. seventy weeks of years". (*Nazir* 32b, Soncino ed., p.118, note 6)
- Isaac Lesser refers to "Ancient Jewish writers", Rashi and other commentators as recognizing "year-weeks". (Isaac Leeser, *The Twenty-Four Books of the Holy Scriptures, 1853,* on Daniel 9:24,25; p.1243, notes 47,48)

So then, the prophecy indicates a period of 490 years (70 x 7 years) allotted to the Jewish nation, during which certain events will occur. You'll notice that the prophecy deals with

a. the coming Messiah, as well as
b. the history of Jerusalem.

Here was a promise that Jerusalem was to be rebuilt and its status restored.

The prophetic pattern

There is a clear structure to this prophecy, in which each verse deals firstly with Messiah, then with Jerusalem.

A: THE MESSIAH	B: JERUSALEM
v. 25 **At the end of 7 + 62 weeks** Messiah will appear.	Will be rebuilt, but under conditions of distress.
v. 26 **After the 7 + 62 weeks** Messiah will die violently.	A desolator prince will destroy it again.
v. 27 **During the 70th week** Messiah will keep covenant with many people.	- - - - - - -
v.27 **In midst of the 70th week** Messiah will cause sacrifices to cease.	The desolator himself will be destroyed as predetermined.

The events of Column A are unmistakably and closely dated to the seventy weeks. However, the events of Column B are not explicitly dated. Nor do they directly fulfill the spiritual purposes of the seventy weeks as specified in verse 24.

Verse 24 says: "*Seventy weeks are determined upon thy people and upon thy holy city, to finish the transgression, and to make an end of sins, and to make reconciliation for iniquity, and to bring in everlasting righteousness, and to seal up the vision and prophecy, and to anoint the most Holy.*"

All these things were to be accomplished by the Messiah. A full explanation of these details appears in my book *Ark of the Covenant.* (<http://www.beforeus.com/abook.html>)

Very well, you ask, this "seventy week" period — which we now know to be 490 years —when was it to commence? If we can find the starting point, the rest of the prophecy should be easy to understand.

"Jerusalem will be rebuilt"

*Know therefore and understand, that **from** the going forth of **the word [decree; commandment] to restore and to build Jerusalem** unto Messiah the Prince shall be seven weeks, and threescore and two weeks: the street shall be built again, and the wall, even in troublous times.* (Daniel 9:25)

It begins from the decree to restore and build Jerusalem.

When did this take place? The Bible itself tells us: it was in the seventh year of the reign of the Persian king Artaxerxes (Ezra 7:1,7,8), when he issued his first "decree" (vv. 11-26) to rebuild the ruined city of Jerusalem.

Leading up to this decree were two others - those of Cyrus and Darius - which related only to the building of the ruined temple.

In 536 BC, Cyrus allowed the Jewish exiles in Babylon to return to Jerusalem and rebuild the temple. (2 Chronicles 36:22-23)

In 520 BC, Darius reaffirmed and expedited Cyrus' decree concerning the temple. And in February, 515 BC, the temple was dedicated. (Ezra.6:13-18. Bright, A *History of Israel* p.372)

Around 520 BC, a governor "beyond the River" by the name of Tattenai (whose name is recorded on a cuneiform tablet) investigated the Jewish Temple rebuilding project which had now been under way for 16 years. As a result, he wrote asking Darius to check the Persian archives to see whether indeed the Jews had been given permission from Cyrus to rebuild he temple.

Darius responded with a thorough search and recovered a memo of Cyrus' decree (Ezra 6:1-5). He then issued the requested information (vv.6-12) in a new decree confirming that of Cyrus (ch.4:1-12).

The specific mention made by Cyrus, Darius and Tattenai was for the rebuilding of the temple. While individual dwellings were erected here and there around the ruined capital, no evidence exists that the city proper was rebuilt as a result of Cyrus' and Darius' decrees. As late as 519 BC, Zechariah was still promised in a vision that plans would be laid for the reconstruction of the city.

But the construction of ***Jerusalem itself*** was accomplished "***according to the decree of Cyrus, Darius, and Artaxerxes king of Persia***". (Ezra 6:14) Ezra the biblical scribe considered the third decree to be the culmination of the three.

His use of the singular word "decree" to cover the three documents indicates the unity of the decrees. It also directs attention to the third one, without which the first two were incomplete.

It was this ***third decree***, "in the seventh year of Artaxerxes" in 457 BC, which ***gave Jerusalem its legal rebirth***, restoring full autonomy in legal judgments, including the death penalty. (Ezra 7:7,24-26)

This made possible the restoration of Jerusalem to capital city status - necessitating its rebuilding as a visible administrative center.

It was this third decree which the prophecy had in mind when it spoke of a decree to "*restore and rebuild Jerusalem*". (Daniel 9:25)

It took the three decrees - of Cyrus, Darius and of Artaxerxes I - to implement the "commandment" of God, as Ezra terms it. (Ezra 6:14) But when 457 BC arrived, the "commandment of God" was complete.

It is ***from this date***, therefore, that Daniel's ***490 years begin***.

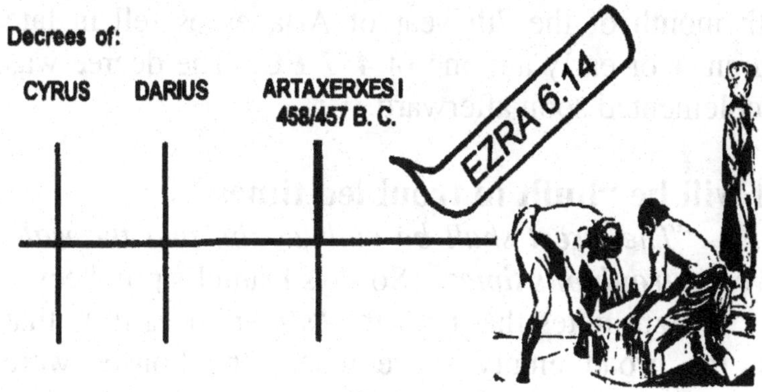

Confirming the date 457 BC

You ask, can this date - 457 BC - be substantiated? Indeed, this date is now firmly established as 457 BC by four independent sources:

- Greek Olympiad dates
- Ptolemy's Canon
- Elephantine Papyri
- Babylonian Cuneiform tablets

For example, one of the Jewish Elephantine papyri written between Tishri, 465 BC, and Nisan, 464 BC, is dated "accession year of Artaxerxes".

All four lines of chronological evidence point unanimously and harmoniously to the fact that ***the seventh regional year of Artaxerxes I*** extended from Nisan (month 1) in the spring of 458 BC to Adar (month 12) in the spring of 457 BC. From the extensive amount of ***evidence*** available, these dates can be considered as firmly and irrevocably fixed.

After Ezra arrived in Palestine in the 5th month of the 7th year of Artaxerxes's reign (Ezra 7:8), he implemented the decree. Since, in old Jerusalem, the Jewish months were numbered from spring to spring, the 5th month fell between mid-July and mid-September on our calendar (depending on the timing of the Jewish New Year's day in a given year). The 5th month of the 7th year of Artaxerxes fell in late summer or early autumn of ***457 BC***. The decree was implemented soon afterward.

It will be "built in troubled times"

*"The **street** shall be built again, and the **wall**, even in **troublous times**."* So says Daniel's prophecy.

Ezra notes that both the "***street***" (Ezra 10:9), that is, the broad empty space where the houses were formerly built, and the "***wall***" enclosing the city (Ezra 9:9), were rebuilt. Nevertheless, the builders were hindered and their plans thwarted by the opposition of the Samaritans, who hired counselors to frustrate them. At the Persian capital, Shushan (Susa),

Nehemiah received a report that his fellow Jews were in "***great affliction and reproach***" and that the newly-built "wall of Jerusalem" had been broken down and the gates "burned with fire". (Nehemiah 1:1-4)

Distressed, Nehemiah sought permission from Artaxerxes to visit Jerusalem and "build it" (Nehemiah 2:5), that is, repair the damage. The Persian king issued letters (v. 7), giving him permission to go to Judah and to receive lumber for gates (v. 8).

In Chapter 3 of his account, Nehemiah used the word "*repaired*" 33 times! "Now it came to pass, when...our enemies heard.., that there was no breach left [in the wall]... they thought to do me mischief" (ch. 6:1,2). Nevertheless (in spite of troubles) "the wall was finished... ***in fifty two days***" (vv. 15,16). A 52 day repair job.

This wall construction in 444 BC was *not* the predicted building of a ***new*** wall, ***but*** the ***repair*** of that damaged by opponents. Indeed, as Daniel predicted, these turned out to be ***"troublous times",*** just as prophesied.

Rebuilding will take "49 years"

The prophecy of Daniel allows for the building of the city and the wall, a total period of "*seven weeks*" (49 years).

Here, then, are our first seven "weeks" in Daniel's prophecy.

49 YEARS

|________________|

"7 weeks"

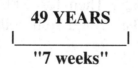

Since historical records from Palestine are so scant, we cannot find independent evidence that Jerusalem was precisely 49 years in rebuilding.

"483 years" to Messiah's appearance

However, the wording of the prophecy that "*from the going forth of the commandment to restore and to build Jerusalem, UNTO MESSIAH THE PRINCE, **shall be 7 weeks + 62 weeks***", provides us with a specific time for the more important event — the appearance of Messiah, the Prince of God.

* 7 plus 62 equals 69 "weeks of years" (69 times 7 years).
* 69 times 7 equals 483.

If we calculate 483 years from the "*commandment to restore and to build Jerusalem*", we should get the very year when Messiah would appear.

Now I suggest you follow this closely and check it yourself. There is no date in Bible history of which one can be more certain.

(There is also no doubt that this prophecy existed. It was translated into a Greek version, called the *Septuagint*, by seventy Jewish scholars in Alexandria between 283 and 180 BC, and circulated throughout the Greek-speaking world.)

Daniel wrote the prophecy. Ezra recorded the commencement date. Then for 400 years there was silence — while Israel and some others waited. The countdown began...

22

Mathematical proof 2 –

AN AMAZING PREDICTION COMES TRUE!

"What's wrong?"

"Oh, she's just found out the baby's a girl."

But why the disappointment? Ah, we shall see why, in this chapter…

* * * * * * *

You remember how the wealthy King Croesus went to visit the oracle at Delphi? He wanted to know whether he should fight the Persians. According to the historian Herodotus, the "wise oracle told him that 'by crossing Halys, Croesus will destroy a mighty power.'"

Croesus took this as a prophecy that he would destroy the great Persian army. So he went into battle. But he was defeated. He ***did*** destroy a mighty power: his own!

Whichever way the battle went, the augury would be true.

Psychic or human prophecy, it matters not which. I shall say it again. They are mere guess work.

But when you investigate Bible prophecy, you will discover it to be as far from human prediction as midday is from midnight. Bible predictions burn all bridges. They are ***specific***.

And Daniel's prophecy, which we shall now pursue further, is a notable example of this – which may prompt us to ask, How did the prophet know?

483 years "to Messiah the Prince"

"Until Messiah the Prince there will be seven weeks and sixty-two weeks." (Daniel 9:25) That is, seven "weeks of years" (49 years) to rebuild the city, followed by 62 "weeks of years" (62 x 7 = 434 years) duration of the restored city — till the Messiah!

The Jewish writer, J. J. Slotki, says:

> Jerusalem will be a fully restored city during a period of 434 years. (J.J. Slotki, J.J. *Daniel, Ezra, and Nehemiah,* P.7)

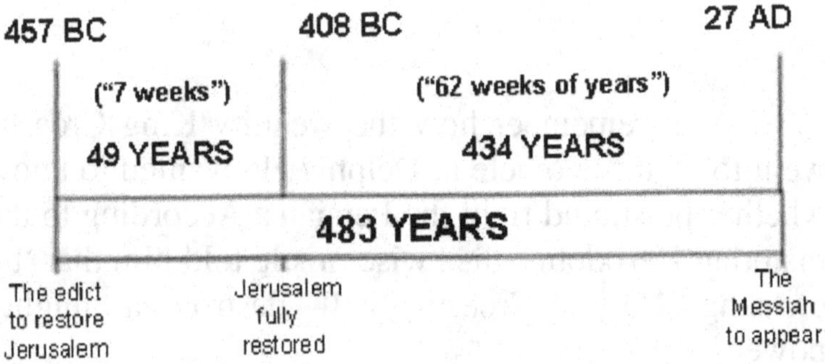

If the rebuilding of Jerusalem was to occupy 49 years this would bring us to the year 408 BC. When we calculate another 434 years, we should get the very year when Messiah would appear.

It must be remembered that there was ***no "0" BC*** (no zero BC) year. Thus, when we count from BC dates to AD, one year must be deducted from the total.

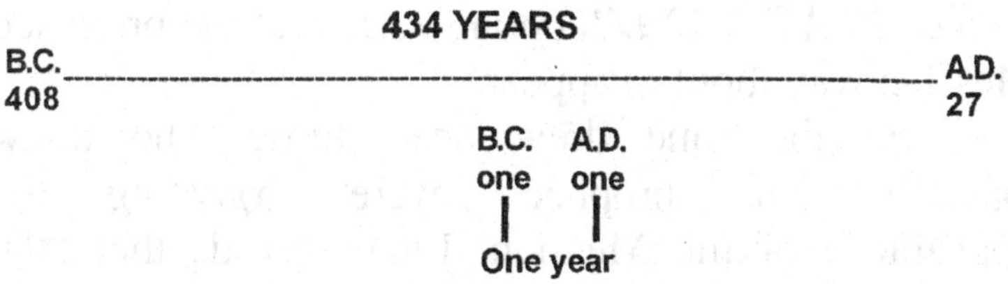

You will see that 434 years after 408 BC reaches to the year 27 AD.

These 434 years would reach to the *Messiah,* a name meaning the "Anointed" one. So ***the Messiah must appear in that year.*** And if that year passed and he didn't come, then we might well say that the prophecy failed. And for that matter, any future claimant to the role is NOT the promised Messiah!!

Do you see how clear that is? The eternal God in His *Intelligence Report* has given you a tremendously solid platform on which to base your confidence.

Did something significant occur during that year? Let's see.

The Jewish expectation

At the time, the land of Judea (Israel) was in the hands of the powerful Roman Empire. Many a Jewish heart longed to throw off the imperial yoke.

Soon news filtered up to Jerusalem that an eloquent speaker had appeared in the Jordan Valley east of the city and was calling on everybody to "repent" (that is, turn from their old failed ways) and "be baptized" (immersed in water to signify a new start).

John the Baptist, as everyone called him, understood the chronology of Daniel's prophecy, and had caused quite a stir by announcing, "*the kingdom of heaven* ***IS AT HAND*"**. (Matthew 3:2), that the promised Messiah was about to appear.

As the time drew near, those who knew Daniel's time prophecy were ***expecting*** the appearance of the Messiah. Luke records that "the people were **IN EXPECTATION"**. (Luke 3:15)

For centuries, almost every Jewish mother prayed with longing that her firstborn son would be the Messiah. Thus there developed a custom that if a boy was born there was great joy. If a girl was born... they wept. Poor girls!

Early Jewish documents, such as the *Septuagint* translation of the Scriptures (283-180 BC) (Hengstenbery, E.W. *Christology of the Old Testament,* reprint; McDill AFB, FL, 1973. 2:824-825 von Lengerke, C *Das Buch Daniel,* 1835, p.410) and the *Testament of the Twelve Patriarchs* (c. 100 BC) (*Testament of Levi* chaps. 14-16) interpret Daniel's time prophecy as referring to the Messiah.

The Septuagint (LXX) interprets the "weeks" in all instances in v.25-27 as ***"years" (ete)*** and ***"times" (kairoi).***

Indeed, whether Essene, Hellenistic, Pharisaic or Zealot, the most usual interpretations of Daniel 9:24-27 within Judaism, until after 70 AD, were of the ***messianic*** kind. (Beckwith, Roger T. "Daniel 9 and the Date of the Messiah's Coming in Essene, Hellenistic, Pharisaic, Zealot and Early Christian Computation," *Revue de Qumran* 40, 1981: 521)

Expectation among other nations

We noted in an earlier chapter that the Promised One was expected by the nations of the world – including the ***Persians***, the ***Babylonians***, the ***British Druids*** and the ***Egyptians*** – independently of each other.

To cap it all, the ancient ***Romans*** were convinced that a master and ruler of the world was to come ***out of Judea***. (David L. Cooper, *Messiah: His First Coming Scheduled*, 1939, p.600)

Tacitus, Suetonius, Josephus and others testify that by the ***first century BC*** there was a widespread expectation of a great Prince to arise in the East – even though general conceptions had become indefinite and incompatible with the character of the Messiah as portrayed in the most ancient prophecies.

In the land of Judea, the Herodian group knew that the time for the appearance of Messiah was at hand. In their worldly perception of the event, they regarded King Herod as the Messiah. (Epiphanius, *Ilanarian*, "The Drugchest, a Refutation of all Heresies," Tertullian, *De praescriptione haereticorum*) From Daniel's prophecy, they correctly found that the period of 490 years was approaching its completion in the time of Herod.

The Essenes of the Qumran community likewise interpreted Daniel's prophecy messianically. That understanding was worked out prior to 146 BC. (Beckworth, p. 525)

The Dead Sea Scrolls have yielded text confirming the Jewish expectation of a personal, individual ***Messiah*** who would ***die and rise from the dead.*** A fragment called "*A Genesis Florilegorium*" (4Q252) reflects belief in an individual Messiah who would be a descendant of David: "*Column 5 (1) (the) Government shall not pass from the tribe of Judah. During Israel's dominion, (2) a Davidic descendant on the throne shall [not c]ease … until the Messiah of Righteousness, the Branch of (4) David comes.*" (Robert H. Eisenman and Michael Wise, *The Dead Sea Scrolls Uncovered*. New York: Barnes & Nobel, 1992, p. 89)

Even the ***deity*** of the expected Messiah is affirmed in the fragment known as "*The Son of God*"

(4Q246), Plate 4, columns one and two: *"Oppression will be upon the earth... [until] the King of the people of God arises,... and he shall become [gre]at upon the earth. [... All w]ill make [peace,] and all will serve [him.] He will be called [son of the Gr]eat [God;] by His name he shall be designated.... He will be called the son of God; they will call him son of the Most High."* (*Ibid.*, p. 70)

"The Messiah of Heaven and Earth" fragment (4Q521) even speaks of the ***Messiah raising the dead***: *"(12) then He will heal the sick, resurrect the dead, and to the Meek announce glad tidings."* (*Ibid.*, p. 23; cf. pp. 63, 95)

Clearly, the general ***expectation of the Jews*** was that ***the time*** for the Deliverer's appearance ***had arrived.***

This is why the Jews sent priests and Levites to John the Baptist, to ask him if he was the Messiah. Although he confessed, "*I am not the Messiah*" (John 1:19,20), there were still many who speculated that John was "*that prophet that should come into the world*". (John 6:14; 7:40)

Certainly John the Baptist understood the chronology of Daniel's prophecy and made it one of the bases of his appeal, "*Repent ye, for the kingdom of heaven **is at hand.**"* (Matthew 3:2)

"The time is fulfilled"

In the crowd pressing around John was a young man approaching thirty. He came to John to be baptized by immersion in the River Jordan.

From this time onward, there followed a series of public statements which, had they been accepted at face value, would have prepared their hearers for what was to occur three and a half years later.

The first was John's announcement upon seeing the young man approaching, whose name was Yeshua: "*Here is the Lamb of God, who takes away the sin of the world.*" (John 1:29) As symbolized by the ancient sacrificial system, this young man would ultimately go "*as a lamb to the slaughter*" (Isaiah 53:7) for claiming to be "*the Son of God*". (John 19:7)

Yeshua began his public ministry by declaring, "*THE TIME IS FULFILLED.*" (Mark 1:15) With his own lips, he announced the termination of the prophetic time period. "I'm here," he declared, "ON TIME."

Thus, one of the crowd who had been to the Jordan reported back to his brother, the fisherman Peter, "*We have found the MESSIAS... the Christ.*" (John 1:41) The term ***Christ*** is the English equivalent of the Greek ***Christos***, "ANOINTED ONE", and of the Hebrew ***Mashiach***, (MESSIAH).

Soon after this, Yeshua entered the synagogue of Nazareth, his home town, and announced, "*The Spirit of the Lord is upon me, because he hath ANOINTED me.*" (Luke 4:18-22)

6 facts pinpoint the year

And what year was this? We're not left to speculate. The first century writer Luke informs us that it was "*In the fifteenth year of the reign of Tiberius Caesar, Pontius Pilate being governor of Judaea, and Herod being tetrarch of Ituraea and of the region of Trachonitis, and Lysanius the tetrarch of Abilene, Annas and Caiaphas being the high priests*" (Luke 3:1,2), that John the Baptist commenced his ministry.

Luke wrote two books: Acts and the Gospel of Luke.

Both books used to be discounted by critics. Among those who doubted their accuracy was William Ramsay.

Honest critic forced to change his mind

Sir William Ramsay is reputed to be one of the greatest archaeologists of all time.

As a student in the German historical school of the mid-19th century, Ramsay was firmly convinced that the New Testament book of Acts was a fraudulent product of the mid-2nd century.

In his research to make a topographical study of Asia Minor, he was compelled to consider the New Testament writings of Luke. Here is how he relates his experience:

> I began with a mind unfavourable to it… but more recently I found myself brought into contact with the Book of Acts as an authority for the topography, antiquities and society of Asia Minor. It was gradually borne upon me that in various details the narrative showed marvellous truth. In fact, beginning with a fixed idea that the work was essentially a second century composition, and never relying on its evidence as trustworthy for first century conditions, I gradually came to find it a useful ally in some obscure and difficult investigations. (Edward Musgrave Blaiklock, *Layman's Answer: An Examination of the New Theology*. London: Hodder and Stoughton, 1968, p. 36 – quoted from Ramsay, *St. Paul the Traveller and the Roman Citizen*)

As a result of that, Ramsay was forced to do a complete reversal of his beliefs. He concluded after thirty years of study that "***Luke is a historian of the first rank***; not merely are his statements of fact trustworthy… this author should be placed along with the greatest of historians." (Sir W. M. Ramsey, *The Bearing of Recent Discovery on the Trustworthiness of the New Testament.* London: Hodder and Stoughton, 1915, p. 222. Emphasis mine)

In fact, Ramsay concluded that "Luke's history is unsurpassed in respect of its trustworthiness." (W. M. Ramsay, *St. Paul the Traveller and the Roman Citizen.* Grand Rapids: Baker Book House, 1962, p. 81)

Since then, further discoveries have shown New Testament writers such as Luke to be careful historians. His reliability shines through details so intricately yet often unintentionally woven into the narrative. His familiarity with particular locations with details suitable only to the times in question stamps Luke as a ***trustworthy contemporary*** of the events reported.

Here also is the verdict of Roman historian A.N. Sherwin-White:

> For Acts the confirmation of historicity is overwhelming.... Any attempt to reject its basic historicity must now appear absurd. Roman historians have taken it for granted. (A.N. Sherwin-White, *Roman Society and Roman Law in the New Testament*, reprint edition. Grand Rapids: Baker Book House, 1978, p. 189)

F. F. Bruce, of the University of Manchester, offers this tribute to the historical accuracy of Luke:

> A man whose accuracy can be demonstrated in matters where we are able to test it is likely to be accurate even where the means for testing him are not available. Accuracy is a habit of mind, and we know from happy (or unhappy) experience that some people are habitually accurate just as others can be depended upon to be inaccurate. Luke's record entitles him to be regarded as a writer of habitual accuracy. (F.F. Bruce, *The New Testament Documents. Are They*

Reliable? London: Inter Varsity Press, 1974, p. 90. Emphasis supplied)

Clark Pinnock, Professor of Interpretations at McMasters University, Toronto, concurs:

> There exists no document from the ancient world witnessed byso excellent a set of textual and historical testimonies, and offering so superb an array of historical data on which the intelligent decision may be made. An honest (person) cannot dismiss a source of this kind. (Josh McDowell, *The Resurrection Factor.* San Bernadino Ca: Here's Life Publishers, Inc., 1981, p. 9)

Yes, you can trust Luke's testimony. Luke gives you six historical facts, in order to pinpoint a date. You can check and re-check.

He informs us concerning the time that John the Baptist commenced his ministry, that it was "*In the fifteenth year of the reign of Tiberius Caesar, Pontius Pilate being governor of Judaea, and Herod being tetrarch of Ituraea and of the region of Trachonitis, and Lysanius the tetrarch of Abilene, Annas and Caiaphas being the high priests...*" (Luke 3:1,2)

You see how historically precise is Luke? He takes pains to confirm the date by ***six independent lines of evidence***.

Tiberius' 15th year

We have an abundance of facts on the Caesars of Rome. And we can identify the fifteenth year of Tiberius' reign. It is 27 AD.

Tiberius commenced reigning on August 19, 14 AD.

The Jewish New Year began in September-October (on the date known in Jewish terminology as Tishri 1).

It was Jewish practice to reckon the years of foreign kings from Tishri 1 (New Year's day by the civil calendar).

Thus Tiberius' short first year (commencing August 19) ended - and the second year of his reign began — on Tishri 1 (in September-October, according to Jewish reckoning.)

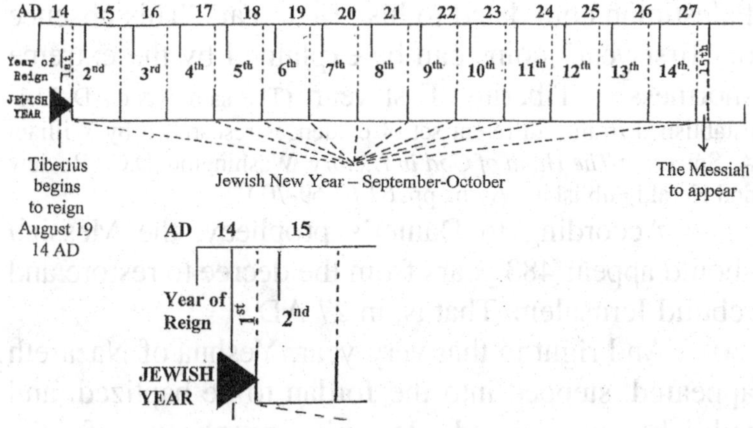

The chart above shows the first fifteen years of Tiberius' reign. ***Tiberius' fifteenth year*** began in September or October, 27 AD.

Tishri 1, Rosh Hashanah, was calculated to follow the new moon of either September or October. A king's "first year" was considered to be the interval between the day he began to reign and the arrival of the following autumn New Year's Day. Jewish clerks and those of some other eastern Mediterranean countries began to date documents by a new emperor's "first year" as soon as they heard the news that he had begun to reign.

Tiberius' second year thus began in Palestine on New Year's Day in September or October, 14 AD even though he had been in power no more than about two months.

Even today in some eastern lands, children are considered to be a year old in the year of birth and to be two years old on the subsequent New Year's Day - even if that New Year's Day comes only a day or two after a child is born. Interestingly, although many Palestinian coins from various years of Tiberius' reign have been found, archaeologists have not found one Palestinian coin dated to his "first year". This absence of "first-year" coins can be explained by the extreme shortness of Tiberius' first year. (The same year AD 27 is established from a different set of evidences researched by William A. Spicer, in *The Hand of God in History.* Washington, D.C.: Review and Herald Publishing Assn., pp. 62-63,69-70.)

According to Daniel's prophecy, the Messiah should appear 483 years from the decree to restore and rebuild Jerusalem. That is, in 27 AD.

And right in that very year, Yeshua of Nazareth appeared, stepped into the Jordan to be baptized, and publicly proclaimed Isaiah's prophecy of the "Anointed One" as predictive of himself. (Luke 4:16-21)

Yeshua was baptized quite soon after John began to preach. Then between Yeshua's baptism and his first Passover (in the following March-April) he spent 6 weeks in the wilderness, gathered disciples here and there, and also attended a wedding feast. On account of all this, we may safely conclude that he was baptized within the year 27.

May one conclude by this public announcement of Yeshua, that Daniel's prophecy given 600 years earlier was fulfilled ***on time***?

Indeed, the prophecy concerning 69 weeks (483 years) to the anointing of the Messiah at his baptism in

27 AD was fulfilled with astonishing accuracy. Paul, a former skeptic, seems to have hinted at this when he wrote, "When ***the time had fully come***, God sent forth his Son, made of a woman." (Galations 4:4)

Yeshua in historical records

Does any skeptic have a problem with the fact of Yeshua's existence? Then listen... It staggered me to discover that Yeshua's' life was attested to by no fewer than ***22 different historians of his day***, such as Tacitus, Suetonius, Serapian, Phlegon, Lucian, Josephus. Many of these historians were antagonistic toward him. He was mentioned in at least four official Roman records:

1 ***Cornelius Tacitus,*** born around AD 55, may have been ***the greatest*** Roman historian. He held the positions of senator, consul, and provincial governor of Asia. He wrote *Annals (16 volumes), Histories, Agricola, Germany*, and a dialogue on oratory. And he mentions that Pontius Pilate crucified Yeshua. (*Annals,* 15:44) Tacitus was a ***scrupulous*** historian who paid careful attention to his historical works. (*Wikipedia)* You can depend on his historical trustworthiness. He was contemporary with many of the events he records.

2. ***Governor Pontius Pilate*** *(31 to 37 AD)* (See Justin Martyr, *Apology,* 1.48)

3. ***Caius Suetonius Tranquillus*** (c. AD 69 – 140), overseer of Rome's libraries (*Lives of the First Twelve Caesars: Life of Claudius,* 26.2)

4. ***Pliny the younger*** (AD 112) (*Letters* 10:96.7)

You can check on the early historical testimony concerning Yeshua by these and various others, more comprehensively in my book *Who's Playing Jesus Games?*, chapters 1 to 3.

But there's more in Daniel's prophecy…

23

Mathematical proof 3 –

WHAT WILL HE DO?

Brenda shuddered. "Jonathan, that makes my flesh creep. All this just coincidence?"

Yes, it was uncanny. It sent a tingle up my spine. And I'm about to share it with you… as we continue Daniel's prophecy. …

Daniel wrote, "*He shall confirm the COVENANT with many for one week.*" (Daniel 9:27) This "week" is the final one of the seventy weeks allotted in a special sense to the Jews.

The covenant to prevail 7 years

An equally valid translation of this passage is: "*One week shall **establish** the covenant*" or "*For one week the covenant shall **prevail**.*" Of course, "one week" denotes seven years.

The prophet Malachi called the coming Messiah "*the messenger of **THE COVENANT***" (Malachi 3:1)

This is the everlasting covenant of mercy (the promise of rescue) that the Creator had made with the human family, the promise that he had given to Adam.

By the events of this seven year period, the covenant would be forever established. And it would prevail "*with many*" of Daniel's people, the Jews. (Daniel 9:27)

This divine covenant was to triumph in the ministry of the Messiah to Israel — a ministry which was to be a unique demonstration of patient, forgiving love.

Mistaken modern interpretations of this passage have had it that some evil character will “make” a covenant with the Jews, then break it. However the original Hebrew word here is never translated “make”. It is usually translated “prevail”. ***Nobody*** was to “make” a covenant.

The covenant already existed. It was now simply to be confirmed. (Daniel 9:27)

For 3½ years Yeshua came publicly to Israel.

Four annual Passovers occurred during Yeshua’s public ministry - between his baptism during September-October 27 AD and his death during March-April 31 AD. (John 2:13; 5:1; 6:4;13:1)

Yeshua’s baptism to first Passover...	½ year
to 2nd Passover...	1 year
to 3rdPassover...	1 year
to 4th Passover...	1 year
TOTAL	3½ YEARS

He confirmed the covenant in person by his life and teachings.

Then, just before his death, he lifted a cup of wine and said to his disciples, “*This is my blood of* ***THE COVENANT****, which is poured out for* ***many*** *for the forgiveness of sins.*” (Matthew 26:28)

Evidently, he was thinking that night of Daniel’s prophecy, “*He shall* ***CONFIRM THE COVENANT*** *with* ***many****.*” (Daniel 9:27)

To become effective, the covenant would require his death.

This period of 3½ years — and a second period of 3½ years that would follow his death — were definitely directed at the Jews (“***thy people***” of

Daniel's prophecy). And as a consequence many Jews did recognize Yeshua as the Messiah.

The New Testament writers bear witness that after Yeshua's death on the cross, the same covenant message was confirmed to the Jewish nation for a further 3½ years.

Fifty days after the crucifixion, on the day of Pentecost, the Jew Peter called his countrymen to turn around and accept forgiveness. "*For the **promise** is to you and to your **children**,*" he said. (Acts 2:38,39)

He testified in the very city where the messianic events had occurred. The evidence was right under their noses. On that occasion, 3,000 Jews accepted the offer. And soon after, another 5,000 men, as well as women and children. The former skeptic Paul added his testimony concerning "*the **COVENANT**, that was **CONFIRMED** before of God in Christ.*" (Galatians 3:17).

70 WEEKS OF YEARS (490 Years)

69 Weeks (483 YEARS)		***1 Week (7 YEARS)***
Jerusalem rebuilt **7 weeks (49 years)**	**62 weeks (434 years)**	**70th week**
Artaxerxes Decree	**Messiah to Appear**	**End of the Jewish Period**

So persuasive was this superlative sort of love, so attractive was the appeal of a God who continued to share his promise in spite of rejection and crucifixion, that (as Luke records) "*the word of God increased: and the number of disciples multiplied greatly in*

Jerusalem, and a great many of the priests were obedient to the faith." (Acts 6:7)

Mark, another writer, states that when the disciples went publicly to Israel, that their Lord was "***confirming*** the word with signs following." (Mark 16:20)

Again, Paul wrote to his Jewish kinsmen, "*How shall we escape, if we neglect so great salvation; which at the first began to be spoken by the Lord, and was **confirmed** to us by them that heard Him.*" (Hebrews 2:3)

Can you see? In a very real sense, the ministry of the disciples was a continuation of the ministry of Yeshua himself.

This is how the Messiah would "***confirm** the covenant*" with "***many***" (that is, the Jews) for "*one week*" (seven years).

Yeshua's use of "Messiah" and "Son of man"

In the popular mind, messiahship had degenerated to the idea of kingship, of one who would violently overthrow the Romans and bring on a Golden Age. Messianic ideas had become nationalistic, destructive and vengeful.

To play that part was the last thing Yeshua desired. Any suggestion that he might do so was a hindrance to his cause. So he told his followers not to say that he was the Messiah, not in public. (Matthew 16:20)

Then, abruptly, he "*began to teach them that the Son of man had to undergo great sufferings and to be rejected,*" that his role was to be essentially that of the innocent sufferer. (Matthew 16:21)

"***Your*** Messiah is a conqueror," he told the disciples; "***God's*** Messiah is a servant." Yeshua accepted the messianic faith of the Jews but interpreted it by means of the suffering servant prophecy of Isaiah chapter 53. He knew what lay ahead and was doing his best to prepare his disciples for it. Rather, he preferred to call himself "the Son of man". That was his favorite title; it identified him with mankind.

However, at the end of his ministry, when he had to confront the high priest preparatory to his arraignment, he was asked point-blank "Are you the Messiah?" And he replied, "I am." It is clear that Yeshua allowed himself to be condemned to death for claiming the messianic role. Even if contemporary ideas of the "Messiah" were mistaken, Yeshua still could not simply repudiate the title to save his life. He was voluntarily taking a course that would lead to his death.

A violent death

"And after the 62 weeks," says the literal Hebrew language of Daniel's prophecy, *"shall Messiah be cut off."* (Daniel 9:26) That is, ***after*** the full 62 week period of the sequence of events in the prophecy, shall Messiah die. ***During the 70th week***, in other words.

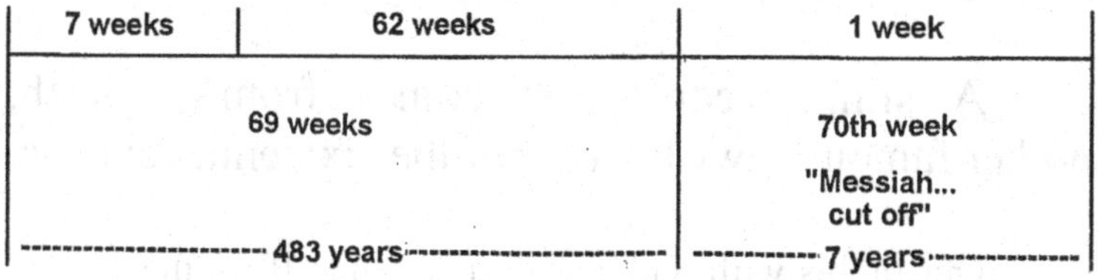
7 weeks
62 weeks
1 week
69 weeks
70th week
"Messiah...
cut off"
483 years
7 years

It does not tell us how soon "after". We need a specific phrase to place the timing of the event. We shall see, shortly, that the prophecy gives that timing in the next verse.

The expression **"CUT OFF"** implies that Messiah would not die a natural death; he would be murdered!

Isaiah's prophecy concurs

The prophet Isaiah spoke in similar terms regarding the coming Messiah. He will be

- *"despised and rejected"*,
- *"stricken"*,
- *"wounded"*,
- *"bruised"*,
- *"brought as a lamb to the slaughter"*,
- *"taken from prison and from judgment"* and
- ***"CUT OFF out of the land of the living"*****.** (Isaiah 53:3-8)

The majority of Jewish scholars understood this as a prophecy of the Messiah.

Concerning Isaiah chapter 53, the Jewish writer Abarbanel writes:

> Jonathan ben Uzziel interprets it in the Targum of the future Messiah; and this is also the opinion of our learned men in the majority of their midrashim. (cited by David L. Cooper, *Messiah: His Redemptive Career* Los Angeles: David L. Cooper, 1935, p.90)

A similar confession comes from Alshech, another famous Jewish writer of the sixteenth century:

> Our rabbis with one voice accept and affirm the opinion that the prophet [In Isaiah 52:13 to 53:12] is speaking of King Messiah. (*Ibid.*, p.90)

The eminent commentator David Baron wrote that:

> The Messianic interpretation of this chapter was almost universally adopted by Jews, ...one of whom says... that in truth 'it was given of God as a description of the Messiah, whereby, when any should claim to be the Messiah, to judge by the resemblance to it whether he were the Messiah or no. (*Ibid.*, p.90)

Many Jews would be amazed to find in their own prayer book this statement:

> Our righteous Anointed [Messiah] is departed from us: horror hath seized us, and we have none to justify us. He hath borne the yoke of our iniquities, and our transgression, and is ***wounded because of our transgression***. He beareth our sins on his shoulder, that he may find pardon for our iniquities. We shall be healed by his wound, at the time that the Eternal will create him [the Messiah] as a new creature. O bring him up from the circle of the earth. Raise him up from Seir, to assemble us the ***second time*** on Mount Lebanon, by the hand of Yinnon. *(Prayer Book for the Day of Atonement,* as translated by Dr. A. Th. Phillips, p.239. Bloch Publishing Company)

Did Jewish sages of old know all this concerning the Messiah when they wrote the prayer books? The answer is obvious. They must have known! ***They are citing Isaiah chapter 53***.

The clarity of this Isaiah prophecy is so anticipatory of the New Testament message concerning Yeshua that some of the Ashkenazi Jews

had this passage removed from their Scriptures. However, the Sephardic Jews retained it.

When the Dead Sea Scrolls were discovered in 1947, among the most prized treasures included was a complete scroll of Isaiah, and right there in it was this same chapter 53. You can see it for yourself if you visit Jerusalem, in the specially built Shrine of the Book, adjacent to the Israeli Museum.

Both Rabbi Yakov Rambsel and Grant Jeffrey describe how the complete phrase *Yeshua shmi* - "*Yeshua is my name*" - appears uniquely coded behind the text of Isaiah's Messiah prophecy in chapter 53. This full phrase occurs *only here*. (Yakov Rambsel, *Yeshua – The Hebrew Factor* and *His Name is Jesus*; Grant Jeffrey, *The Signature of God* and *The Handwriting of God.* All published by Frontier Research Publications, Toronto, Ontario, Canada, 1996 and 1997 respectively)

Yeshua is also encrypted in the heart of Daniel's chapter 9 Messiah prophecy. In fact, the name *Yeshua* appears to lie encrypted behind every major Messianic prophecy!

This code is quite another subject. Since it is not the foundation of my case, I shall neither submit it here as evidence nor go into it further at this point.

It is also significant that the actual name of the coming Messiah is found in the straight surface text of the Hebrew Bible. (See Chapter 24.)

To die on our behalf

Daniel prophesied that Messiah was to die ***"not for himself"***. (Daniel 9:26) He would not die for his own sins, but for those of others; it was to be a substitutionary death.

He told the prophet Isaiah to write that he was coming to die ***"for the transgression [sins] of my people"*** – to be "*wounded for **our** transgressions,*" *"bruised for **our** iniquities,"* so that we can be *"healed"*. (Isaiah 53:4,5,8)

*"... **and shall have nothing.**"* (Daniel 9:26 RSV; also expressed thus in the marginal reading of the King James Version.) — no people, no place, no recognition, no kingdom, no adherents. He shall be deprived of everything. Yeshua was crucified virtually alone and even stripped of his clothes.

"After 3½ years"

*In the **midst of the week [of the 7 years]** he shall cause the sacrifice... to cease.* (Daniel 9:27)

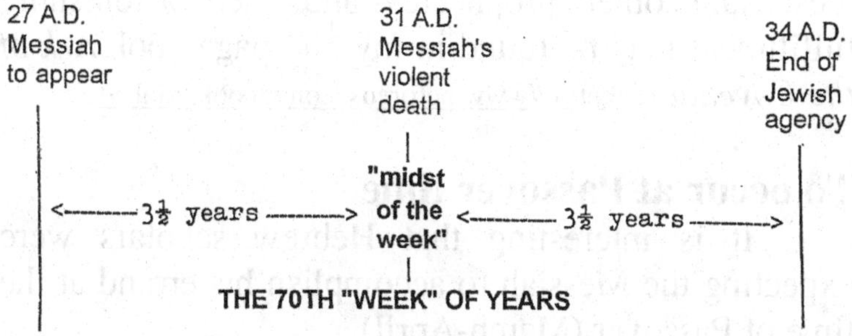

This is the final *"week"* of Daniel's prophecy. From Messiah's appearance to the time of his death would be half of the week, or 3½ years. And, as we have already seen, the disciple John, by recording the annual Passovers that Yeshua attended, provides evidence that three and a half years did indeed elapse between Yeshua's baptism and his crucifixion.

The fourth Passover came in the spring of 31 AD — just 3½ years after his first public appearance — just as the heavenly messenger Gabriel had indicated to the prophet Daniel.

I must agree with Merv Maxwell that "If Gabriel were an athlete instead of an angel, we would stand on our feet and cheer!" (Mervyn Maxwell, *God Cares,* Vol. 1. Mountain View, Ca.: Pacific Press, 1981)

Irrefutable evidences

Other Old Testament prophecies not only identified the year, but the month, the day and the hour in history when that event would occur.

* The year: AD 31
* The month: Nisan (March-April on the Gregorian calendar)
* The day: 14th
* The hour: 3 pm

A mountain of ***historical evidence*** concerning these and other prophecies and their astonishing fulfillment may be found in my 600 page book *Ark of the Covenant.* (<http://www.beforeus .com/abook.html >)

To occur at Passover time

It is interesting that Hebrew scholars were expecting the Messiah to accomplish his errand at the time of Passover (March-April).

The noted Jewish commentator Abrabanel states that

> ...during the month Nisan in which ***the messianic redemption is to occur***, the cup of Elijah ***at the Passover*** meal preserves in symbolism the idea that the new redemption will come during the same season as the exodus from Egypt. (Don Isaac Abrabanal, Commentary on the book of Daniel, titled *The Wells of Salvation* 1497)

Traditional Jewish observance of the annual ***Passover*** feast (*Seder shel pesahh*) is inextricably linked with the ***messianic*** idea. *Zman-heruteinu*, the name by which Passover is known among Jews, means that this is the season of freedom. How significant, when one considers that this event prefigured the Messiah who was to free the sinner from his chains.

Should we be surprised - or not - that other rabbinical writings suggest that during Nisan a much greater redemption will someday be accomplished by the God of heaven?

And that rabbinical tradition holds that Elijah will appear at ***Passover*** time and announce ***the coming of the Redeemer***?

A Jewish tradition expects Israel's ***messianic deliverance*** to be on 15th Nisan, the day after ***Passover:***

> On the same day, the fifteenth of Nisan [the day after Passover], Israel is to be redeemed, in the days of the Messiah, as they were redeemed on that day, as it is said, '*according to the days*'. (*Cabalistae apud Fagium in loc.* cf. Micah 7.15)

Now think carefully about this. Is this a bizarre coincidence, or what?:

Jewish Passover expectation

Firstly, consider the Hebrew understanding of Passover.

1. Hebrew scholars, from their study of the prophecies, expected the ***Messiah*** to bring salvation at the time of the ***Passover***. (*Cabalistae apud Fagium;* Abrabanal, *The Wells of Salvation*;)
2. The Passover service centered around a ***lamb*** that was to be ***sacrificed***. (Exodus12:1-6,11; Leviticus 23:4,5)
3. "In every sacrifice there is the idea of ***substitution***: the victim takes the place of the

human sinner." (*The Jewish Encyclopedia*, art., "Atonement, Day of")

4. Thus the Messiah would become the ***sacrificed "offering for sin"***. (Isaiah 53:8,10)
5. The sinner is thus ***redeemed*** from sin, ***freed*** from its penalty.
6. The time for the Messiah to die as a sacrifice: It will be at Passover.

Jewish Passover testimony

And what happened at Passover time, in AD 31? The man Yeshua ***was sacrificed***. And to this his enemies bear witness.

Is it just coincidence that this occurred at Passover? As the Jewish Babylonian *Sanhedrin*, from AD 95 – 110, testifies:

> ***On the eve of the Passover they hanged Yeshu*** [of Nazareth]…. He hath practised sorcery and beguiled and led astray Israel…. But they found naught in his defence and hanged him on the eve of Passover. (Babylonian *Sanhedrin* 43a – "Eve of Passover")

It surely occurred. And the crucifixion of Yeshua at the precise moment at which it was foretold to occur, has become a pivot of the world's history, just as his birth has become the central epoch of the world's dating reference.

The prophecy of Daniel 9 is irrefutable proof, ***mathematical evidence***, that Yeshua was who he said he was. Yeshua himself constantly appealed to the prophets as proof of his identity.

Prophecy: first, Messiah will die; after that, city and temple destroyed

Daniel prophesied that ***after*** Messiah dies violently (is "*cut off*"), a desolator would come to "*destroy the city and the sanctuary*" – the sanctuary (temple) being the very heart of the sacrificial system. (Daniel.9:26).

And so it was that, in 70 AD, the city and temple were destroyed; Judah lost her autonomy and national life; the scepter of ecclesiastical sway departed from Judah, and the Jewish people were banished from the Holy Land as a result of the wars of 70 and 135 CE. For nearly 2,000 years they became a scattered people.

Accidental coincidence? Not a chance. Accidental coincidence is a mathematical impossibility, even when a few of all the innumerable related factors are taken into account.

Would any honest, thinking person still want to tell us that there was nothing above and beyond mere human power and calculation here? That there was no potent presence of that Mind that knows the end of all things from the beginning? Show me one other historical personage who fulfills this prophecy. There is this one, and no other! As says Adam Clarke:

> The whole of this prophecy from the times and corresponding events has been fulfilled to the very letter. *(Clarke's Commentary)*

Bring sacrifice to an end

> *... he shall cause the sacrifice and the oblation to cease.* (Daniel 9:27)

How would Messiah bring the sacrificial system to an end? And why should he?

You will recall that for millennia there were men and women who anxiously awaited the coming Deliverer, and meanwhile the sacrifices of animals illustrated this belief.

Now Daniel is informed that the Messiah will be "cut off" — will die violently — "*but not for himself.*" Did this mean that the Messiah would die as the substitute sacrifice for the sins of mankind?

Would the Messiah, by his death, abolish the necessity for further sacrifice? Could it be that in the divine plan, Yeshua's death was ***the Sacrifice to end all sacrifices***?

One ex-member of that Jewish ruling body, the Sanhedrin, certainly believed so! Paul wrote that Yeshua's sacrifice "*in the flesh*" had abolished the "*ordinances*" for the sacrifice of animals in the flesh. (Ephesians 2:13- 15 Compare Hebrews 9:8-10)

Another coincidence or divine design?

According to the rescue plan, his sacrifice had terminated the significance of all sacrifices – forever. From now on, all Temple services were redundant. And that brings us to another "coincidence". ***The crucifixion of Yeshua occurred 40 years before*** the destruction of the Jewish Temple.

In the days of the Second Temple there was a custom to fasten a red-colored strip of wool to the head of a goat which was to be sent away on the Day of Atonement. When this red ribbon became white, it was a sign that God had forgiven Israel's sins.

There is a statement in the Talmud that about "***forty years before the Second Temple was destroyed***...the red wool did not become white!"

(Babylonian Talmud, Yoma chapter 39b.) The same passage informs us that the gates of the Temple swung open on their own accord! The ancient rabbis believed that these events were indicators that the sins of Israel were no longer being forgiven and the Temple would soon be destroyed! (Arthur Kac, *The Messianic Hope,* p. 227)

What was the reason for these strange events? Why was this God-given sign of forgiveness removed? Was the Levitical system of atoning for sins through animal sacrifice no longer recognized by God?

Two events in history had virtually synchronised:

1. Yeshua's sacrifice, which he claimed would provide forgiveness to all who would accept it.
2. The red wool stopped turning white, interpreted by the rabbis as indicating no more forgiveness. (They had rejected Yeshua's offer).

Coincidence – or something more?

Condescended to be one of us

Here comes the only one in all history who claimed that he actually chose to be born into this world. Because this is beyond our own limited experience, it is a great mystery that the Creator himself would come to join his creatures. But he tells us it is so.

Rescue mission

If it be true, then talk about AMAZING! This is the most amazing fact of all. Here is what the prophecies say: The great God, ruler of the universe, LOVES us – poor, erring men, women and children – so much that HE PROMISED TO GIVE all that He could to buy us back and make us whole again. He was ready to GIVE HIMSELF in the person of his Son. And He would take the penalty of the broken law upon Himself so that we could be pardoned.

Hearing the cries of His suffering people, the Prince of God was stirred with pity. Nothing was to be desired while man was an outcast, without hope.

So He planned to lay off His royal majesty and step down from His high command over the galaxies, to take upon Himself feeble human flesh.

Now the plan is activated…

The Prince of God enters this enemy territory to save mankind. He will live and suffer with us. He would be targeted for assassination as a human baby and subjected to eleven recorded attempts on his life during his 3½ year ministry. Then he would show by his example how to overcome the Legion of Lucifer.

What humility was this! It stunned the universe.

He humbled Himself to become one of us – and that must have been about as attractive as if we were to become a rat or a slug! The indescribably mighty Lord shrinks Himself to become a fertilized egg in a girl's womb. Nothing less, is the claim. And He did this, among other things, to show human beings what He is like and how much He loves them.

Our free choice

There is pathos in his love letter to us. Firstly, He reveals himself as *"**merciful** and **gracious**, **longsuffering**, and abundant in goodness and truth, Keeping mercy for thousands, forgiving iniquity, and transgression and sin, and that will by no means clear the guilty."* (Exodus 34:6,7)

Then He appeals to us: *"Cast away all your transgressions… and make a new heart and a new spirit: **for why will you die**?"* (Ezekiel 18:31)

He loves every person in the world. That's why He allows each of us free choice.

Who is really keeping this from us?

As you have noticed by now, the Bible does indeed claim to reveal the good news of this Deliverer. And it ***exposes the Legion of Lucifer as a bunch of deceivers***.

Might this explain why this document, more than any other on Planet Earth, has become the focus of such fierce attacks? Especially is this so with the book of Genesis, the section which reports on the Creation and the Fall. (You see, if there has been no Fall, then there is no need of rescue. Our enemy gets us thinking that way, and he has won against us. We are lost.)

So was the theory of evolution ***engineered*** by these same malicious forces simply to discredit the book in the minds of the masses, ***so that millions would reject rescue***? Was Darwin an unwitting pawn in their hands?

It is noteworthy that many well-meaning but pathetically ignorant church leaders have also fallen for the deception. To avoid open conflict with the academic community, theological colleges have retreated under the onslaught of the evolutionists' propaganda. Cowardly behaviour.

Think about this carefully. If there were no Fall, then there is no need for a Rescuer. But – amazingly – it is the very one offering rescue who is, above anyone else, ***spurned*** in our world today.

No wonder the ***Bible*** has become ***central to the "alien" phenomenon***! These so-called aliens are obsessed with the Bible more than any other religious book. They quote it when it suits them. Yet they put it down as being fraudulently written. Yes, these so-called "space brothers" ***especially*** teach New Age philosophy, ***deny Christianity and support the occult***. When you know who they really are, it explains everything.

Rabbis: "Yeshua is Messiah"

As a result of the ***evidence***, many conscientious Jewish scholars have reached the conclusion that Yeshua is, indeed, the Messiah. (See Risto Santala, *The Messiah in the Old Testament in the Light of Rabbinical Writings*, and *The Messiah in the New Testament in the Light of Rabbinical Writings*; Keren Ahvah Meshihi, Jerusalem, 1992; Mark Eastman, *The Search for the Messiah*, California, 1993)

Other rabbis: "Cursed be it!"

Daniel the prophet! "Read him," said Yeshua. "No," said the rabbis. "We'll place a curse on you." And here, again, is their curse:

> MAY HIS BONES & HIS MEMORY ROT WHO SHALL ATTEMPT TO NUMBER THE SEVENTY WEEKS.

And in the Talmud this curse is recorded:

> Rabbi Samuel B. Nahmani said: "Blasted be the bones of those who calculate the end.[6] (Note 6: i.e. Messiah's advent) For they would say, since the predetermined time has arrived, and yet he has not come, he will never come." (Talmud Sanhedrin 97-b, translated in the Babylonian Talmud ed. by Isidore Epstein. 35 vol. London: The Soncino Press Ltd, 1935-1952, p.659)

This statement from the Talmud says:

> The Targum of the Prophets was composed by Jonathan ben Uzziel ... He further sought to reveal by a targum [the inner meaning] of the Hagiographa, but a Bath Kol went forth and said, Enough! What was the reason? -Because the date of the Messiah is foretold in it. *(Megillah* 3a, pp.9,10 Soncino Press)

Footnote 2 on p.10 says:

> The reference is probably to the Book of Daniel.

Now ask an historian who was an ***eyewitness*** at the destruction of Jerusalem, "Josephus, what do you think about the prophecy of Daniel?"

Listen to his reply:

> Daniel also wrote concerning the Roman government, and that our country should be made desolate by them. All these things did this man leave in writing, as God had showed them to him, insomuch, that such as read his prophecies, and see how they have been fulfilled, would wonder at the honor wherewith God honored Daniel. (Josephus, Flavius *Antiquities of the Jews* Vol. 2, Bk. 10, ch.11, sect.7)

PART SIX

THE RESCUER'S NAME

24

The Rescuer's name -

WAS HIS NAME FORETOLD?

Alexander the Great once learned that in the ranks of his army was a soldier also named Alexander. But this man was a coward in battle and a thief among his companions.

Alexander sent for Alexander the soldier.

"Your name is Alexander?"

"Yes, sir."

"You are a man of ill repute in the army?"

The man admitted he was.

"You go from here," ordered the king, "and amend your ways, or change your name."

In ancient times, the meaning of a person's name was considered particularly important. The biblical Lamech, for example, called his son Noah (meaning ***Comfort***), saying *"This same shall **comfort** us..."* (Genesis 5:29) Eber named his firstborn son *Peleg* (meaning ***Division***), *"for in his days was the earth **divided.**"* (Genesis 10:25)

The patriarch *Jacob*'s name was changed to ***Israel***, meaning ***"God's Prince"***, to denote a change of character.

Did you know, ***the coming Messiah's very name*** is predicted in the ***plain surface text*** of the Hebrew Scriptures (the Old Testament)?

Yeshua = Salvation, deliverance

The New Testament writer Matthew records a heavenly messenger's visit to a Jewish man Joseph, concerning the coming birth of a child:

> *And...thou shalt call his name SALVATION* [*YESHUA* - same word]: *for he shall save his people from their sins.* (Matthew 1:21)

Thus the baby was given the Hebrew name YESHUA. The meaning of this name was important – because it indicated his predicted role.

Yeshua (Yahushua) means ***"the Lord saves."*** It is a combination of the name YAWH (*the Eternal One*) and the Hebrew root YASHA.

YASHA is related to an Arabic word, "to make wide," "to make sufficient" – as contrasted with TSARAR (meaning "narrow"). Wideness came to denote "freedom" or "safety", which led to the root YASHA (meaning "to be delivered to a position of freedom or safety").

The Jewish scholar's challenge

Arthur Glass was a Jew who was convinced Yeshua was the promised Messiah. Glass lived in the United States.

One spring day in St. Louis, he met a fellow Jew in the home of a mutual friend. The conversation gravitated to the subject of Yeshua (Jesus).

And the other Jewish man flung at Arthur Glass this challenge:

"If Yeshua is our Messiah, and ***the whole Tenach [Old Testament] is about him,*** how come his name is never mentioned in it even once?"

"But it is," responded Arthur.

"Rubbish. I'm a Hebrew Scholar. And I tell you, you ***can't*** find the name of ***Yeshua*** in the Old Testament."

Arthur paused for an instant. Then he bent down, opened his briefcase and took out his Hebrew Bible.

"My friend," he said, "would you translate into English the passage of Isaiah 62:11, for me?"

The Jewish scholar did so with the utmost ease. He translated rapidly and correctly. And this was his translation of the text, verbatim:

> *Behold, Yahweh has proclaimed unto the end of the world, Say ye to the daughter of Zion, Behold thy YESHUA cometh; behold, his reward is with him, and his work before him.*

Immediately he crimsoned. It dawned on him what he had done. He fairly screamed out, "No! No! You made me read it 'thy YESHUA', Mr Glass! You tricked me!"

"No, I did not trick you," was the reply. "I just had you read the Word of God for yourself. Can't you see that here SALVATION is a Person and not a thing or an event? **HE** comes, **HIS** reward is with **HIM**, and **HIS** work before **HIM**."

The other man rushed to open his own Old Testament. He was talking frantically as he did so. "I'm sure mine is different from yours."

He found the passage, looked it over, and dropped like a deflated balloon. His Hebrew Bible was, of course, identical.

And there it is in the Hebrew Bible (the Tenakh):

ישוע

Save us from what?

Yeshua means ***salvation***, because it indicates the Messiah's predicted role: "*the Lord saves.*"

So from what does he come to save us?
Here's the answer in Ezekiel:

* *They will no longer defile themselves with their idols and vile images or with any of their offenses, for I will SAVE them from* ***where they sinned****, and I will cleanse them. They will be my people, and I will be their God.* (Ezekiel 37:23)

Again:

* *Save me* ***from bloodguilt****, O God, the God who saves me, and my tongue will sing of your righteousness.* (Psalm 51:14)
* *Help us, O God, our SAVIOUR, for the glory of your name deliver us and forgive* ***our sins****, for your name's sake.* (Psalm 79:9)

Indeed, SALVATION is portrayed as a means of HEALING THE EFFECTS OF SIN IN OUR LIFE and our relationship with God:

* *HEAL me, O Lord, and I will be healed; SAVE me and I will be saved, for you are the one I praise.* (Jeremiah 17:14)

Jeremiah also specifies that God's chosen agent to "SAVE" His people is the Messiah. (Jeremiah 23:6)

The ***divine choice of Yeshua as the name for the Messiah*** has an ironclad logic. After all,

* Salvation comes only from the Lord.
* The Messiah is the one through whom God accomplishes our salvation.

No wonder, then, that the heavenly messenger told Joseph: "*You are to give him the name Yeshua – salvation – because he will save his people from their sins.*"

And the record adds that salvation is found in no one else apart from God's appointed Messiah. "*There is* ***no other name*** *under heaven given to men by which we must be saved.*" (Acts 4:12)

Every time the Old Testament uses the word **SALVATION** (especially with the Hebrew suffix meaning my, thy or his), with very few exceptions (when the word is impersonal), it is the very same Hebrew word YESHUA.

Yeshua in the plain surface text

In the Hebrew Scriptures, the expected Messiah is referred to as Yeshua. The name YESHUA is found about 100 times ***in the plain surface text*** all the way from Genesis to Habakkuk! Yes, the very word — the very NAME — that the angel Gabriel used when he told Mary about the Son she was to have. (Luke 1:31)

For example, in Isaiah 12:2 we read: "*Behold, God is my salvation (yeshu'ah).*" (For an excellent discussion on this subject, see *The 490 Year Prophecy,* by S. Howard SAN Enterprises Inc., P0 Box 623,Thorsby, AL 35171, USA. Also Arthur E. Glass, *Yeshua in the Tenach.* Cincinnati, Ohio: Messianic Literature Outreach, P.O. Box 37062)

In Habakkuk (in a prayer concerning the future), we read literally from the original Hebrew:

*Thou wentest forth with the **Yesha** [a variant of **Yeshua**] of [or for] thy people; with **Yeshua thy Messiah** [thine Anointed One] thou woundest the head of the house of the wicked one [Satan].* (Habakkuk 3:13)

Here you have it!... for the Deliverer who shall wound the head of the house of Satan… This refers back to the first messianic prophecy ever given, concerning the Coming One who will wound Satan's head. (Genesis 3:15)

Here you see the very same NAME that is given in the New Testament – ***Yeshua thy Messiah***!

As it is, nearly all Jewish commentators, with isolated exceptions, receive this Genesis prophecy as real history, and agree that the prophecy was messianic in character.

For example, notice this commentary on the Genesis prophecy:

> The Messiah shall restore the good state of the universe which is disturbed by the fall of man. *(Bereshith Rabba,* Ch. xii; *Bamidbar Rabba,* ch.xiii; Targum, Jer. i on Gen.3:15)

The Old Testament was written in the Hebrew language. The name ***Jesus*** in Hebrew is ***Yeshua (Y'shua),*** or ***Yashua.***

The New Testament was written in Koine Greek, because, in the Roman Empire of the first century, Greek was the international common language. The Hebrew name ***Yeshua*** came into Greek as ***Iesous*** because the Greeks did not have a Y or a SH in their language. Then it went into Roman as ***Iesus***, and later into English as ***Jesus.*** However, in the land of Israel where Jesus lived, his family would have called him ***Yeshua***.

Yeshua in the Jewish prayer book

As a matter of fact, even in the Jewish Prayer Book it is written:

> May it be Thy will that the sounds of the Shofar [ram's horn] which we have sounded today be woven into Thy tapestry ***Yeshua, the Prince*** of Thy presence and Prince of might. So mayest Thou receive our pleas and extend to us Thy compassion. (*Prayer Book for the New Year.* Translated by Dr A. Th. Phillips, revised and enlarged, p. 100. Hebrew Publishing Company)

Huh? In the Jewish Prayer Book? How did the sages who wrote the Prayer Book know that the name of the MESSIAH was ***Yeshua*** (***Jesus***), as quoted in the *Mahsor* for the New Year? The answer is that they understood what the Bible teaches concerning the Messiah.

Moreover, on the same page of the Prayer Book is this prayer to God:

> May He appear ***the second time***.

Why did the Hebrew sages write that? Evidently, because ***he already came once*** (though most of the Jewish people are oblivious to it).

Let us remember that among the Hebrew sages were many honest men who knew and wrote truth. And there were others who were not so honest. "May he appear the second time." That some did know the prophecies is evident. Though they wrote honestly knowing that the MESSIAH had to come during the time of the Second Temple, yet, because of prevalent prejudice, they may not have known the true identity of the MESSIAH.

Yet he came — and at the precise time foretold by Daniel. And he fulfilled the predicted messianic role.

Here is another statement in the *Jewish Sabbath and Festival Prayer Book:*

> Hear O Israel, the Lord our God. The Lord is one. He is our God, He is our Father, He is our King, He is our Redeemer. And in His mercy we will hear from Him ***twice*** before the presence of all living beings, and He will be our God. (Rabbi Morris Silverman, Editor, *Sabbath and Festival Prayer Book,* p.139. USA:The Rabbinical Assembly of America and the United Synagogue of America - Conservative Judaism - Jan. 1980)

The key word is *sheynit* (which in Isaiah 11:11 is translated "twice" or "the second time"). This word can only mean "two times" – and clearly alludes to the fact that ***the Messiah comes two times.***

First he comes as "***messianic prophet***". (cf. Deuteronomy 18:15 ff.) The second time, he comes as "***messianic king***". (Isaiah 9:6,7) Do you see?

The words of this prayer are repeated every Monday and Thursday after the 18 benedictions during *Shachrit* before the *Torah* is brought out of the Ark. They are also recited during the *Musaf* service on *Shabat* after the *Torah* is placed back into the Ark.

It seems that Bible prophecies were speaking of the Messiah as fulfilling a dual role:

1. Messiah must come first as God's suffering servant to die in behalf of his people.
2. At a much later time, "*in the end of days*" (Hosea 3:5), he would come to establish and reign over his everlasting, universal kingdom on earth.

25

The Rescuer's name -

WAS HIS NAME EVEN ENCODED?

Is it possible that the name ***Yeshua*** appears ***not only*** in the plain surface text of the Old Testament, but is ***also encoded*** below the surface?

Let me say up front, however, that our case is rock solid without what follows in this chapter. In other words, what I shall now share with you is not offered as proof – but you might call it ***the icing on the cake.***

In 1994, scholars at the Hebrew University and Jerusalem College of Technology announced they had discovered a hidden code in the Bible that appeared to reveal the details of events that took place thousands of years after the Bible was written.

You may have already heard of this code. It was discovered by Dr Eliyahu Rips, a world expert mathematician in quantum physics. It was later confirmed by famous mathematicians at Yale, Harvard and Hebrew University and replicated by a senior code-breaker at the United States Department of Defence.

The "skipping" code

This sub-surface code was discovered in the original language version of the Old Testament, that is, the Hebrew. Hidden under the plain surface text, was found information in the form of equidistant letter sequences. That is to say, letters spaced at regular, equal distances throughout the text spelled out words containing another message.

Allegedly, so intricate, complex and clever is this code that it was found only with the help of computers.

The amount of information encoded into a limited text - in which the same arrangement of letters can contain multiple meanings - would be beyond the capacity of any individual (or group) to create, whatever computing resources are available.

These are highly sophisticated word games – quite invisible without a computer.

Can you imagine a book constructed with several different layers of coded information hidden under the text… each layer independent of the other and each complete in itself?

Isaiah chapter 53 is a ***prophecy of*** the promised ***Messiah***. The text of Isaiah 53:10 says:

> *But it was the will of YHWH [Yahweh, the Eternal One] to crush Him and to put Him to grief; and though YHWH makes His life a* ***guilt offering****, He will see His offspring [those who are rescued by Him], and prolong His days, and the will of YHWH will prosper in His hand.*

That is the plain surface message.

But ***encoded*** at 20-letter intervals through the text of this Messiah prophecy is the message,

> *"Yeshua Shmi"* (***Yeshua is my Name***).

Both Rabbi Yakov Rambsel and Grant Jeffrey describe how this full phrase occurs *only here.* (Yakov Rambsel, *Yeshua – The Hebrew Factor* and *His Name is Jesus*; Grant Jeffrey, *The Signature of God* and *The Handwriting of God.* All published by Frontier Research Publications, Toronto, Ontario, Canada, 1996 and 1997 respectively)

Now, just try to get your head around this: The chances of that expression, ***Yeshua is my Name***, being encoded beneath the surface of that particular verse, by accident, is ***one in a billion***.

That's only one tiny chance in 1,000,000,000!

Can you grasp that?

Some critic will point out that "even if Yeshua is hidden in the text of Isaiah 53, that does not mean it is referring to the person known as Jesus. Yeshua is quite a common name."

With this criticism in his mind, Rambsel, a Jewish scholar, dug deeper into the prophecy of the Messiah in Isaiah chapter 53. And what his search uncovered was breathtaking!

In just those 15 verses from Isaiah 52:13 to 53:12 he discovered the Hebrew names of 43 people and phrases, ***all connected with the Person and death of Yeshua (the Jesus of history).*** They were sitting there, encoded at various intervals, left to right, or right to left.

> Y'shua… Nazarene… Messiah… Shiloh… Galilee… The disciples… Peter… Simon… John…Matthew… Andrew…Philip…James… Thomas… Simon… Matthias… Thaddaeus… Joseph… Mary (encoded 3 times – there were 3 Marys at the crucifixion of Jesus)…Moriah.. His cross…Let him be crucified… Passover… Atonement – lamb... Bread… Wine… Seed… Water… Obed… Jesse… Herod… Caesar… Pilate… Annas… Caiaphas… Levites… The evil Roman Empire… From Zion… Lamp of the Lord… His signature…

The odds of these 43 people and phrases linked to the life and death of Yeshua all appearing clustered here by chance in this brief messianic prophecy are in the octillions! (Well beyond googleplex). In other words, it is not an accident! This prophecy is definitely and deliberately referring to Jesus Christ – and written 700 years before the event.

Coded into Daniel 9

Yeshua – Jesus – is also encrypted in the heart of Daniel's chapter 9 Messiah prophecy.

In that prophecy of Daniel 9:26 which says ***in the plain text surface message,*** "***Messiah*** *shall be cut off* [killed]," what do we find again but this very same name ***encoded beneath the surface***: ***Yeshua!***

It says quite plainly ***Yeshua Messiah***… ***Jesus Christ***! Right there in a prophecy of the Deliverer written 600 years before the event.

Coded into all Messianic prophecies

According to Yacov Rambsel, ***Yeshua*** is encoded ***in virtually every major Messianic prophecy*** of the Deliverer in the Old Testament. He has written a 264 page book on the discovery. (Yacov Rambsel, *His Name is Jesus: The Mysterious Yeshua Codes.* See also, Yacov Rambsel, *Yeshua. The Name of Jesus Revealed in the Old Testament.* Tulsa, USA: Frontier Research Publications, 1996)

Let's repeat that. Beneath the surface, the appearances of the name ***Yeshua*** are found ***especially clustered*** around the ***Messianic prophecies***. Are you grasping what this all means?

The "sevens" factor

We have already noted the astonishing design of interlocking ***7s (sevens)*** found throughout the Bible. Like wheels within wheels, this pattern is woven together ***below*** the surface, in every conceivable way. (And more is to come in later chapters.)

But we might note in passing that this same amazing pattern is especially attached to the name ***Yeshua!*** For example, in the Torah (the five books of Moses), at least 12 times ***Yeshua*** is encoded ***at precisely 7000-letter intervals***. (Not 6997 or 7001… but always 7000 exactly!)

The prophecy of the coming Messiah was also encapsulated in the Hebrew Passover, which centered upon the sacrifice of a lamb. (See Chapter 23 of this present work.) Exodus 12:27 speaks of this Passover ritual. Beginning here, we find three significant words encoded:

* Starting with the last letter of the fifth word, and reading the last letter of each subsequent word, we find *ha'rachel* (***the Lamb***) spelt out.
* At five-letter intervals, the word *Mashiach* (***Messiah***) ppears. (In biblical numerics, the number 5 denotes "grace" - the undeserved mercy of God).
* And also, starting in this verse, the name *Yeshua* (***Jesus***) is spelt out ***at 777-letter intervals. 7-7-7.*** How more perfect could it get?

Oh yes, and something else. As already noted, in Hebrew and Greek, ***each letter*** of the alphabet also ***doubles as a number*** (just as in Latin, v equals 5; x is 10; c is 100, and so on). By adding up the numeric value of each letter in a Hebrew word, you get a numeric value for that word.

The name *Yeshua* is composed of four Hebrew consonents, YOD, SHIN, WAW, AYIN. (Y-Sh-W-A)

ישוע

The total numeric value of the four letters of Yeshua is **386.** And – just get this – twelve times in the Torah, that name *Yeshua* is spelt out at **386**-letter intervals.

Has Yeshua placed his signature on every page of his written Word, like a barely visible watermark on a bank note?

* * * * * * *

Among the nations

Without a shadow of doubt, the message of the Promised One was also known to the nations of the world – ***each nation independently of*** the other. They testified that they had inherited this knowledge from the same great father from whom all were descended. This was ***outside the Bible*** and other sources derived from the biblical text. They knew that:

- Originally this was a perfect world with no suffering.
- There had been a rebellion in the heavens.
- Man had followed the rebels and had himself fallen.
- The Curer of all ills was coming to restore man.
- He was to appear in Judea. He has a Hebrew name.
  (References are given in the respective chapters of this current work. The next two chapters will give further examples.)

On this, we shall see more in the next two chapters. However, it would be appropriate to find among the Hebrews a fuller revelation (such as we discover in the Bible), since through that branch of the human race he was to make his appearance. And logically such a source should carry more weight.

26

The Rescuer's name -

OTHERS KNEW THE COMING ONE'S NAME

Among the numerous popular fallacies we've been taught is that the Druids of Britain were pagans who practised human sacrifice. This propaganda was deliberately promoted by their Roman enemies, to defame a gentle people they could neither coerce nor conquer.

Would it surprise you to know that in pre-Christian times the Druidic universities were the largest in the world? Yes, both in size and attendance. Records from that time list sixty large universities, with an average attendance of over 60,000 students. (Gildas, *Cottonian Ms*. See also Morgan, *History of Britain*, pp.62-65) This fact is substantiated both by Greek and Roman testimony. Records affirm that the noble and wealthy of Rome and other nations sent their children to Britain to study law, science and religion.

Integrity of Druid faith

Examination of the ground around and under the altar at Stonehenge by the eminent archaeologist Sir Flinders Petrie has completely demolished the human sacrifice accusations. His discovery of only the fossilized bones of sheep and goats established, rather, the affinity of the Druid religion with the patriarchal Hebrew faith. In each case the sacrificial burnt offerings were the same as those stated in the biblical record.

Organized by a man called Hu Gadam (Hugh the Mighty), the faith took on the name of Druid. Some claim that the term ***'Druid'*** is derived from the Keltic word 'Dreus', meaning 'an oak', from their custom of worshipping in the open within the oak groves of the island. However, it is more likely derived from ***'Druthin'***, which means ***'Servant of Truth'***. The motto of the Druids was, in fact, 'The Truth against the World'.

Druids awaited the Messiah

The Druid Triads emphasised the omniscience of One God, the coming of the Messiah and life beyond the grave. They believed that the Coming One would sacrifice his life to atone for each man's sins.

They looked for the coming of a "Curer of all ills", who was symbolised by the emblem of the mistletoe – which was identical to the coming "Branch" of which Israel's prophets spoke.

That harmonises well with a statement made by an arch-Druid of the early Christian days, named Taliesin:

> Christ, the Word from the beginning, was from the beginning our teacher, and we never lost His teaching. Christianity was a new thing in Asia, but there never was a time when the Druids of Britain held not its doctrines. (Frederick Haberman, *Tracing Our Ancestors*, p.88)

Research now suggests that the Druids, simultaneously with the wise men of Persia, discovered in the sky the Star of Prophecy, which heralded the long-expected One who was to lighten the world – that same "Star" that, according to a Bible prophecy was to "arise out of Jacob". (Numbers 24:17)

And now – are you sitting down? – here is a discovery even more astonishing: Not only did the pre-Christian Druids know of the coming Messiah. His actual name was known to them – hundreds of years before Jesus Christ even appeared! It was a name familiar on the lips of every Briton. This has astounded students of theology.

They knew the Coming One's name.

In the ancient Celtic Triads this was recorded:

The Lord our God is One.
Lift up your heads, O ye gates, and be
Ye lift up, ye everlasting doors, and the
King of Glory shall come in.
Who is the King of Glory? The Lord ***Yesu;***
He is the King of Glory. (George F. Jowett,
The Drama of the Lost Disciples, p.7. Emphasis added)

There it is, as easy to see as your hand. The Druidic priesthood knew the name ***'Yesu'*** ('Jesus') hundreds of years BC. This name ***'Yesu'*** was incorporated in the Druidic Godhead. In Britain the name ***'Jesus'*** was always the pure Celtic ***'Yesu'***. It never changed. (Procopius, *De Gothici, bk. 3*)

Druidism's influence on the ancient world, as well as its peaceful and ready reception of the Christian faith, proves its noble structure. Druidism prepared the way for Christianity in Britain.

27

The Rescuer's name -

ANCIENT STAR CHARTS RECORDED HIS NAME

This is ***not*** about astrology. It is the archaeology of the ancient star maps.

Just as all nations once shared a ***common language*** (For evidence, see my book *The Corpse Came Back*, chapter 8), likewise all nations had ***an original zodiac*** derived from a ***common source***.

Very early in human history, the stars were named and arranged into groups (constellations) and drawn on sky charts as pictures of animals, people and other objects. Significantly, the same names and figures are consistent throughout history and throughout the cultures of the world. And they have survived on astronomical charts to this day.

These constellations extend in a belt about 16 degrees wide, encircling the earth. If the stars could be seen in daytime, the sun would appear to move through this belt in the course of the year, in a path called the ecliptic. It is this belt, with 12 months for its steps or stages, that we call the ***zodiac*** (not from the Greek "*life*" as is commonly supposed, but from a more ancient Hebrew word meaning "*a way by steps*").

Each stage of the yearly cycle contains its own group of stars designated by a picture, or sign. These are the ***12 signs*** of the zodiac. Each sign is accompanied by 3 more adjacent signs, called ***decans*** (***pieces***), which explain the main sign. This makes a numbered and well-ordered set of ***48 signs*** (12 groups of 4). (Actually there are 88 constellations in all, but only 48 lie within the band across the sky known as the zodiac.)

The world has looked in vain for the origin of these hieroglyphics. Current attempts to guess the zodiac's origin are amusingly absurd, with no supporting fact. The various theories and why they are not valid, are covered in my book *Sting of the Scorpion*. (<www.beforeus.com/shopcart_ebook.html>)

There is ***evidence*** that the most ancient peoples uniformly acknowledged the star pictures and names as sacred in meaning - a pictorial scientific coordinate system which told a story.

So many of us have assumed that star signs were invented to tell peoples' fortunes through the stars. However, the ***historical evidence*** shows that in the earliest times, star sign hieroglyphics had nothing to do with astrology. They are much, much older than astrology. Of 48 zodiac signs, astrology later hijacked 12.

According to Hugh Thurston, the constellations have been scientifically dated at least to about 2700, and a latitude of 36° north (Hugh Thurston, *Early Astronomy*. New York: Springer-Verlag, 1994, pp. 135-137), but there is evidence that they are even older.

As you may already know, each year the stars rise and set some 50.2 seconds later. In 2,156 years they fall back 30 degrees. It has been calculated that when the earliest zodiac sphere was drawn, the position of the stars in relation to earth was almost 90 degrees different from now. The Southern Cross was visible in the Northern Hemisphere from 40 degrees N. latitude; Alpha in Draco was the North Pole Star; Taurus opened the equinoctial year in March; and the summer solstice was in the first degree of Virgo –

about 4000 BC. And other supporting testimony comes from the ancient world. (Flavius Josephus, Book I, chs.1-3; Jonathan Gray, *Modern Religious Myths About Genesis*, pp.26-29)

Names and signs basically unaltered

The Arabs are among the greatest astronomers and historians this world has seen. Albamazer, astronomer for the Caliphs of Granada, speaking of these constellation signs, says that:

> ***None*** of these forms ***from their first invention*** have varied in coming down to us, nor one of their words [names] ***changed***, not a point added or removed. (Albamazer, *Flores Astrologias.* Written in Arabic and translated into Hebrew by Aben Ezra. A Latin translation is in the British Museum Library. Emphasis added.)

Did you get that? The star maps of his day – about 850 AD – and which are in use today, have ***basically never been altered*** since their origin thousands of years ago. They ***were essentially the same as now***. Not only the ***names***, but also the ***figures*** drawn around these groups of stars, have remained basically the same. There are, to this rule, a few exceptions – which can be traced. (Jonathan Gray, *Sting of the Scorpion*, pages 44, 45).

The star maps recorded a prophecy

When you translate the constellation and star names into English (according to the best lexicons and philological authorities) you get meanings such as these:

- "the serpent of Eve" (ancient Persian name for the Hydra constellation)

- "the coming lamb to be slain" (ancient Arabic name for the star sign Lupus, also called Victima)
- "the enemy of the coming" (the Arabic name Arnebeth, for Lepus)
- "the sacrifice slain" (The star Al Dibah, in Capricornus)
- "bruised in the heel" (star name in Aquila)
- "who comes to save" (meaning of the Egyptian name for Taurus)
- "the pierced; the slain" (Arabic star name El Nath, in Aries)
- "the coming judge" (Denebola, star name in Leo; Deneb, star name in Cygnus)
- "this one comes to reign" (Per-ku-hor, Egyptian name for Cepheus)
- "the Serpent bruiser" (Egyptian Fent-Har, star in Ursa Major)
- "rejoicing over the Serpent" (Egyptian Shes-en-Fent, name for Argo)
- "the punished deceiver" (Arabic star name Minchir al Sugia, in Hydra)
- "Satan's head" (Hebrew star name Rosh Satan, in Perseus)

…and so on.

So unlikely are such names for stars or groups of stars, that the question naturally arises, Was there a deeper meaning intended? Was there some message portrayed in the star maps?

It turns out that these 48 ancient pictures with their hundreds of star names were carefully chosen and set ***in sequence*** to tell a story. According to the ancients, they depicted ***an important prophecy.***

And this ***same star chart story*** was known across ***the whole ancient world*** – separately among the different nations.

So, what was this prophecy? It was about a coming Deliverer. The ancient civilizations believed that a serpent (representing the Devil) had taken control of the earth. They believed that a virgin's baby would fight the serpent, defeat him and bring life, peace and happiness back to mankind.

Hieroglyphic pictures on the maps showed this. So here we have star maps thousands of years old, overlaid with pictures and names – and predicting a world Deliverer!

The promised rescue

A clue to what the star charts are saying is found in this ancient cryptic prophecy, dated about 4000 BC:

> [There will be] *enmity between Satan* [symbolised by the Serpent] *and the **woman's Seed**. He [the woman's seed] will **bruise the Serpent's head*** [ultimately destroy Satan]. *But,* Satan will ***bruise his heel*** [wound him]. (Genesis.3:15)

Carefully researching these star maps, I discovered no less than 116 absolute parallels between (a) these star messages and (b) prophecies in the Hebrew Scriptures concerning a coming Deliverer. Both sources told the same, identical story – from beginning to end… the prophecy of a Messiah who would come to rescue men and woman of Planet Earth.

In the star sign ***pictures***, the ***parallels with the Scriptures*** become striking, such as the Fishes (common symbol for the followers of God) being bound by the "bands of death" to the Sea Monster, with the Ram's (Lamb's) leg apparently breaking those bands. Every picture symbol is paralleled in the Bible. ***None of this imagery depends on the star name translations.*** Another example is the "Healer", bruised in the foot, restraining the serpent which reaches for the crown of rulership.

The 48 signs (not 12) commence with Virgo and her child (the woman's "Seed" in the book of Genesis) and end with Leo (the "Lion" of Revelation) – in the same sequence as the Bible. The synchronisation between the Bible and the star charts, of both words and symbols, is amazing. (See the step by step details in my books *Sting of the Scorpion* and *Modern Religious Myths About Genesis*, Chapter 2.)

Recorded on the sky maps

And so it was that on the star maps, over the stars of the Virgo constellation, was superimposed a picture of a "virgin" with a child in her arms - the virgin-born Messiah who will come to deliver mankind.

Here let me stress that this concept did ***not*** originate with the religions of India, China, the Americas, Europe or Egypt. It ***already existed*** BEFORE they emerged.

The same meaning worldwide

Despite their later differences of language, the nations of the world inherited this prophecy. The ***meanings*** of the star symbols remained virtually the ***same*** among the nations. A coincidence? Not on your life!

Consider that group of stars known as ***Virgo***. The hieroglyphic for this constellation is the picture of a woman. But not just any woman… she is a virgin.

This star group was called:

- *Virgo* by the Romans
- *Bethulah* by the Hebrews
- *Parthenos* by the Greeks
- *Kanya* by the Indians.

And every one of these names means "VIRGIN".

You may well ask, Why a virgin? Why not just a woman? There is surely no reason on earth to specify that a group of stars is a "virgin" in preference to a "woman" –unless there already existed some deeper reason for calling this woman a virgin. And if we ask the ancients to explain this, they will tell us they were expecting the coming Deliverer ***to be the "seed" of a virgin.***

And so we find that in this constellation Virgo, the brightest star is ***Spica***, a Latin word which means ***"Seed".*** But, long before that, the Hebrews called it ***Zerah*** which also means ***"Seed".*** The ***various languages each have similar star name meanings.*** The "seed" of the virgin – not the seed of a man. In other words, a child conceived without an earthly father. That's the prophecy.

A common origin

The sameness of meaning worldwide suggests that the ***stars were named before the scattering of the races***, so that, even though the name would differ in each new language, ***the meaning did not change.***

So there you have it! The global pattern of a single story in different languages, recorded in each constellation. The same story was told in all the world's great civilizations. The star charts gave it in 48 pictures and the names of hundreds of stars.

It makes perfect sense that there must have been ***a common source*** for such a phenomenon – ***a source older than the different cultures.***

What astrologers don't tell you

Troy Lawrence was a New Age devotee. This motivated him to do thorough research into the practice of astrology. He discovered, to his surprise, that ***astrologers could not tell him*** the origin of the signs. What he discovered blew him away. Troy recalls that:

> I started my quest by comparing various astrological charts and found that other cultures do not always use the same signs we use. The Chinese, for example, use such things as a horse, dog, chicken, etc. The ancient Chinese signs ***had been the same*** as our occidental version, but a long time ago, a Chinese emperor had changed them. (Troy Lawrence, *The Secret Message of the Zodiac.* Here's Life Publishers, 1990, p. 14. Emphasis added)

Note that East and West, the signs were originally ***the same!*** He continues:

> I also discovered, surprisingly, that the ***earliest*** charts of the zodiac were ***Hebrew.*** The Greeks derived their knowledge of the zodiac from the ***Hebrews***; the Romans got their information from the Arabs, who also had received it from the ***Hebrews***. (*Ibid.* Emphasis added)

That led New Ager Tony Lawrence to the record of the Hebrews, the Bible, ***to solve the mystery.***

Yes, it's a fact! Most of the names on those ancient star charts have stemmed from ***Hebrew-Arabic-Noetic*** roots.

There is substantial ***evidence*** of a single language spoken throughout the world, in earliest times. This language, which Gary Vey calls "The First

Tongue", was in use ***before*** the historic splitting up of languages occurred. (See *The Corpse Came Back*, Chapter 8.)

It is also significant that even the Egyptians, when speaking of the "sacred" language, and citing examples of it, quoted words that are ***Hebrew***. All of this strongly suggests that the "sacred" tongue was what we might today term proto-Hebrew. (This was not a Jewish language. Today's Jews have merely inherited a modern version of it. Rather, proto-Hebrew appears to have been the ***universal*** language, spoken by the ancestors of us all.)

If the "First Tongue" was akin to archaic Hebrew, that would explain why the ***nations of the whole planet,*** in preserving their ancient star names, continued to use ***names*** and ***meanings*** which were ***derived from proto-Hebrew.*** And why so many of today's star names survive in the Hebrew and Arabic form, two languages spoken by descendants of the Hebrew patriarch Abraham.

In the beginning, not only was there one global language, but the star names were identical worldwide.

Then, about 2200 BC, during the reign of Nimrod, occurred a dramatic confusion of languages. (See *The Corpse Came Back*, chapters 10 to 12; *UFO Aliens: The Deadly Secret*, chapter 29) In the resulting dispersion, the migrating groups took into their new languages the ***same*** constellation and star name ***meanings*** with them.

Ultimately, the star sign book in the sky was forgotten by most people. But now archaeology is able to retrieve it.

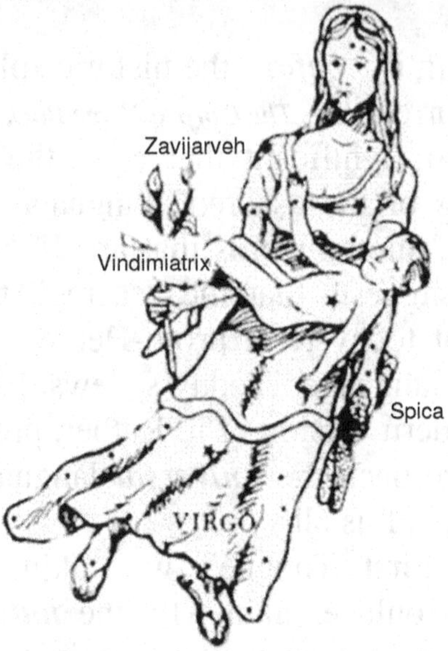

Older than the "christ" legends

We noted earlier the vast antiquity of the star signs. According to the ***evidence***, the promised Messiah portrayed on star maps goes back ***thousands of years earlier than the various "christ" legends*** of the world.

This prophecy was known to mankind LONG BEFORE the time of the Sumerians, the Indians or the Egyptians. The ancients themselves claimed it had been handed down from the first parents of the human race. And, whether we like it or not, that's also precisely what the biblical book of Genesis tells us!

So what is the sequence of history revealed by the evidence? Just this:

Stage 1 – c. 4000 BC: A prophecy is received concerning a coming Messiah.

Stage 2 – To portray this Messiah prophecy, star names and symbols (surviving to this day basically unchanged) are created in the "First Tongue", a language akin to proto-Hebrew. Internal evidence from the positions of the constellations within the sky maps themselves enables them to be dated to as early as 4000 BC. (See *The Corpse Came Back*, ch 8; *Stolen Identity*, ch. 4; *Sting of the Scorpion*, ch.1) Later, the Greeks would make some changes, but these are traceable.

Stage 3 – c. 2200 BC: Queen Semiramus of Babel seizes on the expectation of the Coming One to glorify her dead hero-husband, Nimrod, and establishes the pagan Mysteries. Egypt, Sumeria and other nations adopt this Mystery symbolism of the "hero christ "into their religious systems. (*Stolen Identity*, chs.11-13.)

Stage 4 – Recording the original 4000 BC prophecy, the Bible goes further to predict the precise year of the Messiah's appearance. In numerous details, the "Messiah" prophecies found in the Bible are identical to those in the star maps. (See *Modern Religious Myths About Genesis*, ch.2.)

If you have heard someone say that the "christs" of Hinduism and other religions came first, it is well to note that the first messianic prophecy, recorded on the star maps around 4000 BC definitely pre-dates the 2200 BC confusion of languages which led to the eventual birth of Egypt, India and those other nations with their "christ" legends.

Indeed, would it surprise you to discover that no ***verifiable*** dates for the earliest civilizations – whether they be Egypt, Sumeria, India, China or whatever – go back earlier than about 2200 BC? And increasingly the ***confirmable evidence*** brings the dating closer to our day than previously thought. While it is beyond the scope of this present work to go into the great body of new ***evidence*** concerning this, if comparative dating is an important issue to you, may I suggest that you study my research report on the dating of ancient civilizations. (See *Lost Races: The Big Dating Shock, chapters 6 to 17* <http://www.beforeus.com/dating-civilizations.pdf>)

Considering the above ***archaeological facts***, might one suspect that the world's pagan "christ" legends (2200 BC onwards) are but ***imitations*** of something that was ***already expected***?

In a nutshell, the ancients themselves believed that the 48 zodiac signs were:

- a divine revelation, ***unchanged from the time of the first man***
- a picture gallery of what ***the coming Messiah*** (Christ) will do to save mankind from his mess and end Satan's rule.

Let's say it again. Any notion that the pagan "Christ" legends may pre-date this prophecy of the Messiah finds no historical support. The ***archaeological evidence*** is that, from the earliest age, the world inherited the promise of the Coming One. This original prophecy was ***already universally known***. And ***then***, as the nations scattered out, they ***adapted*** the messianic expectation into their respective mythologies.

Historical versus mythical

A most obvious difference between Yeshua (Jesus Christ) and the "christ" figures of various pagan religions is this. The pagan "christs" exist only as myths. The different religions do not postulate for their "christs" an historical basis, whereas Yeshua is firmly embedded in real time history, attested by an abundance of contemporary witnesses – and the world's calendars are dated from his intrusion into history.

Star maps basically unchanged

According to the great Arab astronomer Albamazer, the star maps, with their ***figures*** and ***names***, have basically never been altered since their origin. They ***were essentially the same as they are today***. Not only the names, but also the figures that were drawn around these groups of stars, have remained basically the same through the centuries.

Critics may point to some changes made. There are some. But they are comparatively minor and generally can be traced.

There is a tradition that Eudoxus of Greece obtained a constellation globe from a temple in Egypt and that this became the basis of Greek astronomy. The same globe was described in detail by the poet Aratus (310-240 BC). (Aratus, *Phaenomena)* However, Aratus described the constellations not as he saw them, but as they were positioned in the sky about 4,000 years earlier. His source, therefore, was an extremely ancient star map. Yet it is noteworthy that the constellations he describes in detail are ***very much the same*** constellations that we have today.

The "lost" constellation

But are you ready for this? Did you know that a whole constellation sign, packed with absolutely explosive information, was ***blasted right off*** the star charts? And a blank space was left where it used to be!

You ask, ***Why*** on earth would somebody do that? Why was it ***deliberately chopped out***? What was so offensive that it had to be removed? The answer may haunt you.

Yet, although lost, this star picture can now be recovered by some wonderfully preserved clues (which we shall soon track).

This brings us to Ptolemy's famous star catalog. Claudius Ptolemaeus, also known as Ptolemy (87-c.170 AD), a Roman citizen of possibly Greek descent, lived in Alexandria, Egypt. And Ptolemy, writing in Greek, actually ***confessed*** that he had ***modified*** some of the constellations.

Not just modified. One complete constellation was somehow ***ripped out*** of the sky maps completely. Ptolemy's celestial map ***left a space*** which showed several unfigured stars.

After Ptolemy's time, astronomy came to a standstill for almost 1,000 years.

And then, during the Renaissance, Ptolemy's star catalog became the standard. The constellations on Ptolemy's map are still used, almost unchanged, today.

But what is this missing constellation sign? Are you curious to know?

Tracking it down

Now comes an exciting piece of detective work. Please follow this carefully.

On Ptolemy's map we can see a blank space which marks the location of the missing star sign.

In the map, which is reproduced below, do you notice the large area with no constellation – near the top in front of the face of Virgo, the virgin, near where she seems to be pointing?

The space contains five stars bright enough for Ptolemy to have recorded there. That is the precise area of the missing constellation.

PROJECTED ON THE PLANE OF THE ECLIPTIC.
NORTHERN.

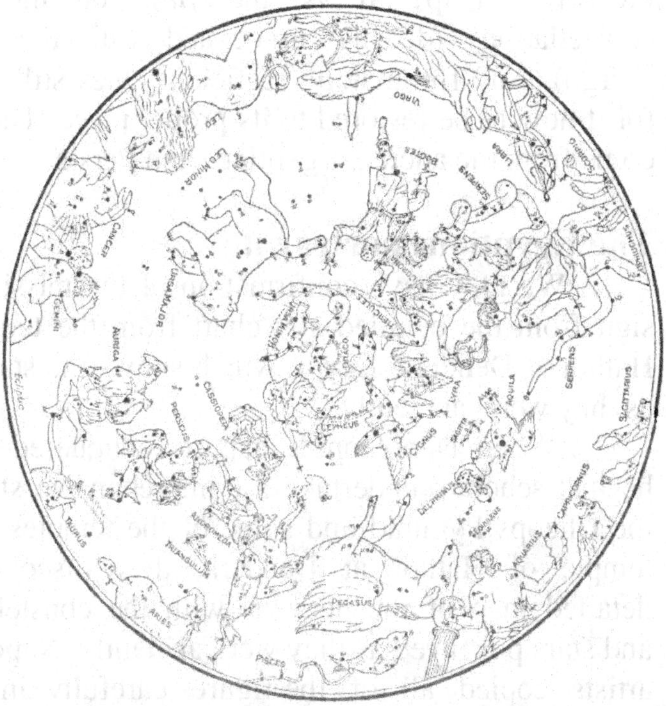

Today the constellation Coma Berenices (Bernice's Hair) occupies the area of sky where this missing constellation should be found.

The Polish astronomer Johannes Hevelius in 1687 created the Hunting Dogs just to fill up the same gap.

The earlier zodiacs identify it

Fortunately, we get some help from Albamazer, the famous Arab astronomer. From earlier star maps, Albamazer knew about and was able to describe this constellation.

He informs us of its location, what the figure looked like, and even its meaning. It was above the head of Virgo – and one of Virgo's explanatory signs.

What star group should be in that position on Ptolemy's map? It is the ***first*** of the three constellations (decans) associated with the Virgin (Virgo). And fortunately, sufficient clues still remain for it now to be restored to its proper place. The clues come from the ancient Egyptians and Persians.

The Egyptians portray it

We now have confirmation of the missing star sign from the detailed sky chart from the temple of Hathor at Dendera, Egypt, which shows the star signs as they were anciently.

When Napoleon Bonaparte conquered Egypt, he had scholars undertake a comprehensive study of the Cheops Pyramid and some of the temples. In the temple of Hathor at Dendera, they discovered a detailed map of the heavens with the constellations and stars portrayed as they were anciently. Napoleon's artists copied all of the figures carefully, in detail. The result was a set of huge volumes filled with drawings. The Dendera map of the heavens is now in the British Museum. Although the temple was constructed in the first century BC, the map revealed features of the sky that could be dated by the precession of the equinoxes to a period much earlier. (Peter Tompkins, *Secrets of the Great Pyramid.* New York: Harper & Row, 1971, p. 174; The sketch below: John Pratt)

Because the Dendera zodiac is centered on the north celestial pole, its projection can be dated simply by measuring where the ecliptic intersects the celestial equator. The intersection of the ecliptic and celestial equator rotates one degree in 72 years.

Using this method, various researchers have dated the time shown on the map to be from 700-1600 BC. The uncertainty is due to the circles not being well defined. Since the temple itself was built in the first century BC, the zodiac (which memorialises a much earlier time) cannot be used to date the building.

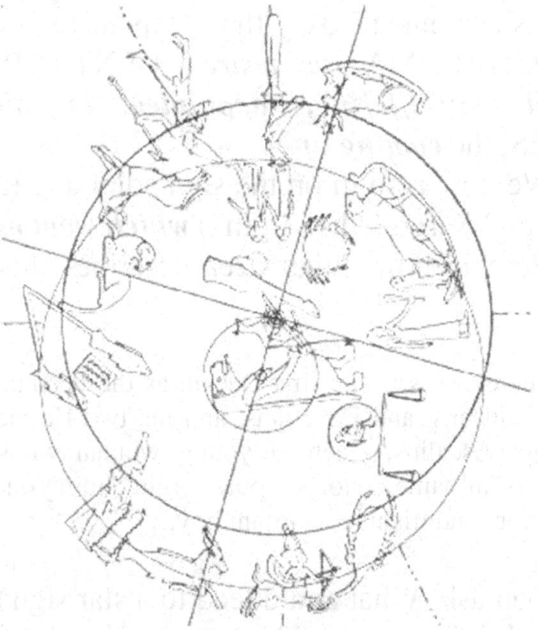

Here is the missing sign

On this ancient map from Egypt, the constellation of the ***Virgin*** (Virgo) is easily found. She is portrayed as a woman holding a branch. Close to her is found a decan, or ***explanatory sign***, of a woman seated on a throne ***holding up a young infant***. This star sign is called Coma. This is the "missing" constellation.

Why would this one get cut out?

What can we discover about this "missing" constellation?

As we saw earlier, the 12 main zodiac signs do not stand alone. Each of them has co-joined with it, either on the north or south side of the zodiac belt, three amplifying signs, equally full, vivid and to the point. These are called decans.

And so, on the oldest star maps, VIRGO (the ***virgin***) is accompanied by three explanatory signs, or side-pieces (COMA, the ***desired***; CENTAURUS, the ***despised, sin-offering, appointed to die***; and BOOTES, the ***coming one).***

We now zero in on the sign adjoining (and thus amplifying) Virgo ("the virgin") ***which went missing.***

Here is how Albamazer describes this zodiac sign:

> There arises in the first Decan, as the Persians, Chaldeans, and Egyptians, and the two Hermes and Ascalius, teach, a young woman whose Persian name denotes a pure virgin, sitting on a throne, nourishing an infant boy,…

You ask, What could lead to a star sign that had been on the charts for 4,000 years, to then be suddenly rejected?

On the page after next, you will notice, in the photo of the virgin and child constellation as found in the Dendera planisphere, that the head of ***the son*** is slightly higher than the head of his mother. This hieroglyphically symbolises that he is to be ***the greater.***

In the Hebrew and Oriental dialects Coma meant "***the desired***", "***the longed for***". Since hieroglyphically, the son is greater than the mother, the "desired one" is not the woman, but her child.

The Virgo ***woman*** (who gives birth to the "Seed") and the ***woman*** in Coma (holding up the infant) are ***one and the same***. And the ***infant*** in all the star signs is everywhere ***the same Promised One***. The focal point of Coma is the child.

Let's continue Albamazer's description of this star sign:

> There arises in the first Decan, as the Persians, Chaldeans, and Egyptians, and the two Hermes and Ascalius, teach, a young woman whose Persian name denotes a pure virgin, sitting on a throne, nourishing an infant boy, said boy having a ***Hebrew name,*** by some nations called ***Ihesu***, with the signification ***Ieza,*** which in Greek is called Christ. (Frances Rolleston, *Mazzaroth; or the Constellations.* London: Rivingtons, 1862, updated in 1875, with the latter version reprinted by Weiser Books, York Beach, Maine, 2001).

Interestingly, the Cherokee nation of North America refer to the Messiah as ***Tsi Sa,*** other nations as ***Chisa***. The English equivalent is ***Jesa***, a corruption of ***Yesha*** which means *deliverance*, all of which resemble ***Ieza*** (***Ihesu***) of the star sign.

So what could lead to a star sign that had been on the charts for 4,000 years, to now be suddenly rejected? Is it becoming clear?

Please take note that Albamazer was not a Christian. He was an Arab astronomer simply stating a fact. According to Albamazer's information, this puts the ***name of Yeshua (Yeshu, Jesus)*** back thousands of years with the ***earliest*** (as he said, ***unchanged***) zodiac maps – identified as the "*desired one*", or the Deliverer the nations were longing for!

In the ancient zodiac he is "***the Desired***", which is precisely how he is denoted in the Old Testament: "***the Desire of all nations***" who "***shall come***". (Haggai 2:6,7)

Two more bombshells:
* He has a ***Hebrew*** name.
* That name is **IHESU**.

Constellation from Dendera planisphere (Photo: John Pratt)

The identity with ***Yeshua*** is unmistakable. Here is ***Yeshua*** the expected Deliverer – on a sky map ***unchanged*** from earliest times (declares Albamazer) – scientifically dated to the period 700 to 1600 BC, with an ultimate origin back to 4000 BC!

Not only did Albamazer preserve for us the Persian interpretation that it was an infant being held by its queenly virgin mother, and that it represented Jesus Christ. He adds that there are ***many testimonies*** that this is correct: and he names them - the Persians, Chaldeans, Egyptians and others.

I'll say it again. This is long before Greek myths were written. So the stars did not come from the myths. Rather, the myths came from the stars. The Messiah's name Ihesu (Yeshua, Jesus) pre-dated the pagan myths that imitated the prophecy.

Now can you guess why this "explosive" star message had to be ***blasted right out*** of the sky maps?

Attempt to stifle the news

As the message of Yeshua the Messiah spread across the earth, it shook paganism severely. Its opponents in Rome and Alexandria (the chief centers of paganism) counter-attacked.

(a) In Rome and Alexandria in particular, they infiltrated the Christian movement to defuse its power;

(b) In Alexandria and Rome, corrupted texts downgraded Yeshua; (but texts elsewhere escaped). (*The Da Vinci Code Hoax*, Chapters 17-18,20-21; *Who's Playing Jesus Games?* Chapters 12-15; *The Sorcerers' Secret*, Chapters 4-6)

(c) In Alexandria, Ptolemy's star map ***chopped out the prophecy identifying Ihesu (Yeshua) by name.***

My turning point

I was staying at a backpacker's hostel in Melbourne, Australia. There I heard a young lady from England proudly claiming that the ***stars*** controlled her everyday life.

"What nonsense!" I thought. Determined to prove her wrong, and with time on my hands, I plunged myself into research at the Victoria State

Library. But as the ***evidence*** on the origin and history of star signs materialised, it not only made astrology look anaemic, it compelled me to come face to face with something that I had long avoided.

Well, I finally confronted Mary Ann with my discovery, and she looked at me incredulously. "Then, Jonathan, why are you not a Christian?" And she followed that up with, "I'm going to get myself a Bible tomorrow." (You don't need to guess, this changed Mary Ann's life.)

A few days later I stood on the corner of Elizabeth Street and Bourke Street, waiting for the pedestrian lights to change.

And right there on that corner, the implications suddenly hit me like a jack hammer on concrete. "So this thing is not just in the Bible, for Jews or Christians. It's on the star charts of the whole world. Wow! Then this God is ***leaving no stone unturned*** to make the evidence available to every person who will listen. He's telling His love... even to me... useless wretch that I am! What love – what huge, enormous love! Incredible!"

That was the moment of truth for me. That day Lucifer lost one of his lackeys. Not that I'm anything great. Believe it!

* * * * * * *

End note: Missionaries have found native tribes that already know the gospel, from seeing it in the stars. (For one example, see *Modern Religious Myths About Genesis*, ch.2)

PART SEVEN

THE RESCUER REJECTED

28

The Rescuer rejected -

WAS HE A DECEIVER?

What kind of person was this man Yeshua… really?

His Words — a puzzling paradox

One thing that stands out about this man is his words. How simple was everything he said, how easy to remember, yet how profound!

Yeshua was not a political activist. He knew that the problem was in the hearts of men. And he worked on the heart!

To estimate his influence on history, consider the difference between Yeshua and all philosophers and moralists. To gather all their wise and good precepts, you must first sift out all the error, immorality and absurd superstition, which would be an enormous job.

The fact is that a single person, unlearned in men's wisdom, not only opposed the practices and maxims of his own country, but formulated a system so admittedly superior to others.

Joseph Parker declares:

> After reading the doctrines of Plato, Socrates or Aristotle, we feel the specific difference between their words and Christ's is the difference between an inquiry and a revelation. (Frank Meade, *The Encyclopedia of Religious Quotations*,. Westwood: Fleming H. Revell, undated, p.57)

Socrates taught for 40 years, Aristotle for 40, Plato for 50—and Yeshua for only three; yet those three years surpass in influence the combined 130 of these three greatest men.

Former Yale historian Kenneth Scott Latourette says:

> As the centuries pass the evidence is accumulating that, measured by His effect on history Jesus is the most influential life ever lived on this planet. (Kenneth Scott Latourette, *American Historical Review.* LIV, January 1949, p.272)

Latourette speaks also of:

> ...the baffling mystery... that no other life ever lived on this planet has evoked such a huge volume of literature among so many peoples and languages, and that, far from ebbing, the flood continues to mount. (Latourette, *A History of Christianity.* New York: Harper & Row, 1953, p.44)

Let's face it. The life, the words, the character of this strange Man are the enigma of history. Any naturalistic explanation makes him a more puzzling paradox, a fathomless mystery.

His words are "the greatest ever spoken" (Ramm).

"He shed more light on things human and divine than all the philosophers and scholars combined" (Schaff).

One cannot fail "to see... that since the days of Christ, in spite of all the progress of thought, not a single new ethical idea has been given to the world" (Thomas).

Erstwhile skeptic Josh McDowell said it all:

If God became man, then certainly his words would be the greatest ever spoken. (Josh McDowell, *Evidence That Demands a Verdict* - Vol. I. San Bernardino, Ca.: Here's Life Publishers Inc., 1986, p.129)

And so I wondered. Could this explain the paradox and solve the mystery?

His preposterous claims

Then who was Yeshua? A superman? A fake?

He made seemingly impossible assertions and promises —strange statements that would normally brand a man either a preposterous liar or a mad fanatic.

Take these, for example:

- *I am the light of the world.* (John 8:12)
- *Heaven and earth shall pass away, but my words shall not pass away.* (Mark 13.31)
- *I am able to give life to whom I wish.* (John 5:21)
- *I have moral authority over all men.* (John 5:27)
- *Only I can save men.* (John 3:36)

Who is this person who places his own authority side by side with the authority of God?

You see? Yeshua claimed to be no mere holy man — he claimed uniqueness.

According to those who personally heard him teach, he said:

- *I am one with God.* (John10:30)
- *I am God's only Son.* (John 3:16, 34, 35)
- *I was with the Father before the world was made.* (John 17:5)
- *Before Abraham was, I AM.* (John 5: 58) (The name of God in Hebrew is YHWH or I AM – the Eternal One.) (Exodus 3:14)

And Yeshua made still other audacious claims:

- *You will see me sitting at the right hand of God the Father.* (Luke 22:69)
- *I am equal with God.* (John 5:17,18)
- *Worship is due to me as it is to the Father.* (John 5:23; 10:30,38) (Hence Yeshua commanded and accepted worship as God.) (Matthew 4:7; John 10:33; 20:28,29)

Then, as if that were not enough, he predicted:

- *I will judge the world, and arouse the dead.* (John 5:27-29)

These were all claims to divinity — and were recognized as such at the time, by those who heard him.

Yeshua is the only religious leader who has ever claimed to be God.

He made the incredible claim that he, a simple carpenter's son among the shavings and sawdust of his father's workshop, was in reality God in the flesh! He never "guessed" or "supposed". His teachings were ultimate, final.

Yeshua was crucified not for his actions; ***the issue was his identity***. This is unique among criminal trials.

He was crucified for blasphemy — saying that he was God. And indeed, unless he were equal with God his words ***were*** blasphemy.

Was he a great moral teacher?

C.S. Lewis, who was a professor at Cambridge University, and once an agnostic, wrote:

> A man who was merely a man and said the sort of things Jesus said would not be a great moral teacher. He would either be a lunatic — on the

> level with the man who says he is a poached egg — or else he would be the Devil of Hell. You must make your choice. Either this man was, and is, the Son of God; or else a madman or something worse. (C.S.Lewis, *Mere Christianity.* New York:The Macmillan Company, 1952, pp.40,41)

He cautions:

> Let us not come up with any patronising nonsense about his being a great human teacher. He has not left that open to us. He did not intend to. (*Ibid.*)

Was he a liar?

If this man's claims were false, there were two alternatives:

1. **He knew his claims were false.** If this is so, then he made a deliberate misrepresentation. He was a liar, a hypocrite, a demon — and he was a fool, because he died for it.

   If he made such claims and none were true, then he was the most unprincipled deceiver in all history.

   He told others to trust him for their eternal destiny, even to die for his claims. If he could not back up his claims and knew it, then he was unspeakably evil. He was a liar and a hypocrite, because he told others to be honest, whatever the cost, while himself teaching and living a colossal lie.

   Yet there is not a skeptic who will admit he was a deceiver. They concede he was honest and earnest.

   A bad man could not have taught such great truths as he taught — truths which perform miracles of character-change on people. And a good man could not have deceived the people for whom he gave his life.

Indeed, how in the name of common sense could an impostor have continued to demonstrate from beginning to end "the purest and noblest character in history, with the most perfect air of truth and reality"? (Schaff *The Person of Christ.* New York: American Tract Society, 1913, pp.94,95)

So I say, he could not possibly have been a fraud.

Was he a deluded nutcase?

That leaves us with the second option:

2. **He did NOT know his claims were false.** If this is true, he was sincerely deluded; he was a lunatic.

   Yet the facts show his mind was so keen that it was more than a match for the sharpest intellects of his day.

   Tell me. How could he be a deluded madman, who never lost the even balance of his mind, who sailed serenely over all the troubles and persecutions, as the sun above the clouds, who always returned the wisest answer to tempting questions, who calmly and deliberately "made predictions which have been literally fulfilled"? (Schaff *History of the Christian Church,* 8 vols. Grand Rapids: William B. Eerdmans Publishing Co., 1910 Reprinted from original, 1962, p.109)

The noted British historian William Lecky, a dedicated opponent of organized Christianity, said:

> The simple record of these three short years of active life has done more to regenerate and

> soften mankind than all the disquisition of philosophers and all the exhortations of moralists. (William E. Lecky,*History of European Morals from Augustus to Charlemagne.* New York: D.Appleton & Co.,1903, p.8)

We will need to face it: if his claims were FALSE, whether he be a deceiver or self-deceived, in either case, if he was NOT God he was not good.

Or were his claims true?

In my search for the truth of the matter, it came back to this. This person is either EVERYTHING for mankind or NOTHING —either the highest certainty or the greatest fake.

If his claims are true, then I, Jonathan Gray, must either accept or reject his Lordship.

There needs to be a moral honesty in this, I told myself.

Yeshua prophesied that he would be the great spiritual magnet that would draw men and women of all nations to himself.

That prophecy has proved true. Something to think about?

What his antagonists say

Goethe wrote:

> If ever the Divine appeared on earth, it was in the Person of Christ. (Schaff *History of the Christian Church.* Grand Rapids: William B. Eerdmans Publishing Co., 1910 Reprinted from original, 1962, p.110)

Said H. G. Wells:

> He was too great for his disciples.... Is it any wonder that men were dazzled and blinded and cried out against him?.... Is it any wonder that to this day this Galilean is too much for our small hearts? (H.G. Wells, *Outline of History.* Garden City: Garden City Publishing Co., 1931, pp. 535,536)

Even Rousseau admitted:

> Yes, the life and death of Socrates are those of a philosopher, the life and death of Jesus Christ are those of a God. (Frank Ballard,*The Miracles of Unbelief.* Edinburgh: T & T Clark,1908, p.251)

And in the *Koran,* the book of Islam, Yeshua is referred to as "the greatest above all in this world and in the world to come." (Al-Imran, v.45)

His contemporary enemies bear witness

Significant was the witness of his personal enemies. When Yeshua asked, *"Which of you convicts me of sin?"* (John 8:46) he received no answer.

Eventually Governor Pilate would testify, *"What evil has this man done?"* A criminal crucified with him would cry, *"This man has done nothing wrong."* And a Roman centurion would bear witness, *"Certainly this man was innocent."* (Luke 23:22,41,47)

However hard his enemies tried to bring forth an accusation of wrong, they could not. (Mark 14:55,56)

Yeshua seems to have lived in an unbroken relationship with God. His character was too far above that of every man, a moral miracle of history.

It had been claimed that the divine law was unreasonable and could not be obeyed by men and women. But Yeshua kept it.

Taking human nature and standing as man's representative, Yeshua said he was out to show that man, connected to God, could obey every divine requirement.

Quite obviously, Yeshua demonstrated that God's laws were given to men and women in love. He showed us what it is like to have heaven in the heart.

Say others:

> In the very perfection of his human nature his life stands forth as miraculous in a degree no other of the miracles of Scripture can attain. (John Morton, *Man, Science and God,* London: Collins, 1972, p.161)

> His sinless perfection is a miracle, in the sense that history is ransacked in vain for another fact like it. (Dr J.S. Whale, *Christian Doctrine.* London: Cambridge University Press, 1941, p.104)

> There never has been a more real or genuine man than Jesus of Nazareth. (W.H. Griffith Thomas, *Christianity is Christ.* Chicago: Moody Press, 1965, p.11)

> When one reads his name in a list beginning with Confucius and ending with Goethe we feel it is an offense... against decency. Jesus is not one of the group of the world's great... Jesus is apart. He is not the Great; he is the Only. (John R.W. Stott, *Basic Christianity.* Downers Grove: Inter-Varsity Press, 1971, p.36)

> Sinless perfection and perfect sinlessness is what we would expect of God incarnate, and this we do find in Jesus Christ. The hypothesis and the facts concur. (Bernard Ramm, *Protestant Christian Evidences.* Chicago: Moody Press, 1957, p.169)

Evidence of other hostile witnesses

Far from denying his miracles, Yeshua's enemies attributed them to the power of evil. It is of historical value that his enemies actually wrote of his miracles. They attributed them to sorcery.

The Jewish Babylonian *Sanhedrin* states:

> On the eve of the Passover they hanged Yeshu [of Nazareth].... he hath practised sorcery and beguiled and led astray Israel. (Babylonian *Sanhedrin* 43a - "Eve of Passover", 95- 110 AD)

Julian the Apostate, Roman emperor from 361 to 363, who strongly opposed Christianity, wrote:

> Jesus did nothing in his lifetime worthy of fame, unless anyone thinks it a very great work to heal lame and blind people and exorcise demoniacs. (Philip Schaff, *The Person of Christ.* New York: American Tract Society, 1913, p.33)

Justin Martyr, around 150 AD, refers to official Roman records:

> That he performed these miracles you may easily besatisfied from the 'Acts' of Pontius Pilate. (Justin Martyr, *Apology* 148-150 AD)

Yeshua's miracles demonstrated power over nature, power over disease, demons and death, as well as powers of creation. This power over natural forces seemed so ordinary to this man. It was a natural and necessary outcome of his life.

The miracles occupied, however, a comparatively insignificant place in his ministry; they were worked with restraint, and only in love and mercy, for the benefit of men and women.

Often they were performed before the public for open scrutiny and investigation by skeptics.

When he raised Lazarus from the dead, it is significant that his enemies did not deny the miracle, but, rather, tried to kill him before all men believed in him. (John 11:48-53)

He loved everybody

Never would there be a man so kind as he, so generous, so helpful, so lovely — or so loving.

While abhorring wrong, he wept with compassion over the wrongdoer. He was able to be on the side of the sinner without ever once condoning the sin.

Though he was not soft on sin, Yeshua had come, as he said, "to heal the broken hearted", not to create new hurts. He was always sensitive to the feelings of others. He never needlessly embarrassed anyone or exposed a guilty one publicly.

He associated with the rejected and approached the frustrated with compassion. He went down to the seamy places of the cities where prostitutes were kept and told them that God loved them, that He would forgive their sins and make them into dignified women again. How they appreciated that! They had never been shown love before. Exploited, lusted after, yes, often. But never loved.

There never was another like him, so tender and compassionate, so wise and strong. Yeshua gave abundant evidence that God is love.

What gracious, lovely things Yeshua said! He always made religion easy to understand. He proved that God was all-powerful and inexorably just, but kind and loving and merciful too. Just being near Yeshua made a person want to be good.

Becoming one of us, here with us for a time, was the best way God could communicate with us what He was like and how He wanted us to live.

His "perfect life" – a miracle?

It is evident that Yeshua believed himself to be sinless. We never read of him confessing or asking forgiveness of his wrongs, although he told his followers to do so. It appears he had no sense of guilt. In their close contact with Yeshua, his disciples never saw in him the sins they saw in themselves.

They got on one another's nerves, they grumbled and argued, but never did they see this in Yeshua. Peter declared that he "*did no sin, neither was guile found in his mouth.*" (1 Peter 2:22)

John went so far as to state that if anyone declared himself to be without sin he would be making God a liar and was a liar to himself. Yet of Yeshua he said, "*And you know that he was manifested to take away our sins, and in him is no sin.*" (1 John 3:5)

And Yeshua allowed his dearest friends to believe this.

If you could…

Here is the 64 million dollar question: ***If***, by the evidence, ***you could convince yourself*** that Yeshua is who he claims to be, would you follow him?

If ***no***, then read no further. The upcoming information will not benefit you.

If ***yes***, then would you please do yourself a favor. Read carefully the Gospel of John in the biblical New Testament – then decide.…

29

The Rescuer rejected -

WHY WAS HE REJECTED?

About 1830, a man by the name of George Wilson killed a government employee who caught him in the act of robbing the mails.

He was tried and sentenced to be hanged. However the president of the United States, Andrew Jackson, sent him a pardon. But Wilson did a strange thing. He refused to accept the pardon, and no one seemed to know what to do. So the case was carried to the Supreme Court.

Chief Justice Marshall, perhaps the greatest chief justice America ever had, wrote the opinion. In it he said, "A pardon is a slip of paper, the value of which is determined by the acceptance of the person to be pardoned. If it is refused, it is no pardon. George Wilson must be hanged."

And he was.

* * * * * * *

Promised rescue… promised pardon… is about to arrive…

The time has come. The stage is set… Heavenly beings are dumbfounded because the Creator of the universe, the King of glory, God the Son, is about to depart for a little planet eaten up with problems, called Earth.

They see Him lay His majesty aside.

He is stepping out of the heavenly domain onto this dark, lonely planet of tears… to teach mankind, to show them what He is like, to rescue them, and to restore relations with them.

What! Can you believe it?

The Creator Himself, who controls every atom, is coming to this rebel planet to die for the hostages!

The Creator of everything, who had existed for all eternity, coming to live as a mortal and among mortals and then to die for them so that they might have life unending also! That's nothing less than godlike.

He descends to this hostile enemy territory.

Isaac's ant

Sir Isaac Newton as a child, was one day out in the garden watching some ants.

In his enthusiasm he accidentally trod on an ant, squashing it.

He ran crying into the house. As his mother pulled him close and wiped his tears, the little boy looked into her face and sobbed, "I did not mean to kill it. I loved that little ant."

"Of course you did," soothed his mother.

"Mom," said Isaac, "those ants could never know how much I love them unless I became an ant and could speak their language."

You and I, like those ants – how better could we understand our Creator's love for us, than if He stepped down, took human form and suffered with us? Think now, wouldn't such an act speak eloquently of His love for us? How better could we know His love than if He became one of us? That's what He promised to do!

And when He has visited us – when His divine Son, from the brightness of the glory of the Father,

- has descended to earth

- and assumed our nature
- to reconcile us to God
- and obtain a never-ending life for us

How has He been received?

- Shunned for His voluntary poverty
- Despised for His humble human parentage
- Hated for His holiness
- Tried before law courts for crimes unknown to Him

So the Deliverer comes, covering His divinity in human flesh. But it took them all by surprise. Very, very few have the slightest idea that their long-awaited Messiah is coming to them in such humble guise.

He comes down to our level. Where our first parents had failed, as one of us He goes over the same ground, to be tried and tested in every way we are, and prove that one could win over Satan's power.

He proves that man, connected with his Maker, could live victoriously.

Then He will offer credit to each person for what He did. He will credit to them His perfect life, and He will die the "sin" punishment for them. We on death row may be pardoned – ultimately rescued. However, only one who has NOT fallen under the Serpent's power is able to take upon Himself the penalty of our failure and secure our pardon.

You might begin with a mind unfavourable to Yeshua. But as you read Matthew's historical report, instead of finding Yeshua to be a charlatan seeking glory for himself, you find Him to be a warm, powerful, caring, forgiving Person who went about teaching and healing, and giving of himself for people.

Healing the brokenhearted

One of the prophecies said that when the Messiah should arrive he would *"bind up the brokenhearted... proclaim liberty to the captives... comfort all that mourn... bestow on them the oil of gladness instead of mourning, and a garment of praise instead of a spirit of despair."* (Isaiah 61:1-3)

In his first recorded public address Yeshua announced this as his purpose. (Luke 3:16-21)

In the window of a repair shop downtown was this sign:

EVERYTHING MENDED
EXCEPT BROKEN HEARTS

That's something you and I cannot do. But that would be the Messiah's specialty. This is the one for whom all history had been preparing.

Confronted with that kind of Messiah, you would expect the world to flock to his feet. But the prophecies said that would not be.

Why did the religious leaders reject him?

The ***rejection*** of the true Messiah was ***prophesied*** in Isaiah, Daniel and the Psalms — in prophecies which were acknowledged by the early Jews to be messianic.

These prophecies indicated that he would be rejected by the very people who foretold his coming:

> ...the Redeemer of Israel, and his Holy One, to him ***whom man despiseth***, to him ***whom the nation*** [of Israel] ***abhorreth***...(Isaiah 49:7)
>
> He is ***despised and rejected*** of men; a man of sorrows, and acquainted with grief: and we hid as

> it were our faces from him; he was despised, and we esteemed him not. (Isaiah 53:3)

> … *despised of the people*. (Psalm 22:6)

But the prophecies also indicated that he would be accepted by others:

> Kings shall see and arise, princes also shall worship. (Isaiah 49:7)

> So shall he sprinkle many nations; the kings shall shut their mouths at him, for that which had not been told them shall they see; and that which they had not heard shall they consider.(Isaiah 52:15)

Yes, they had the knowledge of the coming Messiah, but when he came they didn't want him. The question arises, Why did the nation's leaders reject this Person? Wasn't there enough *evidence* for them to know?

Rescue rejected: why?

It wasn't lack of *evidence*. That was not the problem.

From the contemporary accounts, one can uncover at least ten reasons:

1. **They were biased against him.** The human heart, according to the Scripture, is self-deceived and corrupted by wrong doing. We are all naturally rebellious against spiritual laws.
2. **It hurt their national pride.** The Jewish leaders rejected Jesus because he did not fit their mistaken assumptions; because he did not come in the power and glory of a king, to bring immediate, national deliverance from Roman rule. If only they had read the prophecies more

carefully – and understood his real purpose! Their prejudices got in the way. Even to think that their expectations might be disappointed, enraged them. (He told them he had come to conquer sin in the life.)

3. **His humble way of life offended their snobbery.**
4. **He had not been taught by them.** They were unhappy with this brilliant young teacher because he had not attended one of their schools. He was in no way a product of their teaching. He was independent of them.
5. **His character showed them up.** Jesus' compassion stood out in bold contrast to their own rigid, uncaring attitudes. His large-hearted love made their littleness look exceedingly small. Frustrated and angry, they came to hate him.
6. **In argument he outclassed them.** These learned men asked him one difficult question after another, determined to trap him into saying something for which they could condemn him. His mind was so keen that it was more than a match for them. Jesus silenced one attack after another until his enemies gnashed their teeth in frustration and retreated. He had a way of telling little stories and asking them to comment. And often in their response they condemned themselves before they realised that they were the culprit in the story. Clearly outclassed, they became furious.
7. **His growing popularity endangered their influence.** Jesus' healing was making him ever more popular with the people. His personality was so warm and loving that huge crowds

flocked around him. The religious leaders were thoroughly alarmed. More and more people were coming under his influence. Their own influence was endangered. They were losing their control of the people.

8. **They feared incurring the wrath of Rome.** Since 63 BC a dozen rebellions in Palestine had been subdued — most of them by Roman force. Another uprising under Jesus of Nazareth might bleed Rome's patience dry and lead to tighter occupation. For political reasons, Jesus was perceived as a menace.

Next are two reasons why the nation in general rejected the Messiah.

9. **They were asked by Jesus to leave the majority and follow an insignificant little group.** He told them: *"Broad is the way that leads to destruction, and many...go in thereat: Narrow is the way that leads to life eternal, and few there be that find it."* (Matthew 7:13,14) It was a sad fact of life then, as today. Truth is rejected because of peer pressure. Yet history shows that the majority to be generally wrong.
10. **They were asked by Jesus to "forsake all and follow me."** In those days, the result would be to lose your job, your former friends – and perhaps even your life.

To accept his claims was not easy. It meant there was ***much rethinking*** to do.

If you want to know why they rejected Jesus, you only have to look around and see why people reject him today. It hurts our pride to think that we are sinners in need of a Savior.

Acceptance requires not a superficial surface change, but a total transformation of one's life.

Mind-set blocks evidence

Evidence might be conclusive and even overwhelming, but it does not necessarily produce conviction. The will and the affections must necessarily enter into it.

Once men have committed themselves to a certain position, it is very difficult to look at evidence impartially — and more so when private interests are involved.

The subtleties of the human mind are indeed deceptive. Our opinions become fixed to the point where we stop thinking. This will lead to dangerous errors ***unless*** one is a truth-seeker and examines every matter microscopically with an eye focused upon ***undisputed facts***.

When a man told me he did not accept Jesus, I asked him, "Upon what do you base your rejection? Is it upon ***evidence*** against his existence, or ***evidence*** against his claims? Or lack of ***evidence*** for him?"

His eyes evaded me as he replied, "No. It's a lifestyle issue I have."

I felt sad for the dear man.

Let's face it. If one is honest about this he will go with the ***evidence***... wherever it leads. And with this present book in your hands, you have EVIDENCE. As good as any ***evidence*** you can get.

Cover-up by the elite

Now comes one of the most amazing ***manipulations of historical facts*** ever known. It happened in three stages.

1. The Messiah is rejected
2. The time for the "Messiah" expires
3. So the year count is fiddled to a later date

The rabbis had their calculations right. But they rejected the Coming One when he arrived. So it was that "when the true Messiah was rejected, and the time for His coming had gone by," states Anstey, the Jewish leaders "corrupted their Chronology and ***shortened the duration of the kingdom of Persia***, so as to be able to apply the prophecy to Theudas and Judas of Galilee... and at length to Bar Cochab..." (Martin Anstey, *The Romance of Bible Chronology.* London: Marshall Brothers Ltd, 1913, p.283)

Can you believe that? Just read it again. What happened was this:

1. Everyone knew that the Messiah must come ***within 490 years*** after the decree of the Persian king Artaxerxes to restore Jerusalem – as specified by Daniel.
2. But the 490 years had now completed its time.
3. And since the official story given to the people was that the Messiah had not come,
4. it therefore became necessary to ***cut out some years of earlier history*** so that the 490 years from Artaxerxes could still be stretched into the future. (See more on this in Chapter 41.)
5. This would give opportunity to promote some other possible claimant to the Messiah title – someone who just might be acceptable to the people for the purpose of throwing off the Roman occupation.
6. Among such claimants were Theudas and Judas, and ultimately Bar Cochab (Bar Kokhba).

Smooth ploy!

This shortening of the chronology can be adequately traced. Authorities such as Sir Isaac Newton and D. Davidson have addressed this deliberate corruption of history which occurred in the first century of the Christian era. (Newton, Sir Isaac *Chronology of Ancient Kingdoms Amended,* p.357; Davidson, D and Aldersmith, H. *The Great Pyramid: Its Divine Message* Vol. 1 London: Williams and Norgate, Ltd, 1936, pp.348-350)

It is partly as a result of this shortening of world history, that the Jewish year count (in 2011 AD it would be counted as the year 5771), falls short of the year count as arrived at from the Hebrew Scriptures — a curious anomaly. That's right. The present Jewish year count and the Jewish Scriptures ***do not agree with each other!*** You will receive the details in a later chapter.

The hostility toward Yeshua

We have already referred to the Jewish Babylonian Sanhedrin, from AD 95 – 110, which testifies:

> On the eve of the Passover Yeshu was hanged. For forty days before the execution took place, a herald went forth and cried, 'He is going forth to be stoned because he has practiced magic and led Israel astray. Anyone who can say anything in his favor let him come forward and plead on his behalf.' But since nothing was brought forward in his favour he was hanged on the eve of the passover! (Babylonian Talmud *Sanhedrin* 43a – "Eve of Passover" Compare t. Sanh. 10:11; y. sanh. 7:12; Tg. Esther 7:9)

Another version of this text says, "Yeshu the Nazarene". New Testament details confirmed by this passage include:

* Jesus' "magic" or miracle acts
* that he "led [astray] many in Israel"
* the fact of the crucifixion
* the time of the crucifixion

* the intent of the Jewish religious leaders to kill Jesus.

Also, around AD 95, Jewish rabbi Eliezer ben Hyrcanus of Lydda speaks of Jesus' magic arts. (Ethelbert Stauffer, *Jesus and His Story.* Translated by Richard and Clara Winston. New York: Alfred A. Knopf, 1960, p. 10)

Did Jewish authorities deny that Jesus worked miracles? Indeed not. But they claimed these were acts of sorcery.

Despite the hatred of many Jewish leaders for Jesus Christ and Christianity, they ***never question the historical reality*** of Jesus Christ. His coming is part of their history – quite independently of Christianity. And ***Jewish leaders*** still recognise this, today.

Jesus' alleged illegitimate birth was a slur among the Jews.

Jewish scholars have always conceded the Jesus Christ of Christianity to be the most influential "imposter" in their history. Israel Shahak in *Jewish History, Jewish Religion* (p. 97) writes:

> According to the Talmud, Jesus was executed by a proper rabbinical court for idolatry, inciting other Jews to idolatry, and contempt of rabbinical authority. All classical Jewish sources which mention His execution are quite happy to take responsibility for it; in the Talmudic account the Romans are not even mentioned.

The more popular accounts - which were nevertheless taken quite seriously - such as the notorious *Toldot Yesbu,* are even worse, for in addition to the above crimes they accuse him of witchcraft (*Shabbos* 104b; *Sanhedrin* 43a).

The very name 'Jesus' was for Jews a symbol of all that is abominable, and this popular tradition still persists. (The Hebrew form of the name Jesus - Yeshu - was interpreted as an acronym for the curse "may his name and memory be wiped out," and which is used as an extreme form of abuse.) In fact, anti-Zionist Orthodox Jews (such as Neturey Qarta) sometimes refer to Herzl as 'Herzl Jesus' and found in religious Zionist writings are expressions such as 'Nasser Jesus' and more recently 'Arafat Jesus'.

A different Jesus of Nazareth?

Some critics who kid themselves that Jesus never really existed, argue that these Jewish references must apply to some other character.

But I would ask such a skeptic, What would evoke such continuing strong feelings against Jesus, as are today still expressed? If this was simply some man who was connected with a comparatively insignificant event in the distant past, then why does his name evoke such powerful curses today? Their attitude makes sense only if the Jesus they are cursing is one who founded something formidable - Christianity - which has now become a mighty force. That is why emotions rage so hot. There is no mistaking the fact that this is the Jesus of Christianity they are talking about – as historical in their minds, as Hitler.

And nothing else could explain the fact that the Gospels are equally detested, and they are not allowed to be quoted (let alone taught) even in modern Israeli Jewish schools.

The *Talmud* confirms the execution of Jesus Christ, the founder of Christianity – NOT that of some other character.

Because *some* Talmudic passages place Jesus 100 years before or after his actual lifetime, some Jewish apologists argue that these must therefore deal with a different Jesus of Nazareth. But this is ***not how the most authoritative rabbinic interpreters***, medieval sages like Nachmanides, Rashi and the Tosaphists, ***saw the matter.***

Maimonides, writing in 12th century Egypt, made clear that ***the Talmud's Jesus*** is the one who founded Christianity. In his great summation of Jewish law and belief, the *Mishneh Torah,* he wrote of "Jesus of Nazareth, who imagined that he was the Messiah, but was put to death by the court." In his *Epistle to Yemen,* Maimonides states:

> Jesus of Nazareth interpreted the Torah and its precepts in such a fashion as to lead to their total annulment. The sages, of blessed memory, having become aware of his plans before his reputation spread among our people, meted out fitting punishment to him.

David Klinghoffer, a columnist for the Jewish *Forward* Magazine wrote in the *Los Angeles Times* (January 1, 2004):

> The Talmud was compiled in about AD 500, drawing on rabbinic material that had been transmitted orally for centuries. From the 16th century on, the text was censored and passages about Jesus and His execution erased to evade Christian wrath. But the full text was preserved in older manuscripts, and today the censored parts may be found in minuscule type, as an appendix at the back of some Talmud editions.

Jerusalem can't fall, because Messiah hasn't yet come"

As we have seen, the prophecies stated that Messiah would come before the destruction of the Temple and the final exile of the Jews.

During the Roman siege of Jerusalem, as famine and fear raged within the city, the religious leaders, who had a tight control, kept reassuring the populace, "We are secure here. The city will stand – because Messiah hasn't come yet. So hold on! Jerusalem will survive this!"

Soothing but fatal words.

The anguish of a disillusioned people

It is probably safe to say that human suffering never anywhere reached a greater degree of awfulness and intensity, as at the siege of Jerusalem prior to its destruction in AD 70.

Exacerbated by the foul stench of the unburied dead, anarchy broke out. (See my book *Ark of the Covenant*, chapter 18, "The Woman Who Ate Her Son"; Josephus, *Wars of the Jews*, Bk. 5, Ch. 13.)

And yet, the physical suffering was nothing compared to the ANGUISH OF A PEOPLE who sensed they were forsaken by God.

And this is the saddest part of the whole story. During the siege, many Jews expected divine intervention.

To the very LAST they held out, assured of eventual deliverance, for did not the prophecies all say that THE CITY AND THE TEMPLE WILL NOT FALL UNTIL MESSIAH HAS COME?

The inspired prophets Jacob... Micah... Haggai... and Daniel... all agreed on that! Every one of them.

And in more than a thousand years of Hebrew history, never had any biblical prophecy been known to fail. Of that, they were certain. THE WORD OF GOD, WHICH CANNOT FAIL, SAID THE MESSIAH HAD TO COME FIRST.

But now, before their very eyes the Temple was falling. Here was destruction — of everything! EVERYTHING! And the Messiah hadn't come. What had gone wrong?

Can you grasp it? — the utter anguish, the unspeakable despair, the black hopelessness, that now fell upon "God's chosen ones"?

The desolator predicted by Daniel had come. The holy city and Temple were in ruins, the desolation accomplished.

A greater rejection, a greater desolation

Looking back through history, we note that the Jewish Temple was destroyed, with Jerusalem city, on two occasions. Each time, the nation was subsequently dragged or driven into exile.

The first time, in 586 BC, was for their rejection of the prophets and their failure to heed the word of God.

> *And the Lord God sent warnings to them by his messengers... because he had compassion on his people... But they* ***mocked the messengers of God****, and* ***despised his words****, and* ***scoffed at his prophets****,...till there was no remedy.* ***Therefore*** *he brought against them the king of the Chaldeans... He gave them all into his hand... And those that escaped from the sword he carried away to Babylon, where they became servants to him and*

his sons, until the rule of the kingdom of Persia.
(1 Chronicles 36:15-20)

There you have the biblically ***stated reason*** for the first desolation. It was specifically because they ***rejected the prophets*** who were sent to help them turn back to God.

And now, in AD 70, it happened a second time, with the Roman siege of Jerusalem.

Could it be that the reason this time was for their ***rejection of a greater Prophet,*** even the Messiah himself— and a refusal to accept the word of God through him? Was there a connection?

Just coincidence?

And it gets more amazing.

The date the Temple was burned by the armies of Babylon in 586 BC was the 10th day of the month Ab. The date the Temple was burned by Roman armies in AD 70 was the 10th day of the month Ab. (Josephus, *Wars of the Jews*, 6.4.5) The very same date! Does that send a chill up your spine?

These two destructions – were they connected?

Coincidence is when God chooses to remain anonymous.

If the first captivity of 70 years was an adequate consequence for the rejection of their ancient prophets, what can be the enormity of the national sin which brought these people of God to exile, grief and woe for nearly 2,000 years?

According to the Scriptures, it could be nothing less, and nothing more, THAN THE REJECTION OF THEIR MESSIAH... nationally.

Daniel wrote that the Messiah was to come in order to ***"confirm the COVENANT."*** (Daniel 9:27) But this they would despise.

And the Eternal One, speaking through Moses and looking ahead to the Roman siege of Jerusalem, said the result would be the sword upon them, ***"that shall avenge the quarrel of my COVENANT."*** (Leviticus 26:2)

Yes, the Messiah came to CONFIRM THE COVENANT. And he sealed it with his Blood. As predicted, there followed DESOLATION upon Israel. And Jesus gave advance warning why this would be. "*Because you did not recognize the TIME of God's coming to you.*" (Luke 19:43,44)

He told them they were now left "***desolate***". (Matthew 23:38) Soon the "***desolator***" predicted by Daniel would be knocking on the gates of Jerusalem. (ch.24:15; Daniel 9:26,27)

Messiah felt their suffering

Tears were in Jesus' voice as he described to his hearers what was to come upon Jerusalem. In contemplating their suffering he suffered.

The prophet Isaiah predicted that the Messiah was coming to earth to participate in mankind's suffering:

> Surely he hath borne our griefs and carried our sorrows ...he was wounded for our transgressions, he was bruised for our iniquities. (Isaiah 53:4,5)

And so it was from the very start. He was accounted illegitimate, was nearly murdered after his birth in a filthy stable, and became a refugee. He lived in a poor working-class home, then as a teacher. He had no home, no educational privileges, no income. He suffered unjust opposition, unfair trial and undeserved death through the most painful form of execution, crucifixion.

He lived in humble and absolute obedience to his heavenly Father. And he quite ***willingly shared*** in the sufferings of his fellows.

He drained the cup of human suffering to the dregs. So who of us can say to God, "You don't understand"?

Of course He understands! After all, He has been through it all.

And who can say that the Creator has failed to deal justly with human wickedness? He has paid the penalty for it Himself. He has undergone its foul consequences.

And ultimately, although men in their wickedness would demand the death penalty, it would be Jesus himself who chose voluntarily to pursue a course which he knew would lead to his death. After all, that was his reason for coming. His death was a key part of the divine plan to rescue mankind... as many as would accept it.

One person's sacrifice adequate for all?

You ask, How could ***one*** man's death pay the penalty for the sins of ***all*** mankind?

The answer is simple, when you think about it. Because "*all have sinned*" (Rom.3:23), therefore "something special" is required for every person who has been born. Only One whose life is ***equal to all mankind*** could die for the sins of the race. Because Yeshua was the Creator, the Author of all life, the life he laid down was equivalent to all the lives which he had made. Also, such a Rescuer would need to be ***able to rise*** from that death.

Why? So as to apply the benefits of that rescue to all who would ask for it.

The inspired record spells it out: "*There is no other person under heaven through whom we can be saved. Whosoever believes in the Son [Jesus] has eternal life, but whoever rejects the Son will not see life, for God's wrath remains on him.*" (John 3:36). It could not be clearer.

Most priceless of gifts

So the crux of the matter is this. It is by faith in our Creator's mercy that you or I are saved – trusting in Yeshua's sacrifice as the full and complete payment for every wrong we've ever done. Knowing that it is not what you or I can do, but what Yeshua did on the cross, that saves us.

It's only when we understand ***how bad*** sin is that we will understand ***how great*** Yeshua's sacrifice was.

We're all in this together, mate. It's all about living on longer – and enjoying it. Each of us has lost the most valuable gift of all – eternal life. And only our Creator can restore it for us.

If someone said to you, "I'll give you anything you like", what would you ask? I think you would say, "Give me everlasting life." Right? Because, without that, you eventually lose all you have.

Yes, that most priceless of all gifts – simple, straightforward and free – is available to each of us individually, whatever one's past.

And meanwhile, in this present life, knowing one's record is wiped clean, what peace of mind! How much sweeter life becomes! And how your heart will sing!

30

The sacrifice -

REVENGE BY EXECUTION

At his arrest, he could easily have walked away. But he stood there. And let it happen.

He would permit them to bind him, torture him, put him on trial, condemn him and execute him.

He was whisked from one mock trial to another all night, until a verdict could be secured against him.

Yet Yeshua was hardly a helpless victim. He knew he could call a squadron of angels to his side, if he wished. They could have swooped from the heavenly Throne in an instant.

It was no ordinary execution. Yeshua sacrificed himself. Men in their wickedness might choose to crucify him, but it was he who gave himself into their hands to do it.

It is Friday morning. A little after 8 am.

A vast crowd follows Yeshua from the courthouse to Skull Hill. The news of his conviction has spread throughout Jerusalem, and people of all classes and ranks flock toward the execution spot.

At length they reach Skull Hill. Place of death.

The centurion stops... and orders the crosses to be set in the rock, where deep holes have already been cut.

The crosses carried by the two thieves to be executed with him are now thrown down by them, by one with a curse, by the other with a sigh – as he anticipates the agony he is to suffer upon it.

Yeshua's cross is taken by three soldiers and cast heavily upon the rock.

The centurion orders his soldiers to clear a semi-circle with their spears, about the place where the crosses are to be planted.

At the time, crucifixion is the "worst" death, reserved only for the worst criminals. And it serves as a graphic warning to all people.

Crucifixion is an excessively brutal way to die. They strip a convict naked and flog him till his chest and back are in ribbons. Then they arrange his legs uncomfortably and drive blunt 6 to 8 inch nails through his ankles and wrists into a wooden frame.

The Jews, who have crowded near in eager thirst for their victim's blood, edge back slowly and reluctantly before the sharp points of the Roman lances against their chests.

Now the Roman soldiers can get on with their work. It is a terrible work they have to do. And though it is part of the routine of their life, they must hate doing it, especially when their prisoners fight and struggle.

First, a drink

Before they start, they offer each man a drink of wine containing drugs. The effect will not last long, but it will just deaden the beginning of the pain. (Matthew 27:34)

The two thieves gulp their drink thankfully. But Jesus refuses his. He wants to keep his mind as clear as he can. His faith must keep fast hold upon his heavenly Father. This is his only true strength. To becloud his senses will give the powers of evil an advantage.

Then the nails

The first robber, upon seeing the man approach with the basket containing the spikes and hammers, scowls fiercely upon him — and glares defiance.

He is instantly seized by four savage-looking Parthian soldiers of the Roman guard and stripped naked, then thrown upon his back onto the cross.

The struggles of this athletic man are so violent, that it takes six persons to keep him held down upon the arms of the cross.

The legionnaire feels for the depression at the front of the wrist.

One of the crucifiers, with bare and brawny arms, presses one knee upon the arm and drives a heavy, square wrought-iron nail in through the wrist and deep into the wood, by three quick and powerful blows with his short, heavy-headed hammer.

The prisoner gnashes his teeth as the nail enters the quivering flesh.

Quickly the soldier moves to the other side and repeats the action. He is careful not to pull the arms too tightly. Some flex and movement will have to be allowed.

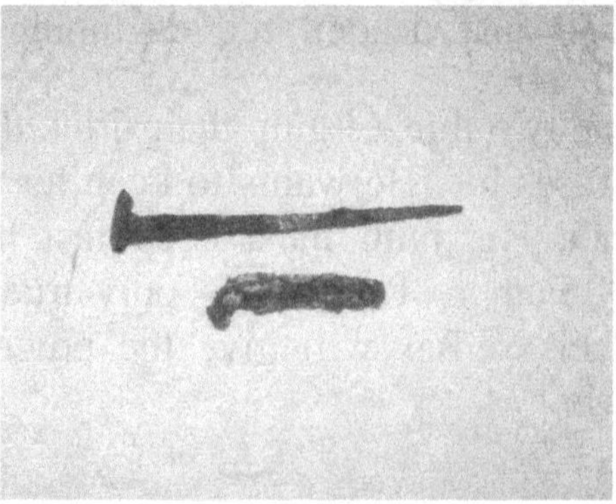

Crucifixion nails

The cross is then lifted into place.

Then both feet are lapped together. The left foot is pressed backward against the right foot. With both feet extended toes down, a long, sharp spear-nail is driven through the arch of each, into the timber, leaving the knees flexed.

A shriek, mingled with curses, testifies to the agony of this wretched man. Thus secured he is left, bleeding and writhing.

The blood-stained crucifiers, with their baskets, cords, hammer and spikes, now approach the other robber.

He, too, wrestles in their hands. After much resistance, his arms are thrust back and nailed to the cross.

When the centurion gives orders to bind Jesus also to the cross, the four soldiers lay hold upon him, remove his robe and begin to strip him of every garment.

But Jesus makes no resistance.

The mother

The mother of Yeshua is there.

Her heart is still throbbing with hope that Yeshua will work some mighty miracle and deliver himself from his murderers.

Again her heart sinks as she recalls the words in which he had foretold the very scenes that are now taking place.

She looks on with agonized suspense. Will he permit himself to be shamed like this? Must she witness his shame and sorrow, without even supporting him or bathing his forehead?

She watches him thrown onto the wood. The hammer and nails are brought.

A few of the disciples stand at a distance. Their hearts faint.

But his mother is bowed with agony almost beyond endurance.

"Oh, don't let me hear the crashing of the nails into your feet and hands. My son, my son! Oh, prove to your mother that you are a true prophet!"

"What's all that wailing?" snaps one of the priests. "Who is that woman?"

"The mother of Yeshua," answers someone.

"The mother of the blasphemer? Let her be accursed!" he cries in a savage tone.

"You see, woman, what is the end of bringing up an impostor to blaspheme Yahweh and the Temple. You wretched woman. Your hopes and his have today miserably died! So die all false Christs and false prophets! You see, if he were the Messiah, he would not stand there and be crucified like a common evil-doer!"

Mary buries her face in her hands... and weeps on a friend's shoulder.

As some disciples bear her from the scene, they can hear the awful preparations... the rattling of the hard cord as they bind him to the cross... and the low, eager voices of the four busy crucifiers... then the ringing of the spikes being taken from the basket... then a moment of silence and suspense.

Next comes the sickening blow of the hammer!

A shriek bursts from the soul of the mother. It echoes far and wide among the tombs of Skull Hill, only to be broken by the crashing of the spikes, as they are driven through the bone and muscle of his tender flesh.

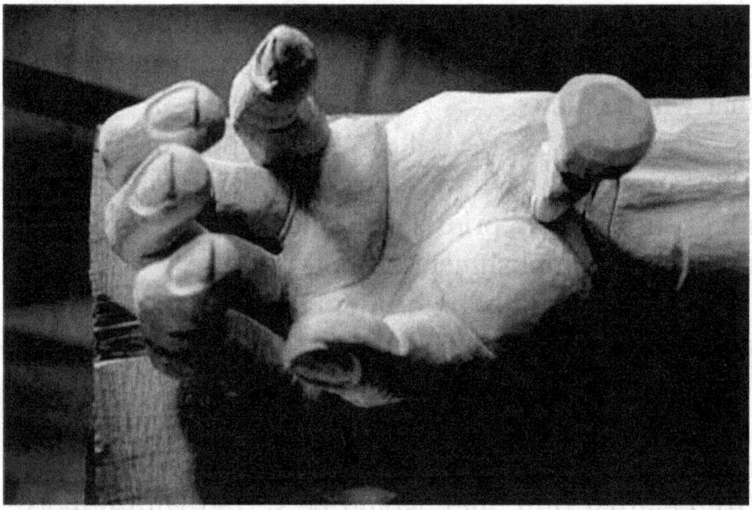

Jesus? He murmurs not, but groans in agony. The piercing nails, tearing his tender flesh, make it quiver. And his face, though calm and serene, turns pale, And large drops of sweat stand on his brow.

Jesus hears his mother's shriek and a deep sigh escapes him.

Pity and forgiveness

While the thieves are cursing their executioners, this Jesus, in his agony, makes no murmur or complaint.

There is no pitying hand to wipe the death-dew from his face. Nor words of sympathy. Nor his disciples' loyalty. Instead there is ridicule.

While the nails are being driven through his hands and the sweat-drops of agony are forced from his pores, from the pale, quivering lips of the innocent sufferer, a prayer of pardoning love is breathed for his murderers:

"Father, forgive them, for they know not what they do!" (Luke 23:34)

His mind passes from his own suffering to the sin of his persecutors — and the terrible retribution that will be theirs.

No curses are called down upon the soldiers who are handling him so roughly. No vengeance is invoked upon the priests and rulers, who are gloating over the accomplishment of their purpose.

Jesus actually pities them in their ignorance and guilt. He breathes only a plea for their forgiveness, "for they know not what they do".

Should they know that they were putting to torture the One who had come to save the sinful race from eternal ruin, they would be seized with remorse and horror.

However, willful ignorance does not remove guilt. It is their privilege to know and accept Yeshua as their Savior. And some of them will yet do so. Others, by stubborn refusal, will prevent Yeshua's prayer being answered for themselves.

It strikes me that, in a broader sense, that prayer includes all of us.

Upon all rests the guilt of the Son of God's death. To all, forgiveness is freely offered. "Whosoever will" may have peace with God... and inherit eternal life.

His cross lifted into place

As soon as Jesus is fastened to the timber, it is raised above the ground by strong men, and with violence thrust into a hole in the rock two feet deep.

This causes most intense pain. The shock brings his whole weight upon the nails in his wrists. It tears and lacerates them, nearly dislocating his shoulders.

The first thief faints from pain at the shock caused by the setting of his own cross. The second, cool and defiant as he has been, utters a loud cry of agony. But Jesus makes no moan — though his deathly pale appearance shows how inexpressible is his torture.

It is 9 am. (Mark 15:25)

The three crosses have now been fixed and raised, with the "feature criminal", Yeshua of Nazareth, in the midst on a level several feet higher than the others. This is the chief place of disgrace.

Now the centurion pushes back the crowd so that the criminals can be left to die.

Someone begins sobbing. "Oh, what a fearful death for Yeshua! For him whom we knew so well. I still love him... although he has deceived us."

They know he might linger on for days, dying slowly... exposed to the fierce sun by day and the chilly winds of night. While above him will hover on steady wings the savage birds of prey, impatient for their feast.

As he slowly sags down with more weight on the nails in the wrists, excruciating, fiery pain will soon shoot along his fingers and up his arms to explode in the brain. The nails in his wrist will put pressure on the median nerves.

In pushing himself up to lessen this stretching torment, he will have to place his full weight on the nail through his feet. So again he will feel the searing agony of the nail tearing through the nerves between the bones of the feet.

The time will come when the arms will fatigue. Cramps will sweep through the muscles, knotting them in deep, relentless, throbbing pain.

With these cramps, he will eventually be unable to push himself upward to breathe. Air will be drawn into his lungs, but to exhale will be difficult. He will then be fighting to raise himself, so as to get even one small breath.

Gradually, carbon dioxide will build up in the lungs and blood stream. Cramps will partially subside. Spasmodically, he might push himself upward to exhale and bring in life-giving oxygen.

Hours of this limitless pain, cycles of twisting, joint-rending cramps, intermittent partial asphyxiation, searing pain as tissue is torn from his lacerated back, as he moves up and down against the rough timber.

Then another agony begins: a deep, crushing pain deep in the chest, as the pericardium slowly fills with serum and begins to compress the heart.

It is now almost over — the loss of tissue fluids has reached a critical level. The compressed heart is struggling to pump heavy, thick, sluggish blood into the tissues. The tortured lungs are making a frantic effort to gasp in small gulps of air.

He can feel the chill of death creeping through his tissues. Finally he can allow his body to die. (From a medical doctor's description)

That is what lies ahead.

All this is recorded in Scripture with the simple words, "*And they crucified him.*" (Mark 15:24)

What kind of love is this, that Jesus is willing to go through this, with each of us in mind?

He could call ten thousand angels from his Father to rescue him, but he willingly endures the agony for each one of us.

The long hours

The sun is high, now, and the heat is adding the misery of thirst to the other torments of the crucified men.

The hours will seem long, and some of the soldiers sit down on the ground to pass the time as best they can.

They divide the prisoners' clothes amongst them.

In spite of the blood and dirt that stains Yeshua's robe, they can see what a beautiful garment it is. It was given to Jesus; it was a gift. They gamble for it.

The mockery

Yeshua's enemies vent their rage upon him, as he hangs naked publicly. Many priests are present at the execution, to witness the climax of their bloodthirsty plot.

What men to lead the nation! How cruel, heartless and utterly devoid of mercy and pity are they, gloating at the suffering of their victim!

Luke records the event:

> ***And the people stood beholding. And the rulers also with them derided him, saying, He saved others; Let him save himself, if he be the Christ, the chosen of God.*** (Luke 23:35)

Jesus, in agony and dying, hears every word.

As the priests scream, "He saved others; himself he cannot save. Let Christ the king of Israel descend now from the cross, that we may see and believe," Yeshua could do just that.

But it is because he will not save himself that you and I will have hope of pardon and favor with God. If Jesus now saves himself, he will forfeit the power to save others. The plan of rescue will have been broken.

Though they know it not, those Jewish leaders give utterance to a profound truth. Jesus' refusal to save himself is the supreme demonstration of divine love.

It is precisely because Jesus chooses not to save himself at this moment, that he will be able to save others.

As Jesus now hangs upon the cross, Lucifer, through his puppets, spares no device, however cruel and false, to shake the Deliverer's hold on his Father's love and overruling providence.

"He trusted in God; let him deliver him now, if he will have him: for he said I am the Son of God." (Matthew 27:43)

Several times during his remarkable, brief career as Messiah, the voice of God had been heard proclaiming Yeshua as his Son. This had occurred at his baptism and again at his transfiguration experience just before his betrayal. The Father had spoken, witnessing to his divinity.

But now the voice from heaven is SILENT! No testimony in Jesus' favor is heard. Alone he suffers abuse and mockery from wicked men.

In their mockery of the Messiah, the men who profess to be the expounders of prophecy are repeating the very words which the old writings had foretold they would utter on this occasion. (Psalm 22:7,8)

Yet, in their blindness, they do not see that they are fulfilling the prophecy.

But the most startling scenes are yet to come.

"For indeed a death by crucifixion seems to include all that pain and death ***can*** have of horrible and ghastly - dizziness, cramp, thirst, starvation, sleeplessness, traumatic fever, tetanus, shame, publicity of shame, long continuance of torment, horror of anticipation, mortification of untended wounds - all intensified just up to the point at which they can be endured at all, but all stopping just short of the point which would give to the sufferer the relief of unconsciousness.

"The unnatural position made every movement painful; the lacerated veins and crushed tendons throbbed with incessant anguish; the wounds, inflamed by exposure, gradually gangrened; the arteries - especially at the head and stomach - became swollen and oppressed with surcharged blood; and while each variety of misery went on gradually increasing, there was added to them the intolerable pang of a burning and raging thirst; and all these physical complications caused an internal excitement and anxiety, which made the prospect of death itself - of death, the unknown enemy, at whose approach man usually shudders most - bear the aspect of a delicious and exquisite release." (Frederick W. Farrar, *The Life of'Christ.* Dutton, Dovar: Cassell and Company, 1897, p. 619)

But it was not the cross that killed him

It began the evening before, when Yeshua went with three disciples to the Gethsemane Garden on the east side of town. He knew the time had come to take upon himself the world's sins, and suffer the retributive justice for them. The agony began.

As he who had never sinned now took upon himself its crushing weight, he began to experience such indescribable anguish as to sweat blood. (Luke 22:44) The death process for our sins had begun. After this, Jesus would have soon died even if they had never put him on the cross. The blood-sweat of agony, when the circulatory system breaks down under extreme mental anguish, is a first sign of approaching death, which will follow within a matter of hours. It was under those trees that he had begun to taste the sufferings of death for every man and woman.

And now, as he hung on the cross, the powers of darkness pressed upon Yeshua. Now, as he felt the crushing weight, the horror, of the sins of the world that he had taken upon himself to shoulder – your guilt and mine – as he felt it descending upon him, the agony grew unbearable. So great was the anguish that his physical pain was hardly felt.

The dreadful thought was pressing upon him, "Even your Father in heaven won't want you now. All this guilt you have chosen to take upon yourself has doomed you. You are finished."

Throughout his life Yeshua had been telling people the good news of God's mercy and pardoning love. Salvation even for the worst of sinners, he had said. But now, Jesus, the sin-bearer, is enduring the wrath of divine justice against sin. Now, as God strikes sin, He strikes His own Son. The guilt of every wrong committed on this planet presses upon his soul. In the place of the wrongdoer, the Son of God suffers the penalty.

Alone Jesus endures this anguish to save us from it. He feels the black despair which the lost rejecter of rescue will feel on the final judgment day... the torment of separation from one's Creator... the torment of the damned, when they realize that, by their own choice, they are God-forsaken and lost forever.

"My God, my God" — Jesus' cry pierces the darkness — "why have you forsaken me?" (Mark 15:34)

How the divine Father must have suffered with His Son! Longing to intervene, He must hold back and let the penalty be paid. What a price was paid for your rescue and mine! The Innocent Ones were the victims.

Now, in the darkness, it seems that even his heavenly Father has deserted him. The hope of rising from the tomb a conqueror now seems a distant illusion. Despair tells him that his separation from his Father will be permanent. Now it appears that he is going down to a grave from which there will be no resurrection. So that we can receive the joy of life in a new world and the company of the Father, he himself must give up life forever.

"My God, my God, why have you forsaken me?" The Rescuer's heart breaks with that cry. He has borne all that even he can bear. It was this sense of the world's guilt, and its terrible effect, separation from God, which made Jesus' suffering so bitter, and crushed out the life of the Prince of God.

What value our Creator has placed upon each person!

31

The sacrifice -

BLOOD AND WATER

That afternoon in Jerusalem, a man clothed as a priest was about his Temple duties, preparing a lamb for slaughter.

It was the annual Passover celebration. And around 3 pm, in accordance with Jewish custom, the priests were to kill the Passover lamb.

But he was troubled. Something very strange was transpiring. Out on the hill to the north — on Skull Hill, the place of execution ***—an eerie darkness had fallen three hours ago***. And it had spread far and wide, even over the city.

He tried not to be distracted by it. And continued his work.

Clothed in his gorgeous robes, the priest stood with lifted knife, ready to slay the lamb for the ceremony.

With intense interest, onlookers stood by.

Suddenly the earth shook. There was heard a loud, sharp ripping noise, from inside the building.

The priest got such a fright, the knife dropped from his trembling hand, and the lamb escaped.

In terror and confusion he rushed inside the first chamber. And looking ahead he saw that the massive curtain which separated the first room from the second, had been torn. As though by unseen hands, it had been ripped violently from top to bottom. (Matthew 27:51)

The Most Holy Place, which was off units to everyone except the high priest, now lay exposed to the view of all.

It was startling. The great veil had been torn not from the bottom upward as men might have done it, but from the top to the bottom. You could call it — if you dared — supernatural.

I understand Josephus says somewhere that the great veil of the Temple was 3 inches thick! It would have taken a team of bullocks to tear it!

Always cautious, I resolved to track down, if possible, whatever sources outside the New Testament were available.

An obvious help would be a Jewish rabbi.

Yes, it was an Australian mid-winter Sunday afternoon - June 29, to be precise - that I went to the home of Rabbi Reubenzacks. The rabbi ushered me into a study crammed with books, mostly on shelves, but also in numerous piles neatly stacked along the wall.

I quickly came to the point. "Rabbi, do you know anything about the tearing of the veil of the Second Temple?"

The rabbi looked surprised.

I added, "It is supposed to have occurred early in the first century CE at the time of Passover."

Initially taken aback by the directness of the question, the rabbi recovered his composure, then guardedly, but with honesty, responded.

"Yes," he said, "there is an unwritten Jewish tradition that the veil was torn mysteriously at that time."

"It is finished"

Outside the city, at that same moment the veil was torn, Jesus cried out "IT IS FINISHED!" (John 19:30) From now on, Temple sacrifices would be meaningless. The symbol was meeting its fulfillment in the death of the Lamb of God.

The Messiah had completed the work his Father had given him to do.

It had been planned from the beginning of the world. (1 Peter 1:19,20; Revelation 13:8) And every step in the plan of rescue had been completed according to schedule.

Lucifer had been unsuccessful in his attempts to overthrow the plan. Jesus' victory assured the salvation of mankind.

As Jesus in his death agony cried out, ***"It is finished,"*** a shout of triumph must have rung through the heavens. The great contest that had been so long in progress was now decided and Jesus was conqueror.

What happened that day to parallel the ancient sacrificial system was almost startling. On the annual Hebrew Day of Atonement (Yom Kippur), the high priest would enter the Holy of Holies with the blood of the sacrificed animal, then sprinkle the blood upon the Mercy Seat, which represented the Throne of God.

After ***three hours in the darkness*** of the Most Holy Place, the high priest would come out with the empty basin, hold it up, and proclaim, ***"It is finished."*** Then the people knew that the sacrifice had been accepted by God and their sins were forgiven.

Yeshua's ***three hours in darkness*** on the cross ended with the triumphant cry, ***"It is finished."*** He had done all he could. We now had a means of rescue.

That did not mean that everyone would be saved. A parachute is manufactured and finished to the extent that it can save a pilot who bails out of a plane. But it still needs something... the action of the man to pull it open as he jumps. His part is also necessary. Although a parachute is ***finished***, the pilot's part has yet to be finished, before he can be saved. In the divine rescue plan, our individual response would be crucial.

Rock split open

Jesus gave one final cry with a loud voice, "Father, I commit my spirit into Your hands." (Luke 23:46) As he submitted himself, the sense of the loss of his Father's favor was withdrawn. By faith, Jesus was victor. He had now become conscious of triumph and confident of his own resurrection.

Immediately a fearful rumbling sound erupted from deep down m the earth. The ground shook violently and the rocks were split open. (Matthew 27:51) Jesus was dead. (John 19:32,33)

From the startled Roman centurion were forced the words, "Truly this man was the Son of God."

Death by crucifixion was a slow process. A victim could linger on for days. Those soldiers were a special dispatch assigned to crucifixions. They were familiar with crucifixion scenes. They were shocked that Yeshua was dead already.

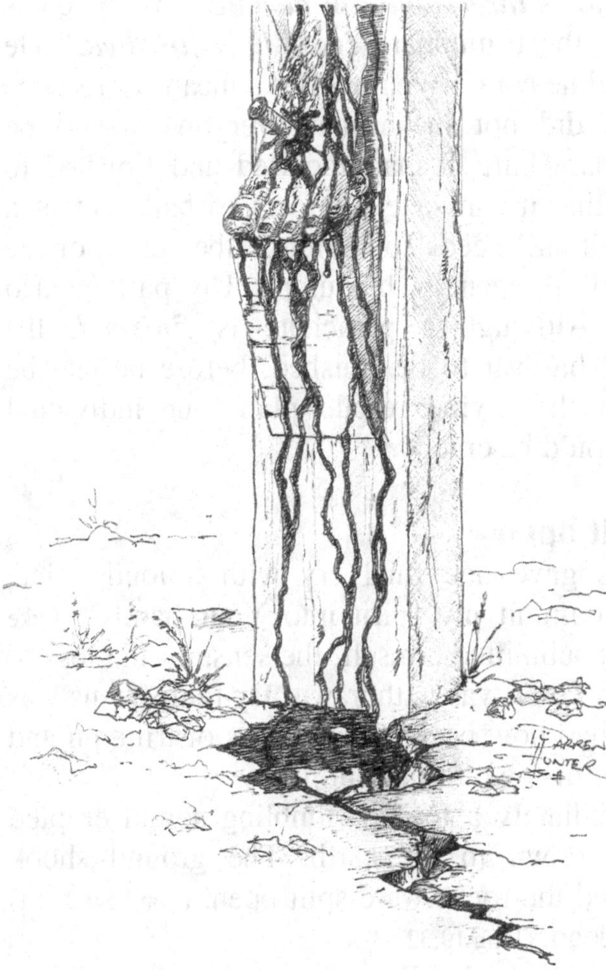

A spear thrust into his side

The priests wanted to be sure Yeshua was dead, so at their suggestion a soldier thrust a spear up into his side.

Notice carefully what happened next. The disciple John writes:

> However, one of the soldiers pierced his side with a spear, and blood and water flowed out. I saw all this myself and have given an accurate report so that you also can believe. The soldiers did this in fulfillment of the Scripture that says, "Not one of his bones shall be broken," and, "They shall look on him whom they pierced." (John 19:34-37)

Did you notice? Out flowed two copious and distinct streams, one of blood, the other of water. This was noted by those who stood by. It was when the semi solid dark red blood poured out, distinct and separate from the accompanying watery serum, that they knew Yeshua was, indeed, dead.

Here was startling evidence that Jesus' death was not due to physical exhaustion, nor to the pains of crucifixion, nor to the spear thrust. His heart had literally burst. Two things — that sudden cry, uttered ***"with a loud voice"*** at the moment of death (Matthew 27:50), and the stream of ***blood and water*** that flowed from his side - declared that he had died of a broken heart. The muscles of the heart may have been actually torn. It can happen under intense mental strain.

Ah, there's more to this than meets the eye.

Blood and water medical testimony

Some years ago, Dr Walshe, Professor of Medicine at University College, London, declared that in heart rupture the hand is carried to the front of the chest and a piercing shriek uttered. Usually death very speedily follows. Blood escapes into the cavity of the pericardium (the heart sac), which sac has, in cases of rupture of the heart, been found to contain two, three, four or more pounds of blood accumulated within it, and separated into red blood and limpid serum ("blood and water").

In 1957, A.F. Sava reported that he had experimented with cadavers less than six hours after death. These experiments proved that when a lance is thrust into the side of the chest, "fluid from the pericardium and the heart will 'flood the space around the lung rather than ooze its way slowly across the pierced lung' to the wound in the chest wall." (Erich H. Kiehl, *The Passion of our Lord.* Baker Book House, 1990, p.146)

Sava believed that in Jesus' case, blood and water would have gathered just inside the rib cage, between the pleura lining the chest and the pleura lining the lung. He also suggested that the scourging (flogging) a few hours before he was crucified was sufficient to cause an accumulation of bloody fluid inside the chest:

> Experience with severe chest injuries has demonstrated that non penetrating injuries of the chest are capable of producing an accumulation of a hemorrhagic fluid in the space between the ribs and the lung. This volume of bloody fluid varies with the severity of the injury and the degree of response to such an injury. Such collections of blood in closed cavities do not clot. The red blood cells tend by their weight to gravitate toward the bottom of the containing cavity, thus dividing it into a dark red cellular component below, while the lighter clear serum accumulates in the upper half of the collection as a separate though contiguous layer.. From a purely anatomic- mechanical standpoint, therefore, the likelihood of hemorrhagic effusion between the lung and the ribs is far greater than a

> similar occurrence within the pericardial sac. (A.F. Sava, "The Wound in the Side of Christ," *Catholic Biblical Quarterly* 19,1957, p.346)

In 1975, John Wilkinson, a medical missionary, analyzed and assessed various theories, and concluded that the issue of blood and water was due to "gravity and the vertical position of the body on the cross. Noting that blood remains fluid for some time after death, Wilkinson concluded that the lance must have pierced the lower part of the heart cavity. On the basis of his medical experience with severe injuries he agreed... that the 'water' originated in the pericardial sac. This fluid 'was thin, clear and colorless and quite distinct from the thick, opaque, red blood it accompanied.' The lance thrust released the fluid and, in penetrating the heart, also released the blood, which came out first. It is probable that more watery fluid flowed out than blood." (Kiehl, pp. 146,147)

> Dr. C. Truman Davis, a medical doctor who has meticulously studied crucifixion from a medical perspective, says that "an escape of watery fluid from the sac surrounding the heart" is evidence "not [of] the usual crucifixion death by suffocation, but of heart failure due to shock and constriction of the heart by fluid in the pericardium."

Samuel Houghton, MD, the great physiologist from the University of Dublin, an authority on the physical phenomena accompanying death wounds, states:

> That rupture of the heart was the cause of the death of Christ is ably maintained by Dr.William Stroud; and that rupture of the heart actually occurred I firmly believe.The importance of this is

> obvious. It [shows] that the narrative in St. John xix could never have been invented; that the facts recorded must have been seen by an ***eye-witness***; and that the eye-witness was so astonished that he apparently thought the phenomenon miraculous. (Frederick Charles Cook, ed.,*Commentary on the Holy Bible.*London: John Murray, 1878, pp.349,350)

John thought it, if not to be miraculous, at least to be unusual.

It had begun the previous evening, in Gethsemane Garden, when Yeshua sweated blood, as Luke the physician noted. (Luke22:44) That's where the "great anguish" began, which was ultimately to snuff out his life.

Jesus did not die from nail wounds or the pain of crucifixion. It was something else. He was slain by the sin of the world that he had chosen to bear. This was not the ordinary death we all die, but the "final" death of separation from God. Jesus tasted that death, in unmeasurable agony, to save us from it.

Then Jesus literally, as well as metaphorically, died of a broken heart.

And with what tenacity! How could one ever deserve such a person?

32

The sacrifice -

PUBLIC EXECUTION: WHY NEEDED?

“Was the cross plan just a gimmick?"

"What do you mean?"

"Well, if he was about to die anyway, then why allow himself to be nailed publicly to a cross? I almost feel sorry for those priests. It’s like God willed it, so they had to act their guilty part. Like they were victims of fate."

Interesting. But no, they were not victims of fate or of prophecy. They didn’t have to do what they did. Jesus had done everything possible to save them from this terrible deed. They ***freely chose*** their course of action. ***And God overruled it to His purpose***.

1. AS UNDISPUTED EVIDENCE THAT THE SACRIFICE HAD BEEN MADE.

The agony of a ***public*** death meant that witness of it could be borne without the shadow of doubt. It was to become the pivot of history.

Consequently we know more about the details of those hours leading up to and during the death of Jesus than we know about the death of any other one person in all the ancient world.

In the 10th century Apaplus wrote:

> We have found in many books of the philosophers that they refer to the day of the crucifixion of Christ. (Shlomo Pines, Professor of Philosophy at Hebrew University, Jerusalem;

David Flusser, professor at Hebrew University, New York Times press release, Feb.12, 1972. carried by *Palm Beach Post-Times,* Feb.13, 1972, "CHRIST DOCUMENTATION: Israeli Scholars Find Ancient Document They Feel Confirms the Existence of Jesus.")

And elsewhere we have cited first century statements from Tacitus, Josephus and also from the Jewish Talmuds, relating to this event.

2. THE CROSS WAS OVERRULED TO REACH MEN'S HEARTS.

Jesus had said, "If I be lifted up [on the cross] I will draw men unto me." (John 12:32) The cross became God's chosen means of winning men and women to His love. (John 12:32,33)

Shame or triumph?

To anyone watching, it was a disaster. Jesus had failed. On the other hand, if he really was the Messiah, choosing to die on man's behalf, one could draw several startling conclusions.

1. SIN MUST BE A TREMENDOUSLY IMPORTANT MATTER

Sin ***required*** the Deliverer's death. And he died because sin was curable.

When does a doctor operate? When there is hope! Certainly not when it is hopeless! So sin is neither hopeless nor incurable, otherwise he would never have died. For sin to be grappled with successfully, God Himself must come right into it.

2. THE CROSS PROVED GOD'S LOVE

His death answered the question as to whether the Creator had sufficient love for mankind to exercise self-denial and a spirit of sacrifice, so that humans could be saved.

The spotless Son of God hung upon the cross, his flesh lacerated with whip strokes; those hands that so often reached out to help people, now nailed to wooden bars; those feet so tireless on errands of love, spiked to the cross; that royal head pierced by a mock crown of thorns; those quivering lips shaped to the cry of woe.

And all that he endured: the blood drops that flowed from his head, his hands, his feet; the agony that racked his frame; the unutterable anguish that filled his soul for lost mankind...

It was for me... and you.

He who calmed angry waves and walked the foam-capped billows, who made devils tremble and disease flee, who opened blind eyes and called dead men to life... offers himself upon the cross as a sacrifice.

And this from his love to us!

He endures the penalty of divine justice for your sake... and, mine. His death proves his love.

What a triumph!

3. IT PROVED WHICH ONE CARED

For thousands of years, the forces of evil had been in a tussle for the control of the human race. (Zechariah 3:1,2; Job 1:6-12; 2:1-7; Jude 9; Revelation 20:7,8)

It was claimed by the prophets that behind man's rebellion were evil entities. They had denied God's truthfulness and His concern for His subjects. Having initially rebelled against the government of heaven, they had been cast out. Rather than destroy them there and then (which could have been misunderstood), God decided to fight the rebellion with LOVE.

Lucifer, their leader, it was held, had shifted his battlefield to planet Earth — and led our first parents into rebellion.

"Go it alone," he urged. "Be independent. You don't need God."

And we fell for it.

When the rebellion began, it had seemed incredible that sin could be as dangerous as God said it was.

But when the universe saw the centuries of hatred, heartache and death on planet Earth, they began to understand. They watched Lucifer's (Satan's) kingdom in operation.

Then they saw God's Son enter this enemy territory to save mankind. He lived and suffered with us — showing us by his example how to overcome.

Then he went to the cross. That showed the value God had placed upon men and women. It was the ultimate evidence of God's great love.

But Satan's unquenchable hatred toward the Son of God was revealed in the way he carefully planned the betrayal, mock trial and shameful crucifixion.

This opened the eyes of the universe to his true criminal character. Heavenly beings were horror-stricken that Lucifer, a former one of their number, could fall so far as to be capable of such cruelty. Now every sentiment of sympathy or pity which they ever felt for him in his exile was quenched from their hearts.

So there is Lucifer, professing to be clothed in celestial light —yet with envy he exercises revenge on an innocent Person, against the divine Son of God who has, with unprecedented self-denial and love, come from heaven and assumed the nature of lost mankind. (John 3:13; 6:33,41; Micah 5:2; John 17:5; 8:58)

Now Satan appears hideous! He has committed such a horrible crime against heaven, that heavenly beings shudder with horror.

The last link of sympathy with him is broken. He is finished, as far as the inhabitants of other worlds are concerned. (Isaiah 14:12-17; Revelation 12:9-12; Luke 10:18)

He has revealed his true character as a liar and a murderer. (John 8:44) Lucifer is discredited. Jesus Christ is vindicated.

What a triumph!

4. IT SATISFIED DIVINE LAW AND ESTABLISHED IT AS UNCHANGEABLE

The death of Jesus was a convincing argument that the law of God was as unchangeable as His Throne.

The fact that God's own Son, the surety for man, was not spared, testified that the divine law, which had been violated, could not be altered to save the sinner.

No, the violation of that law must meet the penalty, death. Therefore, the justice of God must put to death His beloved Son who stood in the wrong-doer's place.

The law must stand as firm as the Throne of God — although the earth shake and the whole creation tremble — as the Son of God dies in agony.

Justice demands that sin be not only pardoned, but that the death penalty must be executed. The very purpose of Jesus' death was to secure pardon for the law-breaker, without destroying the law.

The death of Jesus is the mightiest evidence of the holiness of the law of God.

In the days of the Persian Empire, the monarch Darius labored strenuously, feverishly, to save Daniel from the lion's den. But there stood the "law of the Medes and Persians which alters not." (Daniel 6:8) The majesty of law, the very stability of the government, demanded that the sentence be executed, or else the throne itself would be imperiled.

Even so, had there been another way to vindicate the sovereignty of divine law, Jesus need not have died.

But infinite love and wisdom could devise no other plan, since to abolish the law would have immortalized sin.

The royal law must stand unshaken, even though it cost the life of the beloved Son. The law and justice of God — all-holy — are established. (Romans 3:31; Matthew 5:17,18; James 2:10-12)

What a triumph!

The grandest drama of all

When I finally grasped the grandeur of this event, I realized that beside it all the wisdom of earth's wisest men sank into insignificance.

Just think of the immensity of the drama!

The co-Creator gave himself as a ransom. He laid off his royal robe. He laid aside his kingly crown, and stepped down from his high command over all heaven, and took upon himself feeble human flesh. (Philippians 2:5-8) And as if that were not enough, he so abased himself as to suffer the excruciating pain of the cross, at the hands of people he had created. (John 1: 1-3,14; Hebrews 1: 2; Colossians 1:16)

It is a mystery that he did it. And it is a mystery that God so loved the world as to permit His Son to make this great sacrifice. Science is too limited to comprehend this event. This mysterious and wonderful plan of rescue is so far-reaching that philosophy cannot explain it. The most profound reason cannot fathom it.

Indeed, this was ***the most daring rescue mission of all time.***

For many years I lived as an unbeliever. There are readers who, like myself, will be able to relate to the following true experience of yet another skeptic.

George Vandeman recounts this story of an unbeliever who rescued an orphan boy from a burning building.

"Having lost his own wife and child, he desired to adopt the lad. Christian neighbors were skeptical about the wisdom of placing the boy in an infidel home. But the applicant won his case when he held up his hand, badly burned in the rescue of the lad, and said, 'I have only one argument. It is this.'

"He proved to be a good father, and little Bobby never tired of hearing how Daddy had saved him from the fire. And he liked best to hear about the scarred hand.

"One day with his new father he visited a display of art masterpieces. One painting interested him especially — the one of Jesus reproving Thomas for his unbelief and holding out his scarred hand.

"'Tell me the story of that picture, Daddy', the little fellow pleaded.

"'No, not that one.'

"'Why not?'

"'Because I don't believe it'.

"'But you tell me the story of Jack the giant-killer, and you don't believe that.'

"So he told him the story. And Bobby said, 'It's like you and me, Daddy'. And then he went on, 'It wasn't nice of Thomas not to believe after the good Man had died for him. What if they had told me how you saved me from the fire and I had said I didn't believe you did it?'

"The father could not escape the sound reasoning of a little child. He had used his own scarred hand to win a small boy's heart. Could he continue to resist the scarred hand of the Man who had died for him — and say he didn't do it?" (George E. Vandeman, *The Cry of a Lonely Planet.* Mountain View, Ca..: Pacific Press Publishing Association, 1983, pp.255,256)

It has to be the mightiest argument of all, that cross on Skull Hill. The scarred hands of Yeshua. Hands that were wounded in his encounter with the forces of evil — so that you and I could live!

33

The Rescuer accepted -

THE PROPHECY THAT SAVED MANY LIVES

What a paradox!

During their revolt against the Romans in AD 66, thousands of Jews poured into Jerusalem, considering it to be safer inside the city, than out of it.

Yet, while the Jews were coming ***IN***, all of Jerusalem's Christian citizens were escaping ***OUT*** of it.

In the holocaust which followed, 1,100,000 people perished. Never have so many citizens perished in the fall of any city. Only about one-tenth as many people were killed in Hiroshima as in the fall of Jerusalem.

But here is an extraordinary fact: ***Not one*** believer in Jesus perished in the subsequent destruction of Jerusalem. Of this, you shall soon see testimony.

And how did they survive it? The answer is, they had been watching for the "sign" — and they followed the instructions of someone they understood to be Jesus.

Now, if Jesus never existed, but was merely a later "invention" of someone's fertile imagination (as some like to tell us) – then how shall we explain this prophecy which an "imaginary person" had given to his followers? How is it that every Christian escaped, when about everyone else perished or went into slavery?

What made the difference? Yes, it was a prophecy… one that already existed before AD 66. Jesus, these survivors claimed, had given them a prophecy. They acted on it.

The event is affirmed by history. At this early date, there were already many who not only believed in Jesus, but conducted their lives in harmony with his teachings.

He told them how they could escape this coming disaster. It's an historical record that of those who followed his advice, ***not one lost his life.***

They so unshakeably believed in Jesus and believed that he had personally given this prophecy. And their belief led them to actions which were opposite from the rest of the population – and which saved their lives.

What was this prophecy?

Shortly before his crucifixion in AD 31, Jesus made his final visit to the Jewish Temple. This magnificent structure, according to Josephus, was constructed of white marble stones each of immense size – 25 cubits (43 feet) in length – as large as a bus! (For more on ancient mega size construction techniques, see Jonathan Gray, *Dead Men's Secrets,* chs. 16 and 17. <www.beforeus.com>)

On the way out, he pointed to those mighty temple stones and confided to his disciples, "*Truly I say to you, there shall not be left here one stone upon another, that shall not be thrown down.*" (Matthew 24:1,2)

All these giant stones would be thrown down? An unlikely event!

Puzzled, four of them seized a private moment, to ask the question, "**WHEN** will this be?"

Then Jesus dropped a bombshell. "*All these things shall come upon* ***this generation.***" (Matthew

23:36; 24:34) *"YOU yourselves shall see it happen."* (v. 15)

After that, he ***listed off seven omens*** that would precede that dreadful event - signs that were to find a remarkable fulfillment. (Matthew 24; Mark 13; Luke 21)

Wait for THE sign, then flee

Then he gave **THE** sign — a ***specific*** sign that would alert them:

> *WHEN you shall see the abomination that makes desolate, spoken of by Daniel the prophet, stand in the holy place; WHEN you see Jerusalem* ***SURROUNDED BY ARMIES****, you will know that its desolation is near. WHEN this happens, then get out of the city quickly.* (Matthew 24:15-19; Luke 21:20-24)

Among the Jews an idol or other heathen symbol, such as a banner, was often termed an "abomination", or something offensive from a religious point of view. This would apply to the banners of a Roman army appearing outside the city.

A most unlikely prophecy

"Okay, okay," someone says, "the Romans had no need to attack Jerusalem. It was already part of the Roman Empire, under their jurisdiction. For the love of common sense, ***why would they ever besiege it?"***

Furthermore, to make such an event even more unlikely, Rome had, since the days of Julius Caesar, treated the Jews leniently. They lived by their own religious law, were exempt from military service, and even retained puppet kings, the Herods.

And then, what strange advice about leaving the city after it was already surrounded by armies – ***how ever could they leave?***

I know, I know, it does seem an illogical type of prediction. How on earth could such an ***unlikely*** event take place?

Amazing sequence of events

Let's see what happened.

It turned out that the Roman officials during the succeeding years became more grasping. Crushed by taxation, the Jews turned to the Zealots — a group of fanatical leaders to whom Rome was a foe to be rooted out with the sword.

In AD 65, the Roman agent Floris did something that really upset the Jews. And they revolted. Led by John of Giscala (a rich merchant of Galilee) and Simon bar Gioras, the Jews rose in mass revolt.

Roman garrisons were surprised and cut to pieces. Jerusalem itself was seized by these Jewish fighters and fortified.

Cestius Gallus, Roman legate of Syria, took command of Judea and in the autumn of AD 66 marched against Jerusalem, surrounding it with his troops.

Had it not been for the Jewish rebellion that year, the Romans would have had no reason to besiege Jerusalem. But, 35 years earlier, Jesus foretold it. "*When armies surround Jerusalem,*" he said, "*then flee.*"

Pagan banners betokening the presence of Gentile arms not only appeared near and around the city, but were eventually in the holy place. They fought about the holy temple — attempting in vain to enter.

"*When you see the abomination stand in the holy place*," said Jesus.

THIS WAS THE SIGNAL FOR THE CHRISTIANS. But however could they flee? The attackers were already encircling the city! Furthermore, the furious war party in the city, the Zealots, would have prevented any attempted flight.

Cestius' Roman troops were so successful that the Jews were ABOUT TO SURRENDER. Encouraged by a promise of the loyalist party in Jerusalem to open the gates for him, Cestius gathered his troops to a strong assault. He penetrated as far as the northern wall of the temple.

THEN AN ASTOUNDING THING HAPPENED.

Suddenly he withdrew from the city, "***without any reason in the world***." (Flavius Josephus, *Wars of the Jews*, Bk. 2, ch. 19, sect. 7. Emphasis added)

THE CHRISTIANS KNEW THE REASON.

As the Zealots opened the gates and set out in pursuit of the retiring Romans, the watchful believers knew THEIR MOMENT HAD COME.

Latching on to Jesus' warning of 35 years earlier, every Christian fled out through the open gates at the proper time. They fled to Pella, in the foothills of a mountain range across the Jordan River, a place completely separated from Judea by the Jordan Valley.

There is no doubt that this occurred. It is quite ***openly admitted by a standard Jewish authority***: "Prior to Jerusalem's siege by Titus (in 70 CE)," *Encyclopedia Judaica* states, "its Christian community moved to Pella."

"It is hard to account for this escape if [Jesus'] prophecy was written after the event," G. A. Williamson points out in his introduction to *Josephus – The Jewish War.*

Not one Christian perished in the subsequent destruction of Jerusalem. Why? Because they had Jesus' prophecy. They had been watching for the specific sign — and they obeyed their Lord's instructions. Can you believe it? THE PROPHECY WAS SPOT ON!

A prayer answered

Something else. The Christian believers had been praying, in harmony with Jesus' instruction, that this event would not occur during winter, nor on the Sabbath day. (Matthew 24:20) Graetz, the Jewish historian, has computed the days involved, showing that Cestius must have withdrawn from the city on WEDNESDAY, October 7. The Christians did not have to travel on the Sabbath. Neither did they have to flee in the winter.

Haste necessary

Jesus had predicted that the flight out of the city would require such haste that the man on the housetop or in his garden should not try to gather any extra clothing. (vv. 17,18)

History shows that such haste was necessary. Time was of the essence. To postpone flight would entail great danger. As it happened, the ROMAN ARMIES SOON RETURNED. The temporary respite was the last opportunity the Christians would have to escape.

As the Romans devastated one town of Judea after another, people fled when possible to Jerusalem, swelling the numbers there to be fed and kept in order. This continued, since united action from Jerusalem appeared to be the safeguard. During a comparative lull in the storm, more thousands of people poured in. The moment the Zealots returned, the gates were closed and desperate preparations were begun for the next encounter. No Christian would have escaped then. Before long, the invading Romans returned to the siege. Fearful scenes of famine and bloodshed were to follow, until Jerusalem would be laid waste.

But — and note this point — history records that NOT ONE CHRISTIAN PERISHED IN THE SIEGE OF JERUSALEM....

Oh, and something else. Titus, the Roman general, commanded that the Temple, a world wonder, be spared. Had his command been obeyed, Jesus' prophecy of the Temple stones being dismantled, would have failed. But so infuriated were the soldiers by the defenders' stubbornness, that one soldier cast a burning brand into the Temple. Soon its mighty cedar beams were ablaze. In the intense heat, the adornments of gold melted and ran down between the cracks of the stones. Later, the Romans, in a passion to extract the gold, physically tore the stones apart. Thus was fulfilled Jesus' prophecy concerning "not one stone" being left on top of another.

Critics wrong again

Important: the prophecy of Jesus was already in place – before AD 66.

1. The event is affirmed by history.

2. Jesus' followers at that time believed this prophecy from Jesus. And their belief led them to actions which, in contrast to the rest of the population, saved their lives.

Here again are the events:

1. Jerusalem is surrounded by Roman armies.
2. Romans withdraw.
3. Christians leave.
4. Jews flood into the city.
5. Jerusalem is destroyed

Wake up, Jackie! The Jesus prophecy that saved the Jerusalem Christians in AD 66 was ***not*** made up by some writer ***after*** the event. You have just seen ***actionable proof*** – prophecy in action in real life. This knocks out the "late" first century, even second century origin of the Gospels claimed by some critics.

Why don't they give up? After all, being on the winning side is far more satisfying.

Seals his credentials as the divine Rescuer

But more importantly, the unlikely advice Jesus gave in this prophecy seals Jesus Christ as ***the reliable rescuer.***

This is not some nebulous messiah based on guesswork. This is ***actual, measurable and provable*** escape from death by those who believed Jesus in real historical time, that has ***already*** happened. It is even documented by his enemies.

But it gets better. His ability becomes relevant to every person in this 21st century who is wise to take note. Jesus has also given practical tips on how you and I can escape what's coming on the earth soon. Credible Deliverer? You can stake your life on it.

Thought questions

Concerning these things that the prophet Daniel predicted:

- Was Jerusalem rebuilt? …YES
- Did sacrifices end? …YES
- Was Jerusalem destroyed again? …YES
- Did Messiah come? …WELL?

What about Yeshua's alleged rising from the dead?

There's a related issue we shall ultimately need to face: Did he rise from the dead, or not?

The messianic prophecy of Isaiah 53 stated that Messiah, though "*brought as a lamb to the slaughter*", "*an offering for sin*", "*cut off out of the land of the living*", yet "*he shall prolong his days*", ultimately see the results of his sacrifice "*and shall be satisfied*". (Isaiah 53:7-11) Other prophecies emphatically declare that he shall receive "*an everlasting dominion, which shall not pass away.*" (Daniel 7:13,14)

For these to occur he would need to rise from the dead. We shall now investigate this…

PART EIGHT

BACK FROM DEATH?

34

Eyewitness documents –

HOW EARLY, HOW RELIABLE?

About 950 AD, a Tahitian by the name of Kupe sailed almost 2,000 miles to New Zealand, then back to tiny Tahiti, a mere speck in the ocean.

The Tahitians possessed no writing. They had, however, prodigious memories.

I understand that two hundred years later, other Tahitians, following Kupe's verbal sailing directions preserved by professional memorisers, made a successful landfall at the very same inlet on the New Zealand coastline as their predecessor. They did not return.

Then in 1350 (using sailing directions repeated but never recorded for 400 years) another group arrived in New Zealand.

Oral tradition was computer-accurate in ancient times. There is evidence that man's early ancestors – including the Jews – had incredibly ***accurate memories***. We shall touch on this later in this chapter.

* * * * * * *

The CAUSE of Christianity's early, rapid growth

For a moment, let's just chew over this question: Assuming Jesus did not rise from the dead, then ***what was the catalyst*** for Christianity?

What cause can be pinpointed, to explain the historical fact that Christianity transformed the world of the first century?

The odds of its success were poor. Several religions already existed at that time. Some elements that are also found in Christianity, were already found in them.

Why did Christianity succeed – especially when it was so exclusivist and frowned on compromise with other religions?

And why were its proponents so willing to face death for their claims?

We must be realistic about this. The Christian movement did not just happen. It had ***a definite cause.***

It was said of the Christians that they "turned the world upside down." (Acts 17:6)

What was the cause of this influence? I submit that it was nothing less than the resurrection of Jesus. (And in the next few chapters you will discover my reasons for stating this.)

At no time was there ever a form of Christianity which omitted to emphasise ***the centrality of the death and resurrection*** of Jesus Christ. The resurrection of a divine Jesus from the dead was the explanation that Christianity gave for its very existence. That belief was ***its central driving force***.

As Wilbur Smith recognises:

> Let it simply be said that we know more about the details of the hours immediately before and after the actual death of Jesus, in and near Jerusalem, than we know about the death f any other one man in all the ancient world. (Wilbur M. Smith, *Therefore Stand: Christian Apologetics*. Grand Rapids: Baker Book House, p.360)

You and I both know it. The historicity of many other characters from the ancient world is accepted on much less evidence than this – often merely upon the single appearance of a name.

Christianity is well grounded in the facts of history. The Bible itself is a document of demonstrated accuracy. It is well attested history. You can trust its writings.

Jesus story invented?

"No, no, no, that can't be," yells someone who has just opened the book at this page. "David Icke says the New Testament was written by a fraudulent Roman family, long after the alleged events." (David Icke, *The Big Secret.* Wildwood, MO.: Bridge of Love Publications USA, 2001, pp.106-107)

Okay. So a man wants to invent a modern fiction that some folk will believe? Here's all you have to do. Just think up a name and conjure up some dates… and well, that sort of makes it sound plausible, right? So he tells us that a family with the name of Piso wrote it, between 60 AD and 138 AD?

Yeah, sure they did. And I'm Alexander the Great.

Now get serious.

Go back!

If you started reading this book only five minutes ago and you are already here, I want you to go straight back to Chapter 1. If you do not first read carefully the preceding chapters, you may neither understand nor accept the truth of what follows. And in that case you will not be qualified to make a rational judgment concerning this matter.

If you believe Mr Icke's assertion, it's because you have ***not seen the evidence*** in our earlier chapters. So please do yourself a favor. Go straight back and start again.

Eyewitnesses were still alive when the documents were written

For the establishment of an historical fact, no documents are esteemed to be more valuable than ***contemporary*** letters. Especially letters by the eyewitnesses.

Professor Kevan says of the epistles of the New Testament:

> There is the unimpeachable evidence of the contemporary letters of Paul the Apostle. These epistles constitute historical evidence of the highest kind. The letters addressed to the *Galatians*, the *Corinthians*, and the *Romans*, about the authenticity and date of which there is very little dispute, belong to the time of Paul's missionary journeys, and may be dated in the period A.D. 55-58. This brings the evidence of the resurrection of Christ still nearer to the event: the interval is the short span of twenty-five years. Since Paul himself makes it plain that the subject of his letter was the same as that about which he had spoken to them when he was with them, this really brings back the evidence to a still earlier time. (Ernest F. Kevan, *The Resurrection of Christ.* London: The Campbell Morgan Memorial Bible Lectureship, Westminster Chapel, Buckingham Gate, S.W.I., June 14, 1961, p. 6)

Also, bear this in mind:

> When an event takes place in history and there are enough people alive who were eyewitnesses of it or had participated in the event, and when the information is published, one is able to verify the validity of an historical event. (Josh McDowell, *Evidence That Demands A Verdict.* San Bernardino, Ca.: Here's Life Publishers, Inc.,1986, p.189)

Now may I ask you? Is it likely that a book, describing alleged ***public events*** that occurred 30 or 40 years previously, could have been accepted or cherished if its stories of abnormal occurrences were false or mythical?

Of course not. Why? Because the ***memory*** of all elderly persons regarding the events of 30 or 40 years before, is ***perfectly clear***.

No one could today publish a biography of George Bush's White House days, full of PUBLIC ***event anecdotes*** which were blatantly untrue. They would be contradicted at once. They would not be accepted and passed on as true.

Likewise, there was no way in which the New Testament writers could have got away with pure fabrication. For, as Luke himself records, there were ***plenty of eyewitnesses***.

The assertion that Jesus is just a myth will not bear close scrutiny.

This whole subject calls for intellectual honesty. The ***evidence*** makes perfect sense – enough to engender a deep assurance that the Jesus account is not founded on delusions or cunningly devised fables, but on historical events. These are ***real*** events which, however unusual they may be, are indeed the greatest events which have ever happened in the history of the world.

History is a knowledge of the past based on ***testimony***.

And, just in case someone may not agree with that definition, I shall ask, "Do you believe Abraham Lincoln lived and was President of the United States?"

"Yes," is usually the reply.

But no one whom you or I have met has personally seen Lincoln. We know only by testimony.

Can we know HOW EARLY the New Testament was written?

"Oh," someone says, "the writers only ***claimed*** to be living so close to the events. A pseudo-author writing a century or more after the fact could claim anything."

He could.

But make no mistake. There is good ***evidence*** that the books of the New Testament were NOT written down a century or more after the events they described. They were written during the lifetimes of those involved in the accounts themselves. So scholars today must regard the New Testament as a competent primary source document from the first century.

It is not within the scope of this work to overwhelm you with evidence regarding the authenticity of the New Testament documents. Such evidence is abundantly documented in my book *The Sorcerers' Secret.* But briefly now, we shall see how important is the timing of the documents.

If, as our critic claims, the whole thing was just "made up" on a Roman writing desk no earlier than 60 AD – and as late as 138 AD, then how can we account for the following:

1. An Egyptian witness

Jerome and Eusebius both relate that Pantaenus was sent in 180 AD by Demetrius, Bishop of Alexandria, Egypt, as a missionary to India. There, in a large Jewish colony on the far side of the Ganges River, he discovered descendants of converts made by the apostle Bartholomew, who, they informed him, had arrived there earlier. And to prove it, they showed him the Gospel of Matthew in Hebrew characters which Bartholomew had left with them in ***57 AD.***

Pantaenus spent several months with them, then returned by ship to Egypt, bringing this Gospel back with him.

Do you see the problem this poses for Icke's theory? If the story of Jesus and his disciples (one of whom was Bartholomew) was all "made up" between 60 and 138 AD, then how on earth could a large group of Christians far away in south-east Asia ***be in possession of a Gospel of Matthew*** brought by a fictitious Bartholomew as early as ***57 AD***?

As a matter of fact, although the date Matthew wrote his Gospel has been much discussed, no convincing reason has been offered for discrediting the traditional date of 37 AD. (That is ***a paltry 6 years after*** the claimed resurrection event.)

Come on skeptics... why don't you give up?

2. An Armenian witness

Hundreds of miles further away, in Armenia, an independent record was kept of events taking place there. As an Armenian historian testifies:

> Christianity was preached in Armenia by the apostles Thaddeus and Bartholomew in the ***first half*** of the ***first century.***

> The generally accepted chronology gives a period of eight years to the mission of St Thaddeus (35-43 AD) and sixteen years to that of St Bartholomew (44-60 AD), both of whom suffered martyrdom in Armenia. (Assadour Antreassian, *Jerusalem and the Armenians*, p. 20)

So the story of Jesus was invented by a Roman family between 60 and 138 AD? Oh, come on. As early as ***43 AD*** Thaddeus ***forfeited his life*** for claiming that Jesus Christ had risen from the dead... ***only 12 years after*** the events he was willing to die for. Also, would you die for something you knew was a lie?

3. An Indian witness

Further independent records were kept in India of the arrival of Jesus' apostle Thomas. The Indians claimed that Thomas landed at Cranganore on the Malabar coast in July, ***52 AD***, and each year they celebrate the anniversary of his landing. (Aziz S. Atiya, *A History of Eastern Christianity*. London: Methuen & Co. Ltd., 1968, pp.172,361)

In 1964, the government of India produced a stamp picturing Thomas, to commemorate his arrival on the coast of Malabar in July, 52 AD. At the time of his arrival, there was a large population of Jews, Syrians and Greeks there.

So do you still believe the Jesus story was invented long ***after*** all this – decades after Thomas came to India to give his testimony of Jesus?

4. A Dead Sea Scrolls witness

Among the Dead Sea Scrolls found in the Qumran Caves of Israel in 1947 were 19 fragments of ***Mark's Gospel***. These have been dated to ***50 AD.*** In order for the Essenes to have possessed Mark's Gospel about Jesus at so early a date, it must have been in circulation several years prior to their obtaining a copy. (Elva Schroeder, *Whatever Happened to the Twelve Apostles?* Norwood, South Australia: Peacock Publications, 2003, p. 125)

And it is recorded that Mark took the news of Jesus' death and resurrection to Alexandria within 15 years after the event, in ***46 AD***. (*Ibid.*)

So tell me, what does this do to our friend's theory that a private Roman family fabricated the Jesus story between 60 AD and 138 AD?

5. *A Roman witness*

Roman historian Tacitus (52-120 AD) wrote a number of detailed histories including *The Annals of Imperial Rome, The Histories and The Agricola* and the *Germania.* He informs us concerning the great fire of Rome which took place under Nero in July, ***64 AD***:

> Nero fastened the guilt, and inflicted the most exquisite tortures on the group popularly known as Christians. Christus, from whom the name had its origin, suffered the extreme penalty during the reign of Tiberius at the hands of one of our procurators, Pontius Pilate, and a most mischievous superstition, thus checked for the moment, again broke out, not only in Judea, but even in Rome. (Tacitus, *The Annals of Imperial Rome, XV.44*)

He tells us that ***thousands of Christians*** were ***executed*** for their faith. Clement of Rome states that "a great multitude" were killed at this time. But thousands more remained alive to carry the Christian message. Does that give us some idea of the number of people following Jesus in Rome ***as early as 64 AD***?

If, as our friend Icke wants us to imagine, the Jesus story was ***only starting*** to be put down on paper from the fraudulent heads of some writers in 60 AD, and they wouldn't finish their job until 138 AD, come on, where did ***so many thousands of Christians*** spring from as early as 64 AD?

And worse still for the critic (by 15 years earlier) is the testimony of Latin non-Christian historian Suetonius (69-140 AD). He informs us that Emperor Claudius expelled Jews from Rome in ***49 AD*** because of trouble caused by followers of one Chrestus (Christ), "Chrestus [Christ] being their leader." (Suetonius, *Lives of the First Twelve Caesars: Life of Claudius,* 26.2, us, *Li)*

Ramsay the skeptic

In an earlier chapter we related the experience of Sir William Ramsay, reputed to be one of the greatest archaeologists of all time. Over his long academic career, Ramsay was honoured with doctorates from nine universities and eventually knighted for his contributions to scholarship.

As a student taught by higher critical professors, he believed that the New Testament book of Acts (written by Luke) was a fraudulent product of the mid-second century AD.

However, as a result of 30 years of intensive research, he was forced to do a complete reversal of his beliefs, leading him to testify that "Luke's history is unsurpassed in respect of its trustworthiness," calling the Bible writer "the greatest of historians". (W.M. Ramsay, *St. Paul the Traveller and the Roman Citizen.* Grand Rapids: Baker Book House, p. 81)

More recent discoveries show that this assessment applies to all of the New Testament writers. They were careful historians.

Many New Testament passages were once claimed to be inaccurate, unhistorical or unscientific. Often this was because the New Testament was the only source for such statements.

Subsequent discoveries have confirmed the authenticity of the information in the New Testament books.

William Fox Albright was one the world's foremost Middle East archaeologists. His verdict is:

> We can already say emphatically that there is no longer any solid basis for dating any book of the New Testament after about A.D. 80, two full generations before the date between 130 and 150 given by the more radical New Testament critics of today. (William F. Albright, *Recent Discoveries in Bible Lands*. New York: Funk and Wagnalls, 1955, p.136)

Later, with still more evidence in, he revised the dating to even earlier:

> In my opinion, every book of the New Testament was written... very probably sometime between about A.D. 50 and 75. (In an interview for *Christianity Today*, 18 January, 1963)

Many of the liberal scholars are being forced to consider earlier dates for the New Testament. Dr. John A. T. Robinson's conclusions in his book *Redating the New Testament* are startlingly radical. His research led to the conviction that the ***whole*** of the New Testament was written before the Fall of Jerusalem in AD 70. (John A.T. Robinson, *Redating the New Testament*. London: SCM Press, 1976)

Later church issues unknown by Gospel writers

Another fascinating pointer to the early timing of the Gospels is the absence of 'church' concerns or propaganda. Had the early Christians cooked up the contents of the Gospels, we would have expected them to have put into the mouth of Jesus matters which were of burning concern to themselves, at the time they wrote.

Yet the fact is that, even though circumcision became such a contentious issue in the early Church, it never gets a mention in the Gospels. All the more reason, therefore, to conclude they were written ***earlier***.

The New Testament writers preserved history honestly, without injecting into it any personal bias.

Could the facts have been remembered accurately?

Even so, it might be asked, in the years until they were written down, could the facts have been remembered accurately enough to be reliable?

Well, even the most radical of New Testament scholars will assure you that the oriental memory was "wonderfully retentive" (Professor Dennis Nineham). And there are sufficient parallels in Judaism to show that the disciples could have transmitted the stories of Jesus ***word perfect***.

Shorthand writing

But "oral memory" may not have been entirely necessary.

One of the men called by Jesus to accompany him was Matthew, a despised tax collector. When

Jesus invited Matthew to join the small band of twelve, Matthew dropped everything and followed.

The first thing he did was to organize a lavish feast in his own house for fellow tax collectors and other outcasts from society, to meet Jesus personally. When Jewish leaders expressed shock that Jesus would keep such company, his reply was, "It is not the healthy who need a doctor, but the sick."

Although Matthew left behind his old life, there was something that he brought with him – his pen and his ability to write. He could write both in his native Hebrew (or Aramaic) and Greek.

Being a tax collector, he would have also learned a form of shorthand (*Encyclopaedia Brittanica Macro*, Vol. 16, p. 709) which enabled him to write down quick assessments of the merchandise before him.

A system of shorthand had been devised in 63 BC by Marcus Tiro, for taking down speeches made by men such as Cicero, and later Seneca in the Senate of Rome. The system invented by Tiro was so well received that it was taught in Roman schools and remained in use for more than 1,000 years. From Julius Caesar onward, most emperors were proficient in it. It came into extensive use later among Christian leaders. Reportedly, Origen used up to seven shorthand writers in rotation. During Tiro's time, notes were recorded on ivory tablets with a sharp stylus.

It is possible that Matthew used a wax tablet, which enabled the day's writing to be erased after he had transcribed it. These would have included the famous Sermon on the Mount, as well as Jesus' many parables, and other observations as they happened day by day.

Survival of manuscripts

The ***number*** of available manuscripts of the New Testament is overwhelmingly ***greater than those of any other work of*** ancient literature. That's because the New Testament books were the most frequently copied and widely circulated books of antiquity. (S.E. Peters, *The Harvest of Hellenism.* New York: Simon and Schuster, 1971, p.50)

For quantity, the New Testament comes first and Homer's *Iliad* comes second with 643 surviving manuscripts.

New Testament.......24,970 manuscripts
Iliad........................643 manuscripts

No documents of the ancient world are as well attested bibliographically as the New Testament. There is more evidence in support of the New Testament than all the rest of ancient literature combined. It is in a class by itself. To deny the text of the New Testament is to dismiss the validity of the entire written ancient history of mankind - for none of it can pass the tests that the New Testament passes.

The importance of the sheer number of manuscript copies cannot be overstated.

Time proximity to the originals

But what about the ***gap in time*** between the ***originals*** that no longer exist and the ***oldest copies*** we have?

Let's first consider other ancient authors… say, for example, Homer. Do you know that the oldest complete preserved text of Homer dates only back to the 13th century? (Charles Leach, *Our Bible. How We Got It.* Chicago: Moody Press, 1898, p.145) So there's a time gap between the oldest copy and the original of at least 2,200 years.

- For *Caesar's Gallic Wars* (composed between 58 and 50 BC) several manuscripts survive, but only 9 or 10 are good – and the oldest is some 900 years later than his day.
- For the *Roman History* of Livy (59 BC to AD 17), of the 142 books, only 35 survive. And only one (containing fragments of Books III-VI) is as old as the fourth century.
- Of the *Histories of Tacitus* (c. AD 100), of the 14 books, only 4½ survive.
- Of his *Annals*, of the 16 books, only 10 survive in full and 2 in part. All of this depends entirely of two manuscripts, one of the ninth century and one of the eleventh.
- Of the *History of Thucydides* (c. 460-400 BC), only 8 manuscripts survive, the oldest dating from about AD 900, except for a few scraps dating from about the beginning of the Christian era.

In point of time, the earliest surviving manuscripts of the New Testament are ***much closer*** to the originals than is the case with almost any other piece of ancient literature.

Sir Frederic G. Kenyon, former director and principal librarian of the British Museum, informs us that the earliest virtually ***complete*** surviving New Testaments (with some trifling scraps excepted) are of the fourth century – say from 250 to 300 years later. (Frederic G. Kenyon, *Handbook to the Textual Criticism of the New Testament.* London: Macmillan and Company, 1901, p.4)

However, some virtually complete New Testament individual books date back to ***only one century*** from the original writings. (And we have fragments of them still earlier.)

> The interval then between the dates of original composition and the earliest extant evidence becomes so small as to be in fact negligible, and the last foundation for any doubt that the Scriptures have come down to us substantially as they were written has now been removed. Both the authenticity and the general integrity of the books of the New Testament may be regarded as finally established. (Kenyon, *The Bible and Archaeology*. New York: Harper and Row, 1940, p. 288)

The ***most ancient manuscript*** was discovered in Magdalen Library, Oxford, where it had lain unidentified for almost a century. It was a fragment of Matthew's gospel, which bears characteristics of the ***pre-70*** AD (especially the 65-66 AD) period! Internal evidence, when compared to features in other non-biblical texts of known date, confirms this dating. (*The Da Vinci Code Hoax*, ch.10; *Who's Playing Jesus Games?*, chs.6-8)

Scholars accept the writings of the ancient classics as generally trustworthy. The reliability of the New Testament text is likewise assured.

So what have we? Two things:

(1) the ***overwhelming number*** of manuscripts and
(2) their ***proximity to the originals***.

Such evidence gives the New Testament ***great historical credibility.***

How much in doubt?

> There is an ambiguity in saying there are some 200,000 variants in the existing manuscripts of the New Testament, since these represent only 10,000 places in the New Testament. If one single word is misspelled in 3,000 different manuscripts, this is counted as 3,000 variants or readings. (Norman L. Geisler and William E. Nix, *A General Introduction to the Bible*. Chicago: Moody Press, 1968, p. 361)

*Mathematically this would compute to a text that is **98.33 percent pure**. (Ibid.,* p. 365*)*

Thus the great majority of the New Testament "has been transmitted to us with no, or next to no, variation." (Benjamin B. Warfield, *Introduction to textual Criticism of the New Testament.* Seventh edition. London: Hodder and Stoughton, 1907, p. 14) In this we might compare the *Iliad* of Homer and the national epic of India, the M*ahabharata*, with the New Testament:

* *Iliad* - has about 15,600 lines. Lines in doubt: 764. **5%** textual corruption.
* *Mahabharata* – some 250,000 lines. Lines in doubt: 26,000. **10%** textual corruption.
* *New Testament* – c. 20,000 lines. Lines in doubt: 40. **½%** textual corruption.

Unbroken chain

Because Christianity was a missionary movement from the beginning (Matthew 28:19-21), its scriptures were immediately translated into the known languages of that period and scattered across vast distances.

And, although it is true that corrupters in Alexandria (and thence in Rome) altered portions of texts in their immediate possession, the ***unchanged*** text was being ***preserved*** carefully ***in numerous other places*** which the corrupters could not reach. This text was known as the Peshitta, or Syriac Aramaic. Today, the vast majority of surviving manuscripts are from this source. Hence it is termed the Majority, or Traditional, Text.

It is a material fact that an ancient Aramaic New Testament manuscript exists – and ***has been in continuous use since*** ancient times by the Church of the East – thus ensuring ***an unbroken line of testimony from the beginning.***

Translation copies of the Peshitta were also preserved in the West from as early as 157 AD. (See my book *The Sorcerers' Secret*, chapter 5.)

Now think how amazing this is - that amid the overwhelming thousands of manuscripts - the copyists of different countries and different ages succeeded in preserving a virtually ***identical*** Bible. *Harvard Theological Review* cites Kirsopp Lake's exhaustive examination of manuscripts which revealed this "***uniformity*** of the text exhibited by the vast majority of the New Testament manuscripts."

After the seeming endlessness of the Dark Ages, the long isolated Eastern and Western streams finally yielded their respective Bibles publicly. At this time the Italia in the West and the Peshitta from the East were brought together for the first time in over 1,400 years and when compared were found to be still virtually identical.

Of course, there is a claim that Jesus' so-called resurrection is a "hoax" – that he never rose from the dead. If so, then all who pin their hopes on Jesus, are in deep trouble.

So why don't we now grab this by the horns and shake out the truth…

35

Risen? -

"THE DEAD MAN'S ALIVE!"

The following could have been an "on the spot" news account by a reporter in Jerusalem on Nisan 16, in 31 AD:

NAZARENE REPORTED ALIVE

Executed Victim Reported Alive by Roman Guards City in Uproar

JERUSALEM, NISAN 16, 3rd Hour.

Early this morning, not long before daybreak, several Roman soldiers were seen running toward the city from Skull Hill north of Jerusalem. According to witnesses they were very frightened. As they ran by in frantic haste they cried, "HE'S ALIVE! The dead man's ALIVE!" They sped past the tower of Antonia, on by the Temple area, and were just passing the Council Chamber when several priests stepped out and hurried them inside.

Those soldiers were a special detail that was assigned to guard the tomb of the man who was crucified the day before yesterday. He was a teacher from Galilee, called Yeshua.

Quite a crowd had gathered by the time the Romans left the building. The soldiers passed the word through the crowd that the disciples of Yeshua had stolen the body out of the sepulchre while they were asleep. Gradually the people dispersed, but there are some unanswered questions in the minds of many in Jerusalem this morning.

Why did the soldiers go into the Council Chambers telling one story and come out telling quite another? Why were they so self-assured in confessing to sleeping on duty? The death penalty is mandatory for this offense. It very much appears that this tale about sleeping on duty is concocted to keep the truth from the people. But what is the truth? Where are the facts?

This whole affair has been conducted with unusual secrecy as if there were something to hide. The accused was taken prisoner sometime after midnight the day before yesterday in an olive garden east of the city on the west slope of the Mount of Olives. He reportedly put up no resistance and would not permit any of his followers to resist.

The authorities and the mob were led to Gethsemane Garden by a disaffected disciple, Judas Iscariot. He was aware of this private retreat used by Yeshua and his followers.

The trial was conducted before daybreak, which is highly irregular — in fact, illegal. Before the city was awake to what was happening, or before the followers of Yeshua could organize an opposition to the proceedings, they were faced with a "fait accompli". The trial had been held and the Roman Procurator had reluctantly given his consent to the execution.

Yeshua was crucified about three hours after sunrise. Six hours later he was dead. It is very unusual for death to take place so soon after crucifixion. If Yeshua had been sick or old it would not be so surprising, but he was only a little over thirty-three years of age, and was in perfect physical condition. He was buried in a tomb near Skull Hill, the place of the execution.

It seems highly probable that an innocent man has been accused, condemned, and put to death. If this proves to be so, the responsibility for this act will rest on the Sanhedrin, and especially the chief priests Annas, and Caiaphas, his nephew. Their hatred and jealousy of Yeshua of Nazareth have been obvious for quite some time.

The story is circulating that the trial was conducted under these secret conditions because the authorities were afraid of the people. As a matter of fact, Yeshua had a tremendous following, especially among the common people. He is said to have healed their sick, and some say that he raised a man from death in Bethany a few weeks ago.

He has on several occasions made astounding predictions which have happened just as he said they would. For several weeks he has been predicting his own death. He also predicted that on the third day after his death, he would miraculously rise from the dead. Today is the third day!- *Simon Abrahams.*

If it was a hoax that established worldwide Christianity, if its central character Jesus Christ never rose from the dead, then what became of his body within three days after burial must be THE WORLD'S MOST INTRIGUING UNSOLVED MYSTERY.

We all love mysteries. And I think about the day I sat in a backpacker's hostel discussing this very matter with a tourist from Sweden. His name was Leif.

Jesus' "resurrection": a later invention?

"For starters," said Leif, "I do not believe that Jesus Christ rose from the dead. That story is history's biggest fraud."

"Oh yes?"

"That tale was inserted into the writings years later, to glorify a dead hero." Leif was serious.

"I see. Tell me, Leif, the people involved in this fraud, as you call it... that sect known as Christians. When did that group of people actually come into being? Would you agree it was during the reign of the Roman emperor Tiberius?"

"I suppose."

"Leif, that is firmly established, historical fact, is it not?"

"No contest on that, Jonathan. But the resurrection tale, that evolved later."

I leaned forward. "Let me ask you, Leif, what was it that brought these Christians into existence IN THE REIGN OF TIBERIUS? May I suggest to you, it was nothing less than the **belief** that Jesus had recently ***risen from the dead*****!** Even pagan writers and scholars attest this.

"Since this is so, Leif, then how could the resurrection of the dead be a ***later*** invention of Christians? Rather, it was the ***very beginning*** of their belief, the very strength and impetus of their faith. It was the very ***reason*** for their religion and their fervent hope!

"What I am saying, Leif, is that the CAUSE and BEGINNING of Christian faith was the believed bodily resurrection of Jesus."

"Oh, come off it, Jonathan, the story of Jesus was not written down until the second, third or fourth century. Quite a long time after the alleged event!"

It just happened that in my bag was some information on this question. I bent down, opened my briefcase and pulled it out. "Have you heard of Professor William Albright?" I asked.

"Who's he?"

"One of the world's foremost biblical archaeologists, no less. Listen to his summary of the findings:

> Regardless of whatever else the Dead Sea Scrolls tell us, one thing is certain. We know now that none of the New Testament could have been written after AD 80. (William F. Albright, *Recent Discoveries in Bible Lands.* New York: Funk and Wagnalls, 1955, p, 136. See also, Albright in an interview for *Christianity Today,* 18 Jan.1963. Albright. *From Stone Age to Christianity.* Baltimore: Johns Hopkins Press, 1946, p.23)

Leif stared at the statement.

"This means, Leif, that the complete account was already written before the death of the first disciples, and much of it a long time before."

"You mean," he said, "it did ***not*** come to be accepted, or inserted, into the Bible later."

"Right," I responded. "These people ***at first*** had no written records of Yeshua's resurrection. Rather, they had PERSONAL attestation, LIVING eye-witnesses, PERSONAL EXPERIENCES OF THEIR OWN upon which to base their faith. They rested their sound and fervent faith, NOT on some 'records' but on what they had seen WITH THEIR OWN EYES! Any subsequent ***records*** of a LATER date ***were the*** **RESULT OF THEIR FAITH**. What I am trying to say is, ***it was not written records that brought their faith into existence***.

"Paul, himself a one-time skeptic, could later say before King Agrippa, 'For the king KNOWS of these things [of the resurrection of the dead], before whom also I speak freely, for I am persuaded that NONE of these things are HIDDEN from him, for **THIS THING WAS NOT DONE IN A CORNER.'** (Acts 26:26)

"The resurrection of Jesus was a TALKED-OF, DISCUSSED, WELL-KNOWN EVENT that swept the entirety of the Roman empire in a short time."

Leif flushed a little. "Whatever. But look, might it not have been a face-saving device on the part of a small bunch of fanatics?"

"OK, Leif. Suppose you're right. Tell me this. Do invented stories of that kind have the power to transform character and inspire men and women, and even boys and girls, to suffer indescribable horrors of persecution and die martyrs' deaths? If it was just deception, then how do you explain the radiant joy on the faces of the sufferers and the prayers upon their lips as they asked for the forgiveness of those who inflicted the pain? Nothing, absolutely nothing, could withstand their testimony. WHAT THEY SAID 'TURNED THE WORLD UPSIDE DOWN.' When challenged, they replied simply, 'We cannot but speak the things which we have seen and heard.' (ch.4:20)

"How do you account for this?"

Leif looked thoughtful.

"Peter, on Pentecost day 50 days later, did not speak to the crowd as a man who knew he was proclaiming a lie, but as one conscious of the undeniable fact that Jesus Messiah had risen from the dead. That was the main theme of his gripping message. Nobody could contradict him. No one attempted to deny it. The evidence of Jesus' resurrection swept on, to close pagan temples, to cast down idols, to lift men into nobility, and bring hope to a society in despair.

"Jesus had said, 'I am the resurrection and the life.' Let me ask you, my friend, Could YOU say that?"

"Yes, I could say that!"

"But could you make anyone believe it?"

There was silence.

This greatest of all miracles was ***universally believed*** throughout the entire confines of the early Christian movement. A powerful impact was felt because the immediate followers of Jesus who had SEEN HIM PUBLICLY EXECUTED and PUBLICLY BURIED, these same people had even WALKED AND TALKED WITH HIM AFTER HIS RESURRECTION.

A forceful, firm belief in all that he was, and in all that he claimed to be, has gripped men, delivered them from the power of enslaving habits and accomplished miracles of transformation in human lives, for multitudes in each generation ever since.

If Jesus had not risen from the dead, ***there would never have been Christianity*** — nor the New Testament writings.

But let me tell you about the strange experience of Gilbert West and Lord Lyttleton...

36

Risen? -

WHO STOLE THE BODY?

Two bright young men — avowed skeptics — went up to Oxford. One was the eminent Gilbert West, and the other was Lord Lyttleton, the famous English journalist.

These two men agreed that Christianity must be destroyed. They also agreed that to destroy it, two things were necessary:

1. They must prove that Jesus never rose from the tomb.
2. They must prove that Saul of Tarsus, a hired assassin and killer, and fiercely anti-christian, was never converted to Christianity.

Now they divided the task between them, West assuming the responsibility for the RESURRECTION, and Lyttleton and his great mind, caring for the EXPERIENCE OF SAUL on the Damascus road.

They were to give themselves plenty of time - twelve months or more, if necessary.

West entered the driveway of the Porteur mansion. It had been the second snowfall that winter. Smoke spiraled up from the living room chimney. West's neighbor was a "religious nut", a good "victim" upon which to sharpen his wits.

He was ushered into a large office. Porteur looked up.

"Gilbert, my dear man. Such a rare thing... To what do I owe this pleasure?"

The men sat for a time, exchanging gossip. Then West moved in.

"Porteur, I am going to demolish the resurrection myth. Do you dare give me an hour of your time?"

"Why not?" grinned the other man. "So what's on your mind?"

Did not die?

"Well, to be frank with you, Jesus didn't even die on the cross."

"Interesting," responded Porteur. "Then what happened?"

"He took a narcotic drug that fooled the Romans. Or else he was in a swoon when they took him off the cross and put him in the tomb. Somehow he escaped it, and journeyed off to a far place to live out his natural life and die of old age. That's what happened."

Porteur smiled. Was West serious? Yes, he looked like he meant it.

Porteur spoke. "What you say about him taking a drug to induce unconsciousness on the cross, let me tell you something. The fact is, that is incompatible with the very nature of crucifixion."

"What do you mean?" asked West.

"In crucifixion, the arms being spread out and the hanging body, raises the rib cage and drops the diaphragm to the maximum. This means the victim can breathe only by raising the body - and this requires the use of the large muscles of the legs, if it is to be maintained for any length of time. This is why the legs of those crucified were broken to hasten death: death by suffocation would follow within minutes.

"I tell you, Gilbert, if Jesus had taken a drug in sufficient quantity to induce unconsciousness while hanging on the cross, it would not have taken a spear thrust to hasten his death. He would have been dead before his friends could have taken him down. Your idea falls apart with this one elementary fact."

"Just a minute," retorted West. "The Bible says that after Jesus was laid in the tomb that 'they prepared spices and ointment' and brought these to the tomb. If Jesus was dead, what were the ointments for? A dead body needs no medical treatment." (Luke 23:56; 24:1)

"Spices and ointment? My dear friend, they were simply to treat the body of the dead, according to custom," smiled Porteur. "A practice related to embalming. Surely you must know that. And ponder carefully: his own mother and others with her had actually seen him die. They weren't coming to treat a sick man.

"And something else. Just think! When a person has been BEATEN and WHIPPED until he is so EXHAUSTED he literally COLLAPSES on the public streets, when he has been UP all one day and all one night, and part of another, being BUFFETED ABOUT, KICKED and SPIT UPON, when he has been WITHOUT FOOD OR WATER, and LASHED WITHIN AN INCH OF HIS LIFE, finally to have SPIKES driven through his hands and feet, to HANG IN THE BLAZING SUN for hours, then to have a huge spear PLUNGED INTO HIS SIDE, with great spurts of gushing blood and fluids pouring out of his body; when his lifeless, limp body has been TAKEN DOWN from the stake, carefully wrapped in grave clothes and laid away in a tomb - COULD THERE BE ANY QUESTION THAT HE WAS **DEAD**?

"... suppose there could be the ***remote*** chance that Jesus wasn't dead? Tell me, how could he ever, in such a horribly wounded condition, weak and exhausted, remove a huge stone to escape the tomb, a stone that required several Roman soldiers, in all their youth and strength to move?

"Remember, the Jews were carefully ***guarding*** against this possibility. They had said to the governor, Pilate, 'Sir, we remember that deceiver said, while he was yet alive (showing they FIRMLY believed him now to be DEAD), After three days I will rise again. Command therefore that the sepulchre be MADE SURE until the third day, lest his disciples come by night, and steal him away, and say unto the people, He is risen from the dead, so the last error shall be worse than the first.' Pilate co-operated. He replied, 'Ye have a watch, go your way, MAKE IT AS SURE AS YE CAN.'

"To suggest that Jesus had only 'swooned', as you say, is to deny logic, reason, historical fact, and sanity itself!

"You see, West, they made sure the stone could never even be opened FROM THE OUTSIDE - let alone from the INSIDE, by a mortally wounded man. The record says, 'they went, and made the sepulchre ***sure***, SEALING THE STONE, and setting a WATCH.' (Matthew 27:63-66)

"When the stone WAS rolled back, it was NOT done by secretive men at night, but by a powerful heavenly being. The watchers who had been set to guard the tomb FAINTED DEAD AWAY AT THE SIGHT OF HIM. This was ***not*** some ***secretive*** thing, but a TREMENDOUS, AWESOME, GLORIOUS EVENT. (ch.28:2-8)

"Yet there is even stronger proof that it was more than just a swoon from which he recovered."

"What do you mean?" asked West.

"I mean," replied Porteur, "that it is impossible that a man who had stolen half-dead out of the grave, who crept about weak and ill, wanting medical treatment, who required bandaging, strengthening, and care, could have given to the disciples the impression that he was a conqueror over death, the Prince of Life - an impression that lay at the bottom of their future work. It could hardly have changed their sadness into enthusiasm, or lifted their reverence into worship of him."

"I suppose you've made a fair point," conceded West. "So he died. We all die. But it's really this resurrection nonsense I refuse to swallow."

West excused himself. He would begin his investigation in the town library. Then he'd tear the biblical account to shreds.

Historian, concerning Jesus

However, he was soon a little perturbed to discover what Josephus – a 1st century contemporary who was not a Christian – had written concerning Jesus:

> Now there was about this time Jesus... And when Pilate, at the suggestion of the principal men among us, had condemned him to the Cross, those that loved him at the first did not forsake him; for he appeared to them alive again the third day... And the tribe of Christians, so named from him, are not extinct to this day. (Flavius Josephus, *Antiquities of the Jews,* Vol. 3, Bk.18, ch.3, sect.3)

Joseph Scaliger, a man highly familiar with Josephus' work, concludes:

> Josephus is the most diligent and the greatest lover of truth of all writers: nor are we afraid to affirm of him, that it is more safe to believe him, not only as to the affairs of the Jews, but also as to those that are foreign to them, than all the Greek and Latin writers, and this, because his fidelity and his compass of learning are everywhere conspicuous. (Joseph Scaliger, In the Prolegomea to *De Emendations Temporum,* p.17)

Typical of the accuracy tests which Josephus has passed is his mention, for example, of the Masada events. An extensive archaeological excavation of Masada was completed in 1965. Commenting on the finds, *The New Encyclopaedia Brittanica* (1987) states: "The descriptions of the Roman-Jewish historian Josephus, until then the only detailed source of Masada's history, were found to be extremely accurate."

Josephus was not to be dismissed out of hand.

West was not unduly worried. He knew the New Testament writers would trip themselves up and be easy to discredit.

The empty tomb

This was a fact no one disputed: three days after the crucifixion, ***the tomb was empty.*** Romans, Jews and followers of Jesus all checked it - and all admitted that.

Unless they went to the ***wrong tomb***!

Yes, that was it. Those women who came on Sunday morning and reported the tomb was empty must have gone to the wrong tomb.

But as West thought about it a little more, he saw some difficulty there.

How could three or more people so soon forget the place where they had laid a loved one? After all, they had seen exactly which tomb the body was laid in, because they themselves had put it there! (Mark 15:45-47)

In any case, would not Jesus' enemies soon have found the right tomb, and exposed those deluded women and other followers of Jesus who said he had risen?

West the skeptic was determined to be thorough. He noted that this was the private tomb of Joseph of Arimathea. Would this man forget the location of his own donated tomb?

But more problematic for the "wrong tomb" idea was that the Jewish chief priests and elders never questioned that the tomb was empty.

That was it! Somebody must have moved the body ***to another location***. Joseph of Arimathea probably changed his mind and removed the body of Jesus - so emptying this tomb.

But, if that were true, then WHY DID THE GUARDS NOT SAY SO? Why guard the tomb if they knew the body had been moved to another spot? It would have had to be shifted before the stone was rolled over. And if it was empty, it would obviously be seen to be empty by those who sealed the door. Moreover, it would have been a simple story for the soldiers to tell, if Joseph had simply moved the body earlier - ***a much safer story,*** as far as the soldiers were concerned!

For several days, West turned it over in his mind.

It kept nagging at him. WHY WOULD JOSEPH HAVE DONE SUCH A THING so quickly after he had, at a great risk to himself and to his future popularity, begged to have the body that it might be placed in his own tomb? He made no such explanation to the disciples, who now fully believed that Jesus had risen from the dead.

Joseph was an honorable counselor, who "also waited for the kingdom of God", "a good man and a just." (v.43; Luke 23:50)

Would a man of this caliber and character perpetrate a FRAUD?

West thought not. If there had been any trickery, sooner or later it would have been exposed.

On the other hand, the Roman soldiers had a possible chance to hide his body, secretly, and to bury it elsewhere at a later time.

Not likely. Military law could demand the death penalty upon soldiers who lost their prisoner. (Josh McDowell, *Evidence That Demands a Verdict.* San Bernadino, Ca.: Here's Life Publishers, Inc., 1986, pp. 212,213)

The fear of punishments produced faultless attention to duty, especially in the night watches. Why should the guards want to risk death? And what would be THEIR motive for removing the body?

No motive.

Did the Jews steal the body?

Perhaps, thought West, the Jewish leaders hated Jesus so much that they stole the body and secretly buried it in another location. Perhaps that's why it was never found.

West held on, like a bulldog. He continued to study and weigh all the inter-playing factors.

The Jewish leaders steal the body? No, it didn't make sense. On many different occasions they had tried to have Yeshua killed. The religious leaders, that was.

They were jealous of his influence and character. They would have done ***anything*** to discredit Jesus as the Messiah. Yet, even when he was in the tomb there was something about his prophecies that bothered them.

Firstly, in their own Scriptures were predictions about the anticipated Messiah.

Secondly, in Jesus' life, those prophecies, one by one, were claimed to be coming true. One of those prophecies hinted that the Messiah was to come alive again after a violent death. (Isaiah 53:7-11) Yeshua had claimed that he would die and rise again after three days.

So to make sure that Jesus' body could not be snatched from the tomb, the Jewish leaders had themselves called upon Roman help to ***keep that body in the tomb***. At their own suggestion and under their supervision, the tomb was sealed. (Matthew 27:62-66)

So well was it sealed, that no one could break it open - and Roman guards were ordered to watch it.

West continued his investigation of the four New Testament gospel accounts.

That third day after the crucifixion - what a morning it was!

Several Roman soldiers were seen running toward the city.

According to witnesses, they were very frightened. As they ran by in frantic haste, they cried, "HE'S ALIVE! THE DEAD MAN'S ALIVE!"

As they passed the Council Chambers, several priests stepped out and hustled them inside.

WHY DID THE SOLDIERS GO INTO THE COUNCIL CHAMBER TELLING ONE STORY - AND COME OUT TELLING QUITE ANOTHER?

The record said that the Jewish leaders themselves "gave large money unto the soldiers, saying, 'Say ye HIS DISCIPLES came by night, and stole him away while we slept.' And if this comes to the governor's ears we will persuade him, and secure you. So they took the money, and did as they were taught, and this saying is commonly reported among the Jews until this day." (ch.28:12-15)

West asked himself, WHY WERE THE SOLDIERS SO SELF-ASSURED IN CONFESSING TO SLEEPING ON DUTY - when the death penalty was mandatory for such an offense?

AND WHY WERE THE JEWISH LEADERS SO ANXIOUS TO MAKE THE SOLDIERS CHANGE THEIR STORY? The ***Jews themselves*** paid a large sum of money to the soldiers to ***spread the story that*** Jesus' disciples had ***stolen his body*** away. If the Jews had stolen the body, why would they bribe the soldiers to say the disciples had done it?

It hit West like a thunderbolt: WHAT WOULD HAVE BEEN ONE OF THE GREATEST PROOFS TO THE PEOPLE THAT JESUS WAS **NOT** THE MESSIAH and that he was still dead?

SURELY THE FINDING AND EXHIBITION OF HIS BODY!

Yes, indeed. Had the Jewish leaders, or any of the Jews of Jesus' day, been able to find Jesus' body, ***they would have PRODUCED that body!***

I shall throw my own bit in here: just as the fickle Italian public dragged the body of Mussolini through the streets of Milan, to hang it ignominiously in a public square, upside down beside the body of his mistress, so would the Jews of Jesus' day have paraded Jesus' broken body through the streets of Jerusalem and all the other towns and villages around, and displayed it publicly as PROOF for all the world to see. You can count on it.

So it dawned on West that all the Jewish leaders had to do to destroy Christianity was to DISCOVER AND PRODUCE THE BODY OF JESUS.

Such an event would have been the most important talking point for Jews from that day to this.

If the Jewish religious leaders had stolen his body - and KNEW where that body was, and could produce the dead body, THEN WHY DID THESE SAME JEWS FINALLY PERSECUTE AND EVEN MURDER AT THE JEOPARDY OF THEIR OWN LIVES, IN ORDER TO STOP THOSE WHO WENT ABOUT TEACHING THAT YESHUA HAD RISEN FROM THE DEAD?

Would it make any sense to take vows, as they did, to eat no food or drink no water until they had killed the Christian apostle Paul? Would it make any sense to kill James the brother of John? Or to martyr and butcher numerous other disciples and Christians for teaching Yeshua had RISEN from the dead - if the Jews absolutely knew he had not risen from the dead - and could ***prove it by producing his body***?

A man would have to be a literal fool in the face of such compelling evidence, to believe that the Jews stole and had Jesus' body.

ALL THEY HAD TO DO TO DISPROVE THE RESURRECTION STORY, WAS TO PRODUCE THE DEAD BODY OF JESUS.

Gilbert West knew it! There was no way that the Jewish leaders stole Jesus body.

The investigation must continue...

37

Risen? -

DID HIS FRIENDS STEAL THE BODY?

Somebody must have stolen the body. West was sure of it.

Who else, then, but the disciples of Jesus? They must have come while the guards were asleep, rolled away the stone, stolen the body, reburied it, and covered up the affair, so as to trick people into thinking he had risen from the dead.

He would have to investigate this critically. But Gilbert West felt sure this would turn out to be the answer and he would prove it.

His research indicated that ***the chief priests never questioned that the tomb was empty***. They knew that the guards' report was true.

However... if the disciples had stolen the body, WHY DID THE JEWISH PRIESTS FIND IT NECESSARY TO ***BRIBE*** THE GUARDS TO SAY SO? (Matthew 28:15)

If the guards had slept at the tomb, would not those angry Jewish priests have been foremost in accusing them to the governor? But instead they secured the safety of the soldiers, for telling that story.

Again, if those soldiers ***slept on guard***, if while sleeping, their prisoner was taken away, then by military law they merited the death penalty for failing to prevent it. SO WHY WERE THEY NOT PLACED UNDER ARREST BY PILATE'S ORDERS IF THE STORY WAS TRUE?

West was getting more uneasy the more he thought about it.

Was it that Pilate knew the guards had ***not been sleeping*** when the body came out - but that something else had happened?

THE SOLDIERS' EXEMPTION FROM ARREST WOULD SUGGEST THAT THE BODY OF JESUS WAS NOT STOLEN AWAY WHILE THEY SLEPT!

For that matter, if the body was taken while the soldiers ALL slept on duty, then how could they be sure it was the disciples who had done it?

Perhaps one of the soldiers saw the disciples, West reasoned.

OK, suppose he did. Would he not instantly have alerted the other guards, rather than them all face the death penalty?

Anyway, even if all those guards had been asleep, surely they would have been awakened by the heavy noise of the rolling of that massive stone door along the hollow pavement outside the tomb?

But something else nagged at Gilbert West. WAS IT LIKELY THAT ALL THE SOLDIERS WOULD BE ASLEEP - ALL AT THE SAME TIME? Especially since provision was made to avoid weariness by changing the guard through the night watches.

Could the disciples really have stolen the body? Frankly, West was now beginning to wonder.

Breaking the seal meant death

And how about the stone? That massive seal-stone had been rolled into place against the door - and then sealed with the official Roman seal, a seal no human power dared break, the strongest seal of authority in all the world. To break the Roman seal was punishable. So if the disciples had broken it, THEN WHY WERE THEY LET GO FREE?

I would like to share with you an interesting discovery.

Roman decree in Nazareth

From Nazareth, Jesus' home town, there came to light in 1878 a most interesting slab of marble, inscribed in a Greek text.

For many years it lay in the Froehner collection, its value unrecognized until 1930. It is now in the Louvre, Paris.

The text contains a decree issued by an unnamed Roman emperor prohibiting under penalty of death, any kind of tomb robbery, including tombs of relatives, or the moving of a body to another place. It is believed to be from the early days of the Imperial period.

> Ordinance of Caesar. It is my pleasure that graves and tombs remain undisturbed in perpetuity for those who have made them for the cult of their ancestors, or children or members of their house. If, however, any man lay information that another has either demolished them, or has in any other way extracted the buried, or maliciously transferred them to other places in order to wrong them, or has displaced the sealing or other stones, against such a one I order that a trial be instituted as in respect of the gods, as in regard to the cult of mortals. For it shall be much more obligatory to honor the buried. Let it be absolutely forbidden for anyone to disturb them. In the case of contravention I desire that the offender be sentenced to capital punishment on charge of violation of sepulture.

The dating of this inscription has been placed somewhere between 44 and 50 AD, which was during the reign of Claudius Caesar, who was noted for his persecution of the Jews. (Acts 18:2) This was not many years after the death of Jesus. It is believed that the preaching of the resurrection had already begun in Rome by this time. Perhaps this decree reflected the fact that the enemies of Christianity had faced up to the empty tomb story.

The placing of the decree on a rock in the little, unimportant town of Nazareth where Jesus was reared, indicates a possible relationship between the decree of Caesar and the empty tomb of Jesus.

If it came at a time preceding the crucifixion, it would prove that there was evidently no ground for the accusation that the disciples stole the body of Jesus. Otherwise the authorities would certainly have brought the disciples of Jesus to trial. And the fact that this was not done would show that the rulers of Judea had no hope of making such an accusation stick.

Gilbert West did not know of the Nazareth inscription, but he was a man of clear perception.

If the disciples had been proven guilty, he reasoned, of stealing Jesus' body, would not their enemies, the priests, have been the ***first to demand their execution***? Was it not strange that, instead, the priests ***tried to hush up*** the whole matter?

This was puzzling.

And yes… Nazareth DID exist then

Some skeptics would want us to believe that Nazareth did not exist in the time of Jesus. But think about this. If there was no settlement here in the first century, then what would have been the point in placing this marble slab decree here? (For actual archaeological evidence that Nazareth existed in the 1st century, just email me.)

More problems

West would spend weeks more on the resurrection question. He was no longer sleeping well.

He recalled how the disciples had deserted Jesus and fled in fear from the scene of the trial and crucifixion. Eleven timid, terrified men. How would they dare face a guard of armed soldiers?

And the size of the stone... how could eleven of them even move a stone which, according to a fourth century manuscript, the *Codex Bezae,* required twenty men to move? (This is in the Cambridge library.)

West knew he was in trouble.

Unexplainable behavior… unless

The thing that threw West most, was the conduct of the disciples themselves.

The faith of the disciples had collapsed after Jesus' death on the cross. (Luke 24:21,22; Mark 16:14)

Each was in abject fear for his own personal safety. At the trial, Peter cringed under the taunt of a maid.

They began their defection by denying Jesus, deserting him, flying in all directions, studiously concealing the fact of their former connection with him. They were not only moved by ***fear*** to conceal themselves, but by ***shame***. They were sorely mortified at having been led astray by him. Because they were ***honest***, plain, sensible men. They had originally followed him because they saw in him that moral purity and truth, which formed the elements of their own characters.

To them, the whole thing was now over. They thought it had been 'nice' while it lasted, but now their leader had been martyred. And ***they were about to go their own way,*** back to their respective jobs and positions of earlier days, and give up the whole thing.

Those disciples were very reluctant to believe he had risen again, according to the records. So they scattered to different areas to forget it, to fishing or some other humble way of life. (John 21:3)

BUT... WHAT DO WE BEHOLD!!!

WITHIN JUST SEVEN WEEKS AFTER THIS, THE RESURRECTION OF JESUS IS MADE KNOWN *BY THEM*, THROUGH THE LENGTH AND BREADTH OF THE LAND! Those men who had cowered and hidden in dismay, now came ***boldly forth***, full of confidence in Jesus... to follow him everywhere. Even back to Jerusalem they came - of all places! To the very place from which they had fled! Now they walked everywhere with ANIMATED STEPS AND HEADS HIGH, like men no longer serving a defeated convict, but like men whose Master was Lord of heaven and earth.

What restored their faith?

***What had re-established their faith*?** What caused this virtually miraculous change?

These men - all cowards, ***timid and afraid*** of the Jews who had killed Jesus - how come they were ***suddenly*** so filled with power and conviction, that they went out enthusiastically announcing against all opposition, ***even at the risk of their lives*,** that Yeshua had risen?

West was really troubled now. He asked himself, Would numerous men be torn limb from limb, thrown to wild beasts, drawn and quartered, sawn in two, hung upside down, burnt at the stake -

FOR SOMETHING THEY KNEW TO BE A DELIBERATE HOAX?

No one ever could have believed (or would have believed) upon the dead Jesus as the Son of God, had he not had the ***evidence*** for the resurrection.

Gilbert West hated to admit it. But the idea that the ***disciples stole the body***, so defied all logic, reason, and known facts, as to appear ***ludicrous***. They could NOT have done it.

I shall add something that was not a part of West's investigation. That is, that the Jews are the most resourceful and untiring race on earth! They searched the whole world relentlessly, until they discovered the whereabouts of Nazi war criminal Adolf Eichmann. They investigated, searched, scanned, scoured, until they ***found him***.

They were able to find Eichmann, even though he was in South America... yet they were unable to produce the dead body of Jesus - in tiny Judea!!!

Because there **was** no dead body.

That much was now clear to West. But he also knew that if there was no dead body - that if the resurrection had occurred - there would have to be people who saw him alive.

West's investigation now took this unexpected turn…

38
Risen? -

THE WITNESSES

Only 50 days after the tomb of Jesus was burst open, the ***erstwhile cowardly*** disciple Peter suddenly ***stood up before a huge crowd*** and addressed them.

Thousands of visitors were in Jerusalem for the Pentecost festivities.

In his speech, Peter explained why the ancient ***prophecies*** had said that the coming ***Messiah's body***, when he died, ***would not suffer decay***. (Acts 2:24-31)

Peter's logic convinced 3,000 Jews in that audience that the only solution to the empty tomb was that Yeshua was bodily raised from the dead.

"We all are WITNESSES," said Peter. (v.32)

It was significant that Peter's first public speech was in that ***very same city*** where the resurrection was claimed to have happened.

If it was all a hoax, how ever could he have hoped to gain believers among those who were there - among those who were in a position to know whether he spoke truly? Only weeks after the death of Jesus, their ***testimony*** right there in Jerusalem was ***received as true***, and multitudes became disciples.

Peter told them, THE EVIDENCE WAS RIGHT UNDER THEIR NOSES!

Local reaction an important indicator

Think about this. After the alleged resurrection of Jesus, here were the established religious leaders telling the people that Jesus' body had been stolen. And there were Jesus' disciples teaching and doing miracles in his name. The citizens of Jerusalem were forced to make a decision.

The Bible records the public reaction. With women and children factored in, it appears that perhaps as many as 15,000 residents of Jerusalem (about 15 percent of the population) became believers within days of the event. Such a change in religious orientation was unheard of. Especially when you realise that this was a monotheistic culture which would have difficulty in accepting the concept of Jesus also being God.

* * * * * * * * *

Gilbert West went over the ***evidence*** that he had been amassing. He had not expected this to happen. Like Lord Lyttleton, he had been sure it would be easy to discredit the whole thing.

He had started out believing there was no evidence. That the resurrection was a total fake.

Now he went over the facts again, looking for a flaw. And he kept coming back to this: THERE WERE TOO MANY WITNESSES TO THE EVENT FOR IT TO BE DENIED!

These witnesses were ***not*** resting their faith on an empty tomb, but upon ***appearances*** of Yeshua after the event - ***on many*** different occasions!

West had already begun to list them.

Firstly, the soldiers

Because the Jewish authorities made special effort to prevent any resurrection, placing armed guards around the tomb, securing the entrance with a Roman seal over a mighty stone barrier - this very act had resulted in ***more positive and conclusive proof*** of what happened.

The greater the number of soldiers placed around the tomb, the stronger it made the testimony that the dead man had risen. A whole guard of pagan soldiers became eyewitnesses.

Knowing that to let a prisoner escape attracted the death penalty, the Roman soldiers were compelled to admit to their own peril that this very thing had taken place, even though the tomb was securely sealed as though for eternity.

Secondly, the Jewish religious leaders

The proof that forces exceeding the power of a group of armed soldiers, had opened the tomb, stunned the religious leaders.

The fact that

(a) they bribed the soldiers to hush up the facts, and that

(b) they bribed the Roman governor not to punish the soldiers for their story, - these two actions demonstrated that what they were trying to hide was AN ADM1SSION OF THE FACT.

Efforts to prevent the resurrection and to circulate a false report concerning it, served only to provide additional confirmation of it as an historical ***fact.***

Thirdly, the witnesses to Jesus' actual appearances

Jesus had been ***seen alive*** after the "event", not once or twice, but at least ten times, according to records. He was seen, not by just one individual, whose word could be doubted, but by GROUPS of two, seven, ten, eleven, and even 500. More than half a thousand people had seen him after his resurrection and under many different circumstances.

Jesus TALKED, WALKED, ATE, OPENED THE SCRIPTURES, PREPARED A FIRE FOR BREAKFAST, AND SHOWED THE NAIL SCARS. He permitted them to touch his real body. Thomas skeptically examined the wounds and scars.

During all those occasions, the favored ones ***spoke with him, touched him*** and ***dined with him***. And he gave the order to spread the news to the world. (Matthew 28:5-10, 16-17; Luke 24:86-48; John 20:19-29; 21:4-13; 1 Corinthians 15:6)

The verdict of a doctor named Luke was that these were *"infallible proofs"*. (Acts 1:3. The book of Acts is attributed to Luke.)

Mass hypnotism?

But West was not to give in easily.

These alleged appearances of Jesus after his death could, he considered, have been mass hypnotism, or perhaps an hallucination, resulting from a fervent desire in the hearts of the disciples. Or even an apparition.

But there was a problem with that. The disciples ***did not believe he would rise.*** They ***doubted*** that he had risen. They called it an "idle tale". (Matthew 28:17; Luke 24:10,11)

They did not even WANT to believe he had risen! (Luke 24:13-31)

All the way through the gospel accounts, the writers themselves attest to a very great ***reluctance*** on the part of his closest disciples to ***believe*** in his resurrection.

Could the "appearances", then, have been an hallucination?

Do men "conjure up" a vague or nebulous dream in something they are "hoping for", if they really ARE NOT EVEN HOPING FOR IT? Would they have an ecstatic "vision" of something they DIDN'T BELIEVE WOULD OCCUR in the first place?

West had to admit, that would not be logical.

What was more, DIFFERENT GROUPS of people kept on seeing Jesus in DIFFERENT PLACES at DIFFERENT TIMES. It could be neither mass hypnotism nor a dream. The same dream does not repeatedly keep occurring to totally different people in widely separated areas at totally different times.

West actually found twelve different occasions recorded when Jesus appeared after his resurrection. It was unlikely that men of such diversity of character would all be deceived and deluded. One could hardly imagine Peter becoming delirious, or Thomas hysterical, or the group of 500 all simultaneously suffering from an hallucination.

It was crystal clear that the disciples of Jesus DID NOT BELIEVE the resurrection of Jesus until they simply HAD to believe it.

An ardent unbeliever convinced

As he researched, West came upon the account concerning a man named Saul. A Pharisee, Saul was well educated. His logical mind would not be readily deceived. Yet he gave testimony of his meeting the resurrected Yeshua on the way to Damascus - ***while he was an ardent unbeliever***. That meeting turned his life around.

Only one explanation made sense. All these people saw Jesus, the same Jesus. Alive again. They were all skeptical. They DID NOT BELIEVE his resurrection - until they simply HAD to believe it.

While unlikely for us...

West saw himself in this. His problem was, he was asked to believe something that was really unbelievable. He was asked to believe that a dead man rose from the dead. And he had NEVER SEEN A MAN WHO DID THAT.

West was confronted with testimony that a "miracle" occurred. He could not produce witnesses that it did not occur. All he might do is introduce witnesses who would say they had never seen anything like this happen.

Was he to say that no fact was to be taken as testimony unless he, Gilbert West, had experienced it? Anyone who took his own experience solely as his criteria would cut himself off from the greater part of human knowledge.

In West's mind, there was a tremendous presumption against an ordinary man rising from the dead. However, coming to know Jesus as he was portrayed in the gospels, West saw that, whereas it was unlikely that any ordinary man should rise from the dead, in his case the presumption was exactly reversed. It was unlikely that THIS man should not rise. It could be said that it was impossible that he should be bound by death.

Yes, the evidence for the resurrection was shaping up to be GOOD EVIDENCE.

Other scientists speak

For a moment I shall interrupt this story of Gilbert West.

As I write this chapter, I have before me some interesting comments by a chemical scientist and an historian. Let me share them with you.

Dr. A.C. Ivy, of the Department of Chemical Science, University of Illinois, states his faith in the bodily resurrection of Jesus Christ. He says:

> On the basis of historical evidence of existing biological knowledge, the scientist who is true to the philosophy of science can doubt the bodily resurrection of Jesus Christ, but he cannot deny it. Because to do so means that he can prove that it did not occur. I can only say that present-day biological science cannot resurrect a body that has been dead and entombed for three days. To deny the resurrection of Jesus Christ on the basis of what biology now knows is to manifest an unscientific attitude according to my philosophy of the true scientific attitude. (Cited by Wilbur M Smith, in article, "Twentieth Century Scientists and the Resurrection of Christ', *Christianity Today,* April 15, 1957}

Professor E.M. Blaiklock, former Professor of Classics at the University of Auckland, New Zealand, says:

> I am a classical historian, and as an historian I look upon the empty tomb and the only available explanation of it, as a better authenticated fact than almost anything else I have taught about that century in all my university years. (Jonathan Gray, private files)

The two skeptics, West and Lyttleton, met again as planned. Each was a little sheepish, as he approached the other. Each was apprehensive of what the other's reaction would be.

For when they compared notes, it was realised that they had both come independently to disturbing conclusions. West had found the evidence pointed unmistakably to the fact that Jesus did rise from the dead. Lyttleton had found, on examination, that Saul of Tarsus did become a radically new man, through his conversion to Christianity.

Both men had become, in the process, strong and devoted followers of Yeshua. Each had experienced a remarkable change in his life, which had occurred through contact with the risen Messiah.

39

Risen? -

LEGAL VERDICT

If you went into court with such evidence, how would you come out? I wanted to be sure. Not being a lawyer myself, I went in search of the best I could find.

And here is what happened. But first let me say this:

When an event takes place in history and there are enough people alive who were eyewitnesses of it or had participated in the event, and when the information is published, one is able to verify the validity of an historical event.

Sir Edward Clarke, K.C., wrote:

> As a lawyer, I have made a prolonged study of the evidences for the events of the first Easter Day. To me the evidence is conclusive, and over and over again in the High Court, I have secured the verdict on evidence not nearly so compelling. (Wilbur M.A. Smith, *A Great Certainty in This Hour of World Crises.* Wheaton: Van Kampen Press, 1951, p.14)

Professor Thomas Arnold, author of a famous three-volume *History of Rome,* who was appointed to the chair of Modern History at Oxford, stated concerning the evidence for the resurrection of Jesus:

> Thousands and tens of thousands of persons have gone through it piece by piece, as carefully as every judge summing up on a most important cause. I have myself done it many times over... I know of no one fact in the history of mankind

> which is proved by better and fuller evidence of every sort. (Wilbur M.A. Smith, *Therefore Stand: Christian Apologetics.* Grand Rapids: Baker Book House, 1965, pp. 425,426)

Lord Lyndhurst, one of the greatest legal minds in British history, who in one lifetime held the highest offices which a judge in Great Britain could ever have conferred upon him (Solicitor-General of the British government; Attorney-General of Great Britain; three times High Chancellor of Cambridge), wrote:

> I know pretty well what evidence is; and I tell you, such evidence as that for the Resurrection has never broken down yet. (*Ibid.,* pp.425,584)

While still Professor of Law at Harvard, Simon Greenleaf wrote a volume entitled *An Examination of the Testimony of the Four Evangelists by the Rules of Evidence Administered in the Courts of Justice.* In it he says:

> The laws of every country were against the teachings of His disciples... Propagating this new faith, even in the most inoffensive and peaceful manner, they could expect nothing but contempt, opposition, reviling, bitter persecutions, stripes, imprisonment, torments, and cruel deaths.... They had every possible motive to review carefully the grounds of their faith.... If then their testimony was not true, there was no possible motive for its fabrication. (Simon Greenleaf, *Testimony of the Evangelists, Examined by the Rules of Evidence Administered in Courts of Justice.* Grand Rapids: Baker Book House, 1965, pp.28-30. Reprinted from 1847 edition)

A former Chief Justice of England, Lord Darling, said concerning Jesus' resurrection:

> On that greatest point we are not merely asked to have faith. In its favor as living truth there exists such overwhelming evidence, positive and negative, factual and circumstantial, that no intelligent jury in the world could fail to bring in a verdict that the resurrection story is true. (Michael Green, *Man Alive.* Downers Grove: Inter-Varsity Press, 1968, pp.53,54)

What does the resurrection prove?

Throughout this investigation I had been jotting down some common sense facts. It dawned on me that if Jesus' resurrection really happened, then this would affect my life. Like it or not, no person on earth could remain unaffected. Here's why:

> ***Firstly***, Jesus' resurrection placed a seal on the genuineness of certain Old Testament prophecies. (Psalm 16:10; Hosea 6:2)
> ***Secondly***, it placed a seal on Jesus as being who and what he claimed to be. (Romans 1:4; Acts 13:30)
> ***Thirdly***, the resurrection proved Jesus' inherent power. (Romans 1:4; John 10:17,18)
> ***Fourthly***, it marked him as the conqueror of death.
> ***Fifthly***, unless it happened, we are still without hope beyond the grave. (1 Corinthians 15:14)

But more than that, such a resurrection would place a seal on his full authority as King and universal Judge. It would make the Judgment of all men certain. If so, then one should take seriously the Scriptural claim that our Creator has "*appointed a day, in which he will judge the world in righteousness by that Man whom he has ordained; whereof he has GIVEN*

ASSURANCE unto all men, in that he has raised him from the dead." (Acts 17:31)

So, ***sixthly***, Jesus' historical resurrection makes certain our own future resurrection at that day. Each person will be raised - to eternal life or judgment.

And it struck me. By accepting his claims, I had nothing to lose - but the possibility of everything to gain.

On the other hand, if it was true and I did not accept, I had everything to lose. (1 Thessalonians 4:14,16-18)

The event itself

Just try to imagine that resurrection morning. Picture yourself there. The night of the first day of the week has slowly worn away. The darkest hour, just before daybreak, has come. Jesus is still a prisoner in his narrow tomb. The great stone is in its place; the Roman seal is unbroken; the Roman guards are keeping their watch.

And there are unseen watchers. Hosts of the Legion of Lucifer are gathered about the place. If it were possible, the prince of darkness with his antagonistic army would keep forever sealed the tomb that holds the Son of God.

But a heavenly host surrounds the tomb. Angels that excel in strength are guarding the tomb, and waiting to welcome the Prince of Life. And behold, there is a great earthquake; for the angel of the Lord descends from heaven. Clothed with radiance from God, this messenger leaves the heavenly courts.

The bright beams of God's glory go before him, illuminating his pathway. His countenance is like lightning, and his clothing white as snow. And for fear of him the keepers shake, and become as dead men.

Now, priests and rulers, where is your guard? Brave soldiers that have never been afraid of human power, are now as captives taken without sword or spear. The face they look upon is not the face of mortal warrior; it is the face of the mightiest of the messengers of God. This messenger is he who fills the position from which Lucifer fell. It is he who on the hills of Bethlehem announced Jesus' birth.

The earth trembles at his approach, the hosts of darkness flee and as he rolls away the stone, heaven seems to come down to earth.

The soldiers see him removing the stone as he would a pebble, and hear him cry, "Son of God, come forth. Your Father calls you."

As he exits the tomb in majesty and glory, the angel host bow in adoration before him and welcome him with praise.

The decree of heaven has loosed the captive. Mountains piled upon mountains over his tomb could not have prevented him from coming forth. (Based on Matthew 28:2-4)

* * * * * *

So where was this tomb that was burst open? After all this time did anything remain? Was there anything physical left behind that could supply ***archaeological evidence*** of such an event?

It was a tantalizing question. And one that deserved an answer. I began to probe... not totally prepared for the surprise.

40

Risen? -

THE TOMB AT SKULL HILL

Some very precise clues (for future archaeologists?) were given in the New Testament concerning the crucifixion, the burial site and resurrection of Jesus.

Skull Hill execution site

The writings inform us that Jesus was crucified "outside the city" (John 19:17,20; Hebrew 13:12) at a place called "the Skull" (Matthew 27:33; Mark 15:22; Luke 23:33; John 19:17) "***Skull***" translates to "***Calvary***" from the Latin, or to "***Golgotha***" from the Aramaic.

There is only one place around Jerusalem which has borne, and still bears, the name Skull Hill. It is just outside the North Wall, about 250 yards north-east of the Damascus Gate. A portion of this hill bears a striking resemblance to a human skull.

It is also the traditional site of burials for Muslims, Jews and Christians. Here it was, according to local tradition, that criminals were stoned to death. In the *Mishna* this place is called ***Beth ha-Sekelah***, literally, "***House of Stoning***".

Nearby is St. Stephen's Church, built over an old basilica that was erected to commemorate the stoning of Stephen, the first Christian martyr here, in 34 AD.

This was the recognized place of public execution for Jewish criminals. As late as the beginning of the 20th century, Jews would spit at the hill, throw stones and curse the "destroyer of their nation". It is such a site that the Roman authorities would have selected for executions.

"Outside" the city

Skull Hill is just a short distance outside the Damascus Gate, the only direct exit from the Castle of Antonine (the alleged place of Jesus' illegal night trial).

Recent archaeological opinion also holds that the Damascus Gate, which today marks the northern boundary of the Old City, likewise marks the northern boundary of Jerusalem in the 30s, the time of Jesus' crucifixion.

All this tends to add weight to the feasibility of Skull Hill, outside the wall, advocated by Otto Thenius (1842), Colonel Couder (1875) and General Gordon (1883), being the actual site.

One might note, in passing, that this rocky outcrop contains also what is known as a large complex of Jewish tombs dating from the First and Second Temple periods - and in particular, what is known as the "Garden Tomb", in which many believe Jesus was buried. The quarried face is hundreds of feet long.

Excavation begins

During excavations by an American team from January, 1979 to January, 1982, in front of the escarpment of which Skull Hill is a part, a crucifixion platform was uncovered. It extended out from the cliff face for about eight feet.

Skull Hill, Jerusalem (note the facial features at the right)

The excavation crew found four squarish holes, each 12 to 13 inches wide, cut into the bedrock — holes which, apparently, had once held crosses.

One of the holes was elevated above the rest, cut into the shelf-like platform behind. It appeared that this was the place where the "featured" criminal-victim was crucified, being elevated several feet above those crucified around him.

Had this hole held the cross of Jesus Christ?

Stone "plugs" set into the cross-holes had the obvious use of preventing the holes from filling up when not in use, as well as preventing people and horses from breaking their legs.

After the removal of debris, one of the cross-holes was measured and found to extend 23½ inches into the solid bedrock.

The Romans liked to crucify victims as an ***example***, or a ***warning***, to the populace. And to erect the crosses beside a crowded thoroughfare fulfilled this purpose well.

Pertinently, this crucifixion site was found to be up against the Calvary escarpment close to the place of the Skull. It was north of the Damascus Gate, on a ledge facing toward a public road, the old highway that led to Samaria.

"A very great stone"

Continued clearing of the area exposed a portion of a large, flat rock, which was a little less than ***two feet thick***. I would like you to remember that measurement. We shall meet it again.

The exposed edge was curved, somewhat like that of a large, thick, rounded table-top.

As the men cleared away more dirt and debris, it became apparent that the stone was enormous.

They stopped digging. The dirt and debris piled over it was ten feet deep. It would be several years later before its true dimensions were to be determined by sub-surface radar from above the ground. The diameter was found to be ***13 feet 2 inches***! Thirteen feet two inches. Remember that measurement also, as we shall meet it again.

A building had apparently been constructed at one time to enclose BOTH the crucifixion site AND this great, round stone.

What could be the significance of this stone?

Nearby... a tomb

The New Testament describes a nearby garden which contained the newly cut out tomb of a wealthy man, Joseph of Arimathea. It states that the owner of this tomb, who had witnessed the crucifixion of Jesus, was so moved that he went to the governor, Pontius Pilate, to ask for the body of Jesus to be placed in his – Joseph's – own unused tomb. This request was granted.

> *Now in the place where he was crucified there was a garden; and in the garden a new sepulchre, wherein was never man yet laid. There they laid Jesus. for the sepulchre was near at hand.* (John 19:41,42)

John, a first century witness, furnishes us with a THREE-STRAND LINK:

1. the Skull Hill crucifixion site
2. a surrounding garden, and
3. a nearby tomb.

In 1867, in the same cliff face not far from where the crucifixion-site excavators would later work, a landowner was digging a cistern on his property, when he discovered a tomb cut into the cliff face. As with the crucifixion site, this tomb was beneath the current ground level, covered in the debris of many centuries.

Several cisterns were also unearthed at this spot. These suggested that an olive grove could have existed here. One of the cisterns was very large — and it dated back to the first century or earlier. Lying some twelve feet below the pavement against the east wall, it could hold about 200,000 gallons of water, sufficient to keep a large plantation green throughout the eight dry months of the year. In 1924, a very fine wine press was excavated near the present main entrance to the garden. This indicated that there had been a vineyard nearby.

Of special interest

Of course the discovery of a tomb in this vicinity could hardly be described as sensational. Many tombs had been found in this large, ancient burial area of Jerusalem.

But this tomb was of special interest.

When a tomb is seen to be unusual (and we shall address that shortly), and is seen to be adjacent to an ancient execution site, as well as in the setting of a garden, such a combination of factors is not to be taken lightly.

In 1883, General Gordon, the notable British soldier, came to the area – and became convinced that the "skull face" was the true Golgotha.

This prompted him to go looking for a tomb that was "*near at hand*", as indicated in the Bible.

And just a few hundred feet away was this tomb, today known as the Garden Tomb.

Although first discovered in 1867, it was not excavated until 1891. At that time, Dr Conrad Schick prepared a report with diagrams, which was published in the *Palestine Exploration Fund Quarterly* of April, 1892.

This tomb became the prime suspect for being the tomb of Jesus Christ. However, strenuous opposition arose from adherents of the traditional "Holy Sepulchre" tourist site inside the Old City.

The Church of the Holy Sepulchre had been built by the Roman emperor Constantine in 333 AD, on a site selected by his mother, Helena.

Many scholars have asserted that this site of the Holy Sepulchre church could have been outside the city wall in Jesus' time. It is INSIDE the wall today.

The Garden Tomb

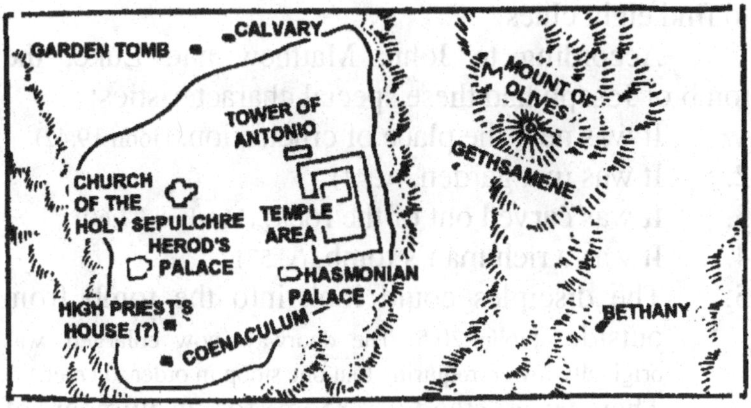

However, prevailing archaeological opinion is that the wall is now just where it was in Jesus' day. And also that the actual place of Jesus' crucifixion was the "Skull Hill" outside the city wall.

Soon this new tomb site, the "Garden Tomb", gained some supporters.

"First century"

Once excavation of the tomb was completed, characteristics were noted which did prove it to be dated to the first century of the Christian era, the time of Jesus.

Dame Kathleen Kenyon, the famous British archaeologist, said in 1970, "It is a typical tomb of about the first century AD." (Jonathan Gray, private files)

Eight vital clues

Very well, then, we have here today a first century tomb. But that is a far cry from identifying it as the tomb of Joseph of Arimathea.

There would need to be some reasonably good ***evidence***. Is there any way the biblical accounts might assist us? Indeed, in those ancient writings I was able to find eight clues.

According to John, Matthew and Luke, the tomb of Joseph had these special characteristics:

1. It was near the place of crucifixion. (John 19:42)
2. It was in a garden. (v. 41)
3. It was carved out of the rock. (Matthew 27:60)
4. It was a rich man's tomb. (v. 57)
5. The disciples could look into the tomb from outside. (John 20:5. The doorway, now enlarged, was originally lower, requiring that one stoop in order to enter.)
6. There was standing room for a number of persons. (Luke 24:1-4)
7. It was a new tomb and not an old tomb renewed. (John 19:41)
8. The tomb was closed by rolling a GREAT stone over the entrance. (Matthew 27:60)

In every one of these particulars, the tomb discovered in 1867 matched the biblical description. It fitted like a glove.

A rich man's tomb

Entering the tomb, one is impressed with the size. Certainly, only a rich man could have afforded a tomb such as this. Inside the tomb, to the right, was a spot for the owner of the tomb to be laid – and close to that, another spot, possibly for his wife. To the left, a large room was cut out for mourners to stand.

Used by a different person

But this tomb was not used by the person or persons for whom it had been cut out. Inside the tomb, one section carved out of the rock to fit one man, had clearly been enlarged for somebody else —someone who was taller than the man for whom the tomb had been measured.

This enlarged section indicated that not the owner, but ***some other person***, was laid in this rich man's tomb.

The ancient record states that Joseph, a member of the Sanhedrin, took the body of Jesus and *"laid it in his own new tomb", "wherein was never man yet laid."* (John 19:41) This spot in the tomb that was enlarged for someone's feet, was this another link in the evidence?

A most remarkable feature of Jesus' entombment is that, although he was executed as a criminal and so should ***not*** have received the dignity of normal burial, yet his body was rescued from 'disgrace' and laid in a grave of highest rank!

Yet this very event was prophesied concerning the Messiah, many centuries earlier:

> *He made his grave with the wicked but with the rich in his death.* (Isaiah 53:9-11)

The mathematical odds against such an event are enormous.

Inside the tomb: the receptacle for the body

A new or uncompleted tomb

The existence of the cavity in the receptacle at the tomb's north-east corner, and the absence of this cavity in the south-east receptacle, as well as the unfinished groove toward the north end of the west wall, show clearly that the tomb was never completed.

A "great" stone

Something else. Matthew records that Joseph, after placing the body in his own new tomb, *"rolled a great stone to the door of the sepulchre, and departed."* (Matthew 27:60)

The text goes out of its way to say "***great***" stone. This clue, that it was a GREAT stone, is another evidence that the owner of the tomb was a rich man.

How the seal stone was secured in front of the tomb between two metal pegs, and with the Roman seal attached

Someone else was also interested in this tomb. The Jewish chief priests and Pharisees went to Pilate, the Roman governor, saying:

> *Sir, we remember that that deceiver said, while he was yet alive, After three days I will rise again. Command therefore that the sepulchre be made sure until the third day, lest his disciples come by night, and steal him away, and say unto the people, He is risen from the dead, so the last error shall be worse than the first. Pilate said unto them, Ye have a watch: go your way, make it as sure as ye can. So they went, and made the sepulchre sure, sealing the stone, and setting a watch.* (vv.62-66)

The missing seal stone

Immediately in front of the tomb is a stone trench, or trough. This was for the rolling of a stone to seal the doorway.

At the left end is an incline. The stone was rolled onto the trough at this end.

Late in 1995, I took an archaeological team to Jerusalem. We measured this trough which was built to channel the rolling stone. We found this trough to be — wait for it — about ***two feet*** wide!

At the right hand end of the trough is a large stone block, positioned to prevent further movement of the seal-stone toward the right. Above that, on the right hand face of the tomb itself, a ridge was cut in the rock, which would block the stone from rolling further in that direction.

In the face of the tomb were two evidences which showed that a very, very large seal-stone was once used to seal this tomb.

In the right side of the tomb face, team member Dr Nathan Meyer had on an earlier visit pointed out a hole which was pierced into the cliff face. The hole held the oxidized remains of an iron shaft. This has since been removed, but the hole remains.

On the left hand side of the tomb face, another hole had been pierced into the rock for the insertion of a metal shaft, to prevent the seal-stone from being rolled to the left and the tomb being opened.

That Friday, October 20, at 4 pm, team members Dr David Wagner and Peter Mutton measured across the tomb face from the shaft hole on the left to the ridge at the right. The distance was discovered to be — you guessed it — ***precisely 13 feet 2 inches*!**

Examining the groove which blocked the seal stone from rolling any further to the right

Jonathan Gray points to the shaft hole which held the seal stone in place on the left

This shows that the seal-stone was, indeed, "a very great stone" - over twice the diameter of any other seal-stone found in Israel! To our knowledge, the largest seal-stone previously found was 5 feet 6 inches. This and the size of the nearby buried stone were a PERFECT MATCH.

Mystery of the iron shaft

Now let me share with you something intriguing.

We photographed and video-taped the spot where the Romans drove the iron shaft into the stone face of the tomb at the left edge of where the thirteen foot seal-stone would have been. They had done this in an attempt to prevent the stone from being rolled to the side and the tomb being opened.

The record states that the stone was "sealed". (Matthew 27:60,66)

The metal shaft on the left which held the stone in place was about two fingers in thickness. It would be impossible to bend this shaft, much less snap it off, simply by pushing the seal-stone against it. To move the great stone even one inch, the shaft must first be taken out.

However, when we examined the hole that held the metal shaft, we found that ***the shaft was still in there***! What was left of it, that is. It was sheared off, level with the wall. The appearance of the metal was consistent with its having been sheared off when struck with a tremendous force from the right-hand side.

According to an engineer, the shear strength of this peg was approximately 60 to 80 tons. To put it another way, a metal peg of such thickness would withstand 60 to 80 tons' pressure before it actually snapped off.

Imagine, if you can, ten tip trucks all compressed together - or all the materials for two brick houses squeezed together - and suddenly dropped onto the iron peg. That is the pressure involved.

However, being soft and malleable, the peg might have taken more than 60 to 80 tons' pressure, bending first before it sheared right off.

The engineer confirmed my conclusion. "I could see that the end had been torn slightly sideways - perhaps a quarter inch - to the left, even though it was now rusted some," he said. "It was an incredible sight, to witness what had happened. Accomplished by moving the stone in one simple move." He calculated that the stone itself weighed around 13.8 tons.

It would be impossible, humanly speaking, to snap off that metal shaft ***from a dead stop.*** There was no leverage.

The seal-stone has gone.

Someone pushed the stone aside without taking out the metal peg... Who was it?

The disciple Matthew informs us that the power involved was non-human:

> *... the angel of the Lord descended from heaven, and came and* ***rolled back the stone*** *from the door, and sat upon it. His countenance was like lightning, and his raiment white as snow: And for fear of him the keepers did shake, and became as dead men.* (Matthew 28:2-4)

The evidence shows that the stone was moved ***with great speed***, by some colossal force WITHOUT TAKING OUT THE METAL ROD.

Could that sheared off metal shaft still visible in the wall be ***evidence*** of a supernatural opening of the tomb? Is this a physical witness to the miraculous resurrection of Jesus?

Critics versus confirmation

For several years after I first reported this discovery, a critic asserted, "No, no, you are mistaken – that metal spike is no more than a stray bullet which hit the wall during the 1967 war."

Oh, okay, that's clear! Now we know! Thankyou Madhatter!

We asked the police department. "What would happen if you fired a bullet into a stone cliff? Would it embed into the wall?"

"No," was the answer. "It might shatter a hole in the stone wall, but it would not fix itself into it."

Then... advance forward to 2004. The metal was at last being tested by the Israeli Antiquities Authority (IAA).

Eventually further information was released. IAA archaeologist Yehiel Zelinger wrote a short article stating that the metal object found in the wall of the Garden Tomb was consistent with metal pins used in ***Roman*** construction. He stated that samples taken from the metal object were tested at Hebrew University and shown to contain both iron and lead.

You see, it was common in ancient times to set metal pins in molten lead. This would make them easier to drive into solid objects. While these tests do not determine the date of the metal object, they do show a consistency with metal pins used to construct the Coliseum in Rome and with those found in other ***Roman period*** sites.

Bottom line... the findings are consistent with my conclusion that this metal pin was used by the Romans to seal the Garden Tomb. The metal pin is

NOT shrapnel from an exploded shell, nor a stray bullet. It IS of ancient origin.

Could this, then, be direct archaeological evidence of the supernatural shearing off of the peg to wall level as the seal stone was superhumanly rolled at high speed against it? Is this archaeological evidence of the resurrection event?

The remains of the metal peg, the outer end of which was sheared off by some tremendous force

PART NINE

THE COVER-UP

41
Cover-up -
WHY PERSIAN HISTORY WAS COMPRESSED

Is there really a 241 year discrepancy? Is it true that the Jewish Bible and the Jewish year count ***disagree with each other***?

That's right. In the 130s of the present era, Jewish history was deliberately shortened to make the messianic prophecy of Daniel chapter 9 extend into the second century.

This was the last of a series of moves to curb the alarming growth of the Christian movement within the Jewish community.

The truth not being told

Is it true that ***an acknowledged hoax*** is being perpetrated upon the ordinary Jewish people and they are generally unaware of it? You've said it, Simon. And sadly, the history of early Judaism has also been misrepresented to the Jewish people by standard Jewish literature and/or by their rabbis.

Something here just doesn't smell right. How could this happen?

Although most rabbinic literature has mischaracterized first century Judaism as being almost totally pharisaical, the truth is that the religious situation was one of great flux, with six or seven different groups struggling for ascendancy within the Israeli Jewish community. Most of these were represented on the Council (Sanhedrin).

That diverse representation initially included the so-called "Nazarenes" or followers of Yeshua of Nazareth.

However, with the Roman siege of Jerusalem in 70 AD, virtually no one escaped except the Nazarenes, who had been prophetically forewarned to re-locate to Pella, east of the Jordan. Only the lead-Pharisee, Rabbi Jochanan ben Zacchai, was able to fake his own death, be removed alive from the city during the siege, and re-organize the Sanhedrin in Jamnia (Yavneh) on strictly pharisaical grounds.

About 90 AD, his successor, Rabbi Gamaliel (II), in order to drive the Nazarenes out of the synagogues (they were numbering approximately 20-25,000 by that time in the region), added the "curse against the *minim*" (heretics) to the Eighteen Benedictions recited at every "authorized" synagogue.

Despite this, it seemed impossible to curb the growth of the Christian movement.

Scholarly fiddling with prophecy texts

Finally, in the 130s, Rabbi Akiva, "the father of the Mishnah", attempted to answer the Nazarenes (Christians) by promoting a new (non-Septuagint) translation of the Hebrew Scriptures into Greek, which ***ripped out key words in the texts*** that were especially used by the Nazarenes to demonstrate Jesus as the Messiah.

Very thorough, this boy! Akiva also ***chopped out*** at least 160 years of known Persian history, so that the 490 years prophesied by Daniel, during which Messiah must appear, would reach into the second century.

Then, around 140 AD, Rabbi Yose Ben Halafta, one of Akiva's main disciples, codified this mutilated

Jewish chronology in the *Seder Olam Rabbah* ("Book of the Order of the World").

The *Seder Olam* cuts out 60 years between Adam and the birth of Abraham and 17 years between Solomon and the consecration of the Second Temple in 515 BC, but a whopping 164 years is deleted from 515 BC to 70 AD.

The chart on the next page indicates a deletion of 160 years for the Persian period. (By an alternative reckoning, 167 years have been deleted.) Average it, say, to a 164 year deletion.

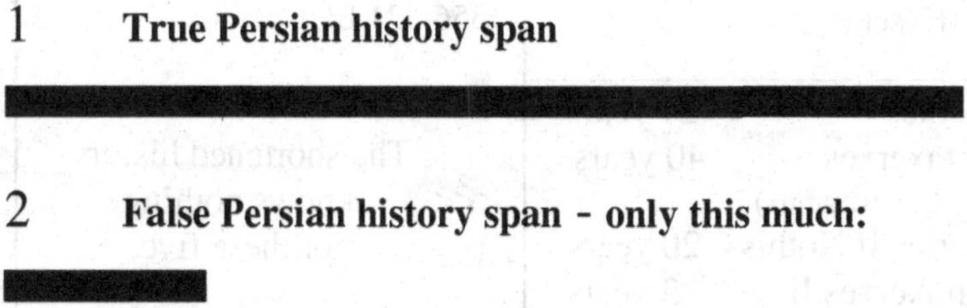

Do you see the time-span difference between ***the fake*** and the reality? And it is the second time-span which is today ***used*** by modern mainstream Jewry. An ***officially*** accepted fake!

It may asked why cuts were made in the Persian period, rather in the Greek Seleucid era that followed it? The answer is that Akiva and Yose ben Halafta could not make cuts from the Greek Seleucid era, because the chronology of that period was still in use, was firmly fixed among the Jews, and was well understood. It was too well known.

They could pull off their deception easier if they kept to the earlier period, the Persia Empire period.

TRUE HISTORY	FALSIFIED HISTORY
Some ten Persian kings ruled during the relevant period.	It records only five Persian monarchs.
Darius the Mede 25 years (575-551 BC)	Darius the Mede 1 year (374-373 BC)
Cyrus the Great 22 years (551-529 BC)	Cyrus the Great 3 years (373-371 BC)
Cambyses 7 years (529-522 BC)	Cambyses (Artaxerxes) ½ yr. (370 BC)
Pseudo-Smerdis 7 months (522 BC)	Ahasuerus 14 years (370-356 BC)
Darius the Great 35 years (Hystapes)	Darius the Great 35 years (356-321 BC)
Xerxes 21 years Artaxerxes 40 years (Longimanus) Darius II Nothis 20 years Artaxerxes II 3 years Darius III 6 years	<<< The shortened history knows nothing of these five.
Date of Temple's dedication: Feb. 10, 515 BC	Date of Temple's dedication: 355 BC
Alexander defeated Persia: <u>331 BC</u>	Alexander defeated Persia: <u>331 BC</u>
184 yrs	24 yrs
	"The Persian Empire existed during the time of the Temple for 24 years." (*Seder Olam, Rabbinic View of Biblical Chronology* (transl. Heinrich Guggenheimer (Jason Aaronson, Northvale, NJ, 1998), 260.)

And since the prophecy of Dan. 9: 24-27 dealt with a decree that was issued by a Persian monarch, the empire which preceded the Greeks, this left only the Persian period of history for them to exploit.

Thankyou, honest teachers.

It is important to bear in mind that Josephus, writing *Antiquities* one short generation prior to Rabbis Akiva and Jose, knew how many years there were in Persian history. He states that there were 408 years from a prophecy Daniel gave in the third year of Belshazzar until Antiochus' Epiphanes' desecration of the Temple in 167 BC. (Josephus, *Antiquities of the Jews*, X.xi.4)

Therefore, any argument that this shortened chronology among the Jews precedes Josephus rings hollow.

Jewish sources admit year count is falsified

You ask, do any of today's Jewish scholars know about this deliberate date fiddling? Oh yes.

The *Encyclopedia Judaica* has this to say about Rabbi Yose's "compression of the Persian period":

> The most significant confusion in R. Yose's calculation is the ***compression*** of the Persian period, from the rebuilding of the Temple by Zerubabbel in 516 BC, to the conquest of Persia by Alexander, ***to no more than 34 years***. (*Encyclopedia Judaica*, article: "Seder Olam". Emphasis mine)

Quite a number of Jewish scholars are aware of this problem, and some, such as Rabbi Simon Schwab, have tried to justify this chronological cover-up with the following amazing words:

> The gravity of this intellectual dilemma posed by such enormous discrepancies must not be underestimated... How could it be that our forebears had no knowledge of a period in history, otherwise widely known and amply documented, which lasted over a span of 165 years and which was less than 600 years removed in time from the days of the Sages who recorded our traditional chronology in Seder Olam? Is it really possible to assume that some form of historical amnesia had been allowed to take possession of the collective memory of an entire people?. our Sages - for some unknown reason - had 'covered up' a certain historic period and ***purposely eliminated and suppressed all records and other material pertaining thereto.*** (Simon Schwab, *Dr Joseph Breuer Jubilee Volume*, "Comparative Jewish Chronology". New York, NY: R. Samson Raphael Hirsch Publications Society, Philip Felheim Inc., 1962), pp.182, 188. Emphasis Achwab's.)

Did you get that? A frank admission that this was a purposeful suppression of the truth!

Now notice how Schwab attempts to justify this chronological sleight-of-hand:

> If so, what might have been their compelling reason for so unusual a procedure? Nothing short of a Divine command could have promptedaintly 'men of truth' to leave out completely from our annals a period of 165 years and to correct all data and historic tables in such a fashion that the subsequent chronological gap could escape being noticed by countless generations, known to a few initiates only who

were duty-bound to keep the secret to themselves. (*Ibid.*)

Do you get what he's saying? A Divine command to cover up and deceive the Jewish people about their own history and that of the world? Could it be that their own prophet Amos puts his finger on the real problem?: *"Their lies have also led them astray, those after which their fathers walked."* (Amos 2:4)

Attempt to excuse it

So what is the reason for this hoax? According to a number of Jewish scholars, including Schwab, God directed the second century sages to falsify the data so as to confuse anyone trying to use the prophecies of Daniel to predict the time of the Messiah's coming.

So just get this. God gave the prophecy to Daniel so that everyone ***would know*** when to expect the Messiah. And then, God tried to cover up what He had revealed – so people ***would not know***? Methinks that statement is cosmically silly!

Very well, then, what was accomplished by this historical cover-up?

By ripping out 165 years of real time from Persian chronology and throwing it away, Rabbis Akiva and Yose ben Halafta apparently hoped to

(a) derail the evidence which Christians had successfully argued since 31 AD that Daniel's 490 year prophecy was fulfilled by Yeshua of Nazareth.

(b) extend Daniel's 490 years into their own day, and thus whip up support for a "messianic" revolt against the Roman occupation, a move which led to the Bar Kokhba revolt of 132-135.

If one ever needed evidence that Daniel's ***messianic prophecy*** was ***understood by the Jews of the first and second centuries,*** one need look no further than the *Seder Olam*. Its hacked chronology:

(a) deflected attention away from Yeshua's fulfillment of Daniel 9, and

(b) facilitated Akiva's effort to support Simon Bar Kokhba as the fulfillment of the prophecy.

It was taught that Bar Kockba would overthrow Roman rule, then rebuild the Temple.

Indeed, there are 483 years between the *Seder Olam's* bogus date for the dedication of the Second Temple (355 BC) and 129 AD, when Jewish deliberations over Emperor Hadrian were deadly serious.

Therefore one may deduce that ***the falsification*** of Jewish chronology was ***deliberate***.

True dating till Messiah appears
I←--→I
457 BC 483 years 27 AD

False dating till Messiah appears
I←--→I
355 BC 483 years 129 AD

And what was the result of this misidentification of messiahs?

It led to all Judea being laid waste and Jews forbidden to live within ten miles of Jerusalem. As if that were not enough, all Jews throughout the Empire were required to pay a head tax to support a new pagan temple in – of all places – Jerusalem.

What is so astonishing is that Jewish historians still consider Bar Kokhbar as their "most important messianic figure."

"Ban and burn" the book that exposes the hoax

By the 16th century, some Jewish writers were challenging the *Seder Olam.* Rabbi Azariah de Rossi of Mantua, in his work, *Ma'or `Einayim* ("Enlightenment of the Eyes"), demonstrated that the year count was severely flawed, some 165 years short of reality!

Although de Rossi's conclusions were irrefutably correct, the revelation was hotly resisted. Some traditionalists tried to appeal to Rabbi Joseph Karo, author of the *Shulhan `Arukh*, urging him to ***ban*** Rabbi de Rossi's book. Karo did in fact compose an order for the ***burning*** of the *Ma'or `Einayim*, but died before it could be implemented.

This alteration of Persian/Jewish history remains in use. Yet no secular, Persian or Christian scholars anywhere in the world accept the compressed version of history. And many Jewish scholars also now dispute it.

When one discusses the "Jewish" date of the world, the source used is the book *Seder Olam.* In fact, this is *the* source where we get to our counting of the year 2011 being the 5771 year of the world. This is in conflict with calculations which we derive from the ***Hebrew Bible***. Using the Bible, when we calculate back from the reign of Solomon (a date which is fixed in history), we arrive at a date for Adam which ***disagrees with*** today's fabricated ***Jewish calendar.***

Although the *Seder Olam* is not a formal part of the Mishnah or Talmud, it is a work of Talmudic authority which no orthodox Jew would think of openly contradicting (Floyd Nolen Jones, Th.D., Ph.D., App. G, *The Annals of the World.* Master Books, 2005, 934), despite the realization that it is missing around 240 years.

In all this, one feels the hot breath of ***something bigger***. This is ***no ordinary hoax.*** One can perceive behind it the intense antagonism of the Legion of Lucifer in its long-running feud against the Prince of God.

Where + when = why

Approximately the ***same time*** (130 -140 AD) that rabbis were mutilating the Jewish calendar to exclude Yeshua from being the Messiah, and at the very ***same location*** which was the heart of an anti-Christian paganisation campaign, Ptolemy's star chart scratched out the Ihesu (Yeshua) prophecy (as we saw in Chapter 27). How they hated that dangerous ***forbidden secret*** – Yeshua's rescue plan for us!

Look for the Messiah now, in vain

To anyone who still looks for Messiah to come, let it now be declared: It is certain that Daniel's 490 years *"from the commandment to restore and build Jerusalem"* expired almost 2,000 years ago. So one is for ever *without excuse,* who will not admit that the Messiah has come when we have gone so far beyond the utmost reckoning for his coming. If he has not already come, then he never will come.

Watch for the impersonator

Do not be surprised if, before this is all over, Lucifer himself poses as the returning Jesus Christ.

Jesus did warn there would be persons staging a fake Second Coming.

> Then if anyone tells you, 'The Messiah has arrived at such and such a place, or has appeared here or there,' don't believe it. For
>
> false Christs shall arise, and false prophets, and will do wonderful miracles, so that if it were possible, even God's chosen ones would be deceived. See, I have warned you.
>
> So if someone tells you the Messiah has returned and is out in the desert, don't bother to go and look. Or, that he is hiding at a certain place, don't believe it! For as the lightning flashes across the sky from east to west, so shall my coming be, when I, the Messiah, return. And wherever the carcass is, there the vultures will gather. (Matthew 24:23-28)

Fantasy? Not quite. In his book *Dark Secrets of the New Age* (pp.68,69), Texe Marrs reveals that the New Age movement expects the increasing earth changes to develop into utter world chaos. Then, at the time of a great earthquake in Jerusalem, the New Age "Christ" will appear on the Mount of Olives, and will proceed to become king of Jerusalem.

Can you imagine it? A being of dazzling radiance... majestic... and escorted by a vast procession of people. The people prostrate themselves before him. He lifts up his hands and utters a blessing over them. His voice is melodious, soft and subdued. He speaks heavenly truths and heals sick people, just as Jesus did. Then he gives a blessing to the New World Order and says that all those who will not come together under its laws have no right to exist. Just think of the effect that would have!

The 'big event'

How will you know it is not the Second Coming? No sweat. According to the prophetic Scriptures, when Jesus Christ returns, the world is heading for the greatest spectacle in its history. The

sky will light up from London to Los Angeles - and from Melbourne to Moscow. Every eye shall see him. And it'll be noisy. Something else: He won't at that time set foot on the earth. That's the difference. (Revelation 1:7; Matthew 24:27,30-31;1 Thessalonians 4:16,17)

It pays to know Bible prophecy. Then you won't be conned.

42

Cover-up -

THE REVENGE MOTIVE

Jack and Ellen bought their 11-year old son and 9-year-old daughter a beautiful little black German Shepherd pup. Bijou grew up as a loved member of the family. He played with the children, licked them affectionately, followed them everywhere.

Frequently they would go off out through the gate and into the adjacent forest. The parents knew that whenever the children were with Bijou they were safe. Somehow he always knew to bring them home for dinner on time.

…Until one day… when they failed to appear.

Ellen glanced at the clock. It was half past six. She went out to the gate. She called out. No reply. She called again… and again.

Worried, she went back to the house. Jack was already scrubbing up for dinner.

"Have you seen the children?" she asked.

"No," shrugged Jack. "They should have been back half an hour ago."

Then it was 6.45… then 7 o'clock. Now they were really concerned.

Jack strode out through the gate and into the forest. "Johnny…are you there? Kerry… can you hear me?" Silence.

Jack pushed deeper into the forest, calling as he went. He lumbered back home and they began phoning neighbours.

At almost 8 pm there was a scratching at the door. And there was Bijou, splattered in blood.

A dreadful thought overwhelmed Jack. His shock turned to anger. "What have you done to my kids!" he screamed. Grabbing a heavy slab of wood, he lashed into the dog... wham!... wham!... WHAM!

As the blows tore into his flesh, the helpless dog looked up into his master's eyes. Jack roared and raged at him, beating the dog harder and harder. Bijou lay still. Very weakly, he raised his head. With one last pitiful look at his master, his head dropped. Bijou was dead.

A search party that night failed to find the children. At daybreak, the search was resumed. Eventually, they came upon the children huddled at the base of a tree. Nearby lay a dead wolf.

The older child stirred, looked up at his father, and asked, "Where's Bijou?"

"The wolf came after us," explained the children. "Bijou fought it and killed it. Bijou saved us!"

Come to think of it, didn't someone do just that… for you… and for me? So what shall we do with this Jesus? Ignore him? Let the enemy slander him? Or wake up and benefit?

If the message of Jesus is true, then it must be the most wonderful news that you or I could ever receive.

Yet the widespread hostility against it seems to be almost an obsession. Who is orchestrating this hostility?

Ask yourself, ***who has the most to lose***? That's right, the Legion of Lucifer have the biggest motive in the world… REVENGE!

Satan the real god of the Mysteries

And those various pagan 'Mystery' religions with their imitation messiahs: Why were they set up? To divert mankind away from the rescue plan, no less. And to bring them under Lucifer's control. (Alexander Hislop, *The Two Babylons*; London: S.W. Partridge & Co., 1969, Jonathan Gray, *Stolen Identity*, chapters 12 to 16 – <http://www.beforeus. com/stolen-id.php>)

At the time the real Messiah put in his appearance, mighty Rome ruled the world. Rome was already a prisoner to that 'Mystery' religion – which meant Lucifer was the secret god of Rome.

Throughout history, ***Lucifer's emblems*** were the ***serpent*** and the ***sun***. That's what the name Lucifer means – Day-star. And, according to the fundamental doctrine of the Mysteries, as brought from Babylon to Pergamos, thence to Rome, the ***sun*** was ***the one only god***. (Macrobius, *Saturnalia*, lib. I. cap. 17,23, pp. 65, C, and 72, 1, 2)

Thus Teitan, or ***Satan***, had become the one only god. And Janus was just an incarnation of this same only god. ***Now the secret is out… the real name*** of the supreme great god of Rome. Worship of Satan (Lucifer) was the secret purpose of the Mysteries.

This secret was most jealously guarded. So much so, that when one of the most learned of the Romans, the high-ranking Valerius Soranus, incautiously divulged it, he was mercilously put to death. (Hislop, *The Two Babylons*. p. 279)

Eventually ***Satan*** was regarded with awe and dread under the name of ***Pluto***, the god of the underworld, as the great god on whom every person's destiny depended. To him it belonged 'to purify souls after death.' (Taylor's *Pausanias*, vol. iii. P.321, Note)

And his other symbol, the ***serpent,*** was worshipped in all the earth with extraordinary reverence! Therefore, to claim that one had been born as 'the serpent's seed' potentially attracted great honor to the claimant. That's why Olympias, the mother of Alexander the Great, declared that her son had not sprung from King Phillip, her husband, but from Jupiter, in the form of a ***serpent***! And why the Roman emperor Augustus pretended that he had issued from Apollo in the form of a ***serpent***.

Strategy 1: destroy Christianity from outside

The bottom line was this: Rome ruled the world. And Lucifer was the unseen ruler of Rome.

Well aware were the Legion of Lucifer that if the news of Jesus being the true and only Deliverer should triumph, then the pagan altars and temples of Rome would disappear.

So the Legion of Lucifer, through their Roman puppets, declared full scale war… open season on the followers of Jesus. Police were searching for these 'traitors' everywhere.

But the fiercer the attacks, the bolder the Christians became. Their love of Jesus meant more to them than their own lives. As thousands were imprisoned and executed, more sprang up to take their places. Instead of liquidating Christianity, persecution made it explode. And paganism began to fall back on its heels.

Strategy 2: sabotage it from within

Lucifer and Co. figured they had better put an end to this crisis once and for all. They decided to change tactics – infiltrate the movement and destroy it from within with a phony system of Christianity. Smart and sneaky, it would work like a charm.

The local Christian church in Rome, the capital city of the empire, became the target. By stealth, infiltrators got themselves planted in positions of influence within the group. Then they gradually sneaked in their pagan gods and idols – outwardly giving them new names… so that to the ordinary people the pagan Jupiter was "just a memorial to the Christian apostle Peter." Venus became the Virgin Mary. The sun god's December 25 'birthday' became the birthday of Jesus, and so on. The unsuspecting members had no idea that their new leaders were pagans who worshipped these images in honor of Lucifer. The Christian movement in Rome had been taken over. And this subterfuge is documented by numerous historians.

Today's religious Roman leadership knows their allegiance is to the same Lucifer cult as ancient Rome. As I write, at the ***highest*** levels of initiation, priests are being taught that their leader is not Jesus, but Lucifer. Of all systems on earth today, this is the ancient Babylonian system in its purest form – in at least 80 of its features. (Hislop, *The Two Babylons,* 330 pages) Despite this, the hierarchy allows the ***ordinary*** members and priests worldwide – millions of genuine, loving people – to think their organization is set up for "Mary" and "Jesus", ***so as to maintain their support***. Sad, but true. These poor people are unwitting victims of a takeover.

A continuation of the Roman Empire

So it was that as the Roman Empire disintegrated in the 5th century, Lucifer's paganised church in Rome stepped into its place. Papal Rome was, for all practical purposes, the continuation of the Roman Empire. Listen to the historians:

> Out of the ruins of political Rome, arose the great moral Empire in the "giant form" of the Roman Church. (A.C. Flick, *The Rise of the Mediaeval Church.* 1900, p. 150)

> The Roman Church…privily pushed itself into the place of the Roman World Empire, of which it is the actual continuation; the empire has not perished, but has only undergone a transformation…. It still governs the nations…. It is a political creation, and as imposing as a World-Empire, because the continuation of the Roman Empire. The Pope, who calls himself "King" and "Pontifex Maximus," is Caesar's successor. (Adolf Harnack, *What is Christianity?* New York: G.P. Putnam's Sons, 1903, pp. 269,270 – italics in the original)

Once it was established with armies at its disposal, the church in the capital city then set out to eliminate all opposition within the Christian world to the imitation Christianity it had set up.

The faithful retreat into wilderness regions

Real Bible Christians everywhere were appalled. They knew Lucifer had taken over the church in Rome and that although called Christian, it was phony, satanic and totally unchristian. So to save their families, millions of true believers withdrew to secluded areas where they could continue their uncorrupted way of life. Pure Christianity went underground for about 1,000 years.

Meanwhile, the political-religious power became the visible, ruling body over kings and nations. During those centuries it would slaughter from 50 and 120 million true believers. And where Bibles were found, they were burned by order of the church. (John Foxe, *Foxe's Book of Martyrs*, 432 pages) This history, once available in our libraries, is book by book being checked out and "lost".

Manuscript corruption

The Legion of Lucifer recognized what a powerful tool in the hands of the Christian movement was the written testimony of the witnesses to Jesus. You can kill people. But you can't kill what they've written. It can spread like a fire.

So in Alexandria, Egypt (the center of pagan philosophy) the corrupters very early got busy altering Bible texts within their reach, to downgrade Jesus' divinity. Prominent in this was a teacher by the name of Origen. Later, the Roman emperor Constantine, in a political bid to unify pagans and Christians, adopted Origen's corrupted manuscripts. However, only about 45 surviving Greek manuscripts of the New Testament (***1 percent of all***) stem from Constantine's corrupted copies. And these represent only ***one tiny geographical area*** – Alexandria.

99% not corrupted

The majority of New Testament manuscripts were beyond the reach of the corrupters. These remained safe, not in one location, but in Asia Minor, India, Greece, Syria, Africa, Gaul, Italy, England, Ireland and numerous other places. Of these, over 5,000 manuscripts have survived (99 percent of all surviving Greek New Testament manuscripts).

As the Dark Ages dispersed, and the carefully preserved manuscripts ***in the East*** were compared with those hidden safely ***in the West***, they were found to be ***virtually identical.*** And these formed the basis of the King James Bible in use today. (Jonathan Gray, *The Sorcerer's Secret*, 186 pages)

Counterfeit mistaken for the true

Again, may I stress, this is not about individual people – many of whom are decent, honest men and women – but about a corrupt system. My own dear wife used to belong to it, and she's a wonderful woman. It is the uncensored truth you want, right? I raise this topic only because it is essential to our understanding of the Jesus-Lucifer feud.

Today, although most don't know it, the world's largest, wealthiest and most powerful "Christian" organization is on the side of the hijackers. Founded primarily on politics, it does not promote the Christianity taught by Jesus, but answers to the Lucifer Legion. Its primary aim of world rulership is now almost within reach. This political power's "Christian-looking" front has the world mesmerised. Its public relations has been so successful that when most people think of "Christianity" or even "religion", this organization comes to mind.

And modern critics of Christianity have fallen for the trick. They see its 80 pagan features tagged with the name of "Jesus". So they jump to the conclusion that Jesus himself is just another item of "recycled paganism". These writers may sound scholarly. But their research is pathetically shallow. Critics, wake up! Get to know your history!

Is Christianity recycled paganism? Well, you know the answer to that. But the Lucifer Legion have done their job well. Just be sure you understand the difference between pure Christianity and Romanism. That's your key. It will explain so much! (For evidence, see my books *Stolen Identity* and *Welcome, Then Betrayal.)*

Lucifer or the Creator

Rome's Jesuits have successfully infiltrated or control all key world organizations. The Supreme Jesuit General is "in command of the Sovereign Military Order of Malta, Scottish-Rite Shriner Freemasonry, the Knights of Columbus, B'nai B'rith [Jewish Masonry], the Nation of Islam, the Mafia, Opus Dei, and the Ku Klux Klan, along with a host of lesser Brotherhoods." (*Saturday Evening Post*, January 17, 1959) Whether it be the CIA, the Federal Reserve Bank, the Bank of America, the FBI, KGB, FEMA, Freemasonry, Mossad, German BND, the British SIS, or M16, the top is invested with Jesuits (Jonathan Gray, *Welcome, Then Betrayal*, 2008, pp.155-157,170-179,207-216), as are the New World Order, the New Age movement, the Trilateral Commission, the C.F.R., the Illuminati, UFOism, the world's governments, the judiciary, military, universities, the pharmaceutical industry, sports and entertainment industries – Rome is pulling the strings. She has the best intelligence service on the planet.

The top leaders in the various Jesuit infiltrated religions, as well as leaders of nations, are high Masons – who take orders secretly from the highest Mason who wears the ephod – the pope. They are the "intelligent people" called "esoterics". By the time they get that far in their training, they know that they are really following Lucifer. The well-meaning members who have joined at the lower levels (whom the "esoterics" mockingly call "catechumen" = human cattle) do their chosen "good works", unaware that their respective organizations are set up to follow Lucifer.

The heads of Rome, the heads of Masonry, and the heads of the Church of Satan are basically of the same religion worshipping the same god, Lucifer. In acknowledgement of this, the top men all give the same two-horned-fingers satanic hand signal.

Ordinary honest people in "the one true faith" are lulled into acceptance by hearing "Jesus" words, seeing "holy" pictures, and kissing images of saints. When they wake up and discover what this is really all about, there will be a perfect storm!

All roads to ruin lead through Lucifer and his invisible government.

Mankind is indeed in the malignant grip of a satanic cult. Too sick to diagnose its deformity, it is afflicted by a debilitating spiritual disease. The aim of the Legion of Lucifer is to bring the human race to self destruction.

All Lucifer's various strategies have one common root – their hatred toward, or degrading of, Jesus Christ. So then, what is it about Jesus that evokes so much opposition? The Legion of Lucifer will never bother to counterfeit something unless it is important. Satan (Lucifer) authored paganism to denigrate his hated enemy – Jesus – so that people would reject the Rescue offer. He desires your destruction.

This plan of destruction for the human race could only have been ***strategized by a genius far beyond the ingenuity of man***, orchestrating and synchronizing it from behind the scenes.

Citizens of pagan New World

The grand final showdown will be, in effect, between New World Order Satanism and Bible Christianity. And it will lead to the end of man's control of this planet – and a new world.

The Legion of Lucifer proposes a universal religion ***made from all kinds of faiths except that of Jesus*** and obedience to his law.

The biblical book of Revelation prophesies that this global religion will indeed emerge, headed by the man with the number 666. The three sixes are ***three coiled serpents***, the emblem of Satan himself.

What's going on here?

Is it possible that many of us here on earth have made an awful mistake? That we've been misled by teachers who do not have the answer? Is it possible that there is not only a God who loves you and me, but there is coming a Judgment?

Is it possible that the Bible – the most widely translated and read book in the world – is, after all, telling us the truth about our origins and our destiny?

You'd better believe it! According to the evidence, the *Intelligence Report* (the Bible) offers the only effective explanation (and solution) for the problems of our real world. And the only permanent future.

* * * * * * *

Now, in case someone has been asleep up to this point and therefore has some lingering doubt about ALL the Bible having been generated ***supernaturally*** (especially the New Testament – the message concerning Yeshua, which the Legion of

Lucifer are hell-bent on suppressing), I have saved up a shocker for you.

Do you have the guts to look at this?...

* * * * * * *

Detailed information on these questions:

*** Has the Bible been changed?**

*** Are there books "missing"?**

is available in

The Da Vinci Code Hoax (chapters 7-12,14,20-21)

The Sorcerers' Secret (chapters 3-7)

Who's Playing Jesus Games? (chapters 10-15)

The Weapon the Globalists Fear (chapters 10,20)

Further information on:

* **Lucifer's top human agency, Rome**

*** The man with the number 666**

Stolen Identity (chapters 42 and 43)

Welcome, Then Betrayal (pages 150-256)

PART TEN

THE FINGERPRINT

43

Fingerprint of the author -

UNIQUE WATERMARK

In an earlier chapter we discovered how the very same 7s design that we see in nature has also been found embedded ***on and beneath*** the surface of the Old Testament.

We noted that both the Bible and nature bear ***similar identification marks*** – just as surely as various papers from the same mill bear beneath their surface the watermark of ***that mill alone.*** The truth is that quite independently of the biblical text is a "watermark" design woven through the surface message –a ***pattern of 'seven'***, if you please!

Whilst the Old Testament was composed in ***Hebrew***, the New Testament was in ***Greek***. These are the two languages in which every letter of the alphabet also doubles as a number.

Thus every letter, word and sentence has a numeric value, the sum total of each letter value. So when you read a word or sentence, you are simultaneously looking at a string of numbers.

We noted that the discovery of the "watermark" in the text was made by a Russian scientist, Ivan Panin, one of the ten top mathematicians of his day in the United States.

The New Testament also?

It turns out that this hidden design is not only in the Hebrew Old Testament (as we found) but also in the Greek New Testament. It contains the very same hidden design complex.

Now, just suppose you were asked to construct ***a genealogy of real people***, but with certain constraints:

- The number of words in the genealogy must be evenly divisible by 7 (with no remainders)
- The number of letters must be exactly divisible by 7
- The number of vowels and consonants must each be divisible by 7
- The number of words that begin with a vowel must be divisible by 7
- The number of words that begin with a consonant must be divisible by 7
- The number of words that occur more than once must be divisible by 7
- The number of words that occur in more than one form must be divisible by 7
- The number of words that occur only in one form must be divisible by 7
- The number of names in the genealogy must be divisible by 7
- The number of male names must be divisible by 7
- The number of generations in the genealogy must be divisible by 7

Is there such a genealogy?

Yes, there is. Just go to the very first passage of the New Testament - Matthew 1:1-11. This lists the human ancestry of Yeshua.

Here is what Panin discovered ***in the Greek***:

- The vocabulary contains 49 words (7 x 7)
- 28 words start with a vowel (4 x 7)
- 21 words start with a consonant (3 x 7)
- 7 words end with a vowel (1 x 7)
- 42 words end with a consonant (6 x 7)

- The 49 words have 266 letters (38 x 7)
- Of the 266 letters, 140 are vowels (20 x 7)
- Of the 266 letters, 126 are consonants (18 x 7)
- Of the 49 words, 14 occur only once (2 x 7)
- Of the 49 words, 35 occur more than once (5 x 7)
- Of the 49 words, 42 are nouns (6 x 7)
- Of the 49 words, 7 are not nouns (1 x 7)
- These remaining common nouns have exactly 49 letters (7 x 7)
- Men's names occur 56 times (8 x 7)
- The names of just 3 women appear in the passage; the Greek letters of their names add up to 14 exactly (2 x 7)

Panin calculated that it would have taken Matthew, working 8 hours a day, several months to construct this genealogy, even if that were possible.

"Oh, surely not that long," I hear someone protesting. "After all, he could surely just choose his words to make the numbers add up."

Not so simple.

You see, to compose this ancestral list Matthew ***could not choose*** the names to be used. The fact is, those names were chosen BEFORE Matthew was born! This is a direct father-to-son list of people who had already lived and died centuries earlier.

Another example

Let's take another passage – ***regarding the birth of Yeshua*** – Matthew 1:18-25. This comprises 161 Greek words (exactly 23 times 7).

Dr Panin has challenged anyone to produce a similar passage of 161 words in three years.

"Oh, that should not be so difficult," I hear someone saying.

You think it's easy? Just try it.

"But it's only 161 words – a mere third of a page."

Indeed. But its 7s pattern is so complex that according to the mathematical law of probability, the ***chance of*** such a pattern appearing stands at ***ONE in 200-odd quintillion***, a number which consists of 21 figures.

These amazing numerical features forming even one small passage, to say nothing of the thousands in the entire Bible, could not possibly have occurred by accident.

If these features did not occur accidentally, then there is only one alternative. These features were ***purposely intended*** …planned …designed.

Let me illustrate. Suppose you are carrying a bag of oranges. Suddenly the bag breaks and the 25 oranges fall to the floor. What chance would there be for the oranges to fall into five perfect rows, with five in each row, each orange being exactly opposite the other, like this?

Suppose we arrange the oranges on the carpet, in five even rows, thus:

o o o o o
o o o o o
o o o o o
o o o o o
o o o o o

Well? Could they arrange themselves this way?

That would be impossible, you say. And I would have to agree with you.

So if you came into a room and found the oranges arranged this way, you would arrive at only one conclusion, right? That they were purposely designed or arranged in this specific manner. If I insisted that this occurred accidentally you would call me insane!

Likewise, these profound numeric features found in the very structure of the original Bible text… ***you can be sure*** that they are ***not*** there by sheer chance or accident, but by design. They are arranged according to a definite plan; they form thousands of perfect and uniform designs.

Another example

Now turn to ***the next chapter of Matthew - chapter 2.*** This tells the story of the childhood of Jesus. And it likewise has a vocabulary of 161 words (23 sevens). These occur in 238 forms (34 sevens). And these have 896 letters (128 sevens). And their total numeric value is 123,529 which is 17,647 sevens. (You understand that every letter in the Greek alphabet also doubles as a number.)

Furthermore, each of the 238 forms has, in turn, alphabetical groups of sevens, which it would be too tedious to enumerate.

This chapter consists of at least four logical divisions - and each division shows individually the same 'sevens' phenomena found in the chapter as a whole. Thus the first six verses have a vocabulary of 56 words (that is, eight 7s), and so on.

Also, there are some speeches here: Herod speaks, the Magi speak, the angel speaks. Their numeric phenomena are so pronounced that though they are, as it were, a dozen rings within rings, wheels within wheels, yet each is a perfect pattern of sevens in itself… even though each forms only a part of the rest.

If you, the reader, can write a chapter like this as naturally as Matthew writes, and build into a mere 500 words so large a number of intertwined yet harmonious mathematics - if you can write a short chapter like this ***in five years*** you will do very well indeed.

You want the truth? There is ***not a single paragraph*** out of the hundreds in Matthew ***that is not constructed*** on exactly this same plan!

Yet ***with each additional paragraph*** the difficulty of construction increases, not in arithmetical but in geometrical progression. Exponentially! Because you will need to plan your paragraphs so as to develop constantly fixed numeric relations to what has gone before and what follows. Every additional letter, word, and sentence makes the matter tremendously more complicated and comprehensive.

Now are you ready for a bombshell? Do you know ***how long it would take*** for any man to write that one Gospel – Matthew's?

We ask Dr Panin. And he tells us that it would have taken Matthew ***over one thousand years*** to have constructed the Gospel on these lines. And that's assuming it to have been possible for him to do so, which, of course, it was not, because of the many circumstances over which he had no control.

Did you get that? One of the world's greatest mathematicians affirms that Matthew (the writer of the first book in the New Testament) ***could not have written that book in 1,000 years***!

But here's the problem: Jesus was crucified in AD 31 – so Matthew's Gospel (which reports that event) could not have been written earlier. And in AD 70 Jerusalem was destroyed (an event still future when

Matthew wrote) – so it could not have been written later.

The truth is, Matthew didn't have a thousand years to write the book. So how he managed to do it in those ***mere 39 years*** between AD 31, when Jesus Christ was crucified and AD 70, when Jerusalem was destroyed, let any sane man explain.

Yet Matthew did it. We thus have a miracle – an unheard of piece of literary mathematical artistry, unequalled, hardly even conceivable.

This is a vital 'fact' for the skeptic to contemplate.

"Sevens" in Mark

Now turn to the very next book, the Gospel of Mark. You will find it shows exactly ***the same 'sevens' phenomena*** as Matthew. Let's take, for example, ***the first eight verses*** of Mark, which report on the ministry of John the Baptist, the man who announced the arrival of Jesus.

* This passage contains
- 126 words (18 times 7)
- 294 syllables (42 x 7)

* Its vocabulary has 77 ***different*** words (11 x7). The sum of the factors of 77 is 14 (2 x 7). And it is divided again between tens and units exactly by 7s!

* These 77 words of the vocabulary have 427 letters (61 x 7). And the sum of its factors amounts to 14 (2 x 7).

* Of those 427 letters,
- 224 are vowels (32 x 7)
- and 203 are consonants (29 x 7)

* In it, John the Baptiser uses exactly 21 of the vocabulary words. (3x 7)
* The words he doesn't use amount to 56 (8 x 7)

* 42 of the words begin with a vowel (6 x 7)
* 35 of the words begin with a consonant (5 x 7)

… and so on.

Now, if the cleverest man in this world sat down to produce similar phenomena of 7s, his brain would soon reel, because ***every time he adjusted one portion it would upset another***!

If a man was able to struggle through, it might well take months to produce these mere eight verses, even choosing his own words. But where would he be if, like this example, he had to use unbroken, several phrases by two other writers - one being a quotation from the Old Testament?

How can this be explained? Peter tells us: These writings '*came not by the will of man... but... by the Holy Spirit.*' (1 Peter 1:21) That is the Bible's own explanation of its Author. Might it, after all, be true?

Another example

Now turn to ***the last twelve verses of Mark.*** This passage, which critics sometimes slur as 'a forgery', presents (among others) these phenomena:

- It has 175 words (or 25 sevens).
- Its vocabulary has 98 words (14 sevens).
- Of these, the ones Jesus uses in His speech, are 42 (or 6 sevens).
- In like manner, of the 175 words in these same twelve verses of Mark, the ones Jesus uses total 56 (or 8 sevens).
- And all this, too, with the usual break-up into alphabetical groups of seven in each case.
- Then again, of the 98 words of the vocabulary, 84 (or 12 sevens), are ***used before*** by Mark.
- And 14 (or 2 sevens), are used ***only here***.

Mark, then, is another miracle, another unparalleled mathematical literary genius. Remember this: ***with each additional sentence the difficulty greatly increases,*** and owing to the limitations of human intellect, soon becomes hopeless.

Modern attempts have failed

Scholars who have set out to accomplish a similar thing admit that after struggling for days their efforts were in vain without reducing the passage to a meaningless jumble.

A single author?

Both the Hebrew Old Testament and the New Testament give evidence of this amazing phenomenon.

Now here is the problem. The New Testament, comprising 27 books, was penned by at least eight different writers – yet, from the hidden design which runs right through, it appears there was one single Author! I ask you, does this suggest ***a single Intelligence*** behind the writing of all 27 books?

In any case, it became apparent to Panin that ***whoever*** had organized the New Testament had arranged its words and letters precisely in numeric order, and guided them into combinations of numbers. And this Intelligence was careful to weave designs and intricate cross-patterns into ***every section*** of this 27-book volume.

So what had Panin found? Simply this, that the New Testament, in Greek, was ***like a single skilfully designed artefact***... nothing less than the product of some mathematical mastermind. Panin had discovered a deliberate structuring that was far beyond human possibility to invent.

No ordinary book collection

You see the problem now, don't you? We're no longer talking about an ordinary piece of literature. We are face to face with a phenomenon that required an outside, above-human Intellect.

Are we to understand that the whole Bible is like this?

You've got it, George… ***every paragraph, passage and book*** is constructed in the same astonishing way. Amazingly, there is not a single paragraph out of the thousands in the Bible that is not constructed on exactly the same plan.

And it's even more remarkable, when you consider that Luke is a Greek, Mark a Roman, and Matthew a Jew. Yet they all wrote with the same sub-surface pattern. And although each of them wrote in his own different style, when it was all completed, the same identical pattern under the surface emerged all the way through each book!

Say that again? Many writers, all so different – yet ***one Master Mind*** right through.

But are you ready for an even more amazing discovery?...

44

Fingerprint of the author -

THE CROSS-OVER MYSTERY

Here's something else to blow you away! Other chain features of 7 running through the Bible are completed ONLY when you have the whole 66 books together.

Certain special words are scattered through many different books of the Bible to form amazing chain-designs. A particular word extends over several books of the Bible until it is used just 7 times or a multiple of 7 times!

A startling feature of this arrangement of '7s' is that an uncompleted portion of a series of 7 will cross over from one book to another, until it totals 7 and then stops. A particular feature will appear to a total of 7 (or multiples of 7) times, but only when you place all the books together... scattered through several different books until it totals 7 appearances overall.

For example, the name *David* appears throughout the Old Testament exactly 1,134 times (162 x 7). The name *Jeremiah* occurs in 7 Old Testament books, with exactly 147 (21 x 7) mentions. The term *Hallelujah* (Greek *Alleluia*), meaning "*Praise Yahweh*" (God) occurs 28 times (4 x 7) over the whole Bible.

The index that made a mistake

A certain Bible concordance (indexing every word in the Bible) was prepared by C.F. Hudson, supervised by H.L. Hastings and checked by Ezra

Abbot. It listed what were thought to be all of the Bible references to the word "*Moses*". It catalogued the name as appearing 846 times. But according to our numeric discovery, that had to be wrong – because 846 does not divide evenly by 7. However, 847 does. Could it be that the concordance was in error – and that it had omitted one reference?

Yes. The scholarly gentlemen who prepared that index had overlooked a reference in the book of Hebrews! The error was detected by applying the numeric design occurring in the structured Bible text!

The whole Bible is like this! Every paragraph, passage and book is constructed in the same astonishing way.

These patterns are indeed real. They are too consistent to have appeared by accident. They appear deliberate, yet could not have been contrived by the authors unaided. They constitute irrefutable ***evidence*** underscoring the integrity of the entire "message system". They hint at its non-human and infinite origins.

Can you explain it? This same numeric pattern crosses from one book to another, independent of each writer, bringing the whole into harmony.

This chain feature forms ***only when all the books are brought together***. No single writer could have produced it. Neither could all the 40 or so different writers have collaborated to produce it – since most of them never knew each other.

The discovery of such ***word-chains*** requires careful searching in all parts of the 66 books of the Bible.

How did each writer know what to do?

Take, for example, the design of sevens in the name '***Moses***'. This could not have been planned and carried out by the Bible writers themselves. It must be remembered that those writers did not all live at the same time; they lived many years apart.

We've already noted that the 66 books were written by about 40 different persons. These persons were scattered throughout various countries of the world. And they were men of widely different backgrounds. Many of them had little or no schooling.

So I ask you, how could each one of the 40 writers, the last writer separated by 1,600 years from the first, insert the name '*Moses*' just enough times to keep the numeric design in suspense until it came to John, the last writer who used it in the book of Revelation? He needed to use it just once to complete the design!

How could each writer have known that he should use a particular word a certain number of times so that when all would be finished centuries later the total would divide perfectly by seven and would show numeric design?

Certainly such design could not possibly have been planned by the writers themselves. The case of Moses is only one example of chain design extending throughout the entire Bible. Literally hundreds of other cases like this can be pointed out.

Every word linked in an inter-book chain

By one method or another, each word of the whole Bible is ***linked and connected*** in one amazing pattern.

Let's face it. There are only two possible ways in which these intricate sevens patterns could have occurred:

1. They came about by sheer chance, or
2. they were purposely arranged.

An integrated message system

This is just another ***evidence*** that the Bible is an integrated message system, ***the product of supernatural engineering***.

Matthew, uses just 140 words (20 times 7), found nowhere else in the New Testament.

But how on earth did Matthew know that the other writers, Mark, Luke, John, James, Peter, Jude, and Paul would not use those same words? How did Matthew know that he should use certain words which would not be used in any of the other 26 books of the New Testament?

So how did he accomplish that particular feat of 7s? Did he have an agreement with them that ***they*** would ***not*** use those words? You and I both know that's impossible.

Alternately, did he have all the other New Testament books before him when he wrote his own book? But that would require that Matthew's book was written LAST.

Each writer wrote last?

And in the same manner in which we saw that Matthew wrote ***last***, it can be shown that Mark also wrote ***last***. So we have this fact established: Matthew surely wrote after Mark, and Mark equally surely wrote after Matthew.

It is, however, an additional fact that ***Luke's Gospel*** contains exactly the same phenomena as those of Matthew and Mark. And so does John, and so do the books of James and Peter, Jude and Paul. We have, then, no longer two great unheard-of mathematical literati, but eight of them, and ***each wrote after the other???!!!***

That's right - ***each of the other writers*** does exactly the same thing – each other writer likewise uses exactly 'x times' 7 words found ***nowhere else*** in the New Testament. And for this to deliberately occur requires the impossible scenario that every one of those different writers wrote his own book LAST.

So there you have it. Not only is each of the 27 books they wrote constructed on the same interlocking 'sevens' pattern. But each book by the same method already mentioned, can be shown to have been written last. So we have 27 New Testament books ***each written last***. This incredible phenomenon is not a theory. It is fact.

The features are there, and there is no human way of explaining them. Eight men simply cannot each write ***last***. 27 books simply cannot each be written ***last***.

How to solve the problem

But once we conclude that ***One Mind*** supervised the whole, then the problem is solved as simply as an algebraic equation.

But do you do realize what this means?

Since the discovery of a design is proof of a designer, the next logical question arises: WHO PLANNED AND CARRIED OUT THESE AMAZING NUMERICAL DESIGNS? Again we have two possible alternatives:

1. Natural human intelligence, or
2. A supernatural intelligence

Let's consider these:

1. Natural human intelligence

Were these amazing numeric designs planned by the men who wrote the books of the Bible? As we noted, ***many*** of the writers were ***just ordinary men*** from different walks of life, who had ***little or no schooling*** at all.

So how long would this have taken them? If Matthew, Mark, Luke or John, for instance, had attempted to construct and produce the harmonious numeric features and designs which are found in their books as a whole, and if they had attempted to produce separate numeric schemes and designs which occur in each division, and in each subdivision, and in the words, forms, vocabularies, letters, etc., how long would it have taken them to construct their books?

Centuries upon centuries!

Can you tell me that mere human intelligence planned and worked out the amazing designs of numeric features which occur in the very structure of the Bible text?

Let's get real! The limitations of the human intellect and the shortness of human life make it impossible. So no man or any set of men combined could accomplish such stupendous feats.

This phenomenon is uncanny! And you have ***scientific, mathematical proof*** of it.

2. A supernatural intelligence

This cross-over pattern contributes to a broader design that was ***beyond the horizon of the writer himself***, It evidences a supernatural influence weaving a broader tapestry.

Not only that, but it has survived the jamming and interference of its enemies (attempts to corrupt the text) over many centuries, without material damage.

Let's move on now to scientifically analyse this incredible phenomenon…

45

Fingerprint of the author -

WHAT ODDS?

Do you know about the law of chances?

Of course you do!

We all know how to play a game with a six-sided dice. To throw a ***six*** is not easy. At least on the law of averages you should throw a six once every six throws.

If I throw ***2 consecutive sixes***, you may call me 'clever'. If I throw ***3 sixes one after the other***, you'd say I'm 'too lucky'. If I throw ***4 consecutive sixes,*** you might look at me as though I'm cheating.

If I throw ***5 sixes in a row*** you'll tell me that's 'impossible'. But then I throw ***6 sixes in a row*** – what then? You'd say that the dice is definitely ***rigged***.

Suppose I do that just once more, you might grab the dice and examine it, right? On the law of averages, I could not throw ***seven sixes in a row*** by accident.

Now, what if you make 24 throws of the dice and they all come up as a 6? What are the chances that this will happen ***24 times in a row***, accidentally?

"Oh that's easily calculated," you say. "There is a standard, recognized, scientific method of calculating chances… an established ***law of chances***."

You are right.

And if you don't mind, I'd like to apply this same law to the number 7. As you are aware, whatever number we use, the law of chances works in the same way.

Only one number in every 7 is a multiple of 7 – 14, 21, 28, 35, 42, 49, and so on. According to the law of chances, for any one number to be a multiple of 7 accidentally, there is 1 chance in 7, right?

According to the law of chances, for any 2 numbers to be multiples of 7 accidentally, there is only 1 chance in 7 x 7 - that is, only 1 chance in 49.

According to the law of chances, for any ***3*** numbers to be ***multiples of 7 accidentally*** there is only 1 chance in 7 x 49, or only ***1 chance in 343***.

As we have just noted, for any 1 feature to occur accidentally there is only 1 chance in 7.

For 2 features - 1 chance in 49
For 3 features - 1 chance in 343
For 4 features - 1 chance 2,401
For 5 features - 1 chance in 16,807
For 6 features - 1 chance in 117,649
For 7 features - 1 chance in 823,543
For 8 features - 1 chance in 5,764,801
For 9 features - 1 chance in 40,353,607
For 10 features - 1 chance in 282,475,249
For 11 features - 1 chance in 1,977,326,743
For 12 features - 1 chance in 13,841,287,201
For 13 features - 1 chance in 96,889,010,407
For 14 features - 1 chance in 678,223,072,849
For 15 features - 1 chance in .. 4,747,561,509,943
For 16 features - 1 chance in 33,232,930,569,601
For 17 features - 1 chance in . .232,630,513,987,207
For 18 features - 1 chance in ...1,628,413,597,910,449
For 19 features - 1 chance in .11,398,895,185,373,143
For 20 features - 1 chance in .79,792,266,297,612,001
For 21 features - 1 chance in 558,545,864,083,284,007
For 22 features - 1 chance in 909,821,048,582,988,049
For 23 features - 1 chance in 368,747,340,080,916,343
For 24 features - 1 chance in 581,231,380,566,414,401

So for 24 features to occur in any situation accidentally, there is only 1 chance in 191,581,231,380,566,414,401 - only 1 chance in one hundred and ninety-one quintillion, five hundred and eighty-one quadrillion, two hundred and thirty-one trillion, three hundred and eighty billion, five hundred and sixty-six million, four hundred and fourteen thousand, four hundred and one.

Consider that there are in excess of three million words or twenty million characters in the 66 books of the Bible. And bear in mind that the "evidence" would be null and void, in most cases, if EVEN ONE CHARACTER WERE DELETED, CHANGED OR ADDED!

Here are the results of a complete Bible investigation and analysis. Within the whole Bible:

1. The NUMBER of WORDS in the VOCABULARY divides evenly by SEVEN.
2. The NUMBER of WORDS that begin with a vowel divides evenly by SEVEN.
3. The NUMBER of WORDS that begin with a consonant will divide evenly by SEVEN.
4. The NUMBER of WORDS that begin with each letter of the language's alphabet will divide evenly by SEVEN.
5. The NUMBER of WORDS that occur more than once will divide evenly by SEVEN.
6. The NUMBER of WORDS that occur only once will divide evenly by SEVEN.
7. The NUMBER of WORDS that occur in only one form will divide evenly by SEVEN.
8. The NUMBER of WORDS that occur in more than one form will divide evenly by SEVEN.
9. The NUMBER of WORDS that are nouns will divide evenly by SEVEN.

10. The NUMBER of WORDS that are not nouns will divide evenly by SEVEN.
11. The NUMBER of LETTERS in the vocabulary will divide evenly by SEVEN.
12. The NUMBER of LETTERS that are vowels will divide evenly by SEVEN.
13. The NUMBER of LETTERS that are consonants will divide evenly by SEVEN.
14. The NUMBER of PROPER NAMES will divide evenly by SEVEN.
15. The NUMBER of MALE PROPER NAMES will divide evenly by SEVEN.
16. The NUMBER of FEMALE PROPER NAMES will divide evenly by SEVEN.
17. The TOTAL NUMERIC VALUE OF ALL THE WORDS will divide evenly by SEVEN.
18. The NUMERIC VALUE OF THE VARIOUS FORMS in which the words occur will divide evenly by SEVEN.
19. The NUMBER OF WORDS THAT ARE FOUND in the Bible will divide evenly by SEVEN.
20. The NUMBER OF PROMISES FOUND in the BIBLE will divide evenly by SEVEN.

There is a term called a Google (sometimes spelt as Gugle), which is ONE followed by100 Zeros. (Some definitions enlarge on this and claim that Google is a BILLION TO THE BILLIONTH POWER!) GOOGLEPLEX is a GOOGLE to the power of GOOGLE.

Let's illustrate the immensity of this figure, say, in terms of years. Suppose we had a mountain the size of Mount Everest that was solid DIAMOND - and a bird came ONCE A YEAR and MADE ONE PECK against this mountain. IT WOULD TAKE A

GOOGLE NUMBER OF YEARS TO ERODE THAT MOUNTAIN TO SEA LEVEL!

Now let's apply this to the Bible numerics phenomenon. Going through the ***20-point*** list above, what are the odds of these features in the Bible occurring by accident? Well, by the time we get to just Point 9, the odds of the listed phenomena occurring by chance have already blown out to GOOGLEPLEX.

Many brief Bible passages have as many as ***70 or 100*** or more features of 7 in the very structure of their text. If there is only one chance in quintillions that ***24*** features of 7 could occur together accidentally, what would the chance be for 70 features of 7 to occur together accidentally?

In the field of physics, it is commonly defined that any probability smaller than 10^{50} (10 with 50 zeroes after it) is manifestly absurd.

When there is only one chance in thousands for something to happen accidentally, it is already considered highly improbable that it will occur at all. When there is only one chance in hundreds of thousands, it is considered practically impossible.

But here there is one chance in ***not only*** millions, ***but*** billions and trillions, that just 70 features could occur together in a passage accidentally.

All right, what about the skeptics? And what about other holy books - do they contain this code pattern?...

46

Fingerprint of the author -

SKEPTICS STUMPED

As you can imagine, this “sevens” discovery was to change the course of Panin’s life. For the next 60 years, he would use every working moment to painstakingly write out over 43,000 pages of data – all based on this intricate matrix revolving around the number 7 and prime factors of 7.

He had discovered the Bible, in its original language, to be ***a skilfully designed artefact***. It was nothing less than the product of a mathematical mastermind. What Panin had discovered was a phenomenon far beyond any human possibility of deliberate structuring.

Panin would later present his findings – all 43,000 pages of them – to the Nobel Research Foundation. He also presented to them his conclusion that the Bible could only be the work of Someone with the Mind of the Creator. Nothing less. The reply of the Nobel Research Foundation was:

> As far as our investigation has proceeded we find the evidence overwhelmingly in favor of such a statement.

The challenge

Now Panin issued a challenge through the world’s leading newspapers. He challenged anyone to either submit a ‘natural explanation’, or refute the evidence.

Did they?

To date, no person has successfully done so.

Some time later, copies of the Bible numerics report were submitted to over 500 of the best known centers for agnostic or atheist beliefs, including universities and centers of learning conducted by non-religious organizations. This challenge was issued:

(a) ***Disprove*** the report and its data, OR

(b) ***Produce*** any other text written by men that will contain any of the same phenomena!

ONLY one condition was stipulated: the phenomena MUST be from inherent factors of the language and not "contrived" by manipulation. In other words, the phenomena must occur in a natural feature of the language in which it was written. (Translations are unable to maintain such phenomena.)

All evidence for numeric structure of text will qualify as "scientific" in the sense that it can be repeated, and "we invite such scrutiny."

No one has been able to meet the challenge. Does that speak for itself?

What about other holy books?

"But," I hear someone asking, "there must be some other books with this numerical code?"

That's a good question. So are you ready for the truth? Here's the verdict:

This interlocking numeric phenomena is found ***in no other literature.*** Mind you, there have been sincere efforts to find such numerics in the Greek classics (Homer's *Iliad* and others), the *Septuagint*, the *Apocrypha,* the *Koran* and other works, but they have proven unsuccessful.

This numeric pattern cannot be found in other holy books. ***Not in any of them.***

If you add the Apocryphal books to the Bible, as one religious group does, the numerical pattern of the Bible as a WHOLE is thwarted. Not one of the phenomena, such as Number of Proper Names, Number of Words Grouped Alphabetically, and so on, remains when these books are considered.

For that matter, not one of the apocryphal books contains ANY numeric pattern phenomena of any ascertainable sort!

The fact that these books do not contain even ONE of the numerical phenomena is sufficient evidence that these books should not be considered in the same class as the Bible.

Let's say it again. NO WORKS OF MAN SHOW EVIDENCE OF SUCH DESIGNS. It seems that man just cannot do it.

Prove it for yourself

Now, this can be ***scientifically tested***. So here's my personal challenge to the skeptic. Before you reject my claim that ***man cannot*** do it, you must provide evidence that man ***can*** do it.

So why don't you try this? Write a passage – any passage – yourself. And see how long it would take you to produce a passage as long as Matthew's (161 words) containing an equally intricate pattern!

You can appreciate that with each additional paragraph the difficulty of construction increases, not in arithmetical but in geometrical progression. Because the writer must write his paragraphs so as to develop constantly fixed numeric relations to what has gone before, as well as to what follows.

And there's the point. With each additional sentence the difficulty greatly increases, and owing to the limitations of human intellect, soon becomes hopeless.

Scholars who have set out to accomplish a similar thing admit that after struggling for days their efforts were in vain without reducing the passage to a meaningless jumble. One such attempt was made by a Dr D.B. Turkey. He reports:

> I gave numeric values to the English alphabet, and tried to prepare a message which would adhere to the numerics, and make every section a multiple of seven, and present all the other features of Biblical arithmography, without letting the meaning of the passage descend to nonsense. After working on it for days, I could get no satisfaction. Yet this feature is accomplished in every one of the thousands of Bible paragraphs without the slightest visible effort.

One letter can change the result

Let's say it again. If you sat down to produce similar phenomena of 7s, your brain would soon be reeling, because every time you adjusted one portion it would upset another! It's just too complex. Every piece impacts on every other piece.

You can't pull out one word, without upsetting the pattern. No wonder it is written, *'The Scripture cannot be broken.'* (John 10:35)

Now, just think how crucial to a message one important detail can be:

On October 13, 1945, a citizen of Durham, North Carolina, was brought before Judge Wilson of Traffic Court for parking his car in a restricted street right in front of a sign forbidding parking. But instead of pleading guilty, the defendant protested that he was not extracting ore from underneath the street.

This was not a facetious reply, for when the sign was brought in as evidence, the defendant triumphantly pointed out that it read "NO STOPING". And ***stoping,*** he was able to prove with the help of an unabridged dictionary (Webster's *New International Dictionary,* p. 2,485), means "extracting ore from a stope, or loosely, underground."

"Your honor," said the defendant, "I am a law-abiding citizen. When I saw that sign I noted it carefully. And being a law-abiding citizen, I said to myself, 'Bill, whatever you do, don't extract any ore – it's against the law.' Judge, I didn't do any stoping – and I move the case to be dismissed."

The judge decided that the defendant had lived up to the letter of the law – the single letter – and the case was dismissed. (Maxwell Nurnberg and Morris Rosenblum, *How to Build a Better Vocabulary.* New York: Popular Library, 1961, p. 174)

So who says the Bible has been tampered with?

Do you see the point? With the biblical numeric pattern turning out to be so precise, we can neither pull out, nor add, ***one letter*** of one word. Yes, one letter makes all the difference. This is a ***self-checking, self-verifying*** protection factor.

Seriously now, this application of the number 7, both to the Bible as a whole, and to each separate book in detail, enables us to determine ***the question of whether there are "missing" or "extra" books*** with demonstrable certainty.

And also, if any passage did not fit the numeric pattern, we could determine precisely where any tampering had been done! Do you see? It's fail proof.

In any case, you might like to try writing a comparable passage of interlocking sevens yourself – with the surface script still making sense as a written work? – and you'll see how ridiculous is the claim that someone just thought up the story of Jesus then wrote it into a book. Or that the Bible has been so ***tampered with*** over the centuries that you can't know what the original writings said? Yeah… and I'm Julius Caesar.

Be on your guard. There are half-informed critics who play on our gullibility – assuming that, like other books, the Bible is just a collection of man-made myths. But, apart from the numerics feature, even the **evidence** of manuscript history is against them. (See *Who's Playing Jesus Games?* ; *The Sorcerers' Secret*; *The Weapon the Globalists Fear*; *The Da Vinci.Code.Hoax*.)

You now have a clear advantage over the critics

You now have the advantage. You have just learnt something of which most critics are still unaware – that the Bible is composed not of words alone, but is also an astonishing design of interlocking 7s – like wheels within wheels – woven together in every conceivable way, ***both on and below*** the surface.

Now would you be kind enough to answer this: In a toss-up between (a) documents stamped with the ***authentication code*** and (b) books that ***lack*** the authentication code, on which would you rather stake your life?

What does COMMON SENSE suggest?

Integrity of texts assured

Has this ***self-checking, self-verifying*** protection feature been actually applied to testing variations in Bible manuscripts?

Indeed, it has. By means of the numeric designs, Ivan Panin settled every one of the alternative readings left by the translators Westcott and Hort in their Greek Bible text. The result was his scholarly *Numeric Greek New Testament* and his *Numeric English New Testament*.

So, Dan "Vinci Code" Brown, you want us to believe it was Constantine's scheming politics that determined which books should be included in the Bible – and which not?

Stick to fiction, Dan. You're better at that.

QUESTION: The number of books in the Bible is 66, but since the number 7, denoting perfection, is found as a pattern right through the Bible, shouldn't there really be 77 books? Although you say no books are missing, doesn't this indicate that some books are lost?

ANSWER: If you ever hear that there are "lost books of the Bible", don't fall for the trick. The books were originally grouped so that they would eventually number ***49 (7 x7).***

Josephus, the first century Jewish historian, confirms that were only 22 books in the Hebrew Bible (The Old Testament). (Josephus, *Against Apion*, Book I, Section VIII) The 22 books that Josephus wrote of correspond exactly with our 39 books of the Old Testament. Some of the books that we classify today as two separate books were classified as one book. That is, although the contents remain the same, the grouping into the number of books was different.

Now, to those 22 books, add the 27 New Testament books, and what do you have? 22 + 27 = 49… whose factor is 7. This 49 is precisely 7 multiplied by 7 – it is the multiplication of perfection by perfection.

You can be sure that nothing is missing.

Yes, there are other books around that some people think should be in the Bible – like the so-called books of Enoch, Adam, Jasher, the so-called Gospels of Thomas, Philip, Mary, the Gospel of Truth, the Testimony of Truth, and what have you… but none of these qualifies. The "impossible" sevens code is absent from every one of them. That should tell us something.

Whatever their merits, they are not what you can call "God-breathed" records. They should not be classed with the Bible.

Why doesn't the world hear about this 7s code ***evidence***? It will.

Of course there will always be detractors who try to explain it away, but their reasoning is pathetically weak. One can't argue with mathematics. It's an exact science. And we are dealing here with ***mathematical certainties***. The scientific method… the hard logic… the sound laws of reasoning. What can one say? It is astounding.

Foolproof, too. It can withstand any amount of honest testing. Then why don't we all swallow our pride and start taking its message more seriously?

The claim of authorship

Why was this 7s pattern encoded into the text?

Is it the Author's way of assuring us at this particular late moment – where our scientific materialism has pushed us to the brink of radical skepticism – that He is precisely who He said He is? This ***integrated, deliberate, detailed design*** running through the entire Bible, might this actually be His signature?

Certainly, it is not the work of many minds, but of ***one Mind***… a Master Mind. The Bible must stand or fall – or rather, be received or rejected – as a ***whole***.

Does it claim for itself divine authorship? Indeed, it does:

> ***All** scripture is given by inspiration of God.* (2 Timothy 3:16)
> *For the prophecy came in old time **not by the will of man**; but holy men of God spoke as they were moved by the Holy Spirit.* (2 Peter 1:21)

All these years the Bible has been insisting that it is the Creator's message to man… and not man's ideas about God. At least 3,800 times it claims to be the spoken word of the Eternal One set to writing.

"The Spirit of God took charge of me as I wrote," say the writers. And now we see it demonstrated in this 7s code. In the precise letter-by-letter sequence, one perceives in action a supremely intelligent and purposeful Mind that paid excruciating attention to detail. This sevens code is of the same caliber as the DNA code programmed into your body.

So I ask you, may we not regard this as ***scientific evidence*** that the Eternal One actually did write Scripture by his servants' hands – that it is *God-breathed?* Does any other explanation make sense?

Good scholarship will follow Aristotle's Dictum:

> The benefit of the doubt is to be given to the document itself, not arrogated by the critic to himself.

In other words, we should accept what the writer tells us, unless there is compelling reason to believe otherwise.

Do you have any compelling reason to negate this ***evidence*** you have been discovering? You have just seen something that is scientifically testable. You can try it yourself. But I assure you that repeated scientific, mathematic demonstrations prove that humans cannot replicate it. If you want ***actionable proof in real life,*** here it is.

The message of the book

One of the most important messages the Bible brings us concerns our ***origins.***

To determine the truth of our origins, we need an eye-witness account from someone:

* who knows everything,
* who does not lie and
* who has written down (through the agency of human hands) all we need to know about the past.

And we have just such a document in the Bible which, I believe, we have discovered to be our Creator's written word. That is a faith statement, of course, but a very reasonable faith statement because the ***Bible's history*** is ***exactly consistent*** with what we observe in the world around us.

(And, as we have discovered, repeated scientific, mathematic demonstrations prove that humans cannot replicate the book itself. Again, if you want ***actionable proof in real life,*** here it is.)

On the other hand, the ***evolutionary account of history*** is ***not consistent*** with the evidence we see around us, so faith in evolution is not a reasonable faith.

The Bible reveals that you and I are pawns in ***an unseen warfare*** and that our individual destinies are entirely determined by our ***personal*** relationship with the Ultimate Victor.

It informs us also that ***a rescue project*** is in progress. Whatever you do, you'd better play safe and not knock it. What if, after all, it turns out to be very, very ***real*** – and your future does indeed hinge on it… What then?

I'm not talking about ways to survive economic collapse, new deadly diseases, radiation, and so on. That is already covered in my book *Will You Survive?* (<http://www.beforeus.com/shopcart_ebooks.html>)– revealing practical steps you can take to reduce your suffering in the coming world crisis – like relocating to the country, then learning how to survive without money, how to store the best survival foods, how to cook and refrigerate food without electricity, or wood, or petroleum, or other fuels… how to enjoy reduced disease risk, greater endurance, more energy, and so on. Important as these are, we're not discussing these right now – but something much more important and lasting… your longer term future… ultimate survival of you and your loved ones. Because the present system will soon come to an end.

The coming shock

In the New Testament, there are hundreds of references to the Messiah's ***Second Coming***. For every prophecy relating to his First Coming (to offer himself as the suffering servant), there are eight concerning his return as King of kings, to ***abruptly interrupt human history.***

How often have we seen men and women oppressing others, flouting the law, and enjoying the fruits of their evil ways until the day they die! On the other hand, we see innocent people suffering. And we ask, Where is the justice?

There is a time soon coming when wrongs will be made right – when all will be made equal. It is called the Day of Judgment.

After driving for several hours, a man was almost home. As he approached a bridge, he sped up and raced across it much faster than the safe speed limit. Then, to his horror, he saw a traffic officer waving him down. He stopped. The officer came over to his car, looked in at him and asked, "Do you know you were breaking the law?"

The shocked driver replied, "I didn't expect to see you here!"

Humankind is about to learn a powerful lesson. The Creator that man has ignored, rejected and generally rebelled against from creation to this day is preparing for the inevitable: to fulfil His prophecy of direct intervention in the affairs of the world, to save man from blowing himself and all life off this planet:

> And except those days should be shortened, there should no flesh be saved: but for the elect's sake those days shall be shortened. (Matthew 24:22)

The most-asked question

But meanwhile, the "suffering" problem remains uppermost in our minds. And we may be tempted to ask: What kind of God would allow innocent people to suffer all these years? Has He anything to say about this burning question?

Why don't we investigate this?…

PART ELEVEN

RELEVANCE TO US

47

What kind of God is this? -

WHY DO THE INNOCENT SUFFER?

If you ever testify in court, you might wish you could be as sharp as this policeman. He was being cross-examined by a defence attorney during a felony trial. The lawyer was trying to undermine the police officer's credibility.

Q.: Officer, did you see my client fleeing the scene?

A.: No sir. But I subsequently saw a person matching the description of the offender running, several blocks away.

Q.: Officer, who provided this description?

A.: The officer who responded to the scene.

Q.: A fellow officer provided the description of this so-called offender. Do you trust your fellow officers?

A.: Yes, sir. With my life.

Q.: With your life? Let me ask you, then, officer. Do you have a room where you change your clothes in preparation for your daily duties?

A.: Yes, sir, we do.

Q.: And do you have a locker in the room?

A.: Yes, sir… I do.

Q.: And do you have a lock on your locker?

A.: Yes, sir.

Q.: Now… why is it, officer, if you trust your fellow officers with your life, you find it necessary to lock your locker in a room you share with these same officers?

A: You see, sir…we share the building with the court complex, and sometimes lawyers have been known to walk through that room.

The courtroom EXPLODED with laughter, and a prompt recess was called. The officer on the stand has been nominated for this year's 'Best Comeback' line – and I think he'll win.

The point to be gained from this is that only when ***all*** the facts are known do some situations make sense. Suffering is one of these things. When we know ***all*** the factors involved, suffering is understandable. As is also God's goodness toward us.

"I don't believe in God because…"

After class one day, schoolteacher Amy Spence was accosted by a student who seemed a little offended. "You mentioned God," said the student. "I don't believe in God."

"Oh?" smiled the teacher, "Would you kindly describe for me this god you do not believe in?"

"Look, I don't believe in a god who would be pleased for us all so suffer like we do," said Doria. "How can he delight in terrorist bombings, cancer, school shootings, and all that? Look at the mess he's made. And he doesn't bother to stop it."

Amy listened carefully to the student's complaint. Doria paused, looked Amy straight in the eye, and said, "Well?"

"Oh," smiled Amy, "I don't believe in a god like that either."

"What?"

"When you think it through, the fact that you and I ask such questions shows that we have an inbuilt sense of justice. So where do you think we got our sense of justice from, in the first place? Are we human beings more fair and just than the One who designed us? Tell me, Doria, who knows better – puny, erring man – or the One who designed the DNA in your body?

"Our study of DNA does suggest an all-powerful, all-knowing, wise Creator who knows how not to make a mistake. And there is also good evidence also that He is compassionate, caring and patient with us.

"But there is more involved in this 'suffering' thing than God's character. Let's sit down, and I'll share something with you."

* * * * * * *

The answer to ***why innocent people suffer*** is not so elusive. There are three main reasons which we ought to address.

1. Free will

As we noted in Chapter 16, one of the most priceless treasures implanted within us is the ability to freely make our own decisions. We are not robots, but have been granted the ability to choose, because that gives us the potential for the greatest happiness possible.

However, our Creator has not left us in ignorance to stumble along, making wrong decisions blindly. Just as would a loving parent, He also gave us physical and spiritual laws for our guidance and protection.

Live in harmony with them and we experience joy, satisfaction and peace within. Disregard them and we suffer. And our actions often cause others – innocent though they may be – to suffer.

OUR FAULT, NOT HIS

You ask, how could God allow people to hurt each other?

I believe that God is deeply saddened by this, just as we are, but for years we've been telling God to get out of our schools, to get out of our government and to get out of our lives. And, being the gentleman that He is, I believe that He has calmly backed out. How can we expect God to give us His blessing and His protection if we demand that He leave us alone?

In the *Eighty's Club Newsletter* of March 2005 (the Eighty's Club is a Sri Lankan social club in Melbourne, Australia), appeared the following article, inserted by Richard Young, editor:

> Let's see..... I think it started when Madeline Murray O'Hare complained she didn't want any prayer in our schools. **We said OK.**
>
> Then someone said you better not read the Bible in school... it says thou shalt not kill, thou shalt not steal, and love your neighbour as yourself. **We said OK**.
>
> Dr. Benjamin Spock said that we shouldn't spank our children because their little personalities would be warped. **We said OK**.
>
> Then someone said that school teachers and principals should not discipline children when they misbehaved because they did not want any bad publicity, and

they surely did not want to be sued. **We said OK.**

Then some of our top elected officials said it did not matter what we did in private as long as we did our jobs. And, agreeing with them, we said it did not matter to us what anyone did in private as long as we had jobs and the economy was good.

Then someone said, "Let us print magazines with pictures of nude people and call it wholesome, down-to-earth appreciation of the beauty of the body." **We said OK.**

Then someone else took that appreciation a step further and publicised pictures of nude children and then went further still, making them available to all and sundry on the Internet. **We said OK** - they were entitled to their freedom of expression.

Then the entertainment industry said, "Let's make TV shows and movies that promote profanity, violence and illicit sex. And let's record music that encourages rape, drugs, murder, suicide and satanic themes." We said, "It's just entertainment; it has no adverse effect and nobody takes it seriously anyway, so go right ahead."

Now we're asking ourselves why our children have no conscience; why they don't know right from wrong and why it doesn't bother them to kill strangers, their classmates, and themselves. Probably, if we think about it long and hard enough, we can figure it out. I think it has a great deal to do with **'WE REAP WHAT WE SOW'.**

"Dear God, why didn't you save the little girl killed in her classroom? **Sincerely, Concerned Student"......**
"Dear Concerned Student, I am not allowed in schools. **Sincerely, God."**

Funny how simple it is for people to trash God and then wonder why the world is going to hell.

2. Caught in a cosmic war

Indeed, there is a common racial memory concerning a once perfect world… of an age that ***did not know suffering***.

It changed when Lucifer's (Satan's) mob dropped in.

As we have seen, our planet is caught up in a conflict between the forces of good and those of the Lucifer Legion. Satan is trying to get revenge on Yeshua for what happened in heaven.

Might this help us understand why our world has descended into such a mess?

It is true that we are responsible for our own actions. But we need to lift our eyes to see the bigger and more sinister play going on behind the scenes – super-energised by evil forces.

There can be no doubt that these forces have permeated politics, religion, science, the media, education and business.

Yes, it is time we all faced the truth, however startling. This cosmic war being waged by Lucifer and his hosts for the control of the human race is no myth! And they work through human leaders to attain it.

When the facts are known, these entities are the REAL driving force behind the poverty, violence and corruption.

WHY GOD KEEPS "HANDS OFF"

At the time of his rebellion, Lucifer accused God of being a tyrant who would not allow him (Lucifer) freedom to have his own way. Thus, when Lucifer claimed he could set up a better government than God, it was necessary that he be given the opportunity and time to discredit himself, so that when he is finally destroyed, no one will have any doubts about justice.

So, speaking of justice, the Creator's "hands off" policy must prevail – unless you or I, as free agents, specifically ask him to intervene. (And generally that's why people pray.)

Like it or not, we are all involved. Our first parents' choice to allow Lucifer's rule placed the whole world in jeopardy. And individually, by not wanting God in our lives, we have placed ourselves under Satan's dominion. Our Creator simply honors our individual choice.

NATURAL DISASTERS

Lucifer's forces have the ability to interfere with weather and generate hurricanes, droughts and floods. They can manipulate natural forces, to trigger earthquakes and tsunamis. However, their destructive powers are restrained from fully destroying this rebellious world by the power of our merciful Creator.

Are natural disasters acts of God? We are pointing the finger in the wrong direction – although, as we've noted, God can and does intervene for our good when, as free-choice beings, we give Him our permission.

WHY NO END TO IT?

One thing we all recognise is this that our world has become a great mess. And it may well be asked, If there is a Creator who cares about His subjects, then ***why doesn't He stamp out wrong and stop all this suffering?*** He could...

But we need to consider that if He were to stamp out evil now, He would do a ***complete*** job. Suppose God were to decree that at midnight tonight ***all*** wrong was to be removed from the universe – who of us would still be here after midnight?

3. How suffering can benefit us

Our big problem is sin – violation of our Maker's instructions for happy living. ***Our own actions can bring us suffering.***

One wealthy man up for murdering a business associate managed, through his minions, to have one of the jury bribed to persuade the other jurors to find not guilty of murder but guilty of the lesser charge of manslaughter. The accused was duly found guilty of manslaughter and sentenced to five years – a lot better than life.

The corrupt juryman went to prison to visit him, and was thanked by the businessman.

"It wasn't easy," said the ex-juryman, "the others were all for acquittal."

(I can't vouch for the truth of this story, but it does drive home the point. We are often, by our own deviousness, responsible for our own suffering.)

Our all-wise God allows some destructive calamities to come upon the world in order that men and women may be aroused to turn from their evil path. He allows them to suffer calamity, that their senses may be awakened.

He permits a man to be tested on points in which his character is weak, so that those deficiencies can be addressed. Situations in which I have suffered have been the best teachers to accomplish this. In suffering such tests we are prompted to make decisions.

If we decide in harmony with the Eternal Law, then our character is strengthened. If we decide wrongly, in His mercy He does not blot us out, but rather allows us to be brought again and again into a similar testing situation until we gain victory on that point.

And thus we can be led progressively into a closer relationship with our Maker. That is His loving desire for us. But the final choice is yours.

Kirsty, Melissa and Stephanie's mid-morning ritual in the school toilets was regular. They would stand in front of the big mirror, lean forward to apply their lipstick, stand back to admire the result. Then they would press their lips against the mirror, to impress their lip prints.

But least of all impressed was the principal. Something had to be done, she decided. So all the girls were called to the toilets. And there on site it was explained to them that those lip prints were posing quite a problem for the cleaner.

She then turned to the cleaner. "To demonstrate how difficult it is to clean those prints," she said, "would you please clean the mirror."

The cleaner did so – using a long-handled squeegee that he dipped in a toilet bowl.

Since then, I understand, there have been no lip prints.

A deterrent. Sometimes parents need to impose a penalty (a suffering experience) upon a rebellious child, to encourage a behavior improvement. This does not mean the parent is cruel. Rather, a caring parent wants his child to develop behavioral characteristics that will make him a responsible and likeable adult. So all of us need, at times, to endure an unpleasant experience, a deterrent, to straighten out our behavior. Suffering is a great teacher. It can help us learn quickly.

Is your Maker not wiser than you? Is the wisdom He implanted in you greater than the wisdom that He possesses? Are you kinder and better than He who made you?

God's response to our suffering

The Creator's ultimate response to our suffering is dramatic, costly and effective - and is well illustrated by this parable:

At the end of time, billions of people were scattered on a vast plain before God's throne. Some groups talked heatedly. "How can God judge us?"

"What does he know about suffering?" snapped a young woman. She jerked back a sleeve to reveal a tattooed number from a Nazi concentration camp.

A black man lowered his collar. "What about this?" he demanded, showing an ugly rope burn. "Lynched for no crime but being black. We have suffocated in slave ships, been wrenched from loved ones and toiled till only death gave release."

Many other people recounted stories of suffering. Each had a complaint against God for the evil and suffering he permitted in this world. How lucky he was to live where all was sweetness and light; where there was no weeping, no fear, no hunger, no hatred. All agreed that God seemed to lead a pretty sheltered life.

So each group sent out a representative. There was a Jew, a black woman, an untouchable from India, an illegitimate child, a victim from Hiroshima, a sweatshop worker and a prisoner from a labor camp. In the center of the plain they consulted.

At last they were ready to present their case. It was very daring. Before God could qualify to be their judge, he must endure what they had endured. So the decision was made: God should be sentenced to live on earth - as a man! But, because he was God, they set certain safeguards to be sure he could not use his divine powers to help himself:

- Let him be born a despised Jew.
- Let the legitimacy of his birth be doubted, so that none will know who his father really is.
- Let him champion a cause so just, but so radical, that it brings down upon him the hatred and condemnation of the establishment.

- Let him try to describe what no man has ever seen, tasted, heard or smelled.... Let him try to communicate God to men.
- Let him be betrayed by his dearest friends.
- Let him be indicted on false charges, tried before a prejudiced jury, and convicted by a cowardly judge.
- Let him be terribly alone and abandoned.
- Let him be tortured.
- Then let him die a humiliating death alongside common criminals.

As each leader announced a portion of the sentence, there were shouts of approval from the people. But after the final statement, there was a long silence. No one uttered another word. No one moved.

For suddenly all knew God had already served his sentence.

The self-sacrifice of the Son of God furnishes the answer to whether He cares.

* * * * * * *

Yes, you can be sure that He cares passionately about you, that He will listen to you and is able to intervene for your good. As the shipwrecked agnostic and the imprisoned killer were to discover…

48

The living power -

DUMPED ON CANNIBAL ISLAND

"Into the sea, men! The ship's going down."

The trading vessel was about to be wrecked on one of the South Pacific islands. On board was a sailor who had been to this island before. He knew the natives were cannibals.

As they were tossed onto the shore, the men feared there was no hope for them to escape a gruesome fate at the hands of the natives.

This sailor cautiously ascended a hill to spy out the area further.

Soon his shipmates saw him swinging his arms in great excitement. Two of them ran forward to communicate with him.

"What is the matter?" one of them shouted.

"We're safe! We're safe!"

"How do you know?"

"I've just seen down on the other side. Our necks are safe."

What had he seen? A group of government soldiers? No… just a church steeple. He knew the message of Jesus Christ had reached that village before him. And its influence made things safe… even for him, an agnostic.

To be realistic about this, there are a whole a lot of fake Christians in our world who have given the Way of Jesus an undeserved bad name. And one day they shall face their Judge.

Yet, there is no disputing the fact that, wherever Christianity has been demonstrated by true example and word, it has transformed lives for the better. Wherever the influence of Jesus has prevailed, it has had a refining influence on a community or a nation. Not to mention the prosperity and technological advancement in such societies, as compared to others.

Charles Darwin noticed during a globe-encircling voyage the effect of Christianity in New Zealand, and wrote this admission:

> The march of improvement consequent of the introduction of Christianity throughout the South Seas probably stands by itself in the records of history. (Charles Darwin, *Journal of Researches*)

William Lecky, British historian, was a dedicated opponent of organized Christianity. But speaking of Jesus, he could state:

> The simple record [of Jesus] has done more to regenerate and soften mankind than all the disquisition of philosophers and all the exhortations of moralists. (William E. Lecky, *History of European Morals from Augustus to Charlemagne*. New York: D. Appleton & Co., 1903, p. 8)

For the whole world

Behind bars for life, Damon was having a struggle. Here, in his confinement, he was examining these issues and battling his prejudices. Any talk of Jesus really bugged him. "Oh come on," he reasoned, "that guy was a Jew, and he lived in another time. What relevance has that to me?"

He expressed his doubts to fellow inmate Baggs. After all, Baggs, one of the dirtiest desperados in the whole clink, had suddenly changed. Somehow, he had "got to know" this Jesus guy. And his fellow jail mates couldn't believe the change that had come over Baggs!

Baggs faced Damon. "Hey, look at it this way. If Jesus had to become ***one of us,*** to be the universal life-line, wouldn't he have to enter the human family as a single individual of a particular race at a particular time and place?"

"Er… yeah." The words dragged out of Damon's mouth reluctantly. He actually felt awkward talking about this.

"Okay," said Baggs, "Suppose a vaccine for polio was discovered by just one guy, at a particular time and place, so that those of his family had the first chance to know it, does that disqualify it from being a universal remedy for all of us?"

"Stupid question, man," replied Damon. "The vaccine will still help everyone."

And then it struck him like a fist in his face. Just because truth might be revealed at a single place and time, does not make it less valid for ***all*** men.

Baggs leaned toward him. "Okay man. You, me and the whole bang lot of us in here have the same human mould. We've all got the same needs:

- A need for meaning
- A need for forgiveness
- A need to be changed, personally, socially
- And a need to beat death.

"And this guy Jesus fits the bill. You could call him the ***universal*** remedy. Look, mate. What I did was downright low. That's why I'm in here. But, boy, am I sorry, now – because I've got to know this guy Jesus. I tell you, he's for all of us. He's ***the world's answer.***

"He doesn't dig any special nation. What he said and did was good for people in Iran… Kurdistan… Germany… Israel… the U.K.… and all of us in this slammer. It was good then and it's good for you and me now. He says he came to rescue the worst of us. Was he a liar? Look at me. Has he hooked me? Sure has!"

A compulsion to confess

As I received Damon's letter written from his cell, my mind drifted to Max the big American. Max loved his wife deeply. Never would he let a word to be said against her. But secretly he burgled and burned houses and barns, just for kicks.

Then one day Max and an accomplice were lying back in a tent. Max picked up a book. It was the biblical Gospel of John… and he started browsing. Suddenly something twigged inside his head. He felt a strong urge to confess what he'd been up to.

What! Was this really happening to him? Whatever it was pulling at Max's mind, he couldn't resist it.

He got up and stood outside. Now he was tormented by the memories of his actions. He came back into the tent. He went back outside and in again, several times.

From his heart there drifted up a prayer. And suddenly he knew things were going to change

His accomplice stared at him. Max's usual defiant look seemed to be melting.

Max turned to his companion. "Bud, I've gotta do somethin'. I nabbed 31 sheep from a guy in Selma. I've gotta go and confess to him."

"Oh, come on," said Bud. "You can't let anyone know that. You'll be locked up."

"Bud, I have to. I would rather go to the slammer and stay there than to think that Jesus has not cleaned away my wrong."

Half an hour later, Max was on his way to visit the farmer. And with him went his partner.

Tramping along the road, to their surprise, they came face to face with the farmer himself. And they stopped him. The man began to shake like an aspen leaf.

Then Max did the unexpected. To his own surprise - and that of his accomplice and the farmer - he dropped to his knees on that road, before the two of them, and begged to be forgiven.

The farmer was astonished. "What on earth brought this on?" he asked.

Max explained.

Absolutely thrown, the farmer blurted out, "What in the world brought this on? I did not know there was a power that could do this!"

Max and his accomplice handed themselves in to the authorities. "Do with us as you see fit," they said. They confessed everything – their burning down of houses and barns… everything. And they went to the grand jury and confessed to burglaries in various places.

A council was held over the matter. Predictably, an attorney moved that the men be locked up.

The judge looked at Max – and what he said shocked everyone in that courtroom. "What! Should I put this man in? Put a man through that God is putting through? Would you take hold of a man that God is taking hold of? A man whom God's forgiving power has taken hold of? Would you do that?"

The judge moved his eyes from one to the other. "No," he said, finally, "I would rather have my right arm cut off to the shoulder."

Such a scene in court was never before remembered. Something got hold of those men present, and they all wept as children. The report of that experience went far and wide.

The golden key to personal victory

Questions were asked. What power was in that "Jesus book" that was not in anything else? Was it the Bible itself? Or some kind of power behind the Book?

Now I would like to ask this question: Why do I keep hearing more and more testimonies like this? Could it be that Jesus provides not only an ***example*** to follow but also the ***power*** to do so? Does Jesus really instil something of his own life into a man or woman? He did say he would send his Spirit into people who accept his offer. Is this what is happening?

It seems one's chief need is not a change in circumstances, but in ***oneself***. Well-being and happiness come not from the outside, but from inward virtues.

Freedom from guilt

Anyway, Damon kept reporting to me. A few weeks passed. And for the first time since the gates slammed behind him, Damon was sensing peace in his heart. He had discovered Jesus' promise that he could be ***justly*** freed from guilt – and be accepted by his Maker without a slur on his character.

As more time passed, so grateful was Damon, that he found himself adopting a very different lifestyle.

And he knew this for sure: No teacher, no guru in all history had been able to offer complete forgiveness and an utterly new start like that.

This was a living thing! Damon knew it!

How radical that this Jesus could deal so neatly with Damon's crimes! That he was taking Damon's filth upon himself, so that this no-hoper, in here for life, might never have to bear it?

No wonder, thought Damon, that people love him! No wonder they worship him! There's nothing like that anywhere among the religions of the world.

The Hindu idea of ***karma*** says, "You sin, you pay." Jesus' death on the cross shows God saying, "You sin, I pay." Boy, that's out of this world!

A power to achieve quality life

One morning Damon was in the exercise yard. He saw one of the meanest of skull-bashers lurching toward him. For a moment Damon's stomach tightened.

About four feet away, Tornado stopped. He stood there just staring… and opened his mouth.

"I don't know you any more, Killer. What's happened?"

"What do you mean?"

"We're all watching you, man. Look, when you were dumped in here, you were an arrogant pig, vengeful and fist-smart like the rest of us. Now you seem to have some sneaky secret. It's in your eyes. Suddenly you're super cool. What's wrong, Killer? You got an escape plan… or what?"

"You could say that," grinned Damon. "It's Jesus."

And that moment Damon knew for sure. He'd put this character Jesus Christ to the test. And now he knew it. This change was a tangible thing… Others could see it - the written life of Jesus had come alive in his life.

He looked at Tornado. "Tell me, what has your way done for you? You're as pitiful as ever! But you know what? I've now got power man… ***real power***."

Sure, it would take some more time, just as it took Michelangelo time to transform a block of rough marble into a stunning statue like "David". But the Messiah was already chipping away at Damon to produce a similar result.

Damon had studied under Eastern gurus. But now he knew there was only one teacher in the world who offered to change a man's character by taking up residence inside him… Jesus. How different from the ethical system of any other faith!

Tornado just shook his head. "I envy you, man," he said.

"Yeah?" asked Damon, smiling. "You know what? Here's the good news for us guys: This new life is not for an elite few – it's ***a reality event*** we all can dig into… and all be ***winners***!"

That foolish bug

How this reminds me of that silly little June bug!

It happened one night, as Dr Don Feist was giving the college commencement speech on "The Challenge of the Impossible". He glanced down and noticed a June bug crawling in the tin trough among the footlights.

The bug would crawl part way up the sloping tin, then slide ludicrously down to the bottom of the trough. Often it landed sprawling on its back. There it lay and struggled until it righted itself.

During the address, that persistent bug kept crawling and slipping back, until at last it crawled into the speech.

"All the while I have been talking about doing the impossible," said the speaker, "a June bug has been trying to get out of this tin trough, vainly climbing up and slipping back. The foolish bug! It has forgotten that it has wings!"

That bug never saw it could escape from above, but persisted in trying to find some other way out through the sides.

Yes, like that bug I can decide my own rules. I can ignore the divine escape plan, but have only myself to blame if I eventually don't make it.

When our Maker gave Himself through Yeshua for the sin of the world, He ***undertook the case for every person***. He now follows that up by promising His Spirit to empower us in overcoming enslaving habits, so we can be fit candidates for His coming new world. Meanwhile, we can right now begin to function at our highest level.

The formula is wonderfully simple, really.

- Empty oneself of one's misconceptions
- Know God loves you personally
- Believe, and commit oneself to follow Him.

No compulsion. It is my choice… your choice. That's the beauty of it.

Could it be that the ***best evidence of the Creator's involvement with the human race*** is seen in the amazing changes taking place in the lives and marriages of those who ask for His help?

49

The living power -

INCREDIBLE SAFETY IN A NAME

More than 4 million Americans claim to have been abducted by "space beings" (numerous polls – Gallop, Roper, PBS/Nova). Here comes a most amazing discovery concerning alien abductions. Did you know, there is a group of human beings which, by and large, is notably exempt? But, before revealing who they are, let's learn how this startling fact was discovered.

One alien abduction research group in particular deserves credit for the discovery. It was CE-4, founded by Joe Jordan and Wes Clark. Each of its dozen or so Florida-based members was also a trained field investigator for MUFON (Mutual UFO Network). MUFON is unquestionably ***the most respected clearing house in the world*** for UFO reports. CE-4's president, Joe Jordan, also serves as a state section director of MUFON in Brevard County.

Due to the enormous number of abduction victims in the Florida region, CE-4 initiated its own research independently of MUFON. They began probing for patterns or other factors that may have been overlooked by other UFO researchers.

They drew a blank until their research turned in a spiritual direction. ***Clark had a belief in God, but it went no further*** than that. ***Jordan was a "crystal-rolling" New Ager***.

"Neither of us had ever even considered a spiritual origin of the phenomenon," recalls Wes Clark. "We had a hunch we were onto something." ("A Letter to the *Mufon UFO Journal*,"<www.alienresistance.org/ce4mufonletter.htm>, August 1, 2003)

Their investigation took in spiritual groups such as ***Buddhists, Jews, Muslims… and agnostics***. At first it bore no result. All appeared to have experienced abductions.

They studied more case histories. And there emerged a puzzling trend. It had to do with a group who were ***Christians***.

Two categories

And here, the researchers ran into a puzzle. They found that some Christians were abducted – and some left alone. And the question arose – Why?

Where to go from here?

Further investigation turned up confirmation that Christians fell into two categories.

1. The first type was those had given mental assent to Christian ideals or morality, but did not necessarily apply these personally to their lifestyle – either because they hadn't learned to, or didn't want to.
   The researchers found in this group some who regularly claimed ***abduction***.

2. However, the other type of person had given his life over to following Jesus Christ. This type of Christian applied biblical/Christian principles in his daily life.
   The researchers found that this group was notably ***exempt from abductions.***

Remember, ***neither Clark nor Jordan was a Christian***. But, in an attempt to get to the bottom of this, the CE-4 researchers enrolled in a Bible study course. Please note that this was decided upon simply as a means of practical research, and ***not*** from any pre-existing belief in Christianity.

This led them, inevitably, to find information concerning a ***spiritual battle*** being waged between the angelic forces of Lucifer (Satan) and those of the Creator. They discovered that the Bible provided answers concerning the nature of this spiritual battle.

This enabled them to perceive the difference between the Christians subject to abduction and the group that was not.

Group 1: The researchers described a Christian of this group as a "***talk the talk***" Christian. This type of person seems unable to discern spiritual things. Thus he remains open to spiritual attack from alien entities.

Some of these ***regularly claim abduction***.

Group 2: This other type is the "***walk the walk***" Christian. He looks for a spiritual reality in the world around him. This would lead him to view abduction experiences as a spiritual attack. As a result, he would deal with them in a unique manner – by calling on the authority of Jesus Christ to intervene.

This class of Christians are ***left alone*** by the abductors. Very few born-again Christian believers show up among abductees. ("UFOs and Alien Abductions," December 20, 2002, website recently wiped out) It's as though the ETs tend to avoid this group.

This intriguing reality had been more or less ignored by many UFO researchers.

Abductions... halted???

Then, to their astonishment, came a discovery that abductions can be halted!

Florida resident Bill D. was lying in bed when his abduction began. It was Christmas of 1976 – and late at night (a typical time for abductions).

Earlier that evening, looking out through his living room window, he had seen some anomalous lights over the forest to the north. A police helicopter, he thought. It must be searching for drug runners, or something.

The dogs had been agitated and several hours later they were still barking. He turned in for the night.

Kept awake by the barking dogs, he just lay in his bed, wanting to sleep. Suddenly he felt his body being paralysed. He couldn't even cry out. Nothing was visible but a whitish grey, like a fog or mist. But he sensed that someone or something was in his room. His wife remained asleep.

Suddenly, he was being levitated above the bed. Then he sensed that he was being suspended by what felt like a pole pushed into his rectum. He was overcome with terror. But he couldn't scream.

What happened next was astonishing. Here is a direct transcript from his interview :

> I thought I was having a satanic experience, that the devil had gotten a hold of me and had shoved a pole up my rectum and was holding me up in the air.... So helpless, I couldn't do anything. I said, 'Jesus, Jesus, help me!' or 'Jesus, Jesus, Jesus!' When I did, there was a feeling or a sound or something that either my words that I thought or the words that I had tried to say or whatever, had hurt whatever was holding me up in the air on this pole. And I felt

> like it was withdrawn and I fell. I hit the bed, because it was like I was thrown back in bed. I really can't tell, but when I did, my wife woke up and asked why I was jumping on the bed. (Interview with CE-4 Research Group, August 1996, cited in "The Premise of Spiritual warfare," <www.alienresistance.org/ce4premise. htm>, March 7, 2003)

An abduction being stopped? This was the first such report these experienced field investigators had ever heard. And here was a man who did it by just calling on the name of Jesus!

It should again be pointed out that such escapes were experienced only by persons who were strictly ***living*** their beliefs.

Although other researchers had identified the spiritual nature of abductions, none had ever looked so closely at this aspect. Rita Elkins of the *Florida Today* newspaper extensively interviewed Jordan and Clark. The resulting article in her paper drew other experiencers to the surface. Here was one response:

> Recently I read the *Florida Today* account of your research. I'm especially interested in the 'religious component' that you seem to be discovering in some UFO abduction cases. Back about 1973 my wife had a strange experience in the middle of the night. At the time we knew nothing about UFO abductions, so we had no category in which to place it other than extremely 'lucid nightmare.' It has many of the abduction 'components.' The point is that she stopped the entities and the whole experience with the name of 'Jesus.' … It's vital to get this information out. ("CE-4 Case Files," <www.alienresistance.org/ce4casefiles.htm>, August 2, 2003)

As the investigation spread wider, other similar reports were documented. Clark recalls:

> As the number of cases mounted, the data showed that in every instance where the victim knew to invoke the name of Jesus Christ, the event stopped. Period. The evidence was becoming increasingly difficult to ignore. ("The Premise of Spiritual Warfare," <www.alienresistance.org/ce4 premise.htm>, March 7, 2003)

After the *Florida Today* article also appeared online, the Internet news journal *CNI News* took it up.

When Europe's most high-profile and respected UFO journal, *The Flying Saucer Review*, published it, responses came to CE-4 from all over the world. These included dozens of reports of abductions being halted in the name of Jesus Christ.

Not only did researcher Jordan speak with fellow directors of MUFON. He also got in touch with several of the leading abduction researchers in the United States. Each requested anonymity. But ***every single one of them*** told Jordan, off the record, that they had cases of abductees halting their experiences in the name of Jesus Christ.

You ask, why would they suppress such findings? One reason would be fear of damage to their credibility.

Jordan, himself a New Ager when he began his investigations (he is now a Christian), explains that most UFOlogists share New Age beliefs. They "go from one thing to another looking for development of a higher consciousness… Any place but in traditional religion." ("'Spiritual warfare?' Some Look to Bible for Answers to Alien Abductions," <www.flatoday.com/space/explore/stories/1997b/081797b.htm>, January 6, 2003)

One can understand that these researchers did not want their pre-existing belief system challenged. It should also be understood that with the abduction phenomenon at plague proportions, a "specialist" can make a good living.

However, it appears that other forces whom the "aliens" fear are also busy. Many "preventions" simply go unseen, unrealised (and unthanked). Evidently, the Creator has ***not*** washed His hands of us and left us all to the mercy of the Lucifer Legion for whatever they choose to do with us.

It is also apparent that the real Jesus Christ is not really on good terms with the UFO phenomenon at all! One commentator has related the following UFO account: "A friend of mine had a UFO appear to him on one of their sacred mountains. It came in over his house and he said 'I challenge you in the name of the Lord Jesus Christ' - and it disappeared."

Lucifer Legion spirits are "spooked" by this name

Now here comes the obvious question: ***What*** is there about Jesus Christ that "spooks out" these aliens? ***Why*** does the mention of Jesus' name affect the UFO beings so badly? ***Why*** be afraid of a name that is so often ignored, ridiculed, or used as a swear word in present day society?

If Jesus is a fantasy, or just another famous name and nothing more, then, please tell me, ***why*** do so-called "aliens" (the same spirits as seen in séances) "let go" of their victims when Jesus' name is called upon? Will somebody just answer that?

Every honest person must ask, WHY DOES "JESUS" SPOOK THEM OUT so much that they release their victims? ***What is so powerful about Jesus – today?***

This is real life – today – that we're talking about – certified by thousands of real, living witnesses. If you want ***evidence outside the Bible – today – practical evidence that is actionable –*** that Jesus is who he says he is, then you can't get more powerful evidence than that.

We have noted that the messages coming from these "space brothers" often aim at discrediting the Bible record of Jesus Christ. These entities frequently assert that Jesus is not the Rescuer of all the human race. Rather, that he was but one of several good religious leaders who have appeared on earth. Or sometimes they claim he is a UFOnaut like them.

All their energy seems focused on undermining the Bible and the status of Jesus as man's Savior and claiming instead that they themselves are the rescuers.

Me thinks they protest too much. It is hard to shake off the impression that these aliens ***do*** really believe that Jesus is the One he claims to be. If he is their Creator, against whom they are feuding, and they themselves are deceivers, then they certainly have a colossal ***motive*** to discredit him.

Joe Jordan has personally documented over a hundred cases of attempted ***UFO abductions*** where simply crying out the name of Jesus or quoting from the Bible actually ***stopped*** an abduction. To these can be added endless thousands of cases worldwide where ***demonic possession*** of a person has been ***terminated*** by calling on the very same ***name of Jesus***. Evil spirits, it seems, can't prevail against it.

No other name works

It should also be noted that calling on the name of Solomon, Mohammed, Buddha, Krishna or *'god help me'* is not effective. You must be specific. Use the name above all names: Jesus Christ the Lamb of God.

Results prove that he is not the first above others. He is the ***only***. Anyone who wants to dispute that had better come up with more than an opinion. Substitute rules of your own? It won't work!

The ***evidence*** indicates real power in this name. Surely the fact that modern abduction attempts – as well as demonic possession – are brought to an abrupt halt by the calling out of the name "Jesus!" (in whatever language) proves the truth of the New Testament claim that *"there is* ***no other name*** *under heaven given to men by which we must be saved."* (Acts 4:12) This is the name of a Person who possesses all power. And they know it.

Compare the difference

Before physical abductions, targeted victims are not asked if they want to be abducted. The time from appearance of an alien to teleport is just a few seconds. Numerous folk have told their captors that "you have no right to do this." The response they always receive is "we have every right." That is, if they do receive an answer instead of a blank stare from cold black eyes.

As James Neff observes, "They are coming in and violating human will – with little or no respect for the person, their emotional state or being, much the way we deal with lab rats (which is equally unnerving to me)." (James Neff, in response to Ted Twietmeyer, "Abduction Research Results Facts," <www.rense.com>, April 17, 2005)

We have noted that many abductees eventually stop fighting abduction and instead become passive and controlled.

On the other hand, it is noteworthy that, time after time, folk who become ***practising*** Christians, whether they be criminals, or simply broken-hearted, or abused, suddenly become energised with new life, as new people. They describe it as like being "born again". The transformation can be rapid. (I'm not speaking of those who profess to be "born again", but are not.)

This is a far cry from the transformations seen in the lives of ET abductees and spirit possession victims - depression, emptiness, mental illness, even suicides. Not to mention the physical deterioration that often sets in.

But rather than controlling people against their will, the message that Jesus taught on earth was one of liberation. The theme of his ministry was one of love, forgiveness and acceptance. Come to think about it, wouldn't you like to live in a world where these virtues rule? The truth is, most people would.

Many, however, don't want what they regard as the "religious baggage" that goes with it. Why? Because they think of Christianity as just another religion.

However, the issue is not about religions. The UFO debate is ***not*** just about a religious viewpoint. It is about a ***spiritual battle***. This is a conflict of epic proportions. And of such importance that not a single person alive on this planet should ignore it.

The Bible records eyewitness reports that Jesus, when walking the streets of this planet, ***used to stop*** demon possession and free people from it. He claimed unlimited power.

The result is the same today. From numerous case histories, it appears that spirits will frequently mention Jesus, if it will help their agenda. But for a person to pry them with questions about Jesus evokes discomfort on the part of a Luciferian spirit.

However, the most violent reaction occurs when a contactee commands the spirit in the name of Jesus. This provokes anger and fear. Spirits are known to confess, when challenged, that they serve Satan (Lucifer) and that Jesus is their enemy.

Now think about this. Today we have evidence that both abductions and demonic spirit possessions are ***being halted*** by calling on Jesus' name. Might this suggest that he is indeed still alive and powerful?

Those two UFO researchers from CE-4, Jordan and Clark did not start out as 'Bible pounders with a point'. In fact, quite the opposite. One of them was a New Ager, the other not particularly religious. Like the rest of us, they were just looking for truth. It was the research they did and the data they found that made believers out of them.

Going by the mountain of ***evidence***, it would seem far better to have a "close encounter" with the power of Jesus than with a deceiver from the Lucifer Legion. The Bible claim that no other name except that of Yeshua (Jesus) can save us is being put to the test worldwide in

(a) successfully halting alien abductions (testified by respected non-Christian New Age researchers)
(b) successfully saving victims from demon possession.
(c) successfully rehabilitating ruined lives.

Actionable proof in real life.

In the face of this ***evidence***, could it make sense to trust Jesus' claim that he can benefit your life and conquer death for you?

He'll confirm your choice

The beauty is, there's no compulsion about it. We are created free. And if a man doesn't want his Creator's way out, then his Creator will reluctantly confirm his choice. He will finally give us what we have really set our hearts on.

50

A fight for our loyalty -

UNSEEN, BUT REAL

Sunday, July 6, 1997, was a day Kerry Kressie will never forget. On the previous evening, Kerry, her husband Brian and their children, travelled 100 miles to attend my seminar on the Ark of the Covenant in the Emerald Town Hall, Queensland, Australia. They enjoyed the program immensely and took home a large quantity of books and videos.

Among these was my book *Ark of the Covenant*. This book reveals startling archaeological evidence concerning that artefact and its spine-tingling link to the crucifixion of Jesus – as well as the coming defeat of Lucifer. It is a story for which a group of would-be assassins ambushed me, soon after. I believe it infuriated the Legion of Lucifer.

Anyway, the very next night Kerry picked up that book and opened it to read. Instantly, some unseen force flicked it out of her hand and threw it against the wall.

A savage sounding voice said, "*Ma! What do you want to read that for? There's nothing in there that will do you any good!*"

Shaken, Kerry again picked up the book. She opened it. The voice was again heard: "*NOW, YOU JUST STOP THAT*!" Again the book was flicked from her hand and hurled across the room.

This time Kerry placed the book on the bench. She told her husband what had happened, and he suggested she pray about it. "Oh God," she asked, "Please protect me."

After that, before picking up the book to read, she would pray, "Lord, please bind up Satan. Get him out of here and send your angels into this house."

But Lucifer's forces did not leave willingly. As she stood at the wash basin, in the presence of her husband, she was suddenly lifted up five or six feet, carried across the room, and then dumped onto her back. When she tried to pray, she felt that someone was choking her; she had to struggle for breath. A strong force also pushed down on her stomach. It felt like someone was sitting on her.

"Dear Jesus…" she began. Suddenly some hostile force was jacking her mouth wide open and pulling her tongue out toward her chin. Her six-year-old daughter Emily watched in horror.

Then the child knew what she had to do. "In the name of Jesus, you let my mother go!" cried the little one. ***And the force on Kerry's mouth let go.***

Now Kerry and Brian are more determined than ever to launch an assault on Lucifer's kingdom and help rescue others.

Just as I was about to go to print, a man in Victoria phoned to tell us about a vivid dream he had just had. In it, a curtain was opened and he saw a blue covered book. It looked like the book *Ark of the Covenant*. And a voice said to him, ***"Share this with everybody."*** So that's what he's now doing.

In this behind-the-scenes war, the hatred is vicious. The Legion of Lucifer has just one insane obsession: to denigrate, discredit and destroy everything to do with Yeshua.

It is a battle for the mind. Your mind. My mind. And it's intense. How easy it is to get caught in the trap they set and blame God for all the hurt! That's what Lucifer wants. He was the inventor of that slander. And he hates you too.

A burning question

Truth is independent of opinion. Truth is truth – empty of error. It doesn't matter what you think of Jesus. He died for you, anyway. That is truth.

The bottom line is that every individual who accepts the appointed rescue plan will live again – forever – in a world without fear. Your Creator, the wise judge, will deal justly.

Until then, it's death. Not reincarnation. Not life as a spirit. Not automatic life in another form. Just death. Like a sleep. At the resurrection day you will wake up to eternal life or to judgment. This is your choosing time, now. (John 11:11-14,23-24; Daniel 12:2; Hebrews 9:27; 2 Corinthians 6:2) God said to our first parents, "You ***will*** surely die." Satan said, "You will ***not*** surely die." (Genesis 2:15-17; 3:4) That's where the "keep living" lie about death began.

A great cartoon

I must tell you about a cartoon I saw In *Punch*. A couple is marooned on an upturned dinghy.

Another couple (the Harringtons) are in a motorboat, racing to the rescue.

The marooned wife speaks up: "I'm not going to be rescued by Bob and Vera Harrington.. not them!"

It really hit home. Just imagine me saying, "I'm not going to be rescued by Jesus …***not by him!"*** (Even if he's the ONLY hope I've got?) Would I be such an idiot?

Or there's a doctor who has treated a hundred people for the same terminal illness – and with the same treatment every one of them recovered. Then I get that very same illness and the good doctor offers that same medicine to me. What would you think if I said, "No thanks, I don't like the taste of that medicine"?

Okay, for my terminal illness of sin, there is only one remedy… Jesus. Nothing else will work. He's not ***a*** way – he's ***the only***!

Now imagine another doctor. You tell him you want to be cured and he says, "Well, I have four or five medicines, any one of which might work. Just pick whichever tastes good to you, and let me know what happens"? With so many decoys crying out, is it safe to pick whatever "life solution" takes my fancy?

Here, then, is ***the question:*** Why on earth aren't you running this Jesus guy? Is it because he might help you out of your problems, and turn you into a winner? Yeah – a winner! But you wouldn't want that, would you?

Here's the good news: You can leave the past behind. Your Creator has designed it so you can always begin where you are right now to live life a new way – God's way. The Christian life is all present and future.

My wife Josephine and I have been enjoying its benefits together for 16 years now - and are determined to, for the rest of our lives. The results are phenomenal. We also receive numerous testimonies from others who are experiencing it – with no harmful side effects.

Okay, if you don't mind, here are a few tips: Fill your mind with positive biblical input: good books and tapes; and friends who will affirm you in your commitment to your Maker. Maintain this total mental commitment to truth or you will be swamped by waves of human opinion and bad advice, sometimes from well-meaning friends who are badly informed.

The detractors should listen to those who are living it – not to skeptics who are missing out on the amazing benefits. I feel sorry for the skeptics because they are the losers, not those who apply this knowledge.

Even if there were no benefits beyond this life, it's worth it – NOW! Just suppose there turned out to be no future as promised, you've still gained in this life. But what if you discover later that there WAS this wonderful rescue plan and you had failed to accept it? What then? So, these tips may help:

- ***Wake up*** from the evolution dream – ***you'll*** be ***better off.***
- ***Break free*** of that "space brothers" delusion – get to know your real enemy, and not be caught by surprise.
- ***Don't trust in*** some imagined reincarnation (an endless succession of lives of pain, suffering and death)
- ***Rise above*** your distrust of the *Intelligence Report* (the Bible) and ***your*** quality of life will improve.
- ***Let go*** of your prejudice against Jesus and ***you*** will start to live better – and be in the running to live longer.

Wouldn't you like to live longer, free of pain, disappointment and fear? How about peace and stability in your life? Of course you would! Then why keep the most wonderful and loving person who has ever lived, locked out of your life? It's over to you, mate…

QUESTIONS THAT DEMAND AN ANSWER

In fact, these questions ***scream out*** to be answered by anyone who denies the overall thesis of this book:

- What scientific laws support the theory of evolution? (Let's be honest about this.)
- How did (a) the DNA ***information code***, and (b) the ***code to translate*** it, originate separately at the same time?
- Who programs the many DNA machines, all so different from one another, to ***interact*** inside a living cell?
- If mankind evolved from earlier life forms, then why are ***human remains*** consistently found ***in all ages*** of strata, even alongside the "first and earliest" fossil life forms?
- If simple life forms evolved into more complex, then why are ***complex fossils*** found perfectly complete in the "earliest" strata, with ***no evidence of evolving ancestors?***
- If one type of organism evolved into another, then why are there ***persistent unbridged gaps between*** major types – with no evidence of transition from one type to another?
- For evolution's "punctuated equilibrium" (a sudden burst of changes into another type) to occur (e.g. for a dinosaur to turn into a bird – a creature of mostly different design), how could the ***genetic code for a large range of brand new, different, fully functioning organs*** suddenly appear out of nowhere?

- If rock strata took millions of years to form, then why do we find numerous examples of a single, undecayed ***fossil protruding through multiple "ages"*** of strata?
- If everything has evolved, then why are today's basic types ***virtually unchanged*** from their first fossil ancestors?
- How does new DNA ***information*** evolve?
- Since mutations are genetic ***copying mistakes***, in which genetic information becomes garbled or lost, how does a mutation ***add new information*** for evolution to occur?
- Since ***natural selection*** is only a selecting from the existing gene pool of what is already there (that is, a dividing of the gene pool, resulting in ***a loss, not gain***, ***of genetic information***) – since it removes information and nothing new is added, while evolution requires an increase of information – how, then, does natural selection facilitate evolution?
- If ***intelligence*** could not evolve on this planet, but needed input from beings of another planet, then how did intelligence appear ***on that first planet***?
- If the Bible is myth, mistakes, and "made up" history, then why is archaeology consistently unearthing ***evidence*** of actual places and persons, as well as ***physical remains*** from specific events narrated in the Bible? And why has ***not one*** confirmed discovery to date controverted a Bible reference?
- Why is it that the Bible comprises ***the only writings*** on earth with clearly worded ***prophecies*** that have proven to accurately foretell centuries of world history?

- Why is it that the Bible (claiming to be the words of God), and the Bible alone, comprises ***the only writings*** on earth with an ***interlocked numeric code*** within the structure of the plain text, that man ***cannot replicate***?
- If the Bible is based on lies, forgeries and deception, then where does it derive its power to ***transform lives*** for the better, as thousands of living witnesses testify?
- If Jesus never existed, or if he possesses no unique living power today, then why do UFO entities (and demonic entities) in real life today ***react so emphatically*** to commands in his name?
- If Jesus is ***not the only*** Rescuer of mankind, as the Bible claims, then why is it that ***only his name*** can physically ***halt an "alien" abduction*** and ***demon possession*** of any person on this planet today in actionable real life? Why does his name, and no other, work?
- If Jesus did not precisely fulfill the prophecies of the Messiah, then why have Jesus' opponents, since the alleged event, acted with apparent desperation to ***cover up evidence*** by (a) deleting specific long-standing prophecies from their own records; (b) chopping out 160 years of related Persian/Jewish history, and (c) imposing ***a curse*** upon the reading of one prophecy in particular?

When, with ***solid evidence*** (not opinion) you have successfully answered these questions, then please go back to Prologue B and disprove the overall thesis outlined there, to collect your $100,000 reward.

STOP PRESS:

Just a few minutes ago, an Internet contact sent me this news from *The Australian*, dated November 26, 2010:

SUICIDE TWINS Kristin and Candice Hermeler had *God Delusion* in their luggage.

Books found in the luggage of the Australian twin sisters who carried out a suicide pact at a Colorado shooting range suggest they were *searching for meaning*. They included… [atheist Richard Dawkins' book] *The God Delusion.*

So, Mr Dawkins, what does your evolutionary lullabying do to our kids? They emerge from it with a wail of despair, a sob of loneliness, a feeling of meaninglessness in life. There follow low self-esteem, animalistic behaviour and depression.

Now would you like some good news?

Another contact named Merrill got a sneak look into the book you are now reading, with this result:

> I read your e-book the other night and had my eyes opened up and it scared the s… out of me! I was feeling hopeless. I was consistently having bad luck. It had finally got the better of me and I was convinced I was a loser and that it was all my fault as a human being. I have felt suicidal several times. Then I read your e-book the other night - and everything made sense. The whole Jesus concept will be very difficult to follow as I was finally reduced to believing there was no God. I think your e-book ***may have saved my life***.

Now, doesn't that kind of news cheer your heart?

EPILOGUE

Yes, our world's ***in a real mess***. Few will deny that. If it's not war, hatred, loneliness, or selfishness, it's death, sickness and pain. And we've all had just about enough of that, right?

Now, here is a fellow that ***wants to help us***. Not only that, but he ***is able*** to. And what are we doing about it?

So who still wants to say Jesus was dreamed up by deceivers in the late first and early second centuries? Hey, come on guys. Can you really believe that a deceiver could invent such supreme truths which perform ***miracles of character change*** on people even today?...changing wife-beating thugs into gentle, caring husbands, and embezzlers into honest men? Anyone who believes such life-altering principles are founded on a forgery, has more faith in the power of lies and fraud to raise man up and inspire him with noble ideals, than he has in the power of truth to uplift him. Let's get real. A Jesus who is dreamed up like any other fairytale or legend, is a Jesus who has no more power to change lives than an Alice in Wonderland.

Look, almost 2,000 years ago, real men with dirt under their fingernails met a real Jesus who challenged them to follow Him. Would numerous men be torn limb from limb, thrown to wild beasts, sawn in two, hung upside down, burnt at the stake, for something they knew to be a deliberate hoax?

Lying "scholars"

Why is it that some scholars can't tell fact from fiction? They glibly quote others who are just as misinformed. Starting from an anti-supernatural bias, they imagine the historical Jesus to be just a powerless piece of fiction. Let's inject a bit of common sense here. These scholars are ***centuries removed*** from the Jesus they speak about. Don't let them con you.

I have laid out ***evidence*** for you that the ***Bible record*** which reveals this Jesus person is

- supernatural in its origin
- supernatural in its design, and can be
- supernatural in its effect on you and your life. Other books inform you. But the Bible transforms you.

What is more, Christianity is the only religion which bases its essential tenets on the facts of history.

If your life depended on it, which would make more sense – to trust:

(a) biased, faulty scholars living 2,000 years later, or

(b) ***eyewitnesses*** who wrote the New Testament and bore testimony ***close to the events,*** and whose lives were changed for the better by what they experienced?

After all, this is testimony of those who ***met*** Jesus… ***ate*** with him… ***worked*** with him. And the first hand testimony of ***a living power that works today***. Can you do better than that?

A skeptic on stage challenged anyone in the audience to ***prove*** Christianity was true. A young man came onto the stage. And standing there before the audience he peeled an orange. Then he proceeded to suck it.

He turned to the speaker and asked, "Wasn't that orange nice?"

"You fool!" retorted the other man, "How can I know? I haven't tasted it."

"Then how do you know about the Christian life, when you haven't tasted it?"

The rescue is testable

You can't judge the Deliverer by the numerous fake "Christians" who talk but don't live it, any more than you can judge whether soap works by looking at countless dirty children who don't use it.

The propositions of biblical Christianity are testable – both historically and in practical, real life. I submit that we have materially and physically proven ***beyond reasonable doubt*** (sufficient to serve as ***actionable proof***):

- That someone who claims to be our Creator has been communicating with us throughout history.
- That the authority of the one set of documents containing this claim (the Bible) has been ***substantiated with actionable proof***
  - by **archaeology**
  - by **prophecy**
  - by its **'sevens' code**.
- The Bible claim that no other name except that of Yeshua (Jesus) can save us, is being ***put to the test*** worldwide in
  (a) successfully halting alien abductions (testified by respected non-Christian New Age researchers)
  (b) successfully saving victims from demon possession (countless testimonials)
  (c) successfully rehabilitating ruined lives (countless more testimonials) - with an abundance of ***actionable proof in real life.***

We're all in the feud

Let's sum it up. There is a master plan. And the sooner you can get over not wanting to believe it, or worrying that to believe it puts you in the ranks of the nutters, then the sooner you have a chance to benefit from all this.

In all fairness, it must be recognised that the architect of the anti-Jesus slander is none other than Lucifer, the original slanderer! Consciously or unconsciously, our minds have been tarnished by his insidious propaganda. The battle is for the mind. Remember, we are all caught up in the feud between Lucifer, hijacker of this planet, and Jesus the Rescuer. The Legion of Lucifer hate the Rescuer and his plan to terminate evil. They are determined to perpetuate Lucifer's rule over this planet.

Their human puppets, installed in positions of power throughout the world, cook up for us one whopper after another. Big, juicy ones. And they go down nice and easy! We've been lied to. Lots of lies: big lies, little lies. They're playing us for suckers.

These leaders have convinced themselves that their supposed evolutionary advancement of competing "units", such as nations, requires war to weed out the inferior.

This plan of destruction for the human race has been strategized by a genius far beyond the ingenuity of man, orchestrating and synchronising it from behind the scenes. And Lucifer's stooges have taken over – in politics, science, religion, education, the media and the entertainment industry. Accordingly it is proclaimed:

> No one will enter the New World Order unless he or she will make a pledge to

> worship Lucifer. No one will enter the New Age unless he will take a Luciferian Initiation. (David Spangler, Director of Planetary Initiative, United Nations)

Amongst all the global governing changes that are taking place to accommodate this globalism many are overlooking the most dominant aspect of it, its religious and occultic nature. The New World Order IS about religion. It is obeying Lucifer.

Their servants the movie-makers in Hollywood are occultists who have admitted that they are out to get peoples' minds. Holly is the wood of a witch's broom. You've heard of "Columbia Pictures" (named after the ancient pagan goddess Columbia). Concerning the torch in her hand, Occultist Edward Schurr said:

> The flaming torch is a symbol of Lucifer. Lucifer, having regained his diadem, will assemble his legions. Attracted by his flaming torch, celestial spirits will descend. Then the torch of Lucifer will signal from heaven to earth, and the new age Christ will answer. (*Mystery Mark of the New Age*, p. 240)…

The hostility against the Yeshua rescue program – the all-out campaign to persuade us to reject it – is based on Lucifer's savage passion for revenge against the One who tossed him out of his original home.

You've been turned off by hypocritical religious people? I understand. So am I. But that's not the issue. The coming final showdown will be, in effect, between Satanism and Jesus Christ. It may surprise you to learn that, under job or social pressure, most professed "Christians", having failed to cement a personal relationship with Jesus, will ultimately cave in and follow like sheep the demands of the Legion of Lucifer and its puppets.

The Legion of Lucifer proposes a universal religion made from all kinds of faiths where neither the real Jesus nor true escape can be found. In fact, it favors all religions – but not Jesus the Deliverer.

However, the prophecies are clear: This coming Luciferian "do or die" dictatorship will be interrupted by the return of the Deliverer – to complete his rescue program and establish his undisputed sovereignty over this earth we've messed up.

The glorious quality of the coming new earth has already been glimpsed through the character seen in Jesus' earthly life. The plan is for a new earth cleansed from all who are in disharmony… free from those who would mess up this earth again. Those who don't want the Creator's way will not be forced to endure it. He will just confirm each person's choice.

Safety in time of judgment

Merrill was worried. "The Bible says we will be ***judged***. That's pretty scary to me, but what would God judge to be a bad person? Also what about disabled, helpless people? And what about people that are born to really bad people and bad is all they know?"

Good questions, Merrill.

The answer is that God is not only just (hence He can't let me into His new world if I choose to continue sinning), but He is also merciful. He will take into consideration a person's birthplace, circumstances and opportunities. Now, isn't that fair?

And in the Judgment, one who has granted Jesus sovereignty over his life has ***nothing to fear***. He is covered by allowing the Deliverer to take his place.

And the best of life now!

Meanwhile, it is worth asking, Why does pure Christianity seem to work so well in the real world now? A Redbook survey of 65,000 people found that Christians live happier, more fulfilling lives than unbelievers. ***Even their sex life is better***!

Keith's kidney transplant

Keith desperately needed a kidney transplant.

His friend Joe came to the hospital and offered his own kidney to save Keith. Joe's generosity landed him with an infection and confinement to a wheelchair.

But would you believe, after that, Keith avoided Joe, wanting nothing to do with him!

Ungrateful?

And Jesus? Does He ***deserve to receive your gratitude***? On the other hand, He has given you the terrifying capability of refusing. Rejectors should be – and will be – held responsible ***for their own decision***.

You want life – with security, joy and hope? It's your choice.

INDEX

INFORMATION AVAILABLE ON RELATED QUESTIONS:

(books by Jonathan Gray)

TRUE HISTORY OF MANKIND

Dead Men's Secrets
http://www.beforeus.com
The Killing of Paradise Planet
http://www.beforeus.com/first.php
Surprise Witness
http://www.beforeus.com/second.php
The Corpse Came Back
http://www.beforeus.com/third.php

EVOLUTION, DINOSAURS, DNA AND SCIENCE

The Discovery That's Toppling Evolution
http://www.beforeus.com/evol.php
Surprise Witness
http://www.beforeus.com/second.php
Men in Embarrassing Places
http://www.beforeus.com/man-in-carboniferous.pdf

THEISTIC EVOLUTION

Modern Religious Myths About Genesis
www.beforeus.com/shopcart_ebooks.html

THE DATING SCANDAL

The Great Dating Blunder
www.beforeus.com/shopcart_ebooks.html
Lost Races: The Big Dating Shock
http://www.beforeus.com/dating-civilizations.pdf

"SPACE GODS" THEORY & THE OCCULT

UFO Aliens: The Deadly Secret
http://www.beforeus.com/aliens.html
Just Sitchin Fiction?
http://www.beforeus.com/sitchin.pdf

ARCHAEOLOGY, SCIENCE AND THE BIBLE

Dead Men's Secrets
http://www.beforeus.com
The Weapon the Globalists Fear
http://www.beforeus.com/weapon-ebook.html
Solomon's Riches
http://www.beforeus.com/solomon-riches.pdf
The Corpse Came Back
http://www.beforeus.com/third.php
Four Major Discoveries
www.beforeus.com/shopcart_ebooks.html
The Ark Conspiracy
http://www.beforeus.com/tac.php
Ancient Book Led Them to Treasure
www.beforeus.com/shopcart_ebooks.html

BIBLE BEEN ALTERED?
(and are there "missing" books?)

The Da Vinci Code Hoax
http://www.beforeus.com/da-vinci.php
The Sorcerers' Secret
www.beforeus.com/shopcart_ebooks.html
The Weapon the Globalists Fear
http://www.beforeus.com/weapon-ebook.html
Just Sitchin Fiction?
http://www.beforeus.com/sitchin.pdf
Who's Playing Jesus Games?
www.beforeus.com/shopcart_ebooks.html

NON-BIBLICAL "GOSPELS"

Who's Playing Jesus Games?, ch. 16-17
www.beforeus.com/shopcart_ebooks.html

EYEWITNESSES WROTE THE NEW TESTAMENT

Who's Playing Jesus Games?, ch. 6-9
www.beforeus.com/shopcart_ebooks.html

THE "EARLIER" PAGAN "CHRIST" MYTHS

Stolen Identity, ch. 11-12, 15, 25, 40-42
www.beforeus.com/stolen-id.php

HISTORICAL RECORDS CONCERNING JESUS

Who's Playing Jesus Games?, chs. 1-3

http://www.beforeus.com/shopcart_ebooks.html

THE IMPOSSIBILITY OF INVENTING JESUS

Stolen Identity, chapter 28

http://www.beforeus.com/stolen-id.php

Illustration credits

Page 85: Ed Conrad
Pages 45,48: Copyright 2003 Illustra Media
from the film *Unlocking the Mystery of Life*
Page 90: Creation Research www.creationresearch.net
Pages 160,178: Review and Herald Publishing
Page 366: John Pratt
Page 407: O.H. Boyd
Page 628: Sony Pictures Entertainment Company

Surprising Discoveries
P.O. Box 785
Thames 3540
New Zealand

www.beforeus.com